W9-AHP-729

THE FATE OF THE SELF

The Fate of the Self

German Writers and French Theory

STANLEY CORNGOLD

New York · Columbia University Press 1986

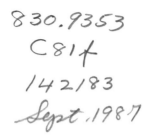

Columbia University Press
New York   Guildford, Surrey
Copyright © 1986 Columbia University Press
All rights reserved

Printed in the United States of America

Library of Congress Cataloging-in-Publication Data

Corngold, Stanley.
  The fate of the self.

  Includes index.
  1. German literature—History and criticism.
2. Self in literature. 3. Self (Philosophy).
4. Criticism—France—History—20th century.
5. Structuralism (Literary analysis). 6. Deconstruction. I. Title.
PT148.S34C67 1986   830'.9'353   85-11292
ISBN 0-231-06174-9 (alk. paper)

Columbia University Press gratefully
acknowledges assistance from Princeton University
in the publication of this book.

Jacket: Paul Klee, "Ein zentrifugales Gedenkblatt," 1923, 171 Aquarell,
Zeitung, kreidegrundiert/ 54,7: 41,7/ Galerie Rosengart, Lucerne. Copyright © 1985 by COSMOPRESS, Geneva & A.D.A.G.P., Paris.

This book is Smyth-sewn and printed on permanent and durable acid-
free paper.

At the bottom
of us, really
"deep down,"
there is . . .
some granite
of spiritual
fatum.

—Nietzsche

Contents

Preface

This book on seven German writers turns on a question of continuing interest, the question of the self, especially as it is involved in poetry, creativity, writing, literature, and poetic discourse. Each writer gives an account of the enigmatic subjectivity that attaches to poetic experience. The self in question is therefore a poetic self, a paradoxical being that must "disown" itself in order to exist. The word in quotes is Hölderlin's as he describes the fate of the "feeling of the sacred" that originates tragic drama: it can "no longer express itself immediately," yet Hölderlin adds "if we cannot carry over our own spirit and our own experience into a foreign analogous material, nothing at all can be understood and given life."[1] The survival of such a self in its analogues is the concern of the writers in this book.

The poetic self cannot be known in advance of its articulation; it can come to life only for a reader. But it is not produced *ab ovo* by that reader. It is present to him as the being which intended by an act of writing to be present to the future of that act. Yet the poetic self is more than the work's ghostly, hypothetical double, its pure aesthetic correlative. It comes to life with the fire and mud of the empirical personality still clinging to it, conveying the thrust of the writer's being to enact, identify, constitute, or bear witness to itself. Literature, for these writers, is the discourse of a subject whose saying, by virtue of how it is said, stands for the self in the future.[2]

The "philosophers" in this book—I omit Nietzsche and think rather of Dilthey, Freud, and Heidegger—tend to celebrate poetic analogues as exemplary and accomplished metaphors of the poetic self (which they define variously as conscious or unconscious).[3] Poets and writers like Hölderlin, Nietzsche, and Kafka do so, but more elliptically. Their work secretes moments of persistence and regeneration in out-of-the-way corners, in subtle effects of sense and style. They are also quick to identify the ways in which the carrying over of the poetic spirit can be threatened and interrupted, can miscarry and fall short.[4] Hence, something of a divide opens up between the philosophers and the poets in this book and also in the work of the poets themselves, in the matter of the continuity between the poetic intention and the self conveyed by its activity.

The consciousness of this difference, however, can widen into a sense of illimitable discontinuity, rift, and rupture, and this has indeed become the exclusive focus of a new French and American critical perspective. The self can never be articulated; it is in no way present to the future of the act of being read in a work for which it holds itself responsible. According to Jacques Derrida, the unconscious is "a 'past' . . . that will [not ever] be present and whose future will never be its *production* or reproduction in the form of presence."[5] And in *The Structuralist Revolution*, J.-M. Benoist also obliterates the conscious self: "The subject is diffracted and caught in the symbolic order, in the structures which pervade, regulate, and express themselves through it."[6] The subject is decomposed and entangled by poetic activity in nets which act of their own accord; the traditional view which understands such activity as the project of a self to overcome a torn or alien state is written off as metaphysical consolation.

Doubts about nonrigorous philosophy drove the German novelist Hermann Broch to literature as "the area where subjectivity is radically legitimate."[7] But today a nonrigorous philosophy contests the legitimacy of this very claim so strongly that the illegitimacy of literary subjectivity has become dogma. The deposition of the self or subject from first position in poetry and poetics is as if ritually assured by a plainsong of negative words like "diffract," "disperse," "fragment," "diffuse." It no longer seems possible to produce a beginning articulation of the question of the poetic self without recourse to the cant of physics and chemistry for metaphors of shattering. I am concerned, however, to provide important grounds for altering this prejudice by examining the work of several German writers—precisely those who have been regularly enlisted in the current discussion to mean the opposite of what they say. These thinkers and writers display a wide range of the constructive positions taken by a cunning poetic subjectivity on behalf of the being that it means to enact in the literary work. Their work thematizes the self as a divided unity and suggests that the thematization itself stands in a relation of complex continuity with the being which impels it.

An account of the poetic self cannot, of course, be detached from general conceptions prevailing in the epochs in which these writers lived, and so their views can also be seen as perspectives on commonly held notions of personality. But the main concern of these chapters is the poetic self, and if older ideas of selfhood are cited, they are meant to clarify the being whose survival into our own time is bound to acts of writing.

Most of these chapters were conceived in response to different occasions. By rewriting them, however, and putting them side by side with other chapters written for this volume, I have seen, and I hope the reader will see, their connections spark. Although the chapters are arranged by the chronology of the authors treated, they do not form a single intellectual history. The desire for narrative or, simply, desire, has instead flowed around the shape imposed on each essay by its original intention. Therefore the reader should not expect a history of subjective poetics in Germany as a linear unfolding of meaning.

The task, however, of writing a book which would include all these authors has brought me back closer to each. As selves they did not suppose that they were inscribing themselves as the next chapter in a single history, and this very fact impelled them to complex self-representations—to literature. And so to respond faithfully to them is to want to keep at the level of form the plural that distinguishes their thrust toward identity, to record the heterogenousness of their ambition.

The selves they embody are to the same extent individualizations of the *many* narratives which preceded these authors and which they did not read as chapters in a linear unfolding. What is true of them ought furthermore to be true of the modern self. My essays, therefore, while oriented to the past, are also projected as features of modern identity, each definite aspect or feature being in Nietzsche's phrase "a semiotically compressed process," a compact narrative of another more complex narrative about the self (BW, p. 516). If the modern self is the congeries of its experiences, it is also writer and reader in the book of itself, a book made up of exemplary narratives about the self produced by major authors. Together their stories organize the self that is responsive to them, and for the power which their engagement with their subject matter produces, they constitute a canon.

I do not want to dispense entirely with linear narrative. Some

of the interinvolvement of these chapters is plainly a function of chronological relation: what Dilthey and Nietzsche wrote, and lived, they took
in part from Hölderlin, just as Mann and Kafka depended in part on what
they read of them. But the historical meaning of these chapters is not
chiefly a product of their chronological consecutiveness. Each chapter
about a canonical work intends to illustrate a representative concern of
literary theory, which is partly the work's own and in whose light other
aspects of the work emerge. Thus each chapter about an author tries to
raise apropos of him a different but important question of method and
philosophy belonging to our present literary culture—for example, the
rhetoric of narration, the politics of reading, and the interrelations of
philosophical, psychological, and literary texts.

Inside each chapter, then, as a feature of the modern self, is
a theory about how such a feature has been produced. Each narrative,
from Hölderlin to Heidegger, can therefore be projected differently by
the theories informing the six other chapters, to produce six additional
aspects. In this book some of these profiles are shown explicitly, while
others are only virtually there for the reader to focus. This gallery of
spectral inhabitants should suggest some of the Breughelian complexity
of the household of the self.

Many writers today are inclined to see critics as standing in
the light emitted by their authors. My feeling is different: I am fascinated by the color that their continuous interpretation brings to my authors' texts. While writing these essays, I have actually strained to look
over my shoulder at other critics, especially the newer ones who have
written about my authors in ways with which I disagree. This looking
about and askance should suggest the profit I have had from the dialectic. Other critics have made possible for me the bracing experience of
discovering the self in a hard place—in writers whose sense of self, and
whose power to constitute a generally intelligible self, has been put severely into doubt. The fact that I respond so much to other critics is
meant to illustrate more than a personal taste. Responsiveness to other
writers on an author ever in question is one of the most rewarding features of contemporary criticism, and I want to heighten the polemical
mood of the scribes.

Acknowledgments

The following material is reprinted with permission: In chapter 1 a much shortened version of pp. 21–37 appeared in *Comparative Criticism*, published by Cambridge University Press (1983), 5:187–200. Chapter 2 was published in a slightly different version in *Interpretation: A Journal of Political Philosophy* (September 1981), 10 (2 and 3):301–37. Chapter 3 was printed with several omissions in *boundary* 2 (Spring/Fall 1981), 9 (3) and 10 (1):55–98. Chapter 4 appeared in abridged form in *boundary* 2 (Fall 1980), 9 (1):47–74. Chapter 6 was also printed in an abridged version in *diacritics* (Spring 1979), 9 (1):84–94. Chapter 7 appeared in a shorter form in *boundary* 2 (Winter 1976), 4 (2):439–54.

This book has taken a long time to write, and my intellectual indebtedness to those who have taught me is great. My greatest debt, both personally and for the light he brought to these authors, is to the late Paul de Man. His seminars on Rousseau and Hölderlin and Heidegger in the late sixties were full of a bliss of intelligent reading. His name and thought run through these pages, though it will be clear that I am opposed to his later work. I should like to thank the Guggenheim Foundation for a grant in 1977–78 which allowed me to conceive several early versions. Finally, of many friends who have stood me in good stead during the writing of the book, I should like particularly to thank Hans Aarsleff, Ackbar Abbas, Paul Becker, Charles Bernheimer, Anne Carson, Josephine Diamond, Joseph Frank, Irene Giersing, Henry Jarecki, Suzanne Keller, all the Kirkhams, Victor Lange, James Laughlin, Constance Meinwald, Laurence Rickels, Howard Stern, Nathaniel Tarn, and David Wellbery. Susannah York has been my eastern lights. I hope those whom I have forgotten to thank by name will forgive me. Bas van Fraassen, Michael Metteer, and Glenn Most gave me the benefit of their thoughtful reading of the manuscript, as did an excellent anonymous reader for Columbia University Press. And David Bromwich showed a valor unusual even in friendship by proposing stylistic changes to the introduction and the first chapter. My friends and students Todd Kontje, Mark Roche, and Robert Tobin helped loyally in discussion and research; Esther Breisacher and Robin Huffman typed, superbly; and Anne McCoy, of Columbia University Press, has been an exemplary editor. Finally, by the logic that connects *denken* and *danken*, I offer this book as a gift to DP, under whose gentle surveillance my words moved into patterns.

ABBREVIATIONS OF WORKS FREQUENTLY CITED IN TEXT AND NOTES

BW   *Basic Writings of Nietzsche*, Walter Kaufmann, tr. and ed. (New York: Modern Library, 1966)

BT   Martin Heidegger, *Being and Time*, John Macquarrie and Edward Robinson, trs. (New York: Harper and Row, 1962)

BU   Thomas Mann, *Betrachtungen eines Unpolitischen* in *Reden und Aufsätze*, vol. 4, *Gesammelte Werke*, vol. 12 (Frankfurt: Fischer, 1960)

GS   Friedrich Nietzsche, *The Gay Science*, Walter Kaufmann, tr. (New York: Random House, 1974)

L   *Letters of Thomas Mann*, 1889–1955, Richard and Clara Winston, trs. (New York: Knopf, 1971)

MH   *Martin Heidegger, Basic Writings*, David Farrell Krell, ed. (New York: Harper and Row, 1977)

NM   Thomas Mann, "Nietzsche and Music," in *Past Masters*, H. T. Lowe-Porter, tr. (New York: Knopf, 1933)

PN   *The Portable Nietzsche*, Walter Kaufmann, tr. and ed. (New York: Viking, 1954)

WP   Friedrich Nietzsche, *The Will to Power*, Walter Kaufmann and R. J. Hollingdale, trs., and Walter Kaufmann, ed. (New York: Vintage Books, 1968)

THE FATE OF THE SELF

Introduction

The past two decades have been heady times for students of criticism. We have experienced in quick succession waves of new literary theory—structuralism, reader-reception theory, and deconstruction. The paradoxical tendency of these movements, however, has been to "attack the notion that a literary or poetic consciousness is in any way a privileged consciousness."[1] Modern criticism flourishes like a Notes from Underground, exultant in the harrowing of its lost prestige.

The trouble goes deep, for it threatens a standard association of belief in the privilege of literature with the assumption of a consciously productive self. The self has been held to be supported by literary or poetic experience, to which in turn it gives a distinctive value. Literature, on this view, speaks for the self and in a sense creates it by shaping the reflexive consciousness of a subject which is part of the self. If literature is therefore vital to the elaboration of personal identity, then to deny literary experience its privilege is also to threaten "the disappearance of the self as a constitutive subject."[2]

This situation is disconcerting, even when the self, as is often remarked, has not disappeared.* The following chapters suggest an intense preoccupation with the self in a number of great German writers, in texts that reach into our lifetime. Their preoccupation survives in their readers. The skeptical attack on the subject, however, raises a crucial question.

---

*The term "self" hereafter implies the constitutive participation of the conscious subject: hence "self" and "subject" are used interchangeably unless plainly distinguished by context.

If writing against the privilege of literary consciousness becomes more and more the expression of literary consciousness, would
not so sustained an attack on the self actually bring about its disappearance? Perhaps this sounds absurd. It did not for Marcel Mauss, who
wrote of the category of the self: "Its moral power . . . is questioned
. . . even in some of the countries where the principle was discovered.
We have a great wealth to defend; with us the Idea may disappear."[3]
What is at stake in this question of the self is more than an adequate
definition of the "self-thing," or the reasons for its resisting definition
and losing qualification as a topic. The question concerns more than
the mood of subjectivity or the way we think about our inner life. The
notion of a self well lost threatens to annihilate many things that matter
greatly to human beings—wholeness, quality, responsibility, even passion. The idea of the self organizes a vast economy of concepts; how we
think about the self altogether determines how we are in the world and
indeed how we resist it.

Yet there are a number of ironies in play in the present critical situation. The first depends on the distinction between what structuralists and poststructuralists have been generally understood as saying on the question of the self, and what, on the other hand, they have
actually written. If it is true that Barthes, Benveniste, Foucault, Lacan,
and Lévi-Strauss have proclaimed in various ways the death of the subject, it is also true that other passages in their work temper this claim
and indeed even assert the opposite. The self can exist as "a person
both in language . . . and outside of it as well," as informing every instance of discourse or as an otherwise rational being. Benveniste, for
example, never questions the existence of a "permanent" subject once
it has arisen from the insertion into the order of language of the being
who says "I."[4] Barthes writes, in *Barthes on Barthes*, under the topic "The
Book of the Self": "He resists his ideas: his 'self' or ego, a rational con-
cretion, ceaselessly resists them. Though consisting apparently of a series of 'ideas,' this book is not the book of his ideas; it is the book of
the Self, the book of my resistances to my own ideas."[5] And in his final
work Foucault was concerned with the technical practices in our tradition "whereby the self . . . is constituted in relation to itself as subject."[6] In the essays that follow I shall sometimes make use of the elo-
quence of structuralist and poststructuralist critics in order to speak on
behalf of the self.

A similar irony is that the argument for the loss of the self
appeals to a modern tradition of thought in which the figures of Nietzsche,
Freud, and Heidegger loom particularly large. But it is not true that these
writers encourage a sort of divestiture of self. A redefinition of self, cer-

tainly—yet this is a distinction which the general reception of the question tends to overlook. Lacan, for example, has been influential in reinterpreting each of these writers. His work has been held to contribute to the dissolution of the subject, but even his invocation of a destructive tradition could lead to a very different conclusion. Citing the phrase from Freud "the nucleus of our being" (*Kern unseres Wesens*), Lacan writes: "It is not so much that Freud commands us to seek it, as so many others before him have, with the empty adage 'Know thyself'—as to reconsider the ways that lead to it." What Freud therefore "proposes for us to attain is not that which can be the object of knowledge, but that . . . which creates our being and about which he teaches us that we bear · witness to it as much and more in our whims, our aberrations, our phobias and our fetishes, as in our more or less civilized personalities." The essential point is that we are asked both by Freud and Lacan to "attain . . . that . . . which creates our being" through the means by which we bear witness to it. In the matter of a privileged witness it may well be that "our more or less civilized personalities" have wasted their privilege. But Freud and Lacan do not assert that literature as a witness-bearer belongs to the unspeaking side of our more or less civilized personalities.[7] For them, as for the writers in this book, literature opens a way into our being. The entire jagged arc of poetic activity from writer to reader—to which, I will add, the subjectivity of the poetic intention necessarily belongs—is privileged evidence of the self.

In another related sense the structuralist and poststructuralist attack on the self has been misunderstood. The attack has been aimed chiefly at the Cartesian subject, the *res cogitans*, a substantial self identified uniformly with the thinking subject and cited in "philosophies of consciousness," where it is erected into the foundation of an epistemology.[8] This is the self that developed under high capitalism into what Fredric Jameson calls "the lived experience of individual consciousness as a monadic and autonomous center of activity."[9] It empowers the author of literary works as a coercive authority "doing something to the narrative of reality" that constrains the reader to reproduce, from the author's own angle, a unified meaning.[10] Now it is only this epistemological or monadic self that the new criticism disavows, and, what is more, it actually produces and affirms in its own right another self—a "decentered" self. Barthes writes in the same text previously quoted, under the head of "Myself, I": "Today the subject apprehends himself *elsewhere*, and 'subjectivity' can return at another place on the spiral: deconstructed, taken apart, shifted, without anchorage: why should I not speak of 'myself' since this 'my' is no longer 'the self' "?[11] The new criticism is therefore misrepresented when readers identify the fate of its self with that of the unitary subject addressed by deconstructive readings. It is only the concept of the monadic self that is claimed to be empty. Yet the received interpretation persists: Structuralists and poststructuralists, it is said, have announced the death of the self,[12] and in a fundamental sense this response is justified. For even if the attack on the self is weakened to exclude the decentered self, the claim it makes is hardly innocent. What is it to recommend a self or subject that is not in any sense a center, an agent, or an origin?

In *Structuralist Poetics* Jonathan Culler tried to rescue the individual subject from the structuralist attack. The self became the necessarily posited "place" in which the "structural process" takes place. It remained the condition of the intelligibility of the individual use of semiotic conventions. In what way, however, is the place where structural operations occur in any meaningful sense a self? "The individual subject," writes Culler, "may no longer be the origin of meaning . . . or even control this process."[13] He or she is the place where it takes place. Yet this place is only the "space in which all the quotations that make up a writing are inscribed" (Barthes).[14] "Emphasis falls," continues Culler, who glosses this point, "on the reader as a function rather than as a person."[15]

I conclude from passages like these (and many others might be cited) that the main tendency of the new French criticism is an attack on the self as it has been understood since German Idealism as the agent of its own development. The polemic goes against more than the self of essences abundantly criticized by Nietzsche, Heidegger, and Sartre. If it were basically a repetition of the existentialist demystification of bad faith, then the new criticism would hardly constitute so serious a provocation. It is different. Nietzsche, Heidegger, and Sartre each reconstructs in the place of the deconstructed subject the possibility of another, authentic self. Poetic language contributes to this edification. That is not at all the tendency of the structuralist "elimination" and the poststructuralist decentering of the self, its agenda of anti-Sartreanism and dismay at the Kierkegaardian rhetoric of subjective ethical concern associated with France's wartime mood. The key question is indeed whether criticism does or does not concern the way literature and thought bear witness to "that which creates our being." And what is it, asks Nietzsche in *Thus Spoke Zarathustra*, that "created . . . value and will?" He answers "the creative self."[16] The project of the new criticism is not finally that of Nietzsche; Lacan introduces "cause" into a subject as an effect of language.

Meanwhile readers on both sides of the question have tended to obscure the issue by their refusal to debate, which harbors uneasiness and derision. In various quarters on both sides, further discussion of the self has been foreclosed.[17]

Who is right? Let us see what the modern self reveals when it is approached head-on in the natural attitude. A swift survey of its concrete experience finds no stopping place, and it has forgotten all the narratives of self laid down in its archives. To try to write directly about it is to solicit the active blank, the consternation that enters where language fails. "Consternation"—precisely; the word returns to a root which means at once "to prostrate" and "to cause to shy or dodge." The task of writing about the self takes on, in an unreflected way, something of the stun and the speed of its subject. The task itself has no immediate certainty about itself.

The question of the self, of the self *in general*, cannot, it seems, be met head on. It might be possible to write about the dogwood outside my window, the child playing beneath it, or even the German writer open on my desk *in general*, and not feel that everything is lost. *That* dogwood, *that* child, *this* text is, really, nothing like the genus, and yet none of them is so unlike the genus as the self. The self is particular, the self as self is precisely what cannot be represented in the concept.

To try, therefore, to analyze the modern self as a particular being will seem paradoxical or impossible. Barthes, on the other hand, attempts to combat the "mythic" opposition between the concrete particular and its intelligible meaning:

> The pure and simple "representation" of the "real," the naked account of "what is" (or what has been), thus proves to resist meaning; such resistance reconfirms the great mythic opposition between the *vécu* [the experiential, or "lived experience"] (or the living) and the intelligible; we have only to recall how, in the ideology of our time, the obsessional evocation of the "concrete" (in what we rhetorically demand of the human sciences, of literature, of social practices) is always staged as an aggressive arm against meaning, as though by *de jure* exclusion what lives is structurally incapable of carrying a meaning—and vice versa.[18]

Overcoming this myth, however, depends on finding the right degree of relation between the concrete and its meaning, between experience and category, and on this score the modern self is likely to be irritable. Its irony is affronted by the forced conjuncture of particular and general. One might be tempted, for example, to find the meaning of the modern self in the very radical degree of its particularity. Its fate might be grasped as the extremity of individuation, the self intended by Fichte being altogether less quirky than the exemplary modern interiority, say, of Leopold Bloom in *Ulysses*. Yet absolute particularity is itself a general term. And whatever heightened sense of its post-Idealist dereliction the self can still recover, its situation—the reflexive situation of self-consciousness—is a general one. The search for principle introduces into it a generality of mode which connects it to other selves and interrupts its supposed concreteness.

Maybe the idea of absolute particularity fails on account of its too great generality. The question may be one of finding a better idea. We can propose with Kafka and Beckett (as did Wylie Sypher in his *Loss of the Self*) the increasing anonymity of the empirical person.[19] But the perception by the anonymous self that it represents a maximum of anonymity identifies it as a radical instance and individuates it. As the exemplary finale of a dissolution, this self inherits a consciousness of itself as a case, which names and hence dispels its anonymity. Precisely these currents and countercurrents disturb the reader of Freud, who stresses "the *peculiar* dispositions and tendencies . . . of each individual ego" as well as its dependency on the *generic* structures of an archaic heritage (italics mine).[20] The difficulty of defining the modern self head-on persists no matter what the ruling idea. When the self touches itself directly, it finds only the antinomy of abstract and particular or both forcibly joined.

As long as the self is considered without historical prejudice as a kind of *system* of particular and general, the bite of Gödel's theorem will be keen. It cannot at once stand inside itself and give a full description of itself. But certainly there has never been only one fold in our self-knowledge, a single system of the self: the articulation of difference within that system always engenders a history. When Nietzsche wrote that only a being without a history could be *defined*, he pointed to the necessity that the self, which resists definition, be rethought within a history.

Confronted by this difficulty, needing to mediate between Kant and Hume, Coleridge wrote: "Now the Self is ever pre-supposed and like all other supersensual subjects can be made known to the Mind only by a representative: And again what that representative shall be is by no means unalterably fixed in human nature by nature itself; but on the contrary varies with the growth bodily, moral and intellectual of each individual."[21] Coleridge's formula rejects the ahistorical claims of the radical particularity and the radical anonymity of the modern self. The task is one of establishing the history of a self neither altogether general nor particular, neither "Self" nor empirically constrained representative. This self is now what Lukács, writing in the Hegelian-Marxist tradition, calls "the specific" (*das Besondere*), and it is only in the specificity of the dialectic of the particular and the general that "the inner constitution of human life is revealed."[22] The specific human self is the being whose concept of itself is constituted by its own activity. The description of such a self could show it embroiled in the dense and refractory particularities of economic, social, and religious life, in which it labors to produce its representative. It could show, for example, as Fredric Jameson suggests, that while the monadic and authoritative self arose within nineteenth-century entrepreneurial capitalism, the emergence of the rhizome-like, decentered self belongs to the growth of multinational corporations.[23]

Like Hegelian and Marxist teleologies, such a history of the self would stabilize it within its own dialectical becoming. The self gains historical density, and it also gains historical ballast—unfortunately, for this is precisely what the modern self rejects. It does not want to carry along a genealogy of dead representatives, let alone a weight of embedding circumstance. From its standpoint, every form of the self's history other than the embodiment of its principle will seem dispensable. Of what use to it are all the archaic masks displaying less completely than itself the features of its being? This being is a self precisely to the degree that it is no longer its own spent possibilities, is different from the residue of lost objects. Whatever comes down to it is alien historical detritus, particular in its own way and therefore not of the self. The particularity of the self is endangered by its history, but so then is its principle, which cannot be other than immanent in a history.

The modern self's aversion to history, however, might apply only to histories too remote—to congeries of illegible names of itself and traces of abandoned struggles. We are selves in light of our own possibility of selfhood; a history of this selfhood would be interesting only in forms entirely transparent to its specific concept of autonomy.

The anthropologist Marcel Mauss sketched out such an exemplary history, recording the emergent features of the idea of the self as the self-conscious subject, in its passage

> from a mere masquerade to the mask, from a role to a person, to a name, to an individual, from the last to a being with a metaphysical and ethical value, from a moral consciousness to a sacred being, from the latter to a fundamental form of thought and action.

This "fundamental form" is the modern category of the subject today under attack; shaped by German Idealism, it identifies "the person with the self, and the self with consciousness as its primordial category . . . . Far from being a primordial, innate idea clearly inscribed since Adam in the deepest part of our being, we find [the idea of the self] still being slowly erected, clarified, specified and identified with self-knowledge, with the psychological consciousness, almost into our own times." [24] The task might well be to elaborate and extend this history in the direction assumed by the "psychological consciousness" as it descends more and more deeply into poetic and critical activity. Such a movement is prescribed by German Idealism, in the sense that aesthetic and critical activity, for Kant, "in the first instance unifies, establishes, vivifies and concentrates the self" (Hermann Cohen).[25] Thereupon the psychological consciousness, having done its work, could disappear, leaving to philosophical anthropology the great task of reconstructing its itinerary.

But here we pause again. The Maussian Idea is only an Hegelian wolf in anthropological sheep's clothing, stunned by the myth whose explosion into fragments announces the modern self. For if this self resists a factual history, it is even less willing to define itself as "the Self which can become for itself an 'object' . . . which dissects its 'inner life' with fussy curiosity." [26] Norman O. Brown rues the "great, and really rather insane tradition that the goal of mankind is to become as contemplative as possible." [27] Never mind that Brown's and Heidegger's critique of reflectiveness is owed to such a contemplative tradition and repeats a moment recurrently identified as an error in Idealist thought; the post-Maussian critique of the self as a possible "object of knowledge" (Lacan) begins to seem compelling. Its implacable skepticism assumes epistemological form: Can a self be itself and know that the act by which it is known "disowns" it? The task of such knowledge is in thinking self-consciousness as nondisruptive. If the self cannot be focused and cannot be centered, it is only this "cannot."

Imagine the self as some substantial entity, some granite of spiritual *fatum*. Imagine that in a privileged moment of self-consciousness it comes to light: *Ecce ego!* How then do we conceive of that being for whom the self has come to light? A notion of self that excluded self-consciousness would be privative. Therefore, the self must be the self together with the self for whom this self has come to light. But if this superself is to come to light as itself an object of consciousness, this apprehension too belongs to it. The process by which the thing becomes itself and also the consciousness of this thing—in a word, the process by which the thing becomes an experience—must, if it is to be comprehensive, be interminable.[28] The self becomes always the future project of the perceiving self; it would fuse an infinite reflection on its experience with its capacity for experience. It recedes forward, so to speak, in a temporal *mise en abîme*, the time of an endlessly recursive self-interpretation. The self is a permanent fugitive, escaping itself into the future of unceasing self-reflection.

This perspective supposes to its advantage that the self is initially a substance. But no geology of the self assures us that what is mined and brought up to the light is granite indeed and not some covering shale. Nietzsche wrote: "It is a tormenting, a dangerous enterprise to dig at oneself this way and descend by force . . . into the shaft of one's being." At what point could one say, " 'This is what you really are, this is no longer the covering' "? [29]

The potential groundlessness of the self leads to the second focus of the epistemological critique. It brings into view the way in which that granite stratum, even if it were visible, could not end with a sharp borderline. Its situation is like that of the *text*, which, for Derrida, is "no longer a finished corpus of writing, some content enclosed in a book or its margins, but a differential network, a fabric of traces referring endlessly to something other than itself, to other differential traces. Thus the text overruns all the limits assigned to it so far . . .—all the limited, everything that was to be set up in opposition to writing [or to a text-like self] (speech, life, the world, the real, history and what not, every field of reference—to body or mind, conscious or unconscious, politics, economics and so forth)." [30]

Edward Said catches both the interior and the exterior scope of this critique:

> The two principal forces that have eroded the authority of the human subject in contemporary reflection are, on the one hand, the host of problems that arise in defining the subject's authenticity and, on the other, the development of disciplines like linguistics and ethnology that dramatize the subject's anomalous and unprivileged, even untenable, position in thought. The first force can be viewed as a disturbance taking place at the *interior* of thought, the second as having to do with the subject's *exteriority* to thought. Together they accomplish one end. For of what comfort is a kind of geological descent into identity from level to lower level of identity, if no one point can be said confidently to *be* irreducible, beginning identity? And of what philosophical use is it to be an individual if one's mind and language, the structure of one's primary classifications of reality, are functions of a transpersonal mind so organized as to make individual subjectivity just one function among others? [31]

Because of its elusiveness, an impression heightened by culturally favored applications of an ambient philosophical skepticism, the modern self has been put into basic question.

What, then, explains the persistence with which writers maintain the sense of self—the self that has "a fundamental certainty about itself" (Nietzsche)?[32] The self is hard to speak of, being neither wholly principle nor history, nor thing, nor solitude, nor figure, as the specifiable relation of these terms. But it need not follow that what is hard to speak of does not exist.

It is a matter of fact that each of the writers studied in this book has given an account of the self. This is the principle of their solidarity. Each author elaborates a conception of the self whose conatus is to communicate itself and to come to light within its work. The chapters that follow speak of the self in Hölderlin as a poetic agency bent on defining textually the lack which disfigures the unconscious; of the self in Dilthey as the "original coordination" of the facts of the age, arising within an "acquired context of the life of mind"; of the self in Nietzsche as a willed openness to interpretation; of the self in Mann as an ironic tautology of writing and history constructed to its own advantage; of the self in Kafka as the suffering that accepts the random disruption of stylistic features; of the self in Freud and the terror-obsessed French Freudians as the enacted myth of cure; finally, of the self in Heidegger as the "existential possibilities of moods."

Each of these writers registers the consciousness of an otherness inhering in his self. In this sense Heidegger writes, "Dasein [human existence] is mainly and for the most part *not* itself" (BT, p. 365). Each writer displays the structure of a divided self that finds it cannot or will not live the other that it is. The definition of this otherness changes from writer to writer, but each self produces an idea of what retards it. Hölderlin suffers the absence of a feeling of the sacred; Dilthey, a culture without center, mere disproportion. Nietzsche finds an ego that must be surpassed, must go under, while Mann shelters against the loss of something domestic and benevolent, a conservative tradition. For Kafka existence outside the condition of being a writer (*Schriftstellersein*) is anxiety long drawn out. Freud and the French Freudians signal the deadness and incitement to terror in the repressed personality; Heidegger finds man "thrown," captivated by his facticity, turning evasively from himself. These writers convert an impediment into a scruple, write to recreate themselves, and attest to a demand: the self must give itself value in surpassing the defect of the given.

Each of these authors lives as a conscious subject aiming through poetic activity to produce the self which it means to be. Each intends this self even as he knows that the self thus realized is also different from the self he is, and so must fall back again into the domain of an adversary facticity. Yet the project continues, sustained by a certain remote intimacy with a third term, a projected totality, which the synthesis aims to approximate. The third term supports the possibility of the transcendence of the adversary other.

It can seem glib to write this way, but these are the putative terms of totality: Hölderlin's poetry is oriented to a non-naturalistic nature, Dilthey's, to the knowledge of society. Nietzsche's work is a transcendental psychology of the creative self, Mann's, the totality of internalized culture. Kafka seeks literature in its promise of a truth outside the phenomenal world, Freud and the Freudians, an ideal of psychological rigor, and Heidegger, a sense of Being as a live philosopheme. (My own postscript summons up an idea of intactness founding the autobiographical project.) The Third is an implicit dimension of representations of self.

In this light too the force of the deconstructive critique can be located. If the totalizing Third is only a linguistic fiction, then the entire system of self, adversary other, and transcendence becomes a myth. To have a sense of its being, the self is thrown back upon itself in versions of blind need, as a radical particularity, or of irony, as the knowledge that it must will its forgetfulness. But writing is unthinkable in such a mode of life, except as avowedly unthinkable *écriture*, so we see these writers energetically organizing their transcendence.

In invoking, now, the essential conditions of a self, I do not mean to invoke a self consisting of essences but rather "a structure immanent in its effects."[33] My purpose is to institute the modern self as the copresence ("structure") of various narratives ("effects") of the self which earlier writers have produced. The self is historical in the sense that it can be made intelligible only by a narrative of this structure—a narrative that engages the self in a hermeneutic circle through exegetical constraints imposed by the chronology of the texts it treats. My chapters will sometimes work against other accounts in which the self has been affirmed in too facile a way (as by Thomas Mann) or alleged not to have been affirmed (as by those writing on Nietzsche).

This study of seven German authors, then, focuses on representations of the self, with the intent of recovering meaning in history. It aims to constitute a kind of intellectual history through a poststructuralist critical awareness. In describing how German writers thematize the self, and in claiming this fact to be *apodictic* evidence of the self, I am not claiming that it is also *adequate* evidence of the self. The self spoken is not in every instance the self that speaks. Indeed a view I share with the new criticism would distinguish between what writers explicitly say about the self and what antithetical concept of self seems often to be at work through their thematic account.[34] The self could get lost in its verbal performance. Even the greatest thinkers of the self cannot say what the self is without unchaining yet another fugitive construction. But this is not to preclude the discovery of patterns of self-loss and self-recovery even in that performance. A cogent description of the modern self, an account of its fate, would be a narration of many authorial narratives about the self. These are the features of the self actually present.

The final question in offering such a story, however, concerns more than the general task of narrating aspects of a structure, to the extent that the self is a structure. There still remains the modern self's historically intensified antagonism toward the historical and hence toward the narrative factor. The figures of narrative have their own history, as strictly speaking structures, ironic or otherwise, do not. Once let history into the self, and surely the self must give up its outline, must unravel and vanish entirely, into a vast library of implicated tropes. Reading too would then become only the internal narrative of the self's resistance to displacement by whatever thesis about itself it encounters. Barthes would be right to make of the self the reader who cannot agree with his own reading and will suspect it as being the arrest of a wash of codes.[35] An arrest, yes—but not, I believe, an arbitrary one. The reader, like Joseph K., is responsible for his arrest, and the text, like the world of the Court, makes its contribution.

The timeliness of these reflections should emerge in relation to the current *dóxa* on the self: the too easy assertion that the self is merely a metaphor, always but a metaphor, always transparent to its constructedness, always a fiction, when it is not an "irrational, unmediated" coalescence of blankness and need.[36] This is a view that cannot be lived. To live it is to go mad, so it will come as no surprise that many a professional killing has recently been made by arguing its necessity. It may therefore be helpful to suggest the hold against this unraveling which the memory of other selves offers. It is for us, really, to decide how far we want to let go of the self—our own and others—and to persist in asking: where does the self unravel? In what place, at what time? To describe it? No, to resist it. This is a good deal better than repeating that the self has always already unraveled. I dislike the brief made for madness by critics of literature; and infinite irony, or what Nietzsche calls "lascivious ascetic discord," is only another name for it.[37] The madness of *literature* without a self no more exists than does the sanity of a *self* without literature.

Thinking, then, that literature has never been made by the mad on behalf of madness to drive the reader mad, I am inclined to see it as tending to sustain coherently the writer's self and receivable only by the reader who is also bent on consolidation and expansion. This political language of consolidation and expansion alerts one again to the real politics in the metaphors of narration. The modern self by virtue of the severity of its refusal of history appears thus to be determined by the history *in* its rhetoric. If what is ordinarily understood as history may seem beside the point for the modern self, nevertheless it is by historical narratives that its features are actually drawn. One is reminded of this constraint when one reads the Germans bedeviled by historical upheavals. Many features of the self in their narratives come into view only in the moment when these authors suddenly shift the rhetorical burden of one element to another, a shift that is overdetermined, and in which the political world plays its coercive part. A plain example of this point is that Nietzsche's phrase "the fate of the self" does not mean the consecutive history of the self but rather its fateful integrity within the course of its wanderings—an exile imposed by injuries suffered during the Franco-Prussian War. The integrity of the self is established by a style open to the history it suffers and perceives—and makes, in the stories it tells, with others' collaboration.

The story in this book too is told with the collaboration of many other authors—of Lionel Trilling, for one, whose *Opposing Self* I read thirty years ago while a student at Columbia College.[38] Rereading it now I am astonished at what I find and glad to record my gratitude. Trilling's book begins: "Most of these essays were written for occasions which were not of my own devising. Yet inevitably an interconnection among the essays does exist . . . . They all, in one way or another, take account of the idea that preoccupies this literature and is central to it . . .—the idea of the self."[39] In this way my book resembles his. Yet, what is Trilling's idea of this "modern self"? "It assumed its nature and fate the moment it perceived, named and denounced its oppressor."[40] Its oppressor is the culture in which it lives. The self's oppressor in my book is different.

The German writer finds himself in a situation different from that of his English counterpart in its feebler actualization of culture apart from religion. Thomas Mann wrote of the German tradition, as well as of our modernity, that the German soul had never identified its life with society: "We are not a people for society."[41] The German writer situates himself between one idea of himself and another. The culture of his age is only one and not often the most important of his leading ideas. In practice, culture can have so small a claim on the self (in inverse proportion to the force with which it could simply destroy it) that even Mann in the 1930s could declare from outside Germany, "Where I am, is German culture."[42] The phrase is striking as the claim to an exemplary maximum of cultural acquisition. It is even more striking as the idea that between the self and its culture there might be no tension at all, however remote from its vicious Nazi form. In Mann's formula, culture lacks institutional refractoriness, its untransplantable intricacy of specification. And indeed, from the beginning of his career, even Mann, as the most cultural-minded of German writers, felt either gratefully at home in the "German tradition from Luther to Bismarck and Nietzsche," or else, as an exile, he rejected it entirely. For always being at home in it or else standing entirely apart, he might escape the anxiety of influence.[43]

We must look elsewhere in the German mind for the oppositional and recalcitrant element against which a preferred idea of the self achieves itself, but we will find this nonhumanity, for it is given. It is the sadness or horror of the human *as the given*. The adversary of the German soul in German writing from Luther to the present is the negative of itself that is given as the burden of its rage and dereliction. Karl Moor in Schiller's *Robbers* says, "Externals are but the varnish upon a man—I am my heaven and my hell," and in this respect he is no different from his adversary, his older brother Franz, who asserts, "What I can make of myself depends on me" (*ist meine Sache*).[44]

Anton Reiser, the wanderer, registers "with eternal vexation and disgust his nature as particular, mangled, disjointed."[45] With cartoonlike plainness, Anton Reiser's heir, Harry Haller, the Steppenwolf, exhibits "his pessimism not in world-contempt but self-contempt; however mercilessly he might annihilate institutions and persons . . . he never spared himself . . . whom he hated and despised."[46]

Even in the work of Lessing, the most humane of the beginners of modern German literature, the earliest "social" comedies are metapsychological. They show less the wickedness of self-willed social exclusion—and hence the oppositional relation of self and culture—than the adversary relation indwelling word and act, intention and performance in each of the characters. Harmony of the will is far off and not only because German culture in the eighteenth and nineteenth centuries offers such a miserable paucity of chances. The German self, I believe, is punished by self-reflection even before its impression of cultural poverty; witness the late position of the "Diatribe Against the Germans" in Hölderlin's *Hyperion*. It is not from culture but from a sense of an original estrangement that the German soul draws its sense of life. This sense impels it to dwell in that rift and assists the hope that by a yet further increase in consciousness it will sublimate and reclaim its given nature. In the post-Kantian phase of German Idealism this separation—from spirit, not from culture—is auspicious as promising the return of the same with a positive difference, which is to say a moment of transparency and unity of the self to itself, as once Greek art perfectly displayed its idea through sensuous form. Goethe is the special case. On the strength of a lucky constitution he was immune, he said, to the temptation of thinking about thinking. Schiller, meanwhile, more typically, could see the back door to paradise opening under the moral pressure of repeatedly struck sublime attitudes: for him and his readers the order of truth, joy, and beauty often seemed near at hand.

The Germans after Hegel, however, did not consider reflection on a self intrinsically self-reflective as the way to the spirit but the stigma of doubt. For Nietzsche social life constituted the order of a secondary degeneration of the ascetic spirit, of the domination of "ideals," which is itself the product of degenerating life. The loss of spiritual elitism meant of course the opposite for Dilthey. It meant the hope of a new institution of culture, and for this he is the exception among the writers in this book. Dilthey was less nostalgic for a specific cultural content (Objective Idealism) than he was for a certain cultural logic—a time when poetry and Bildung stood in a single proportion, a ratio he found in Weimar Classicism. Yet when Dilthey wrote on the Romantic Hölderlin, he was not writing like Matthew Arnold on Wordsworth. Hölderlin did not supply the experienced ground of a possible proportion: Hölderlin was the sign of a misology. Through the history of German writing, Dilthey looked to the past chiefly for signs of a fitness between poetry and the criticism of life, and it is only in the perspective of Hölderlin's collapse that Hölderlin prophesied a reconciliation. Dilthey looked everywhere for hope—to London and Paris, especially, for a new impetus to German epic (What would Nietzsche have thought of this idea?). But Dilthey's gaze, politically sound, was chiefly fixed on the future: he saw in modern city life, formless yet emergent, an immense quarry of raw materials for poetic self-making.

But other political interests were also at work exploding this raw material. During the First World War, while Mann was providing the war party with the legacy of Nietzsche's concept of "life," Kafka was consuming his legacy from Flaubert of a certain concept of "death," of the death-in-life of literature, one that required the renunciation of "all those abilities directed towards the joys of sex, eating, drinking, philosophical reflection." "I need only throw my work in the office out of this complex," Kafka wrote (mistakenly), "in order to begin my real life."[47] His fiction excludes the high culture of modern life, and in his Diaries, which he kept all during the war years, he almost never mentions its inverted image—the war. The end state of Idealism in Germany was the drastically thought-curtailed act, which has since led its infuriated victims (Mann

among them) to denounce Luther, Fichte, and Nietzsche as Hitler's precursors (cf. p. 259n22).

Despite periodic attacks on German Idealism, this lofty anguish is still with us. The modern self has to *force* itself to find in the
institutions of its own culture its brother adversary. In this sense, as Erich Heller wrote, "the modern mind speaks German." The rhetoric which
the modern self speaks to itself is German Idealist without the Idea, a
religion of self-mortification without Abraham or Christ and with the
mortifying element much mollified by habit and a fitful generosity toward the given. Each of the German writers studied here cried out for a
new man, but the man they actually made out of themselves is most
nearly the self unaided, taking its way into an interior poorly lit and not
entirely its own. Some of this is shown in Lionel Trilling's essays to be
the result of the intense quarrel between the self and its culture, but
among the writers under study, excepting aspects of Dilthey and Mann,
few "intensely imagined" that culture. The inside sense of the German
writing destiny is of an estrangement preceding the discovery of social
culture. Much goes unnoted in this inside, especially the coercions of
history, of an historical culture insufficiently imagined, upon the writer
who assumes this neglect as his right, and a political reality which will
avenge itself for the writer's lapse of political attentiveness. This double
register of German estrangement suggests some of the difficulty of writing a German intellectual history. Critics in Germany today are particularly alert to the political coercion in the German decision not to vig-
orously reimagine its culture.

I have now twice signaled my debt to another critic who has
unknowingly sponsored this work. I also read Erich Heller at college and
now reread him. The *Disinherited Mind* and *The Artist's Journey into the Interior*
possess a narrative power which school criticism in the last decades has
done nothing to nurture.[48] Professor Heller describes the "unifying theme"
of *The Disinherited Mind* as "the sense of values as shown or embodied in
the works of some modern German poets, writers and thinkers from
Goethe to Kafka."[49] My own book connects to his because in writing
about the self in the same period I am writing about the agency that
produces a sense of value. That value is the predilection of a self determined to produce itself beyond its own opposition.

Professor Heller's second book retells the story from Hegel's
Aesthetics of how "the perfect unity of inner meaning and outer form which
is *found* in Classic art [was] *left behind* in Romantic art."[50] The spirit takes
its path away from this ideal into the inner life, halting only to seize the
world for company on its inward journey. This story is meant to attach
to the whole development of the German mind since Goethe, hinting

that the immense tragedy which befell it was prepared by its pride, and hinting too of even greater tragedies to come. Certainly German life has forever shown an unusual degree of separation between its literary and political energies, but their tragic outcome cannot be explained by the alleged punishable hubris of Idealism. Professor Heller sees the Romantic journey into the interior as having come to an end; a new beginning must begin with this end. Indeed, a new beginning has begun with the proclamation of the death of the subject. I would oppose this beginning, deflect it in order to reveal in Romantic writers and their heirs the survival of their excess of spirit in the rifts of a philosophical inwardness.

I said before that the inwardness of the Idealist or Romantic mind is not entirely its own, and this points to a last and important distinction between my work and Professor Heller's. I stress that the German Romantic and post-Romantic representation of the self is in no way uniform with "pure spirit" and not even with itself: it is divided, and one side of it is worldly, worldlike, factual. For this is first of all the self of writers who meant to publish their work (Kafka corrected the proofs of his last volume of stories on his deathbed), and in many ways these writers express the consciousness that a writing of the spirit turns the spirit inside out, from spontaneity to fact. Yet they acknowledge the exterior in the interior, and for Hölderlin the self has the duty of empirical existence. If, for Dilthey, empirical existence is a foregone value, artistic creativity is hard. The great writer struggles for a metamorphosis of a superabundant internalized world for the sake of his culture. Nietzsche's great quarrel is Life's quarrel with the ascetic lullaby of inwardness, and Mann is ironical about the relation of the soul to its political success in a more self-dissembling way than has been pointed out by even Professor Heller. Kafka's inwardness is never pure—certainly Professor Heller never maintains that it is—but always compact with the dross of empirical reality to the point of obsession, and therefore what he creates are obverse figures of the spirit, whose degradation is the condition of manifestation in a fallen world. Freud's artistic creator, of course, is as worldly as drive is; beyond his none too radical transformation (*Umformung*) of primary desire, he lives entirely for the world, and transformation amounts only to his arranging a sort of caucus of the instincts, a sly consensus of the desires of mankind housed in art. For Heidegger too (as Spitzer notes) "the seat of the 'world' [is] in the existence of the individual, *within* whom the *um-* [of his *Umwelt*, his environment] is alive."[51] Yet even Dasein's authentic understanding of the world is split into the modes genuine and ungenuine (BT, p. 186), and language entangles itself in things: "In being its *Self* Dasein is, *as* a Self, the entity that has been thrown" (BT, p. 330). Wherever we turn, we see writers represent in their selves an element of facticity alien to inwardness, which by the dialectic enables such a thing as the genuine self to appear in significant distortion, in a revealing concealment. The turn to inwardness is always a turning of inwardness inside out. Hence, the project of living in society as the visible representative of an authentic inwardness is—as Rousseau mentions in the *Confessions*—the most chimerical venture ever undertaken.

Rousseau, perhaps surprisingly, figures in the carpet of almost everyone of these essays. He is my eighth "German writer," a fact which has to do with his intellectual and moral authority, often as a cautionary example, in the German tradition from at least Kant on, who declared in his *Anthropology*:

> The first impression which a reader . . . . has from the writings of Rousseau is . . . of an uncommon clear-sightedness of spirit, a noble soaring of genius, and a sensitivity of soul in so high a degree as perhaps never any writer, whatever his period or nation might be, may have possessed in combination.[52]

And further:

> I am myself by inclination an investigator. I feel the full thirst for knowledge and the anxious restlessness to progress or the satisfaction too at every acquisition. There was a time when I believed that this alone could make the glory of mankind, and I despised the rabble which knows nothing. Rousseau put me right. This dazzling prerogative disappears; I am learning to honor men, and I would consider myself less useful than the common worker if I did not believe that this way of thinking could impart to all others a value in establishing the rights of humanity.[53]

Whenever I discuss Rousseau, it is because the writers I discuss have alluded to him. Their narratives of self are interinvolved with their understanding of Rousseau, as is, I confess, my own postscript on autobiography. But Rousseau's presence in this book is also inspired by the mood of our critical climate. The work of Derrida and especially of de Man has encouraged us to feel the depth of Rousseau's intellectual example. The focus in this book on the question of the self disposes me to favor Rousseau's autobiographical writing, for the amazingly original elaboration of its principle. "My style will itself be part of my story (*histoire*)."[54] Rousseau constitutes the modern identity by conceiving it especially as the mood of the very act of writing its history.

Hölderlin's poetry is responsive to Rousseau's personal example. And with Hölderlin we turn now to the German writer who determined most radically that the mood and language of his poetic practice should constitute his identity. We shall see the forms taken by Hölderlin's quarrel with himself and—I hope not jarringly—mine with his critics. I should like to alert the reader that the first chapter, set in the period of German Idealism, is more explicit than any of the following chapters about the attack made by contemporary critics upon the constitutive poetic subject and so could as well figure as a closing chapter on the fate of the self in the years of the new continental criticism. Furthermore, its critical perspective is owed to some extent to the Heideggerean poetics sketched out in the last chapter.

The subjects of the chapters following Hölderlin—on Dilthey, Nietzsche, Mann—have a kind of objective historical coherence through the likeness of their themes and the provable awareness which several of these writers had of one another. The writers featured in the final three essays have a sort of subjective coherence. They come together chiefly in being treated in the optic of current literary critical concerns to which they themselves contribute. Here the subject matter of this book makes a turn of its helix.

CHAPTER ONE

Hölderlin and the Question of the Self

Changes in literary theory during the past decade have profoundly altered the way in which English and German Romantic writers are being read. The thrust of the new criticism has been to discredit the self or subject as an origin of meaning and value. But what is Romanticism if not an "act of reflection on the fundamentally subjective character of the spirit," on "the isolated self thrown back upon itself"?[1] It is therefore to be expected that Romantic texts should come in for harsh treatment, including more than a little aversion and manhandling, with the purpose of having them turn critic's evidence. The Romantic soul has been asked to sing in an unheard of way, and suspicions of character remain. Thus we read in the influential *Neues Handbuch der Literaturwissenschaft*: "The claim to canonical status, which has been attributed to German Romanticism for more than a century by its historical reception, has today been widely forfeited."[2]

To think about Romantic poetry two decades ago was to feel oneself at the wellspring of modern reflection on the self. It was (wrote Paul de Man in 1965) to grasp writers like Wordsworth, Keats, and Solger as furthering "the most audacious and advanced forms of contemporary thought," especially the distinction between a personal and a "transcendental type of self."[3] To Romantic writers was owed "the experience of an *act* in which, to a certain extent, we ourselves have participated," an act "contributing in an immediate way . . . to the constitution of our consciousness of temporality."[4] Today these words have taken on an odd untimeliness. It is only with a much diminished and ironical sense of self and time that many readers still maintain a feeling of community with Romantic writers.

A new criticism explores in literary texts a repeated moment of the dispersion of self-consciousness into indeterminate fragments. In the more radical view later espoused by de Man, "no discussion of specific experiences of [Romantic] consciousness is any longer conceivable."[5] The dignity of Romantic literature would then consist in the clarity with which it makes plain this permanently "dürftige Zeit," the time of the mind wanting in meaning. The Romantic text has its incoherence to confess, and if in one view it does indeed admit to self-loss as charged, in "metaphorical vehicle[s] of the imperative toward deconstruction,"[6] in another view, which borrows Nietzsche's scorn for the Romantic masquerade, the Romantic confession is made in patent bad faith.[7] Certainly the grounds of poetic and critical authority have shifted.

The once dominant critical discourses of New Criticism and the *critique de la conscience* drew on and acknowledged their filiation from Kant and Hegel, but the new critical theory, in rejecting this older literary criticism, rejects the claims of Romantic metaphysics as they bear on a transcendental or any other kind of centering self. The rhetoric of Romantic poetry is implicated in this attack, since the philosophical vocabularies of Kant's *Third Critique* and of Hegel's *Phenomenology of Spirit* and *Aesthetics* in turn enriched themselves with subjective key words from European pre-Romantic and Romantic poetry. The "beautiful soul" (*die schöne Seele*), for example, figures in Hegel's *Phenomenology* as an exemplary if aberrant form of narcissistic consciousness, but this figure was inspired in Hegel's mind by Friedrich Hölderlin (1770–1843), by the novelistic character Hyperion, by Novalis, and by the aunt of book 6 of Goethe's *Wilhelm Meisters Lehrjahre*.[8] This connection has its own history. Dilthey noted that "in their systems Schelling, Hegel and Schleiermacher carry through on logical and metaphysical grounds the view of life and of the world developed by Lessing, Schiller and Goethe,"[9] and Windelband declared that Kant's *Third Critique* justifies Goethe's (symbolic) poetry, a justification which might extend to unconscious imitation.[10]

Once Romantic philosophies of idealism are read suspiciously, Romantic poetry is bound to be read suspiciously as well. The truth claims of Romantic poetic fictions and the fictive character of many Romantic philosophical texts (e.g., the dialogue in Solger, the conversation in Friedrich Schlegel, and the "journey" of the Spirit in Hegel's *Phenomenology*) make it hard to tell these genres apart. In Hölderlin's poetry, for example, "reflection has been assimilated to such a degree that the traditional treatment of the question concerning the relationship of philosophy to poetry in Hölderlin has become obsolete. In the degree of their reciprocal involvement, Hölderlin's poetry occupies a singular position, . . . one in which reflection enters poetry not simply as a thematic but as a structural element."[11] This intimacy of philosophy and poetry is certainly not unique to Hölderlin. Passages from Rousseau's *Nouvelle Héloïse* and the *Rêveries* (the *Fifth Promenade* especially) have the rigor and argumentative terminology (anti-Lockean sensationalist) of Rousseau's explicitly philosophical writing.[12] The same is true of Wordsworth's *Prelude*, whose "words" would "speak of nothing more than what we are," an ambition that, with its "words," "nothing," "we," and "are," diagrams the metaphysical tradition until recently generating our critical vocabularies. Yet another sort of Romantic poetic authority has been lost with the passing of the German and Swiss existential literary criticism influential in the fifties and early sixties.[13] This is the authority of Heidegger's perspective on Hölderlin, which sees as epochal a revelation occurring in the Romantic period—namely, Hölderlin's perception of the ontological difference between Being and beings.[14]

The difficulty of understanding Romanticism lies in the actual intimacy of our relation to it, our whole critical-interpretive enterprise being a sort of unsettled aura surviving the wreck of Romantic hope. Now, however, it is said that, apart from its complicity with modern rhetorical deconstruction, the Romantic mood is gone, and we read Romantic anxiety with postmodern detachment. The conceptual pairs supplied to the older criticism by Romantic poetry—sentiment/sensation, consciousness/nature, imagination/reason—having lost their cogency, are taken as instances of bad binary thinking. It has seemed possible, for example, to show Rousseau, Wordsworth, and Hölderlin valorizing the pole of Subject (Consciousness), then the pole of Object (Nature), alternately and incessantly. The outcome of such readings cannot therefore be a statement about a unified Romantic consciousness—neither one that registers its triumph or its defeat vis-à-vis stubborn materiality and contingency, nor one that finds itself (or benignly loses itself), having been ministered to by Nature, even in negative pleasure.[15]

The deconstruction of the thought of Rousseau, with Hölderlin soon following, arrives in the wake of Jacques Derrida's deconstruction of the "sovereign" authorial subject.[16] Such projects are part of a structuralist and poststructuralist effort to abolish as illusory the presence of the self to itself and to a reader.[17] But the loss of self even at the level of poetic and critical consciousness is not thought of as a disaster; indeed, reimagined as a necessary divestiture, it is defended as the very condition of writing. The loss of self, wrote de Man in 1980, apropos of Rousseau, is entailed by the arbitrary, mechanical character of "performative" language, including the language of fiction, in whose grip the deluded self pursues its justification. Even the cognitive language produced in justification is only the "aberrant, metaphorical correlative" of the self. "Far from seeing language as an instrument in the service of a psychic energy, the possibility now arises that the entire construction of drives, substitutions, repressions and representations is the aberrant, metaphorical correlative of the absolute randomness of language prior to any figuration or meaning."[18] Neither Romantic poetic nor interpretive language on this view can converge on its concern; neither creates a field demarking or developing a self.

The critical dissolution of the self is accompanied necessarily by the loss of the categorical dialectic of self and other, which is considered an epiphenomenon of the false consciousness of identity arising from the "mirror phase" of development, as a consequence of resentment, or as an intersubjective instance of a metaphysical shell game.[19] Kant and Hegel have been replaced by the master thinkers of the third term—by Marx, Nietzsche, and Freud, who support neither the individual terms of the dialectic nor even this dialectical structure, but rather the textlike system enabling and accommodating them as tropes. Whether society, language, or the unconscious, the system is constituted as an endless and impersonal exchange of negative differential terms.[20]

Certainly this revaluation is occurring too quickly, often without pause or wisdom. Before judging it one needs to know better what has been said on the question of the self by the Romantic poets and by an older tradition of criticism. In the 1920s William Michel described the late "Hesperian turn" in Hölderlin's work and personality as a process of "stabilization" (Verfestigung, which can be translated, with attention to its etymology, as "armoring"). This movement, continued Michel,

> leads from longing and self-deception to what actually is: to the self, to present reality, to the forms and themes of the art of Hölderlin's time and country. . . . Hölderlin's experience of life leads . . . to concentration, to a pulling the self together, to greater boldness in holding fast to the self and everything that belongs to the expanded order of the self. What he inclines to by birth and temperament—the anxious or enthusiastic orientation to the other which tends at one moment to weakness and masquerade and at another to the most exalted dispossession of self—is systematically rejected.[21]

This description of Hölderlin's "turn" poses an exemplary challenge to the reader of Romantic literature. The reader, I will be arguing, also must turn from the appearance of inevitable self-deception and himself speak of the poetic self as "present reality." He must, that is, hold fast to the Romantic understanding of the self as this understanding is given him in spite of critical fashion. This urgency can be situated within Romantic writers themselves in the very rhetoric which today shapes a chiefly destructive criticism.

> Der Mensch will sich selber fühlen. . . .
> Sich aber nicht zu fühlen, ist der Tod.
> (Man wants to have a sense of self. . . .
> Not to have a sense of self is death.)
>
> *Hyperion*

The term "self" persists throughout Hölderlin's work. His conception of the self includes the notion of the otherness of the self to itself. The self is therefore not a simple origin. Yet the recognition of the moment of alterity in the self does not imply that it is only a fiction, a rhetorical figure, or a meaningless because contradictory metaphor. The nonidentity of the self is a given—this is what Hölderlin in the early essay "Judgment and Being" ("Urteil und Sein") calls its divided identity.[22] In *Hyperion*, Hölderlin conceives of the self mythically as "the marriage of poverty and abundance" and metaphysically as the condition of consciousness. This nonidentity he terms "the profound feeling of mortality, of mutability, of . . . temporal limitation."[23] Such perspectives inform his conception of *Bildung*—of education and self-development—which animates and is reflected in the work, as the field of struggle of a particular self-consciousness to realize the historical fate of Western culture.[24] The moment of development demands a moment of self-estrangement:

> One's own being (*das Eigene*) must be as much learnt as what is other. For this reason the Greeks are indispensable to us. But we shall not match them precisely in what is our own, our "national" being, because . . . the *free* use of *one's very own being* is most difficult.[25]

That difficulty is meant to be surmounted. Hölderlin declares, "Put yourself by a free choice in harmonious opposition with an external sphere, just as you are in harmonious opposition with yourself by nature, but in an unknowable fashion as long as you remain in yourself."[26]

The conception of a self that must be learned through empirical separation from itself (from *em-peiros*, "undergoing a risk") persists into the late hymns.[27] The *Bildung* of a self compels it to develop through moments of alienation and return; it is oriented indeed toward a third term, neither self nor particular other. For Hölderlin "the crucial interaction no longer takes place between self and world but between that contact and its negation in time," that is, between having and abandoning such moments of contact.[28] *Bildung* is thus oriented away from particular objects, aspects of personality, other persons, and pastoral and social themes toward a heightened experience of temporality. It turns toward historical and sacred objects and finally toward Nature as that generality enabling, sustaining, and enveloping all such particular contacts and negations. Nature is the condition of the possibility of the self that desires to know it. The momentary loss of immediate experience is the cunning of the self that seeks Nature as a "principle in which time is sustained without loss of that movement of dissolution which defines it for those entities subject to it."[29]

Hölderlin authorizes the traditional concern with self-development in the criticism of Romantic poetry, a criticism perhaps culminating in de Man's essay "The Rhetoric of Temporality" (1971). There de Man identified an authentic Romantic temporal consciousness as follows: "The dialectic between subject and object does not designate the main romantic experience but only one passing moment in a dialectic, and a negative moment at that since it represents a temptation that has to be overcome." Overcoming this temptation "corresponds to the unveiling of time in a natural world to which in truth it bears no resemblance."[30] Precisely this point is anticipated by the young Hölderlin in his novel fragment *Hyperion's Youth* (*Hyperions Jugend*): "It is need which constrains us to lend eternally mutable nature affinity with what in us is immortal. This need, however, also gives us the right [to do so]. This belief is founded on the confines of finitude; as a result it is general in every being that feels itself to be finite."[31] Hence, "when nature co-operates with you, sympathetically . . . , when joyfully surprised, in the realm of the senses your spirit as in a mirror contemplates its likeness, and the forms of nature join with solitary thought, be glad and love . . . but never forget yourself."[32]

I do not hear in these sentences of Hölderlin the ring of delusion, even though time, for him, implies the career of self-development. To feel their force, one could compare them with the caveat of a recent critic of Romantic poetry.

> There can be no consistent progress in the self's process of disabusing itself, because the retrograde tendency of constituting new objects is always at work, continually creating new moments of absolute conviction of "experiences of the real" through interpretative strategies that have not come to be recognized as beliefs because they are (at least temporarily) so deeply held as to be invisible.[33]

Hölderlin also values the moment of insight in which an "interpretative strategy" is unmasked, yet he does not consider as merely retrograde that "tendency of constituting new . . . 'experiences of the real.' " The moment of insight also supplies the legitimacy with which experiences are constituted. For if they are based on a belief, the belief is founded on the very "confines of finitude," the condition of being a self. In what unlivable ascesis could a being deplore as an obstacle the condition standing in the way of its entirely "disabusing" itself of itself?[34] "Ought I to be congratulated or pitied," Hölderlin asked, "that nature had given me this irrepressible drive again and again to develop the forces which are in me?"[35] These forces, he wrote to Schelling, require experience:

> Talent (*Genius*), which is without content, cannot exist without experience, and experience, which is without soul, cannot exist without talent. Each contains the necessity of shaping itself (*sich bilden*) and of constituting itself through art and judgment, of producing an order, a live harmonious changing totality. Art, which organizes, and the drive to development (*Bildung*) from whence it comes—cannot exist and are not even conceivable without their inner element—natural talent, genius—and their outer element—experience and historical scholarship.[36]

Hölderlin exalts experience:

> Viel hat erfahren der Mensch.
> Der Himmlischen viele genannt,
> Seit ein Gespräch wir sind
> Und hören können voneinander
>
> (Man has experienced much.
> Named many of the heavenly beings,
> Since we have been a discourse
> And can hear from one another)
> ("Friedensfeier," third version)

The new object ("experiences of the real"), in being organized, further constitutes a self. Experience, even as error, belongs to truth: "Only that is the truest truth wherein error too becomes truth because truth places it in the whole of its system, into its time and place . . . . That is eternal serenity, divine joy, that one puts everything particular in its place, in the whole where it belongs."[37]

Here "truth"—like "experience" above—is conceived as an act of writing. Is Hölderlin's truth then subject to the general deconstruction of Romantic writing? In his last works de Man found Rousseau deconstructing "cognitive" rhetoric itself, for "writing always includes the moment of dispossession in favor of the arbitrary power play of the signifier."[38] The subject is threatened by the act of writing, threatened with "the loss of something that once was present and that it once possessed"—and which it supposed might be carried over into the poem. Still more it is threatened by an experience of the "radical estrangement between the meaning and performance of any text." Earlier de Man stressed a "transition"—a temporal term—between an inferior blind form of language (the "act") and a superior insightful form (the "interpretation"). Now the threat of self-loss shifts from the space between act and reflection to the space "inside" every act and reflection. An unchanging spatial category of nonconvergence holds apart the meaning of the referential speech act from that of its "performative" compulsion.[39] Now there can be no such thing as "transition" from act to interpretation and no distinction in truth value between act and interpretation. As there could be no self, so there can be no truth.

I do not believe, however, that Hölderlin's work is the record of a sense of failure of a convergence inside language but rather the record by language of a struggle to conserve in a superior mode of self what is threatened with loss. "The feeling of the sacred," for example, in the tragic drama, "no longer expresses itself immediately, it is no longer the poet and his own experience which appear," yet "every poem, including the tragic, must have come forth from poetic life and reality, from the poet's own world and soul, because otherwise the proper truth is lacking, and if we cannot carry over our own spirit (*Gemüth*) and our own experience into a foreign analogous material, nothing at all can be understood and given life." The tragic poet denies his "person, his subjectivity" but not "the spirit, the sacred, as the poet felt it in his world";[40] he sustains himself as the "carrying over," the metaphor, of the given immediate feeling.

This passage comes from the "Philosophical Basis" of *The Death of Empedocles* (1799). Undoubtedly the earlier Hölderlin—a Hegelian Hölderlin—comes under the head of a philosophy of renunciation and recovery. This is the Hölderlin of the *Reflection*: "Only that is the truest truth wherein error too becomes truth because truth places it in the whole of its system into its time and place." For a statement of the difference between Hegel and the later Hölderlin, I turn to Michel Foucault:

> [With Hegel] we find the developing theme of a thought which, by the movement in which it is accomplished—totality attained, violent recovery at the extreme point of poverty, solar decline—curves over upon itself, illuminates its own plenitude, brings its circle to completion, recognizes itself in all the strange figures of its odyssey, and accepts its disappearance into that same ocean from which it sprang. In opposition to this return, which even though it is not happy is perfect, we find the experience of Hölderlin . . . in which the return is posited only in the ex-

treme recession of the origin—in that region where the gods have turned away, where the desert is increasing, where the technè has established the dominion of its will; so that what we are concerned with here is neither a completion nor a curve, but rather that ceaseless rending open which frees the origin in exactly that degree to which it recedes: the extreme is therefore what is nearest.[41]

This region is evidently that of such later poems as the hymns "Andenken" and "Patmos." But here too Hölderlin's question presses for an answer: whose is the activity which ceaselessly rends open and in rending open does not open an abyss but frees "the origin" just as it makes it recede?

The action of rending open and making recede characterizes the poetic activity of a subject vis-à-vis "the sacred." The origin, the sacred, is freed and concealed in a movement of poetic language. This is the responsibility of the poet's self—a responsibility whose history is, in Wordsworth's phrase, "the growth of a poet's mind." It is precisely Hölderlin's increasing distance from Hegel that bears witness to his sense of poetic individuality.[42]

Hölderlin seeks Nature as sustaining time even in the very movement of its dissolution—a form of being that might stay "die reissende Zeit" (time which runs with violent speed, which tears along but also tears what it touches). But Hölderlin writes too that Nature is torn by time and in the tragic moment is "nothing more than time," wholly subject to the "lord of time." If that Nature which encompasses development can itself suffer loss and dissolution, if, in it *beginning and end* |can| no longer allow themselves to be coupled together like rhymes,"[43] then what stability can a self or subject have? Its development would become less the historical enactment of the self than the repeated experience of its death.

Such a perspective gives rise to the view stated by Edward Said that Hölderlin's work reveals an "absolute incompatibility between the realm of totality and the realm of personal interiority . . . . |In his desire for totality| Hölderlin personifies an extremism so complete in its heedless articulation of impossible desires as to exclude the possibility of accommodating one man's inner self to it. |His| works deliver naked desire, totally unconditioned by subjectivity: . . . it is a pure serialism unraveling itself, for its own sake."[44] This is indeed a very French, surreal, and deconstructed Hölderlin, for Derrida too asserts: "Articulation is difference. . . . The relationship . . . is one of seriality without paradigm."[45] At this point, however, the disoriented reader might review

Hölderlin's letter to Schelling, beginning "Talent, which is without content, cannot exist without experience."

Such a conclusion—desire wholly without subjectivity—is paradoxical, Said continues, for how then can poets think like Hölderlin and still retain some semblance of their subjectivity? The answer is that outside of their poetry their subjectivity is indeed only a semblance and a tortured facsimile of it at that. They turn themselves inside out and in the public sphere choose unreason, alienation. They make themselves exterior to social discourse. Hölderlin is therefore only himself, and then only as desire, in his poetry; for the rest he is mad. But this answer does not respond to the fact that throughout the period of his greatest creativity Hölderlin was by any criterion only infrequently mad—a provocative mix of lucidity, rage, and formalized behavior that has repeatedly suggested Hölderlin's lifelong pretense of being mad. The career of Hölderlin's desire for totality is bound up with his madness, as readers of Maurice Blanchot well know, but both themes call first for a clearer description of Hölderlin's self-consciousness.[46]

> If you can stand boldly in a chariot with
> four fresh horses rearing up spiritedly in
> the reins, and can direct their forces—
> whipping in the one that gets out of line
> and bringing down the one that rears up,
> giving rein, guiding, turning, whipping,
> stopping and starting again, until all
> sixteen hooves are moving in rhythm to-
> wards the finishing post—you have
> achieved mastery.[47]
>
> —Goethe

The terms "self" and "self-loss" figure often in Hölderlin's work but not so that either term could be filled with explicit ethical-existential import, to mean "Hölderlin encourages a belief in the primacy of the self" or "Hölderlin calls for an abnegation of the self." He does not encourage self-loss as a testimony to humility in the way that a goal of autobiographical writing has recently been defined—"one's beneficent expropriation in an unconscious circuit of exchange."[48] This latter phrase could not describe a beneficent destiny. It almost literally invokes the end of Hölderlin's poetry—his insanity, his poverty, the state of mind imaged in the second strophe of "The Middle of Life" ("Hälfte des Lebens"): "Die Mauern stehn / Sprachlos und kalt, im Winde / Klirren die Fahnen" ("The walls stand / Speechless and cold, in the wind / Weathercocks clatter").

The term "self" is not pure humility; neither should it be defined as an antithetical claim for a strong poetic ego, bent on an extensive totality of experience or bent on originality and ready to wrestle with nature for it. This error is arraigned early, in *Hyperions Jugend*: "Proudly rejected the help with which nature cooperates in every form-giving activity, the readiness with which the stuff of the spirit proffers itself: I wanted to tame, to constrain."[49] Hölderlin devalues this sort of superiority as bent on an exorbitant consciousness of separation; the self divinizes its own sense of finitude. This consciousness at first exalts the distance between man and "the gods," then, claiming strength, attempts avidly to "constrain" the gods. Hölderlin names and in his poetry avenges—with vacuousness—the titanic blunder.[50]

These, however, are only two of the implications of the terms "self" and "self-loss" which recur in cognate forms in Hölderlin's poetry. They describe a deficient form of the experience of self and of self-depletion, but these forms have to be paired with their authentic counterparts.[51]

In its authentic modes, self mediates the moment of self-loss. The figure of Rousseau in "Der Rhein" illustrates one such mode in his elected withdrawal from the temptation of self-glorification. By choosing simplicity he shuns the danger in the extreme clarity of his understanding of finitude. He grasped as, say, Locke did not, the constitutive priority of consciousness over the sensory representation, and his return to an order of pastoral sensation means at once to remember an innocent "error" and to moderate the force of a truth that would entitle men to blast open the earth. Rousseau chooses to forget—to forget self-consciousness at the point where it might be tempted to call itself a god. Laying on the cloak of forgetfulness is a gesture preparing for what Cyrus Hamlin calls "the hermeneutic": it projects the temporal delay enabling interpretation.[52] The wisdom of such a project is Socratic.

There is, finally, a still stronger mode of self: the self bent on expansion can experience or virtually experience fusion with the god, the dazzlement of immediate or virtually immediate contact. Thus in "The Poet's Vocation" ("Dichterberuf"):

> Der unverhoffte Genius über uns
> Der schöpferische, göttliche kam, daß stumm
> Der Sinn uns ward und, wie vom
> Strahle gerührt, das Gebein erbebte
>
> (Divine, creative Genius came over us,
> Dumbfounding mind and sense, unforgettably,
> And left us as though struck by lightning
> Down to our bones that were still aquiver)

Or in "At the Source of the Danube" ("Am Quell der Donau"):

> Da faßt' ein Staunen die Seele
> Der Getroffenen all und Nacht
> War über den Augen der Besten
>
> (Amazement then took hold of
> The souls of all who were struck, and night
> Obscured the eyes of the best men)

This contact implies a terrible danger, an extinction of personality, like death. From the standpoint of the speaker all life consists in swerving from this moment, in rendering the sacred as a poetic word, "das Heilige sei mein Wort."

The entire foregoing phenomenology is based on the relation of the self to the sacred—the absolute object of desiderative consciousness. In "Homecoming" ("Heimkunft") Hölderlin writes:

> denn, was auch Dichtende sinnen
> Oder singen, es gilt meistens den Engeln und ihm;
>
> (for whatever the poets may ponder,
> Sing, it mostly concerns either the angels or him;)

In "The Poet's Vocation" ("Dichterberuf"):

> Der Höchste, der ists, dem wir geeignet sind
>
> (The Highest, he it is whom alone we serve)

The sacred figures in this poetry as a desideratum, while the reflective consciousness struggles to grasp its absence as necessary. This dialectic originates a poetry evoking the proximity of the divine in the fervor of the recognition that no contact is possible. This fervor develops as the desire for divine names. And if the self (as Jacques Lacan says) is double, involving a "marked" absence, like an empty grave, and a signifier of that absence, like a grave marker—a "ghost" or proper noun—then Hölderlin's poetry of proper nouns is par excellence a poetry of the subject.[53] This subject seeks its place in a symbolic order of names substituting for the absence of the god, which it differentiates as it calls for truer names.

Hölderlin conceives of his ruling desire as in both objective and genitive senses the desire of the absent divinity. Desire exists in a register of fulfillment as felt "degrees of enthusiasm"; the agent of this recognition is the poetic self. "The great poet," writes Hölderlin, "is never abandoned by his self, and he may raise himself as high above himself as he wishes." Thought guards against the dangers of "*falling* upwards as well as into the depths, . . . but feeling is the best poetic sobriety and reflection."[54] Each articulation of poetic self-consciousness therefore corresponds to a moment of felt desire. Each describes a distinctive relation of the finite subject to its origin. In this sense Hölderlin's poetry of the self is a poetry of thought, a poetry that records a history of *types* of contingency. Thus, typically, the speaker at the close of "Hälfte des Lebens" has suffered a devastating loss of original being. In the grip of its need, a wounding hunger for fullness, such a self, as in "Wie wenn am Feiertage," could approach too near "the tables of the gods." The titanic figure in whom the sense of separation is exultant produces from sheer will the aura of illusory divinity. Finally, the self that, like the speaker at the close of "Mnemosyne," takes hold of itself in contemplation does so in the aftermath of a disaster. It reflects on the error, exampled by the Greeks, of having returned too wildly to the fire of the origin. The experience of a fusion with the god is interiorized as a cautionary example.

This field of forms of self-fulfillment and self-loss is diagrammed in the opening lines of "Patmos":

> Nah ist
> Und schwer zu fassen der Gott.
> Wo aber Gefahr ist, wächst
> Das Rettende auch.
>
> (Near is
> And difficult to grasp, the God.
> But where danger threatens
> That which saves from it also grows.)

The feeling of the nearness of the god keeps the self proof against the two kinds of despair at absence: emptying and fury. The difficulty of grasping the god suggests the self in labor—the labor of the concept, but the labor too, through feats of will and desire, cunning and technique, to lay hold of the god. And so each quadrant of the subject's being harbors a different danger, as shown in figure 1.

The danger is one of the invasion by divinity (I), which could consume the self and leave it, after separation, wasted and mute (II). It is the danger too of a divinization of the self-centered effort to take hold of the god (III). Saving grace is then neither the accession of sobriety nor the accession of the god alone but the tension sustaining the right ratio of both elements (IV), already given in the initial statement of the predicates of being: its present absence (nearness), its absent presence

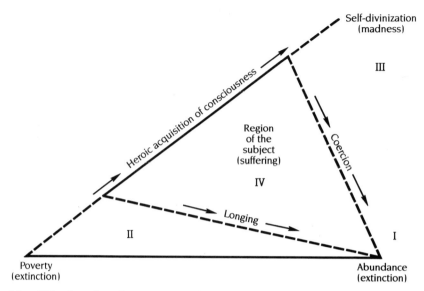

(the difficulty of its being grasped). This tension is the third term—neither phenomenal subject nor other—and has priority within Hölderlin's world as the history of the rapport of the self and the god. The tension is not impersonal:

> Denn nicht vermögen
> Die Himmlischen alles. Nämlich es reichen
> Die Sterblichen, eh an den Abgrund. Also wendet es sich,
> das Echo,
> Mit diesen.

> (For the Heavenly ones
> Cannot do everything. Namely mortals
> Sooner attain to the abyss. Thus the echo turns,
> With them,)

That "the echo turns" is as much the work of man as of "the heavenly ones" ("Mnemosyne"), as much the work of man in the world of the hymn "Griechenland" (second version) as of the "terrible" god of "air and time."

The persistence of a constitutive subject in Hölderlin's work is challenged by Wolfgang Binder's essay "Hölderlin's Poetry in the Age of Idealism."[55] Binder speaks of a three-stage development in the poet's conception of a correct rapport with the god. In the first stage, that of *Hyperion*, Hölderlin claims, through the very self-reflective form of the novel, the primacy of an absolutely self-knowing subject. The mind posits the god. In the second stage, that of *Empedocles*, Hölderlin shows how this hubris shatters, destroying the belief that "it is man who through his language and his knowledge first made the mute gods of nature speak and summoned them into the life of the mind." In the third stage, that of the hymns, Binder says, Hölderlin claims priority for a relation of self-effacing instrumental service ("ein dienendes Gefühl") of the poet to the god. "At the basis of this new understanding is a conception of a Being which no longer needs man in order to come to itself but rather uses him in order to let itself be heard from him and through him."[56] The temporality of consciousness at this third stage is "eschatological simultaneity."

This account, with its language of definitive "overcoming," is too simple and settling: it is regathered religion. It discounts the persistent connection in German Idealism between notions of renunciation and freedom.[57] Binder's third stage dispenses entirely with the constitutive activity of the subject, with self-making through self-conscious language. In Hölderlin, however, there is no such moment of sustained self-abnegation, and explicit references to this constitutive activity can be seen in "The Rhine" ("Der Rhein"), "The River Ister" ("Der Ister"), "The Titans" ("Die Titanen"), and "The Only One" ("Der Einzige"). Indeed there would appear to be no such thing as a selfless language of submission. As Vincent Descombes writes:

> The subject has an original identity to the exact extent to which it constitutes an identifiable place of "enunciation." . . . It is language which produces the singular in its uniqueness. . . . In this sense the subject can well be said to be absolute—liberated from the Other and delivered over to itself alone—on the condition of adding that this absolute being is so to the extent that it is *subjected* to the law of language, which is the law of someone Other than himself.[58]

This kind of subjection creates a subject but not a servant.

A close reading of the hymns shows a persistently combative poetic subjectivity, and through this period Hölderlin's poetics struggles for a form stressing above all Hesperian sobriety and maximum differentiation: "Unterschiedenes ist gut" ("What is differentiated is good").

In the second version of "Mnemosyne" Hölderlin writes:

Ein Zeichen sind wir, deutungslos,
Schmerzlos sind wir und haben fast
Die Sprache in der Fremde verloren.

(We are a sign, without interpretation,
We are without pain and have almost
Lost language in a foreign land.)

This gnome identifies, not an ideal of service but a fatal danger. The assertion of the near loss of language and the advancing logic of the poem show the poet engaged in a movement toward recollection, toward self-assurance, for the sake of commemoration but also for his own sake as a being who names and is not merely a name.

To see in Hölderlin's work the persistence of the self is not to give it the status of an integral origin. In an early essay de Man distinguished "self and language . . . [as] the two focal points around which the trajectory of the work originates, but neither can by itself find access to the status of source. Each is the anteriority of the other."[59] Hence, too, each, in the forward motion of its activity, hurls itself upon, and finds, the other. As Foucault says, "Origin, for man, is the way in which man . . . articulates himself upon the already-begun of . . . language."[60]

The impossibility, however, of grasping the self as a pure origin should not empty the term of its meaning. It does not, for Hölderlin, for whom the self is a divided identity and a perpetual beginning in language. The danger is to suppose that because both terms of self and language are generative together, the self cannot be thought except as an effect of language. This is to invite two kinds of linked misinterpretation. The first asserts an irreparable disjunction within the "trajectory of the work." A machinelike pseudoself, it is said, manufactures sentences that produce the delusion that these embody an intention. A real self is then said to arise by intuiting (with vertigo or restraint) the disparity between this language and its illusory intention. But why affirm that the "real self" is the source of this intuition and attitude and not itself an auratic effect of sentences arising, not to convey, but only to dissemble an insight? So vacuous a self might then indeed seek to escape its impotence by becoming the serviceable instrument of higher powers. Thereafter it would never need to suffer the shock of disillusionment. This turn to mere subjection is the whole of the second misreading.

To stress in this way the difference between active and interpreting selves is, however, to misread a tension which Hölderlin, Rousseau, and other Romantic poets saw as essential. For them, this difference defines the activity of a self that strives to close the disjunction. In the *Hyperion Fragment* Hölderlin invokes a mature ideal of our existence—the condition of "highest cultural development" (*Bildung*), in which "infinitely multiplied and intensified needs and abilities . . . harmonize reciprocally with each other . . . and with everything to which we are connected."[61] This ideal harmony is obtained "*through the organization which we are able to give ourselves*"—through the activity of a self that is the motive of its own development. On the other hand, to value disjunction as such is not to avoid, with fine intransigence, the seduction of positive meaning. It is instead to valorize the meaning of Hölderlin's failure—his madness—and thus to fall captive once again to the mystagogic schemes of a critic like Hellingrath and the worst of his successors, who celebrated this madness.

In "What Is an Author?" Foucault imagines approvingly a culture of the future in which the "tiresome" question "What has [the author] revealed of his deepest self in his language?" would be withdrawn in favor of such questions as "What are the modes of existence of this discourse? Where does it come from; how . . . circulated; who controls it?"[62] He asks for this change, because it is meaningless, he says, to conceive of language as expressing an already constituted self. A work is rather, in Foucault's words, a rift, "a caesura which fragments the moment and disperses the subject into a plurality of possible positions and functions."[63] Said radicalizes this point: "The major feature of the human subject [in the modern period] is . . . that it and its author are fictions together being produced during the writing."[64]

Hölderlin's understanding is fundamentally different, for the model of his thought is not one of "scission" but of reciprocal anteriority. For Hölderlin the condition of the work is a subject, a self, already nonidentical with itself yet bent on determining modes of its near-fullness and depletion. These modes already attune the moment of inscription and are in turn attuned by it. (See the quadrants of figure 1.) The self exists as the experience of this four-fold structure and the intention to determine its ratios in language. This project requires "the best sobriety and reflection of the poet," but what is the result when they are wanting?

Hölderlin's Madness

Hölderlin's "schizophrenia" advanced and disrupted him. By 1804 he could write only occasional poems—and these sporadically and chiefly at the request of others.[65] Yet in the years of the great hymns, when his attacks of madness grew more and more severe, Hölderlin continued to struggle to adhere to himself through an idea of the "general whole." He had written while still young, "I should like to have an effect upon the general whole. The general whole does not exactly put us, the particular individual, into an inferior position, but we no longer live with our entire soul for the particular when once the general whole has become an object of our wishes and strivings."[66] Hölderlin's schizophrenia can be read as the trajectory of moments at which the tension collapsed in a particular being dedicated to the enterprise of a generality.

The form of Hölderlin's striving for generality is the effort to "exist poetically," for man in the full generality of his nature "dwells poetically on this earth."[67] Hölderlin seeks in his poetry an order responsive to, but safe from, the continual flux of shocking experiences of the approach and retreat of being. In such a poetry, as he realized, a single basic tonality (Hauptton) predominates, and there is a paucity of what he called "regulated," perhaps "subordinated," tonalities.[68]

Hölderlin strives to maintain in his poetry a self in its fidelity to a general truth. But how much biographical change can be achieved, how much of a self can be assured, by an act of writing? "To write a poem," says Culler, "the author had to take on the character of the poet, and it is that semiotic function of poet or writer rather than the biographical function of author which is relevant to discussion of the text."[69] But in many Romantic lyrics, as Thomas Weiskel wrote, the lyric "I" representing this very "semiotic function" exceeds rhetorical confinement and literally produces a self:

> The lyric "I" . . . often seems to escape from its contained, dramatic determination and become itself a container. It is as if the "I" were aware of its own presentation in the poem; its progress becomes the successive assimilation or rejection of its former states, so that in the end only a purely theoretical line, not any differential of consciousness, separates it from the present of the maker. Poet, speaker, and reader are merged into one adventure of progressive consciousness . . . . The fusion . . . turns out to be a structural and even programmatic feature of Romantic texts.[70]

In Hölderlin, to an extraordinary extent, semiotic and biographical functions fuse. It is this fact that provokes a reflection on Hölderlin's madness in relation to his poetic career. This enterprise aims not merely to isolate the biographical element, the psychosis, as a foreign body within the poetic intentionality bent on sobriety. More provocatively, it considers the being and the work as fundamentally schizophrenic, in so complicit a way as to allow even the psychosis to be articulated by poetic activity.

Hölderlin's later poetry is marked by striking, indeed exorbitant, revisions. His practice answers to Lacan's view of schizophrenia as the case of an unconscious lacking a decisive regulatory function. "By means of the hole which [this absence] opens in the signified, it attracts the cascade of revisions of the signifier whence proceeds the increasing disaster of the Imaginary."[71] It appears that Hölderlin must write to defend against invasion, in his vulnerable state, of moods without language. This will to defense explains the special intensity with which he rewrites and the degree of attachment to the work he has accomplished. It is as if his hold on being were literally a matter of his clinging to the already articulated work as the point at which he had last left off his personal existence.

He writes as one who is exposed. We imagine in him an extra, an excessive availability to the fate of being moved; this is confirmed by his repeated sense of being "thrown," of being overmastered, by an incalculable destiny. The self thus buffeted struggles to right itself as a relation between the possibilities of its being. This stabilization occurs in poetry. One may say that a generality is the subject of Hölderlin's poetry in the sense that it articulates exemplary relations of the finite consciousness to its desire for totality. Its subject is the possibility of the full human subject.

Hölderlin's madness, then—the fact that the project of his life was so saliently marked—forces the question of the relation of the empirical person to the work. How could a reading of his poems aim at comprehensiveness but omit the fact that they punctuate madness? On the other hand, the enigma of madness slips away from the banal language with which the empirical personality is described—a language which, after it has been put into loose conjunction with the work, is then written off as accidental. How are such connections to be formulated rightly?[72] Where do we turn to understand the power of Hölderlin's madness for his poetry?

We could turn to Paris, for both Foucault and Derrida have written on Hölderlin's madness, each having published an essay on a book directly inspired by the teachings of Lacan.[73] The book, *Hölderlin and the Question of the Father* (*Hölderlin et la question du père*), is a study by Lacan's student Laplanche of the involvement of Hölderlin's schizophrenia in his poetry.[74] Lacan, in a development already well-publicized, undertook from the late thirties until his death in 1981 to reread Freud in a way that makes Freudian categories seem immediately interesting for literary study. Without a sense of Lacan's use of Freud, Laplanche's discussion of Hölderlin would be quite abstruse.

The main point of Lacan's demonstration is that the structure of the unconscious is like the structure of language.[75] This language is to be understood in a Saussurian perspective, as a system of differences between "negative" terms. Terms are negative because each has significance only as an alternative to another term within the system, in the play of compatibility or opposition. Nowhere in such a system is there the abundant and unequivocal meaning that Saussure calls "substance." [76]

As a language, the unconscious is no longer what it has been commonly taken to be, a sort of monolith based on two or three primordial drives or meanings and thus on positive terms, chronologically distinct and vertically inscribed. As a "form and not a substance" the unconscious is, above and beyond the interpretable meaning it could engender, a signifying movement: it transmits meaning to the interpreter through the play of oppositions and resemblances of its signifiers. Like the "monument" of psychoanalysis itself (as Barthes notes), the unconscious "must be traversed, like the fine thoroughfare of a very large city across which we can play, dream, etc.: a fiction." [77]

The structure of the unconscious more nearly resembles, therefore, the structure of explicitly rhetorical, poetic language. The unconscious, as it is revealed in dreams, symptoms, and everyday psychopathology, is first of all a group of signifiers. Their formal relations (say, of condensation and of displacement) are identical with the relations of signifiers in the figures or tropes of rhetoric and poetry. For example, displacement (Verschiebung) which is linked, for Lacan, to the operation of desire, restates metonymy. Condensation (Verdichtung), which is linked to the formation of symptoms, restates metaphor—the symptom then being the metalepsis of desire. Psychoanalysis thus becomes a type of semiotic science. It has to classify the relation of signs—of Wunschbilder in dreams; symptoms, say, in obsessional neuroses; and lapses in everyday psychopathology—just as the critic must identify and organize poetic images, obsessive metaphors, and syntactical lapses (i.e., ellipses or anacoluthons).

The semiotic techniques of psychoanalysis came to be further defined as they were turned on Freud's texts themselves. And it was grasped that Freud's work, seemingly organized on the category of biological, instinctual life, survives in fact as an unresolved play between the rhetoric of two different registers. On the one hand, the work is informed by biological, instinctual, genetic, and adaptational terms; on the other, it stresses the textual character of the unconscious, generated through repression, with its specific modes of doubling and negation, its distortions, ambivalences, and censorings. [78]

What does it mean in any cogent way to speak of the "textual character" of the unconscious? I cite Lacan's "Function of Language

in Psychoanalysis" to make the analogy plausible. Meaning to answer
the old objection of how there could be such a thing as unconscious
thought, Lacan writes:

> The unconscious is that chapter of my history which is marked by a blank
> or occupied by a falsehood: it is the censored chapter. But the Truth can
> be found again; it is most often . . . written down elsewhere. That is to
> say:
> —in monuments: this is my body—that is to say, the hysterical nucleus
> of the neurosis [read, nucleus of the psychosis], where the hysterical
> symptom reveals the structure of a Language and is deciphered like an
> inscription which, once recovered, can without serious loss be destroyed;
> —in archival documents also: these are my childhood memories, just as
> impenetrable as are such documents when I do not know their source;
> —in semantic evolution: this corresponds to the stock of words and ac-
> ceptations of my own particular vocabulary, as it does to my style of life
> and my character;
> —in traditions as well, and not only in them but also in the legends which,
> in a heroicized form, transport my history;
> —and lastly, in the traces which are inevitably preserved by the distor-
> tions necessitated by the linking of the adulterated chapter to the chap-
> ters surrounding it, and whose meaning will be re-established by my ex-
> egesis. . . .
>   [In this account] there is not a single metaphor that Freud's
> works do not repeat with the frequency of a *leitmotif*.[79]

Laplanche's project can now be understood as the effort to
analyze Hölderlin's unconscious as a text. It is true that most "monumental and archival documents" are missing, but this unconscious may
be otherwise constructed as a language, as a certain ordering of signifiers recorded in Lange's *Pathographie*, Beck's biography, and Hölderlin's
poems, letters, and theoretical writings.

The French psychoanalysis of Hölderlin, as performed by Laplanche, means, then, to read the text of Hölderlin's work and his life
not only through explicit Freudian categories but also and especially
through the textual dynamics of Freud's own work. The approach is not
an incursion upon philology but an embrace from within the universal
system of texts and textuality, in which, however, certain textual moments have the force of meanings. And certainly, on the face of things,
Hölderlin ought to be very accessible to such an approach, since he
grasped himself and his vocation in terms of a poetic *Bildung*, and poetic
Bildung as continual mediation—a process of unfolding toward what is
ostensibly other in order to apprehend and return it to the self. This
movement reveals the division of conscious and unconscious; *Bildung* is

the native life of a self that is a divided identity. Furthermore, reflecting on the meaning of man himself, Hölderlin grasped him as a history of Greek and Western modes of *writing*, of representation and of pathos, determined by the experience of the presence and absence of the sacred. Divided identity, poetic language, the consciousness of presence/absence: these are the constituents of Hölderlin's moral being, and they have been rewritten in the vocabulary of psychoanalysis as Repression/Unconscious/Desire. The French psychoanalytical story, of which Hölderlin's life and work is a version, further rewrites these terms as the "mirror phase" and the (absent) "Name-of-the-Father."

"The god within us," Hölderlin declared in his novel *Hyperion*, "is always lonely and poor." This god empties out Hyperion's inwardness. Its mark is the felt absence of life, the mood of mourning (*Trauer*). But Hyperion also knows another god, in fits of dazzling fullness, in moods so rich that they endanger him. A self-sufficient being exposes Hyperion's poverty as the condition of his assuming this fullness as his own. At this moment he wishes the god withdrawn, but if he succeeds, he is abandoned again to the emptiness within. In withdrawing from him, the other god brings the message of death, of pure inhumanity.

Hyperion is organized around such anxious mood swings from stony numbness to fiery dilation. At its highest pitch this oscillation becomes, for Laplanche, a sign of schizophrenia. The subject is racked between desire for the presence and absence of the other, who is at first wanted near, then far. Hyperion's friendship with both Melite, the lover in the earlier *Hyperion Fragment*, and Diotima, the lover in the novel, fits this pattern.

Here is an example from the *Fragment*. Hyperion writes of Melite:

> What I was, I was through her. This good person was delighted with the light which glowed in me and did not realize that it was only the reflection of her own. Only too soon did I feel that I became poorer than a shadow when she did not live in me, and around me, and for me, when she was not mine, that I became nothing when she withdrew from me. It could not be otherwise; I had to question with this deathly anxiety every expression and every sound she made, follow her gaze, as if my life were meaning to flee from me. . . . Indeed every smile of her sacred peace, every one of her heavenly words, had to be a messenger of death for me, telling how she was content with her, her heart. Indeed this despair had to come over me: that the splendid being whom I loved was so splendid that she had no need of me.[80]

The fullness which the other confers is infinite only as the supplement of the subject's insufficiency. This lack requires the subject to conceive of life as outside him and to be appropriated to his nullity. But to the extent that he succeeds in drawing the other near, he is to this degree endangered. For to draw her close is also to draw closer the crushing consciousness of the poverty of the desiring subject. Hyperion is annihilated by the thought that Melite does not need him. The joyous appropriation of a being at once abundant and submissive shatters from the consciousness of the subject's frailty.

Laplanche, following Lacan, calls such object relations "dual." They are specular and narcissistic and involve a moment of identification, as with a mirror image. These terms belong to Lacan's account of the "mirror phase" of development, which is a fiction about childhood. It refers to the moment when small children—confused, powerless, and uncoordinated—achieve through the act of seeing their image a sense of the integrity of their body and of their mastery over it. The victory arises through identification with the image of a being like oneself as a total form (the totality which we are not yet ourselves). The moment is illustrated and realized by children seeing their image in a mirror, though the "mirror" may also be the mother or a caring person.

The mirror phase marks the moment at which an ideal outline of the ego is first drawn by the *Gestalt* thus glimpsed. The mood of the moment is jubilation. Lacan writes of "the triumphant assumption of the image, with its accompanying jubilant mimicry and with the playful self-satisfaction in controlling the mirror identification."[81] This scene establishes the eternally imaginary nature of the ego, which from the start arises as an "ideal ego." From this perspective it is obvious that the self cannot be defined by the ego, an imaginary agency in which it tends to alienate itself.

Now, according to Lacan, the intersubjective relationship, as it is influenced by the effects of the mirror phase, is imaginary, dual, and full of aggressive tension. The ego is constituted as an other, the other as an alter ego. The aggression is plainest in Hyperion's relation to his friend Alabanda. Alabanda's wry smile, when Hyperion shows extravagant enthusiasm, is like the crack in a mirror which introduces a minimal difference between them and shatters the play of identity. Perceived difference, however slight, is at this stage intolerable, vexing aggressively the "narcissicism of small differences." It is as if this perception widened to a breach, disclosing the absolutely unbridgeable separateness of the subject from its ego, its first identification. The subject is thereafter bent on mastery of the distance with which the image of the other manifests itself.

Such mastery might be assisted by the knowledge that the

self is also needed by the other, and it is not as if Hölderlin were insensitive to the other's poverty. His susceptibility extends especially to imperfection, lack, and need. The converse is equally true: his sensitivity to his own lacking provokes the moment of identification with the indigent other. A precarious moment of love occurs as the sense in which the lack in the other answers to the lack in him.

But this moment is also dangerous. The other has always had being only as she remains imaginary. In the moment in which she is recognized as herself human and desiring, she is different—different from the "truth" which constructed her. She is unrecognizable as the fullness she was meant to be. The bliss of Hyperion's intimacy with Diotima is ruined by *her* despair. Hyperion means to live entirely through her; in her needing him he assumes her poverty. The desire of each produces the despair of each. The being who is known is thus as poor as the self; on the other hand, whatever else, in drawing near remains surpassingly abundant, turns desire to abjection.

This oscillation between an abundance born of poverty and one impoverished by knowledge would repeat itself incessantly if another factor did not come to stabilize it. This factor is a crucial third term, which functions to stabilize, regulate, and indeed forbid the unacknowledged, unconsciously inspired ambivalence. The third term is called by Lacan and Laplanche the "Name-of-the-Father"—not the "Father" but the "Na*me*-of-the-Father." [82]

Within the signifying chains constituting the unconscious, the "Name-of-the-Father" occupies the crucial place; it is signifier of the function of rival and interdictor of the son's access to the mother and the mother's total reintegration of the son. "[Such a] conception," writes Lacan, "permits us to distinguish clearly . . . the unconscious effects of this function from the narcissistic relations [of the mirror phase] or even from the real relations which the subject sustains with the image and the action of the person who incarnates it." Thus the "Name-of-the-Father" is not the interiorization of Hölderlin's actual father but a signifier in its place in the unconscious as a language. "It is in the name of the father," Lacan continues, "that we must recognize the support of the symbolic function which from the dawn of history has identified his person with the figure of the Law." [83] The father function subordinates the mirror phase and guarantees the passage of the subject to the symbolic order.

Thus the Name-of-the-Father is not only to be taken literally, it *is* the very letter of the law, of social language and of the signifying function of the unconscious. Within the symbolic order that is essentially language, it assures the permanence of relations arresting an eternal "slippage" between signifier and signified. "This conception," adds

Laplanche, "allows us to postulate that, in a single movement, by means of the father, there is introduced into the primordial pair of mother and child a certain regulatory law and [that there is also introduced] into the symbolic system of the subject an absolute point enabling it to express a certain truth that goes beyond need."[84] The Name-of-the-Father manifests the law of Bildung.[85] It is the condition of Hölderlin's poetry as the recognition of absence and the articulation of desire. But in Hölderlin's unconscious, according to Laplanche, this law, the factor regulating symbolic expression, is missing or defective. What is therefore at stake is the power of the subject's language to inscribe him into the symbolic determinations of the reality that awaits him.

Of the various terms that have been applied to the central concern of Hölderlin's work, the "Name-of-the-Father" is, I think, one of the less abusive. It suggests the "Father God" which recurs in Hölderlin, but it gives that term mainly the sense of a function, which is appropriate to the poetry. The Father God, while occupying a position above "Mother Earth" and mortals, is dependent on them by virtue of their opposite positions—dependent on the patience and conciliatoriness of Mother Earth, who may therefore "receive songs in his name" ("To Mother Earth") and on mortals, who, "since sacred beings are without self-consciousness . . . must feel sympathetically in the name of the gods" ("The Rhein").

The term "Name-of-the-Father" keeps the Father from all specious hypostasis, as if he were a substantial entity which could be experienced in the manner of a sensation or a sentiment within an interpersonal relation. But this missing name could not accommodate empirical father substitutes; for example, it could not be filled in by Schiller. Quite the reverse. In Jena at the time that Hölderlin and Schiller met, Schiller appeared in fact to usurp the functional first position in Hölderlin's being. But in filling the gap, he also rent it, making the absence all the more unbearable. Hölderlin experienced his dependent relation to Schiller as an error. In Laplanche's phrase, "Il rouvrit une faille" in Hölderlin's real being in the form of a psychotic attack, and Hölderlin had to flee Jena abruptly.[86]

We are ready to consider in Lacan's language Hölderlin's madness: "In madness, of whatever nature, we must recognize on the one hand the negative liberty of a Word which has given up trying to make itself recognized . . . and, on the other hand, we must recognize the singular formation of a delusion which objectifies the subject in a language without dialectic."[87] This is ordinary madness. Hölderlin, however, who was schizophrenic even in the years of his greatest poetic power, suffered from no ordinary madness. Despite the absence of the paternal function, his Word struggles to make itself recognizable and to ward off objectification in a language without dialectic. Hölderlin's language suggests this remarkable dialectical power; one need only note the intricate mediations of a text like "The Procedure of the Poetic Spirit" ("Über die Verfahrungsweise des poetischen Geistes"), but it is a dialectic that seems to keep slipping off track. This labor is the preferred form of Hölderlin's desire under the aspect of the law, his way of holding the world at a middle distance. For not to do so is either to die of the poverty of the meanings of things, or else to be engulfed by the excessive meanings of absent things: he has no natural way of regulating their entrance into him.

In Hölderlin the law is at once slackened (he is schizophrenic) and tensed to the utmost (he is the poet of renunciation and the stipulation of differences). In the late hymns the effect is to heighten an austere *consciousness* of the presence and the absence of the gods. This dialectic, in which modes of having language and losing language contend, eclipses for a while the narcissistic oscillations of the mirror phase.

In the psychoanalytic perspective of Lacan and Laplanche, Hölderlin is exemplary, but not as a poet who, threatened by the virtual loss of language, articulated this loss, and in thus representing himself, created himself. Instead he is exemplary because in him poetry arises where in principle the condition of the possibility of the poetic function is absent.

From this perspective, the empirical practice of poetry literally assumes the function of the Name-of-the-Father. The torn unconscious goes over into "an external sphere"; the "Nom du Père" becomes the "Non du Père" of poetic activity. Hölderlin's poetry repeats an unknown, unconscious text, sustaining him, as schizophrenic, for a time. His poetry keeps open this gap, which is not to be accounted a deficiency, because only the openness of poetry could "fill" it; no empirical being could. Hölderlin's isolation testifies to the inevitability of his separation from any being who could fulfill this function for him. He grasps that for poetry, the issue of an absence in being, "God's absence helps" (*Gottes Fehl hilft*).

Hölderlin's poetry, according to Laplanche, articulates a certain absence in his unconscious and functions in its place. The work is a long, irregular paraphrase of the ineffable Name-of-the-Father, which defends against vacuousness, exaltation, or rage. But what answer does this picture give to the question of the self? Do we have in this account a falsifiable argument for the absence of the subject from poetic activity? On the contrary, Laplanche's essay constitutes a partly avowed, partly implicit reaffirmation of the continuity of self, conscious subject, and poetic work.

"Consciousness," writes Lacan, "matters only in its relation [to the question] of recentering the subject as speaking in the very lacunae of that in which, at first sight, it presents itself as speaking."[88] This view shifts ("recenters") the place of the subject but does not annihilate it. Laplanche, too, undertakes to recenter Hölderlin's subject in the position of "the true subject," namely, to cite Lacan, "the subject of the unconscious."[89] When it comes to relating this displaced subject to poetry, however, Laplanche employs a mimetic model in which unconscious self and poetry correspond, despite the fact that the use of such a mimetic model endangers more than a methodology. It puts into question any form of the attack on the subject as it has been understood since German Idealism and as that attack might issue from Lacan and Laplanche.

In Laplanche's view Hölderlin's poetry thematizes, mythologizes, reflects on, and enacts *the negative*; in doing so it doubles the absence of "the paternal signifier." But the paternal signifier has precisely the function of guaranteeing signification. Its absence would induce an unmanageable cascade of revisions. Where then in the absence of the Name-of-the-Father does Hölderlin acquire the signifying function allowing him to articulate this very theme? It becomes necessary to posit and attach to the impoverished unconscious another self, another agent, capable of producing an intelligible poetry of absence. And if this self is to be different from the unconscious, it must be conscious. Now, of course, such a self is said precisely to be absent in schizophrenia as anything other than a hapless oscillation of desire. Yet if such a self is posited but also eclipsed, the work becomes a mere doubling imprint of the unconscious in the torn state in which it lacks the paternal metaphor. But this view is inconsistent with Laplanche's, for it returns to an older and naive conception which he is bent on surpassing—the conception of the psychotic writer as the "living poem," emitter only of "thing-presentations." So we are inevitably brought back instead to a conscious poetic agency endangered by schizophrenia but never absent: the fragile sense of self that seeks to maintain itself in poetry. Only in this way can we imagine Hölderlin seizing the threat to his language, seizing his madness as a question for his poetry: the question of the father, of the absence of the father.

Nothing about the psychoanalytical theory of Laplanche via Lacan controverts the assumption of a mediating subject. Laplanche's account of Hölderlin's psychosis actually constructs such a self around

its schizogenic faults. At the outset he holds to Hölderlin's own governing model of a subject bent on the unfolding, the Bildung, of its forces
and only thereafter identifies gaps in the structure. And when, at the
close, Laplanche exalts its deficiencies by identifying schizophrenia as
"that which opens up the question of the human," he does not annihilate the subject but precisely, rather, "opens it up."

The possibility of such an opening within a clinical and critical dialogue is obtained by Laplanche through a curious refinement of
mimesis. This moment, however, also identifies the error of a poetics of
the unconscious self defined by its likeness to a text. It is as if, despite
the mimetic fallacy—the poem taken improperly as an immediate representation of the inner life—Laplanche could achieve a satisfying degree of conceptual refinement by writing of both poem and life as doublings of a form of *absence*, a modality of *nothingness*, the poem of absence
being explained as a reflection of the absence constitutive of psychosis;
indeed he sees it as enshrining *that very absence*. The crude mimesis of
substantial representation is, in this way, apparently sublated, but actually only deferred. For if we are not now speaking of the poetic presentation of thinglike experiences, we are nonetheless speaking of a
presentation of a non-thinglike experience.

The allegedly aberrant model of correspondence is never actually absent from Laplanche's procedure. He first identifies the nucleus
of the psychosis as the missing Name-of-the-Father, held to guarantee
the tolerable, the human functioning of language as signifying-via-ab-
sence. As Hölderlin nonetheless continues to write poetry, the absent
signifier reappears in a triad of modalities of absence: "the poetic myth
of distancing and of opening—the philosophy of language—the poetic
activity as such, this exercise of language in which language comes closest to its own negative essence." It is toward "these three fields of absence, of the negative, [that] Hölderlin's poetry turns."[90] Laplanche then
suggests an explanation of schizophrenia as itself a turn to the negative,
to a field of absence including these three redemptive possibilities.
Hölderlin's poetry is thus an exemplary repetition of psychotic negativity, for which one would have to reinvent the word "denegation."

But nothing is gained from solutions by neologism. The representation of schizophrenic being in language continues to imply the
existence of an intentional subject. This is plain, for example, in Jean
Beaufret's revealing summary of Laplanche's argument:

> If the poetry of Hölderlin is more and more the incorporation in language
> or, rather, the creation, at the very origin of language, of this negative pole,
> the absence of which made language itself "the great superfluity" [*Hyper-
> ion*], it is because the poet feels more and more the menace which this

absence is for him if he does not succeed in considering it, in its turn, as a means of salvation.[91]

Observe that "incorporation" corresponds to a representative theory, "creation" to a constitutive theory, and Beaufret's balancing of both theories to the copresence, in Laplanche's thesis, of these two perspectives. Since, however, "creation" is the recreation of the absence which already exists "for [the poet]," both theories imply the continuity of the poet's conscious being and his poetry, the conversion by a self of its felt poverty into types of negativity. Beaufret's final conjuration of "the poet" is entirely legitimate.

This is indeed a bemusing state of affairs. For where then does the decisive Parisian attack on the self-constituting subject occur? From the outset we have regarded the thinkers of Paris as the main source of this attack. Have we misunderstood them? Or can it be that, faithful to their own logic, these critics owe their perceptions precisely to blindness to their own theoretical program? We have seen Lacan's and Laplanche's direct or implied reinstitution of the subject. Here now is Foucault's contribution to the same question:

> Hölderlin's experience is totally informed by the enchanted threat of forces that arose from within himself and from others, that were at once distant and nearby, divine and subterranean, invincibly precarious; and it is in the imaginary distances between these forces that their mutual identity and the play of their reciprocal symbolization are constructed and contested.[92]

But who imagines the distance between these forces, who symbolizes their symbols in play and constructs their identity, if not the poet with his "experience" and "scholarship"? Foucault is describing the activity of a poetic self.

It seems to me that neither Lacan, nor Laplanche, nor Foucault endangers the venture of showing the persistence of such a self both as experience and privileged function; indeed they actually give it intellectual support. What of Derrida? In *Of Grammatology*, Derrida writes:

> Freud says of the dreamwork that it is comparable rather to a writing than to a language, and to a hieroglyphic rather than to a phonetic writing. . . . Saussure says of language that "it is not a function of the speaker." With or without the complicity of their authors, all these propositions must be understood as more than simple *reversals* of a metaphysics of presence or of conscious subjectivity. Constituting and dislocating it at the same time, writing is other than the subject, in whatever sense the latter is understood. Writing can never be thought under the category of the subject; however it [the category of the subject] is modified, however it is endowed with consciousness or unconsciousness, it will refer, by the entire thread of its history, to the substantiality of a presence unperturbed by

accidents, or to the identity of the selfsame (*le propre*) in the presence of self-relationship.[93]

But it is very dubious to say that the subject must refer to categories of "substance": consider the entire foregoing account of Hölderlin. It is equally dubious to claim that the "identity" to which the subject refers is any more surreptitiously theological than that of other definite beings or indeed that of beings lacking definite identity conditions, as, for example, the referent of such Derridean categories as "trace," "différance," and "dissémination."[94]

In "La Parole soufflée," a work written at about the same time as *Of Grammatology*, Derrida takes away the sweeping claim to expose the barren "ideological" derivation of the subject through the "entire thread of its history." Addressing Laplanche's work directly, Derrida concludes that the effort to think the historical moment that could bring about a discourse at once critical and clinical—the effort to think the relation of history and "the same"—is an effort for which we are not yet ready. What is entailed, Derrida asks, by the possibility of a discourse in which these two dimensions—the clinical and the critical—could be spoken?[95] It is, I hold, precisely the possibility of a discourse on the self. This discourse is the one actually produced by the French attention to Hölderlin, even when the object is his thematics of absence. For the themes of the mythic negativity of the absence of the gods, the rational negativity of language, and the negativity of poetic practice are poetic decisions taken by Hölderlin on the strength of his experience.

Derrida concludes by asserting the impossibility of thinking history and "the same," that is, the historical situation of the unity embedding the difference between the subject viewed clinically and by literary criticism. This situation entails the impossibility of thinking the unity of the subject except as the factitious replica of a theological object. It also entails, however, the impossibility of thinking *away* the subject as a "divided unity" or as an "harmonious opposition." The deconstruction of the subject is a project that therefore lies always ahead of us. It has not been done, and on the evidence of those who are attempting to do it, it cannot be done, neither factually nor by right.[96]

This chapter has aimed to convey a certain force-field of experience, a four-fold structure organized by the poetic task, within which Hölderlin maintains himself and thus resists the invasions of poverty or blasting fullness or the lure of titanism: the poem represents the sober effort of mediation. I have called this enterprise dialectical, but in doing so have put myself in the way of another criticism that stresses the fragmentariness, heterogeneous irony, and non-self-conscious character of Hölderlin's work. Such a criticism includes within the poetic intention, grasped as the dialectic of the *Bildungstrieb*, another reason and another goal. Blanchot puts the opposition thus: "How can the finite being [literally, the 'determined'] sustain a true relation with the infinite [literally, the 'undetermined']? On the one hand, [we have] the greatest hostility to the amorphous, the surest feeling of the shaping power, the *Bildungstrieb*; on the other, the refusal to be determined, 'the flight from definite relationships,' the renunciation of self, the invocation of the impersonal, the demand for the Whole, the origin."[97] It is not only for polemical reasons that I have been concerned to stress in Hölderlin's poetic enterprise the first position, which associates the concepts of *Bildungstrieb* and dialectic. I believe that the second position can only be comprehensively grasped as belonging to the first. Hölderlin's concern is with maintaining himself as a poetic shaping power responsive to the experience of the Whole; renouncing himself, he cannot write.

Blanchot, the most articulate defender of the constitutive impersonality of the poet's task, describes the destiny of the poet who mediates the sacred. This "torn existence is not only a consequence but . . . is the very division of the poet, his obliteration in the embrace of the word which—existence having disappeared—alone persists, continues."[98] The subject of Hölderlin's poetry is thus the poet's obliteration. But if there is to be more than one poem in his *oeuvre*, then that second poem must do more than affirm the poet's obliteration. It must repeat the previous affirmation, and hence what the poem affirms is the *experience* of obliteration. The subject of poetry is therefore not the effacement of the poet but the *repetition* of the moment of effacement; what survives in the poem is thus the poet's experience, not of self-effacement, but of its impossibility, and hence of the necessity of being a self. Blanchot would have to admit that while there can be a poem, there cannot be a poetry, of self-effacement.

By insisting, then, on the dialectical character of Hölderlin's poetry, I stress the operations of a subject which means to bring into the divided unity of the work the widest possible life under the exigency of densely multiple articulation—connections experienced and explored with a view to proving the maximum of combative interdependence. This dialectic, however, does not produce objectively final results which, stage by stage, could ground Hölderlin's successive poetic ventures, and would never need to be repeated, except retrospectively. The urgency of taking up again and again the combat of the four-fold persists. Hölderlin's experience changes the mood or tonality of his struggle (the linguistic practice anterior to the subject attunes it); experience shifts the weight of his concerns within the struggle, but the spring that keeps the tension, that lives the tension, is the dialectical subject, the mediating self.

Within his task, Hölderlin's poetry offers the picture of a dialectical beginning that either breaks off harmoniously, creating the *impression* of an end stage reached, or breaks off abruptly, creating the impression of a fragment. His next project brings into a "foreign analogous material" the same tension, the same terms in dialectical relation, and so this situation allows for some addition of irony too.

Hölderlin's madness has also been read as a part of the dialectic that establishes dominance over the dialectic and, vulgar prejudice aside, issues into a harmonious end stage intelligible with respect to the previous stages. In this vein, we have Blanchot's rationalization of Hölderlin's madness. "At a certain point," he writes, "and in spite of himself, the poetic destiny requires of [Hölderlin's] personal reason that it become the pure impersonal transparency from which there is no return . . . . Hölderlin himself must become a mute sign, the silence which the truth of the word requires to assert that that which speaks nevertheless does not speak and remains the truth of silence."[99] That which in speaking does not speak is the absolutely absconded sacred. But it is quite incorrect to think of Hölderlin's madness or silence as "the extreme point of the poetic exigency," as accomplishing the dialectic. Hölderlin, of course, thinks silence, thinks madness, as in *Brod und Wein*, and as concepts they can enter the dialectical process. But this is quite a different matter from saying that madness and silence in their brute state themselves enter and fulfill the dialectic. They close it off by wrecking it.

The temptation to construe Hölderlin's madness as accomplishing his poetic destiny can be regarded as a tempting error masking a category mistake. The aspect of Hölderlin that readers must address is his radical desire to develop by *Bildung* a self that will be general. The privileged agency of this development is poetry, and the goal of the poetic career can be grasped as a poetry of the greatest generality and hence as, in a certain sense, impersonal. At this point, however, the parallel between the ideal form of poetry and Hölderlin's madness could become arresting. The madness too could equally well be defined as a type of generality and impersonality; furthermore it is an achieved fact. These propositions could then be easily yoked into a syllogism whose bizarre result is that Hölderlin's madness—as Blanchot alleges—is Hölderlin's final poem. His madness is mute testimony to the poetic career that, defining itself as the effort to speak (determine) the sacred (the indeterminate), must embody as an example the truth of the concealment of being. This result, however, is almost certainly a mistake. And so is the judgment which this proposition reactively produces, namely, that Hölderlin's late hymns themselves represent the achieved sublation of a self, its entire displacement into "the general whole." This view ignores the presence within the hymns of a resolute poetic individuality. Hölderlin does not wish to vanish into a vessel of sacred words but to hold it up: he wishes to sustain himself as namer and named.

I have dwelled on Blanchot even at this late stage of the argument because piety requires that his figure be acknowledged as standing behind both de Man and Laplanche, the oppositional critics of my opening and closing sections. De Man's chiastic surmise, for example, that the so-called drives and representations of psychic energy are only "aberrant correlatives of the absolute randomness of language prior to any figuration" fits as a corollary into Blanchot's metaphysics of poetry, according to which "the work requires of the writer that he lose all 'nature,' all character and that, ceasing to enter into relation with others and with himself by the decision which makes him himself, he becomes the empty place where the impersonal affirmation asserts itself." [100]

Blanchot's formulation allows him to conceive of schizophrenia as the projection at a certain time and on a certain level of the poetic destiny of impersonality. Nothing about de Man's formulation, either, would prevent its being assimilated to a standard description of schizophrenia as the subjection of the self to its language. On the other hand, the two authors must be distinguished. There is nothing in de Man's description of the language of the self that positively belongs to a poetic destiny, nor does he construe Hölderlin's silence as exemplary. Nonetheless, by absolutizing the priority of amorphous language in the sense that the self is made correlative to an "absolute randomness," he destroys the self as a dialectical agent and hence the dialectic itself.

Laplanche in his turn takes issue with Blanchot's idealist, monistic, and unhistorical view of Hölderlin's schizophrenia but equally obscures the persistent operation of an individual poetic agency, a poetic self. He inclines to a view of Hölderlin's poetry as a carrying over into objective analogues, not of a conscious intention, but an absence in the text of the unconscious. Laplanche valorizes Hölderlin's madness as an articulation of the universal question of the "father," of its interiorized signifier, and hence of the absence of the father. In Hölderlin's case even the signifier is absent, and so, according to Laplanche and Lacan, the very possibility of a poetic articulation of absence is jeopardized. In such a situation, therefore, another subjectivity must be posited—an intentional poetic consciousness that, however fragile, organizes the metaphors of the unconscious. Hölderlin's poetry is unthinkable except as a dialectical poetry of the self.

CHAPTER TWO

Dilthey's Poetics of Force

> Your conception of history is that
> of a nexus of forces, of unities of
> force, to which the category of
> "pattern" is to be applicable only
> by a kind of transference.[1]
>
> —Yorck to Dilthey

> What others call *form* I experience
> as force.[2]
>
> —Barthes

> Pomp or force, what does
> the word matter if the idea
> is the same?[3]
>
> —Rousseau

As we have seen, Hölderlin maintains a self in the space of language constructed by a poetic intention (*die poetische Individualität*). The poetic act represents the value and danger of modes of proximity and distance between the finite subject and being. Poetry is itself the mode of being in which for a time Hölderlin finds safety against the crushing disparity between himself and being—a zone of balance.

It is not accidental that in thinking about Hölderlin we are drawn to Wilhelm Dilthey (1833–1911), for he is the author, in *Lived Experience and Poetry* (*Das Erlebnis und die Dichtung*, 1905), of the first synoptic essay on Hölderlin—in which, *mutatis mutandis*, aspects of this picture of Hölderlin's self can be found.[4] Dilthey stresses a feature we have ignored: the barrennness of Hölderlin's social and cultural climate that condemned him to a desperate loneliness. The fear of a culture without a center and voice recurs in Dilthey's critique of his own age, and it is chiefly in thinking of the fate of the self in German literature in the nineteenth century that we now turn to his poetics.

Especially in the United States since the late sixties, Dilthey has been admired as a theorist of the depth and ontological distinction of subjectivity. "In our lie-filled human society," wrote Dilthey, "one kind of work is always truthful—the work of a great poet." This truthfulness consists precisely in its character as "the faithful expression [or 'objectivation'] of a subjectivity (*der wahre Ausdruck eines Seelenlebens*)." The fidelity of the work to the inner life—a work which may indeed also be that of a "religious genius or a genuine philosopher"—assures, moreover, that it can be interpreted "completely and objectively."

Conservative critics have thus been swift to embrace Dilthey for the authority he appears to lend to literary study. Dilthey's work, it is said, dignifies the self on the basis of its expressive and hermeneutic activity. His hermeneutics is seen as promising the recovery of positive and abundant meaning from the objectivations of the inner life, a practice precisely illustrated in the interpretation of literary texts.

It is therefore somewhat ironical to discover that Dilthey's most important work explicitly devoted to poetics should, on close inspection, be a brief as much for individual subjectivity as for the constitutive power of the individual's social and political life, many of the chief "subjective" components of the poetic process figuring as representatives or doubles of social and institutional agencies. This situation tends to produce major ironies, if not downright contradictions, in the prevailing view of Dilthey, since he reverses the relation of source and product, subject and expression. How could abundant, authentic meaning be recovered from a poetic expression if both artist and interpreter are representations of social forces?

In the United States, the political dimension of Dilthey's work is almost unknown, or else it has been noticed in passing in a philosophy chiefly valued for its existential pathos. Yet Dilthey's involvement in politics is unmistakable. It is generally evident in the institutional character of the categories of his critical rhetoric, and it is specific in his fascination with the political struggles of Germany under Bismarck. In Germany today, Dilthey's politics are being scrutinized with subtly polemical intent. One debate turns on the support which Dilthey's alleged vitalism—his "philosophy of Life"—and his view of history as "irrational facticity" is supposed to have lent to Fascism.[6] Other writers question Dilthey's belief in the possibility and urgency of social transformation,

of historical action.[7] Finally, the quiescent, conciliatory, "Goethean" serenity of his political and literary-historical consciousness has been criticized. It led (it is alleged) to a century-long unquestioned installation
of the literature of German Idealism in top position in the canon of German literary history.[8]

The consensus of these views holds that while Dilthey's
rhetoric undoubtedly relies on categories drawn from history and politics, he tends to undervalue the possibility of rational political action.
This is the thesis of Hans-Joachim Lieber, Josef Derbolav, and Bernd
Peschken. The question, however, has certainly not been decided. Frithjof Rodi and Christofer Zöckler, for example, constitute an effective adversary position on behalf of a rationalist, activist Dilthey. All these writers, meanwhile, are richly informative about little-known aspects of
Dilthey's political culture. Yet, what is remarkable is that they leave almost unmentioned in their work Dilthey's major text on poetics—*The Poetic Imagination: Contributions to a Poetics* (*Die Einbildungskraft des Dichters: Bau-
steine für eine Poetik*), 1887.[9] This essay in fact allows us to describe
appropriately the involvement of Dilthey's political consciousness and
unconscious in his poetic theory. It provokes the key question, What must
a poetics be in order to sustain the view that the subjectivity of a poet
may be authentic *and* the representative of institutional forces?

In 1923 Georg Misch, Dilthey's most faithful disciple, declared that "poetics—along with the theory of history—was the germ-
cell of [Dilthey's] ideas about life and about the understanding of life:
he continually nurtured it, continued to work on it" (5:ix). Since then, a
number of general studies on Dilthey have centered on Dilthey's poetics
and especially on his major text, *The Poetic Imagination*. This text confirms
the interpreter's decision to focus on it because it assigns to poetic and
philological analysis an exemplary methodological character and hence
the power to validate a science of the humanities.

This claim is based on the aptness of the literary object for
"causal investigation" (*Kausaluntersuchung*). Dilthey writes:

> We now possess observations on poetic creation and on aesthetic recep-
> tion (the two are related) as well as accounts [by writers] of these pro-
> cesses. We can bring the psychological insights thus obtained to bear on
> the outer history of the formation (*Ausbildung*) of literary works. In analyz-
> ing, finally, the completed transparent structure of these works and thus
> confirming and completing our insight into their genesis, a captivating
> prospect opens up in this domain. Here, perhaps, we could have our first
> success in achieving a causal explanation (*Kausalerklärung*) from generative
> processes. The conditions of performing poetic analysis appear to make it
> possible for it to become the first to achieve by the causal method the

inner explanation of an intellectual-historical totality (*eines geistiggeschicht-lichen Ganzen nach kausaler Methode*). (6:125)

The "totality" named here is that of a single literary work.

This passage goes to the heart of Dilthey's concerns. It bears on intellectual history from the angle of the *privileged kind of research* which poetics does—the depth of its subject matter (genesis), the scope of its explanations (causal relations), and the possibility it holds out of reliable results. Another passage often profiled in studies of Dilthey brings poetics to bear on intellectual history from the angle of the *privileged kind of product* which it treats. In *The Rise of Hermeneutics* (*Die Entstehung der Hermeneutik*), 1900, Dilthey writes: "The immeasurable importance of literature for our understanding of mental life (*des geistigen Lebens*) and for history lies in the fact that only in language does human inwardness find its complete, exhaustive and objectively intelligible expression. Therefore the art of understanding has its center in the explication or *interpretation of the remains of human existence contained in writing*" (5:319).

The first passage, however, makes explicit what the second does not: the royal road to the study of intellectual history is specifically poetics, or reflection on the distinct character of literary language. It stresses, moreover, as the second passage does not, the involvement of an "outer," potentially political dimension in the literary work; as such it is more faithful to Dilthey's poetics as a whole. The passage thus projects a number of lines of inquiry, concerning especially the implications of the claim for the central importance of poetics within a program of intellectual-historical research; the importance within this claim of the power of poetics to exploit a certain notion of causality (*Kausalität*); and the content of this poetics, especially its practical (cultural and political) consequences. These issues are linked; my own remarks will move between them.

It is important to stress from the outset, in the exemplary relation of poetics to intellectual-historical understanding, Dilthey's sense of the practical bearing of poetics, its contribution to social and political praxis. The evidence for this bearing is both general, within the whole of Dilthey's work, and particular, in his essay on poetics.

Consider, first, the general evidence. In guiding the enterprise of the *Geisteswissenschaften* as a whole, poetics guides that "totality of the sciences which take as their object (*zu ihrem Gegenstand haben*) historical-social reality" (1:4). I read this point strongly. The verb *"haben"* (here, "take") is genuinely transitive and implies an active and selective manipulation of experience. This manipulation has practical force, involving, in Gadamer's phrase, "the dissolution of the life bond—the gaining of a distance to one's own history, which is the only way to make it into an object."[10] And this, our own history, Dilthey never tires of repeating, is the history of our social world. "Society is our world. With the power of our entire being, we experience (*miterleben*) the interplay of social conditions. From within, we are aware of the states and forces which in all their restlessness constitute the social system" (1:36–37).

To take "social reality" as an object is therefore to provoke a transformation in the investigator and in his experience—a change which is not in itself theoretical. "He who investigates history," writes Dilthey, "is the same being as he who makes history" (7:278). There is an ideal of mastery, in its way altogether practical, within the "investigation of history," based on the wholeheartedness of "the dissolution of the life bond" (Gadamer)—on the thoroughness of this act of self-distancing and self-alienation that aims at the "re-experiencing of alien states-of-mind" (Dilthey). Indeed, "Action is everywhere presupposed by our understanding of others" (5:317).

Historical investigation is, therefore, an act at once individual and social; rightly understood it is the exemplary form of social praxis, for our task is principally understanding (*Begreifen*)—and no other form of mastery (1:5).[11] The producer and the product of such comprehension are themselves practical: they precipitate more historical life. "Every structure of historical life is finite and as a consequence contains a distribution of joyous strength and force, . . . which similarly releases a new distribution; hence, therefore, actions constantly arise" (7:288).[12]

The key sentence reads, "He who investigates history is the same being as he who makes history." The polemical force of this maxim becomes clear when we recall the banality that is its target. In Goethe's play *Egmont*, for example, a certain Machiavelli (not Niccolò!) repeats to Margarete von Parma her charge to him: "You see too far, Machiavelli! You ought to be an historian. Whoever acts [i.e., *makes* history] must be concerned with the object closest at hand" (act I, scene 2). Dilthey aims to refine this conception of the different tempos informing historical thought and action. Interpretation proceeds only through an action. This action is concerned, it is true, with the object closest at hand—but only in order to put it at a distance, to make it at once past (it is no longer immediate) and future (it will be reproduced by the labor of thought). What is humanly close at hand, moreover, is never simply present. As part of the social-historical order it is always a survival, and it continues to act as the objectivation, as the trace, of inner life past.

In this way objectivity in the historical sciences is itself an

historical action. It takes aim at an object which, as a scriptural monument, can never be self-enclosed or self-identical. And it can succeed
only as the result of an ascesis—an action difficult to learn, but at the
basis of individual development. It is an action which therefore needs
to be taught and for which the university is the traditional site. Dilthey
is speaking in his own voice when he writes of Humboldt's founding the
University of Berlin as a "perhaps not as yet hoped-for sanctuary of the
sciences, . . . a university in the highest sense," where all scientific institutions "cooperate in the one great purpose . . . of arousing new enthusiasm and new warmth for the renascence of the German states"
(12:80–81). A recent writer, Christofer Zöckler, aptly comments, "Scientific freedom [i.e., objectivity] is understood as producible only by reflection on its basis in social interests, not as tied to the fiction of disinterested neutrality."[13]

The immediate point is that the act on which genuine objectivity is founded requires social protection; in turn it contributes to the
truthfulness and cohesion of that society. This idea is plain in Dilthey's
Introduction to the Historical Sciences (*Einleitung in die Geisteswissenschaften*), 1883;
here he spells out the specific contribution which objectivity in the social sciences can make to the society which guarantees it. He writes:

> It appeared necessary to provide a service [similar to that provided by sci-
> entists writing about the basis and method of the natural sciences] to those
> who occupy themselves with history, politics, jurisprudence or political
> economy, theology, literature and art. Those who devote themselves to these
> disciplines are accustomed to approach them from the standpoint of the
> practical needs of society, from the purpose of a professional education,
> which equips the leading organs of society with the knowledge necessary
> for their task. . . . [The isolated professional, the technician] is an instru-
> ment serving society, not *an organ consciously helping to shape it*. This intro-
> duction means to simplify, for the politician and jurist, the theologian and
> the pedagogue, the task of becoming acquainted with the relation of the
> principles and rules by which he is guided to the *comprehensive* reality of
> human society. . . .
>
> Thus conceived, this task, which is founded on the needs of
> practical life, confronts a problem posed by the state of pure [social] the-
> ory [italics mine]. (1:3–4)

This theoretical problem is that of the interrelation and justification of
the social sciences.

To conclude: The "structure of historical life" which Dilthey
is addressing in his *Introduction* (and we in ours) is that of the mind that
produces and reproduces meaning in history. These expressions arise
from a primary act of self-detachment[14] and in turn precipitate new acts,

the "shaping acts of conscious men." Translated into social categories, Dilthey's introduction to the historical sciences, as an educative instrument, addresses the Bildungsbürger—the bourgeois who founds his class distinction on his educability and his powers of self-cultivation, and who requires that his education have a practical result.[15]

In documenting the practical implications for Dilthey of the act of historical understanding, I have made free use of chronology. I have moved back and forth between the "Reorganizers of Prussia (1807–1813)" ("Die Reorganisatoren des preußischen Staates [1807–1813]"), 1872, in volume 12; the Introduction to the Historical Sciences in volume 1; The Rise of Hermeneutics in volume 5; the Plan for the Continuation of "The Construction of the Historical World in the Historical Sciences" (Plan der Fortsetzung zum "Aufbau der Geschichtlichen Welt in der Geisteswissenschaften"), after 1910, in volume 7. I have not followed the conventional account of the increasing predominance of the practical aspect in Dilthey's view of the object of historical interpretation. This trajectory is frequently described in three stages.

In the 1860s, Dilthey conceived a Life of Schleiermacher as a test case for a method that purported to grasp intuitively the inwardness (Innerlichkeit) of the historical subject, but he abandoned this project. It survives as a fragment, as testimony to the felt ineffectuality of his method and his goal. Then, in the 1880s, the key term of his philosophy of historical reading shifted to "inner experience" (innere Erfahrung). The category of experience was held to incorporate a greater measure of constituted social and historical reality. Finally, Dilthey's late turn to the objective spirit was inspired by his suspiciousness of introspection as well as his need to defend against the objectivist scientific position. This turn produced concepts intended to mediate more adequately between inner and outer vitality—concepts of Erlebnis (lived experience) and Verstehen (understanding).[16]

Dilthey perceived that the inwardness of historical beings can be understood even by themselves only through the objectivation of their subjectivity. This understanding has an intrinsically practical character. But this position was not one which Dilthey reached only late. We find it implied in propositions in all his texts, duly stressed at key historical junctures. This view should finally not seem archaic or quaint, as the resurgence of belief in the omnipotence of wishes. Consult, for example, Foucault, whose audacity and modernity are not in question: "Thought is no longer theoretical. As soon as it functions it offends or reconciles, attracts or repels, breaks, dissociates, unites or reunites; it cannot help but liberate and enslave. Even before prescribing, suggesting a future, saying what must be done, even before exhorting or merely sounding an alarm, thought, at the level of its existence, in its very dawning, is in itself an action—a perilous act."[17]

In registering, however, the intrinsically practical character of Dilthey's historical understanding, we do not so much solve as identify a problem. The problem runs throughout the whole of his work, but is articulated nicely in a sentence that we earlier abridged on p. 59. The entire sentence reads "These data of the spirit (*geistige Tatsachen*), which have developed historically within the human world and to which, according to common usage, we apply the term sciences of man, of history, of society, constitute the reality which we do not want to master but above all (*zunächst*) to comprehend" (1:5). *Zunächst* means "above all," "principally," "chiefly," but it can also mean, merely, "to begin with" or "for one thing." What does Dilthey mean? Reading *zunächst* in the first sense we find him saying that the dignity of action is never higher than, or even as much as, the dignity of that act of self-detachment which constitutes the basis of historical thought, of comprehension. The value of voluntary instrumental action is "principally" secondary. A passage in volume 7 confirms this Spinozistic reading. There the energies of action, on the one hand, and the expressed experience to which historical understanding is responsive, on the other, are contrasted. Dilthey writes:

> Through the power of a decisive motive, the act emerges from the fullness of life into one-sidedness. However meditated, it nonetheless expresses only a part of our being. Possibilities which lay in this being are annihilated by it. Thus the act detaches itself from the background of the context of life. And without clarification of the way in which in it circumstances, purpose, means and life-context are connected, it does not allow a full-sided definition of that inwardness from which it sprang. Quite otherwise the objectivation of experience! (7:206)

It is at this juncture that Dilthey's political critics on the left have had their sharpest quarrel with him. In contrasting the truth and authority of expression, to which historical understanding is responsive, with instrumental activity, Dilthey speaks on behalf of expression. Hence it cannot be the practical component of understanding, however conceived, which is the source of its dignity. The understanding of alien states of mind may be the basis for an act. But this does not mean that the value of experiencing alien states of mind lies in the act which issues from it or even in the *active* "dissolution of the life bond" which precedes it—practice meaning at once the enabling condition of thought and its outcome.

There is, however, that other possible reading of the sentence in question. "Zunächst" may indeed imply nothing more than "provisionally," or "for the time being," and may describe a merely interim project. The thrust of this thought is a familiar one from the German Idealist tradition. Schiller's *Letters Concerning the Aesthetic Education of Man* states that the aesthetic cultivation of individuals must precede moral action in the sense that man is not yet ready for moral action. When, however, will he be ready? This consideration is essentially postponed; at the same time it cannot allow the valorization of the aesthetic dimension over the moral, any more than it would allow in Dilthey the valorization of even the most genuine understanding over practical acts (deeds) of mastery.

Only if this interim reading were true could we venture to assert the unquestioned primacy of the practical act in Dilthey. To do so of course is to diminish the intrinsic value of historical and, by implication, aesthetic understanding. The sort of practical bearing they contain leads to further comprehension but not mastery, or indeed only to what a modern writer calls "mastering [the 'relations between things'] by knowing them from outside rather than being . . . in the relationships."[18]

Such ambivalence pervades all of Dilthey's work and is not trivial. It helps explain Dilthey's eagerness to stress the practical character of poetic language and poetic understanding. His ambivalence about the value of practical action makes him reluctant to valorize deeds of political mastery and equally reluctant not to. To argue for the intrinsic political force of understanding is to cover both bets. Dilthey cannot therefore be said to assert unequivocally that the mere decision to perform aesthetic analysis—as it is performed in *The Poetic Imagination*—has itself a measurable practical effect. The idea continues to have a major relevance in Dilthey's thought, but now it will do to stress the plainer point that the analysis that Dilthey—or, by his own account, any aesthetician—performs and publishes has a practical social meaning. This idea, which recurs in *The Poetic Imagination*, is prepared for in volume 1 by the relationship between the cultural system of law and its external organization.

The cultural system of law comprises individual acts and theories provoking and articulating legal consciousness. The external organization of law consists of the legal code and the system of law enforcement. The two, however, are intimately related. Dilthey notes that both the cultural system of law and its external organization "exist always and only side by side and with one another. To be sure, they are not connected as cause (*Ursache*) and effect, but each has the other as the condition of its existence. This relation is one of the most difficult and important forms of the causal (*kausal*) relation." (1:55).

Rudolf Makkreel, author of an important full-length study of Dilthey, comments on this passage in a suggestive way.

> It is significant that in the above passage Dilthey rejects the substantive *Ursache* and uses the adjective *kausal* in introducing a mode of coexistence particularly important for the human studies. What he may have had in mind is that *Ursache* can be etymologically analyzed into U*r-sache*, meaning primary fact. It is exactly this aspect of primacy in causation that Dilthey finds inappropriate in the human studies and wants to exclude from his proposed notion of a reciprocity which is *kausal*. Just as causality in the strict explanative sense was not applicable to psychology when correlating neural processes with states of consciousness, so when considering the relation of the ideal and the actual in the other systematic *Geisteswissenschaften*, we cannot simply make one the primary fact (*Ursache*) of which the other is the mere effect.[19]

Considering, however, the context of Dilthey's reflections on law, one could well leave to one side the psychological parallel and instead enrich the word "causal" by adducing the more cogent word "political." The interaction of legal theorizing and law enforcement occurs as a play of political forces. Dilthey remarks that "even the consciousness of law is not a theoretical state-of-affairs but a state-of-affairs of the will" (1:55). Furthermore, "The study of the systems into which the *practical* action of society has been articulated cannot be separated from the study of the *political* body, since its will influences all external actions of the individuals subject to it" (1:52) (italics mine).

The will is a "context of purposes" bent on objectivation, all objectivations being for Dilthey at once texts and institutions.[20] Institutional force—hence politics—is the key direction of Dilthey's essay on poetics. The practice of poetic analysis bears vitally on the cultural system of literary works, on their mode of production, and on the "political body."

If nowadays (in 1887), writes Dilthey, poetics, the cultural system of literary works, and the external organization of society have cleaved wide apart, that is because

> anarchy prevails in the wide domain of literature in all nations. Our [German] aesthetics, to be sure, is still alive here and there on the lecturer's rostrum but no longer in the consciousness of the leading artists or critics, and only there would it be [truly] alive.
>
> When, ever since the French Revolution, the monstrous realities of London and Paris, in whose souls a new kind of poetry is circulating, attracted the attention of writers as well as the public, when Dickens

and Balzac began to compose the epic of that modern life coursing through these cities, at that moment it was all over for the principles of that poetics which once upon a time in idyllic Weimar had been debated by Schiller, Goethe and Humboldt. . . . Thus today art grows democratic, like everything else around us. (6:104–105)

The vital task is one of "restoring the healthy relation of aesthetic thought and art." This task falls to "contemporary philosophy and the history of art and literature."

Now it is one thing to grant political force to the institutionalized academic disciplines of philosophy and philology, but political force to theorizing about poetics? This position is explicit in the passage above. Elsewhere, the political thrust of inner contexts, texts, and institutions is only speculative. Yet Dilthey, in his essays, encourages us by his example to take up and valorize the inexplicit.

In, for example, a closely linked sequel to *The Poetic Imagination*, the 1892 essay called "The Three Stages of Modern Aesthetics and Its Task Today" ("Die drei Epochen der modernen Ästhetik und ihre heutige Aufgabe"), Dilthey fashions a polemic against "experimental" aesthetics. He concludes by attacking its "isolated analysis of impressions," noting that the "driving interest behind all reflection on art . . . is the question of *the function of art in the intellectual economy of human life*. To the extent that this question can be given a more rigorous answer," he continues, "we must expect it to emerge from the connection of the analysis of impressions with the historical-social study of art. Here, too, there is a point at which a circle in the efforts of the analysts of the impression swiftly makes itself felt. Some sort of inner position toward art, an idea of its inner significance, will guide their work, even where they have no consciousness of such presuppositions" (6:265–266). It is impossible, Dilthey is saying, to practice poetics without bringing into play a notion of the meaning of art. This notion is a reflection of the social and historical situation of the aesthetician. "The understanding of the world (*Weltverständnis*) which [philosophical thought and poetic creation] can have is determined by the historical situation of consciousness and is relative" (6:232). But this line of determinations is a line of force that flows in both directions, so that it is indeed also impossible to assign an "Ur-sache," a primary cause, to its movement. The specific practice of aesthetics in turn modifies the "inner position toward art" which guides it. That inner position (to cite Foucault again) is, as thought, "no longer theoretical. It offends or reconciles, attracts or repels, breaks, dissociates, unites or reunifies." The object of this action is the understanding of the world which inspires it. And that understanding, that consciousness, thus revised, in turn transforms or consolidates the "function of art" in the historical situation, in the "intellectual economy of human life."

Indeed, this circle of cooperating determinations is in its form the very trope of Dilthey's thought and in its thesis here exemplary. Idea and objectivation, poetic imagination and social text, are moments in that reciprocal exchange which Dilthey calls *Kausalität*. And the pivotal terms of the human order are art and the historical situation grasped as foci of an "intellectual economy."

This double privilege is a recurring moment in Dilthey's system. "There appear in the images and structures [of art]," writes Peter Hünermann, "the ruling figures in which the thought, feeling and activity of a generation, a milieu, of this age are reflected. . . . At the same time [these figures] are themselves subject to historical change."[21] The field of this exchange is politics. This word should include both the wide sense of social and historical life and the more concrete sense: the regulation of institutional forces. All objectivations are at once texts and institutions. If art innovates meaningful signs, then politics governs the acts by which these norms, expressive of subjectivity, are resisted or upheld.

It is therefore not surprising to find in the analytical practice of Dilthey himself—the analyst of the *expression*—"a point at which a circle . . . makes itself felt." Dilthey's poetics is informed by a political consciousness, even if he will not or cannot profile this consciousness in its more concrete form. My own concern, however, is to fill in the political context of the "inner significance of art" which guides Dilthey's own poetics. I stress this even in a work ostensibly preoccupied with subjectivity. In fact the path to a political reading of the essay lies through a renewed examination of its subjectivity.

The first obstacle to a political reading of Dilthey's poetics is a general one. Stated briefly, the very possibility of a reciprocal involvement of the terms subjectivity and political power is generally discounted or overlooked in Romantic and post-Romantic texts, so intent are we on reading into these texts the idea that these terms are antithetical, adversary. Writers are at work altering this prejudice. Paul de Man, for example, noted apropos of Rousseau's *Ecrits sur l'Abbé de Saint Pierre*, "Consciousness of selfhood (*se connaître*), whether individual or political, is itself dependent on a relationship of power and originates with this relationship."[22]

This example of the correction of an intellectual-historical prejudice is not haphazard; the fortunes of Dilthey and Rousseau are linked. The conception of Rousseau as promoting individual ineffable subjectivity is one to which Dilthey contributed early in his career, but his understanding of Rousseau necessarily changed direction through his changing conception of the category *Erlebnis* ("lived experience").

Erlebnis, which is an important term current in modern German, is of surprisingly recent coinage: it was not commonly used until the 1870s. Dilthey contributed fundamentally to its naturalization. The word recurs in his biography of Schleiermacher (1870) and above all in the first version of his essay on Goethe (1877), in which he contrasts Goethe with Rousseau. The main event allowing for the naturalization of the term *Erlebnis*, especially in its now almost obligatory association with literary expression, was Dilthey's volume *Lived Experience and Poetry* (*Das Erlebnis und die Dichtung*), although this collection of essays, with its powerful title, did not appear until 1905.

In the 1877 version of the Goethe essay, however, the term *Erlebnis* recurs, although not with the meaning it has in Dilthey's later technical usage. He uses it to describe Rousseau's novel mode of writing from the standpoint of his inner experience. The key point is "inner." In this stage of Dilthey's conception of *Erlebnis*, the word can mean a wholly internal construction. Gadamer, who comments informatively on these matters, notes that Dilthey describes an imaginative construction of Rousseau as one which Rousseau, "in light of his ignorance of the world, spun together as lived experience."[23] But "an *Erlebnis* that has been 'spun together' does not fit the original sense of '*erleben*.' . . . The word '*erleben*' . . . carries the aura of the immediacy with which something real is grasped, unlike something which one also asserts one knows without corroboration from experience." An experience alleged to be entirely imaginary is without "Kausalität." It does not fit in, either, with "Dilthey's own scientific use of the term in his mature period, where *Erlebnis* means the immediate donnée, the basic material of all imaginative constructions."[24]

Rousseau's influence on European Romantic writers was to make *lived experience* the authenticating standard of experience, especially of cognition. But our understanding of such a standard has in turn been shaped by Dilthey's conception of Romanticism and lived experience. When Gadamer writes, for example, "the neologism '*Erlebnis*' obviously invokes a critique of the rationalism of the Enlightenment—a word which in the wake of Rousseau validated the concept of Life," he is invoking a commonplace strengthened only at certain moments and not uniformly by Dilthey.[25] This is the notion that a fundamental difference exists between, on the one hand, political consciousness and activity, and, on the other hand, experience shaped by the requirements of a unique subjectivity. As early as the *Introduction to the Historical Sciences*, however, Dilthey's discussion of natural rights theory stresses as the focus of Rousseau's political thought "the single individual." True, the individual is grasped by Rousseau as a set of unchanging characteristics from which the "abstract relations" constituting society are derived. The theory, however, had a practical result; it "achieved its negative work in the effect of a Rousseau on the Revolution" (1:223). The fact, therefore, that in the Revolution Rousseau's natural rights theory became a political force, suggests the fit between "rationalism" and the relations of force in society reproduced in the experience of a subjectivity, and both terms refer back to the single individual. (See p. 140 of this book.)

What does it mean then when Dilthey is represented as theorist and advocate of the category *Erlebnis*? In his mature work the term is projected as a totalizing category fusing inner and outer, preceding the dissociation of subject and object. But it has otherwise tended (not without Dilthey's support) to be understood as subjectivity pure and simple.

We do not have to return to 1877 to find the subjective sense of *Erlebnis*. In *The Poetic Imagination* itself, for example, Dilthey lines up the term *Erlebnis* with "that vitality which is enjoyed in feeling" and which, by virtue of "the aesthetic process," is only subsequently grasped as form or subsequently represented in an image (6:117).

This terminological difficulty is analyzed by Frithjof Rodi, who identifies Dilthey's retrograde "Cartesian" tendency to write about the category of *Erlebnis* as if it could be split into an inner and outer.[26] But, Rodi points out, this division is contrary to the spirit of Dilthey's thought, for indeed later on in the very text of *The Poetic Imagination* Dilthey writes, "The real core of poetry, *Erlebnis*, contains a relation of inner and outer, 'spirit and garment,' inspiration and materialization, the significance of structure or of phonetic sequence and the figurative visibility of the fleeting psychic moment (6:226). At various moments, then, *Erlebnis* may mean, alternately, a state of mind or the event experienced. Rodi means to iron out this vacillation:

> In reality, Dilthey . . . always has before him, as the dynamic unity of *Erlebnis*, the interpenetration of "inner" and "outer." With this |term| he means neither pulsating inwardness which has yet to assume structure, nor experienced factuality which has yet to be grasped in its significance. When he speaks of two possibilities, he does not mean the two components of the interpenetration ("inner" and "outer"), but two modes of their interplay, two equally privileged forms of the unity of life and form. Both are

called "Erlebnis" and can be differentiated only by the "direction of the process of phantasy" as materialization and inspiration.[27]

This salvaging attempt, however, does not eliminate the division but merely shifts it onto a higher plane of complexity. At first we were forced to distinguish between an "inner" Erlebnis (state of mind) and an "outer" Erlebnis (experienced event). According to Rodi, however, Dilthey always means to name with Erlebnis a prereflexive unity of mind and event, an unvarying interpenetration of inner and outer. This unity nonetheless occurs in two different modes. We are now faced with the distinction between an "inner" inner-outer Erlebnis (fantasy) and an "outer" inner-outer Erlebnis (objectivation) and hence a divided meaning.

Dilthey indeed frequently stresses the subjective dimension of Erlebnis as the felt intensity of inner life and as a result underplays the pressure of metamorphosis which the aesthetic impulse receives in the course of its materialization. The vacillation persists. It is important to determine in each case its logic and position.

If, however, we consult Dilthey's readers, we find that his oscillating concept of Erlebnis has tended to be interpreted entirely on the side of inwardness. It is important to evoke an understanding in which the material and, finally, the political component of the concept of Erlebnis can be given its due.

The resistance to this perspective is particularly entrenched in the American reception of Dilthey. This is certainly puzzling, since this obstacle appears even in a number of American critics whose philosophical awareness and knowledge of Dilthey is beyond question and who, in other places, plainly register Dilthey's effort to enlarge the field of the individual subject in the direction of an "intellectual economy."

Richard Palmer's essay on Dilthey in Hermeneutics opens with the usual stress. "Dilthey," writes Palmer, "began to see in hermeneutics the foundations for the Geisteswissenschaften—that is, . . . all those disciplines which interpret expressions of man's inner life"[28] (italics mine). Dilthey's critique of Kant, Palmer continues, turns on Kant's category "feeling," which did not "seem to do justice to the inner, historical character of human subjectivity" (italics mine).[29] Palmer's manner of constituting Dilthey's full subject is then to add "feeling," "will," and "life" to the knowing subject.[30] What is left out of this addition is the social and political dimension—a nonpsychological or not merely psychological definition of interest.

Palmer's account lacks an appreciation of this sort of Diltheyan language: "Far more intricate, more mysterious than our own organism, . . . Society—that is, the entire historical-social reality—confronts the individual as an object of scrutiny. In it the current of events flows unstoppably, while the particular individuals of which it consists appear on the stage of life and then take their leave. Thus the individual finds himself in it as an element in circulation with other elements. . . . We are forced to master the image of social conditions in perpetually active value-judgments, to restructure it, at least conceptually, through incessant will power" (5:36–37). How adequate, then, is Palmer's paraphrase of Dilthey? "We [do not] experience life . . . in the mechanical categories of 'power.'"[31] Many other examples of such resistances can be adduced.

Fredric Jameson responds to the same crux as did Frithjof Rodi, namely, the subject-object relation. Commenting on Dilthey's essay "The Rise of Hermeneutics," Jameson alludes to Dilthey's "false start" in constituting the *Erlebnis*-like act of understanding (*Verstehen*) as a junction of an understanding monad and an understood monad. Jameson writes:

> Even the doctrine of *Verstehen* itself is not without its own shortcomings; and we may well feel today that thus construed, the dilemma is insoluble; that where the subject is thus initially and irrevocably separated from its object, or the understanding monad from the monad understood, no amount of theoretical or descriptive ingenuity can put them back together again. Any successful theory of understanding must in other words begin after the fact, in the presence of an understanding or an interpretation already realized.[32]

How well-founded on Dilthey's text is this statement? Dilthey is in fact a lot closer to a "successful theory of understanding" on Jameson's account than Jameson credits.

At the outset of the essay, Dilthey describes the object of intellectual-historical understanding in such a way as precisely to extract from it its object-character. He writes, "Human studies (*Geisteswissenschaften*) have indeed the advantage over the natural sciences that their object is not the phenomenon as it is given to the senses, [i.e.,] is no mere reflection in consciousness of something real, but is itself *immediate inner reality* and thus, indeed, as a *context or coherent structure (Zusammenhang)*, is experienced from within" (5:317–318) (translation and italics mine). Jameson's translation omits the word "immediate."[33]

After reading this passage, how can one—as does Jameson—object that Dilthey's theory of understanding fails to begin "after the fact, in the presence of an understanding . . . already realized"? An interior object transparent to its structure is already (at least implicitly) understood.

The same nuance of the "already-realized" character of the object to be understood can be found later on in this essay in Dilthey's definition of "understanding." But Jameson's translation is not quite right: "Understanding [is] the process by which an inside is conferred on a complex of external sensory signs." What Dilthey actually writes is "We term *understanding* the process by which we come to know (*erkennen*) an inner dimension from signs which are given to the senses from the outside" (5:318). The conferring of an inside is not done, as Jameson suggests, by a subjectivity, which with its magnetism and power draws in and endows an external object, meager and halted at the outside. Coherent determinations are not supplied to the naked sign, whence it acquires "inwardness." If there is any conferring implied in this exchange, it is done by the object; an inner dimension is read off from signs, and these signs come in from the outside. This passage complements in an important way the passage cited immediately before. The first passage explained th 't the object of historical understanding is always already "inside" the subject—an inner reality immediately apprehensible to a subjectivity. In the passage defining understanding, Dilthey in turn supplies the signlike outer object an "insideness" which it virtually confers upon the cognizing consciousness.

What we have here is not inconsistency but a fine adumbration of the hermeneutic circle or, if you prefer, that reciprocity of cooperation, of mutual exchange, which Dilthey defines as the causal (*kausal*) nexus. If his shortcomings as a historical thinker are grounded, according to Jameson, on the shortcomings of his psychological hermeneutics, we see that the charge is premature. There is nothing in Dilthey's account of the inner/outer relation in *Erlebnis*, the subject/object relation in historical understanding (*Verstehen*), or the cause/effect relation in causality (*Kausalität*) to warrant the charge of unhistorical subjective idealism. Dilthey insistently marks out the social and political objectivity of the field in which the subject feels its life and the manner in which the subject regulates the claims which life makes on him. The political model shapes even what is alleged to be the most internal of acts—inspirations. The politics of the outer field—the concrete political struggles of a certain stage in the evolution of German society—and the politics of the inner field—in a word "psychology"—are inextricably involved, as we have seen: that is what underlies Dilthey's repeated appeal to a "historical psychology" of the human spirit.

The most comprehensive term for this imbrication of politics and inwardness in Dilthey is "causality" (*Kausalität*). Causality evokes a cause/effect model which resists the attribution of firstness to either term. Indeed it is the uniform operation, in the historical sciences, of this model of causality which, more than the specification of a suitable object, defines the historical sciences. We realize that "data of the spirit" (*geistige Tatsachen*) are precisely those data which submit the investigator to the energizing perplexities of the hermeneutic circle. From this perspective Dilthey has already anticipated Heidegger's valorization of the category of understanding as more than cognition or some activity of cognition; understanding is a constitutive category of *Dasein* (human being).[34] Dilthey still marks out a zone of theoretical activity—that of performing natural science—which is free from the reciprocities of causality. But he does this mainly to signal the special depth of involvement of the historical sciences in such models, in such a mode of being.[35]

Part of the obstacle to appreciating the originality of Dilthey's formulation of the cause/effect relation in interpretive experience will hardly come as a surprise; it is that it has been with us since Dilthey. It would, however, come as a surprise—or, at any rate, as the token of an unsuspected clairvoyance—for literary scholars in countries whose prevailing aesthetics is materialist. We read, for example, in a recent manual from East Germany, a laudatory account of a certain concept of literary reception.

> The concept of reception is shaped from the reader's standpoint. The reader himself "takes" the work as the object which is his donnée. On the other hand, the concept of effect stresses the angle of the work: in being "received" the work itself also takes the reader, operates an effect on him. . . . What we have before us is not therefore a causal relation, in which the work occurs as cause and the events in the reader as effect or, conversely, in which the effects of the work have their cause in the reader. It is a question of a special form of reciprocity, a relation in which both members mutually interpenetrate.[36]

We have here the feeling that the North Pole is being discovered for the second time.

The Poetic Imagination

> In no other period in the history of art have so-called personal cultivation (*Bildung*) and authentic art confronted one another with as much repugnance and disgust as today [1871].[37]
>
> —Nietzsche

> Politics is a realm akin to art insofar as, like art, it occupies a creatively mediating position between the spirit and life, the idea and reality, the desirable and the necessary, conscience and deed, morality and power.[38]
>
> —Thomas Mann

What then is the specifically political dimension of Dilthey's *Poetic Imagination*? To find it out we shall attend to the figures of Dilthey's rhetoric. His images again and again portray political interaction and struggle. Grasped in their real historical context, they explain and indeed generate the tension in his argument.

Dilthey's political consciousness is evident from the outset for all those who read *The Poetic Imagination* in volume 6 of the *Collected Writings*. There, the text is printed immediately following the 1886 essay "Poetic Imagination and Madness" ("Dichterische Einbildungskraft und Wahnsinn"), which was delivered to an audience of students at an academy for army doctors. The concluding sentence of this essay thus appears on the page facing *The Poetic Imagination* and reads inescapably as its epigraph: "May God preserve and defend his majesty our Emperor, in whom we honor an example (*Vorbild*) of all noble, humane and lofty sentiment" (p. 102).[39] *The Poetic Imagination* follows.

What meaning for this work, if any, has Dilthey's gesture of political deference? One trembles a little from this sentence for the fate of the poetological word "example" (*Vorbild*). Presumably the word means one thing when it is written to characterize the relation of poetics to all other intellectual-historical disciplines and another when it is spoken of Kaiser Wilhelm I and all "noble, humane and lofty sentiment." *The Poetic Imagination* might therefore be conceived of as repeating, modifying, or, again, as entirely bypassing this obeisance to the crown. But if we incline to the third view—which is the position of all those commentators who have written on *The Poetic Imagination* without alluding to its political character—we find ourselves from the start having to read against the grain. From the start the work is explicitly oriented to the life of literature as a political institution, as a type of political practice. It is misleading to the thrust of *The Poetic Imagination* to stress apropos of it, as does Makkreel, that "literature constitutes a cultural system where public institutions are of minimal importance."[40] This is to conceive of "institution" in a narrower and more harmless sense than Dilthey does. Literature is an institution because it institutes relations of force between acts of creation, reception, and understanding whose thrust is to enter the public order. Winding through these three kinds of activity is the movement of desire. Where there is aesthetic form, desire acknowledges force.

Literary narratives have plots, and plots, as Peter Brooks points out, "must have *force*: the force that makes the connection of incident powerful, that shapes the confused material of a life into an intentional structure which in turn generates new insights about how life can be told. The powerful fiction is that which is able to restage the complex and buried past history of desire as it covertly reconstitutes itself in the present language."[41] Even as a narrator of literary theory, Dilthey is a political being acting in a field of desire and force. This is especially the case when he writes, not on literary forms alone, but on the genesis of literature as a social institution. For if a genetic account may be understood as an allegory of norms, and if the instantiation of a first state implies the instantiation of a native and natural, hence authentic being, he writes normatively and hence with political force.

The first sign of literature as a social institution appears at the outset of the essay where Dilthey writes about the influence of traditional poetics on philological practice.[42] He does so, however, with the awareness of crisis. "Crisis" is linked at its root (*krinein*) with the concept of separation.[43] When philology is named, it is named as a sign of the separation and divisiveness that has occurred within the institution of literature. It marks the separation of the agencies of production, reception, theory (poetics), and its own analytic practice.

A future poetics will rejoin a once powerful and creative tradition of poetic theory which has fallen into anarchy and impotence. The tradition can be grasped as having functioned in two vital moments—the Aristotelian and the German Idealist. Dilthey specifically considers his program as the enterprise of "supplementing and furnishing a deeper foundation" to the theorem of Idealist aesthetics associated with Kant, Schiller, and Schopenhauer. This theorem "shifts into center-position the importance of feelings for aesthetic processes" (6:119). But as both these moments—the Aristotelian and the Idealist—writes Dilthey, have shaped the practice and self-understanding of philology, it follows that his own psychological and historical poetics will also transform philological practice.

In Dilthey's narrative, Aristotelian poetics dominated the practice of literature and philology until the second half of the eighteenth century. It was "the tool of poets at work and the dreaded standard of critics through to Boileau, Gottsched and Lessing. It was the most effective auxiliary of the philological interpretation, critique and evaluation of Greek literature" (6:103). The hegemony of Aristotelian poetics was usurped in the latter part of the eighteenth century by German Idealist aesthetics. This aesthetics shaped the work of Goethe and Schiller and the critical perspectives of Humboldt, Schelling, Hegel, and the Schlegels; finally it utterly transformed philology.

> It supplemented rational hermeneutics—as it had been worked out in the struggle between Tridentine Catholicism and the Protestants and extended by Ernesti—with that aesthetically-founded hermeneutic praxis whose rules Schleiermacher, following the procedure of Friedrich Schlegel,

derived from the principle of the form of a literary work. It supplemented those value-discriminations and a criticism based on reason, the rules, and grammatical, metrical and rhetorical techniques with that aesthetic criticism which proceeded from the analysis of form and whose important results are evident in the work of Wolf, Lachmann and their successors. Indeed this German aesthetics accelerated the fall in France and England of the old forms and influenced the first still tentative productions of a new poetic age. (6:103)

This German discovery is conceived from the start as having political force, as hastening the fall of older cultural and institutional forms in France and England. German Idealist aesthetics had a revolutionary impact on two societies which, unlike Germany, had revolutions in every area of their life except the aesthetic. If these "old forms" which fell, allude to the old forms of philological practice, then the political force of change in aesthetics is illustrated by its effect upon philology.

The political implications of German Idealist aesthetics adumbrate the political implications of Dilthey's own text. The future transformation of philology is one, and indeed not the least, of the real effects which his text aims to have—a text whose ambitions become graphic at the level of its figures.

Speaking of the hegemony of German Idealist aesthetics, Dilthey writes of this system: "Through these two princes of German poetry [Goethe and Schiller] it dominated the entire empire of literature—with the assistance of Humboldt, Moritz, Koerner, Schelling, the Schlegels, and, finally, Hegel as the Ministers of Fine Arts acting under them" (6:103). Dilthey pictures an efficient empire of German poetry at the turn of the nineteenth century, with a ruling aristocracy still worthy of first rank, served by a loyal bureaucracy of critical talents. The image calls up Dilthey's forever declared admiration for the unified nation-state ("the empire of literature").[44] The image also alludes briefly and polemically to the view—which Dilthey always abjured—of Goethe as an antidemocrat, as the reprehensible tool of "princes," a notion which cost Goethe his popularity in Germany during the middle decades of the nineteenth century.[45] Dilthey, on the other hand, was a single-minded student of Goethe even at the lowest ebb of the latter's fortunes; hence *he* can with good conscience write "prince." A component of Dilthey's political ideal was based literally on what he perceived as Goethe's exemplary wholeness. This view is set out most authoritatively in the text of Dilthey's inaugural lecture in Basel in 1867, where it figures as part of a canonization of the German philosophical tradition. The inaugural lecture, an important document in Dilthey's intellectual development, has often been examined as part of the suspicious scrutiny to which German critics have

submitted Dilthey's political consciousness and good faith. A passage
from Peschken's study is typical of the skeptical thesis.

> After the North German Confederation was founded as the preliminary stage
> of Empire, Dilthey proclaimed, in his inaugural lecture at Basel in 1867,
> the great [harmonious and positive] "life substance" (*Lebensinhalt*) in the
> sphere of the history of [German] philosophy and literature. He seizes this
> moment to offer a total overview of German literary history, in which Clas-
> sicism—including its political dimension—is given a core position. Be-
> cause of the year 1866, Classicism acquires political relevance. With this
> valuation as a starting point, a view of life is canonized which operates on
> the political consciousness and is itself projected as political conscious-
> ness. The point of convergence of the notion of Classicism and political
> consciousness in Bismarck's Empire lies in the *reluctance to admit conflict* within
> both conceptual orders [italics mine]. It brings together fear of the insti-
> tutionalization of political conflict through a parliamentary hegemony as
> well as the resistance to anything problematical in Classicism on the as-
> sumption that its essence is harmony. Political consciousness and the idea
> of Classicism approach one another from different sides, converging on
> this ideology of Empire.[46]

Well and good for 1867, but this reading of Dilthey's concept
of harmony, conciliation, and totality as nourished by the image of the
German nation-state obviously cannot have the last word. We need to
consider the twenty-one years between Dilthey's inaugural address at
Basel and the writing of *The Poetic Imagination*. These years, politically
speaking, were years of uniform consolidation of Empire, of the hegemony of a state over a bourgeois political consciousness, of a steadily
increasing domination by national authority. Yet Dilthey's text of 1887
speaks of the absence of national consciousness, of the felt imperti-
nence of German Classicism as a guiding aesthetic in an age of aesthetic upheaval, of productivity that has lost all familiar bearings. He
speaks of a time of rift, of crisis, of dismaying multifariousness that cries
out for the creation of a national ideology in the form of an epic. Peschken's single link of political and literary awareness will not work: it has
no temporal dimension to it, and it is precisely here that the *décalage*
widens utterly. At the heart of Empire Dilthey discovers not cohesion
but chaos, not conciliation but crisis, not harmony but collision and force.
Peschken is right that in Dilthey acts of aesthetic judgment "acquire, indeed, possess, political relevance," but the direction and implication of
this relevance in 1887 is different from what Peschken finds twenty years
earlier.

It is true that Dilthey continues to look for guidance to the
German tradition defined in its basic directions by Classicism in litera-

ture and Objective Idealism in philosophy. This is not the same as saying, however, that he means to import into the present chaos the values obtained from making a cut into the tradition at, say, 1800. Earlier we read in *The Poetic Imagination*: "Our |German| poetics . . . is still alive here and there on the lecturer's rostrum but no longer in the consciousness of the leading artists or critics, *and only there would it be |truly| alive. . . .* It |is| all over for the principles of that poetics which once upon a time in idyllic Weimar had been debated by Schiller, Goethe and Humboldt" (6:104) (italics mine).

　　In Dilthey's position toward what is valuable and what is dead in Classicism, it is the present that has the last word. "What is *classic*," he writes, "is precisely not what corresponds to certain rules. A work is classic to the extent that it gives human beings in the present complete satisfaction and extends its effect in space and time" (6:236). At the turn of the nineteenth century a princely Goethe dominated with his Idealist aesthetic the "empire" of German literature. For Dilthey, this image of the poet-prince has implications for present policy. It points to that Liberal bourgeois perspective of the 1860s—consistently Dilthey's own—which looked to the enlightened, progressive, bourgeoisified sector of the nobility for political leadership.[47] The figure of the kaiser, meanwhile, goes unnamed in the metaphor. It does not belong, of course, if the image is one only of an earlier state of affairs around 1800. But if we are going to construct a rigorous analogy, so that the image at the same time projects Dilthey's own contemporary political ideal, it interestingly suppresses the kaiser. In this metaphor the imperial figure remains subliminally in play as the *Zeitgeist*, the historical spirit of Idealist poetics, but its only subliminal status also alerts us to an important assertion appearing later in the argument. This is Dilthey's sense of the priority of the individual poetic-interpretive act over the imperial spirit, the *Zeitgeist*. "The *unity* in an age and a people," he writes, "which we characterize as the *historical spirit* of an age, first arises . . . only through the *creative power* and self-glorification *of the genius*" (6:230). This key passage establishes the primacy of genius (including explicitly that of the political figure) with respect to the historical stage of consciousness and also reaffirms a political ideal of the hegemony of enlightened aristocracy. This genius may or may not be an artist. Dilthey writes apropos of the possible unity of a historical age through the "coordination of its facts": "The genius of the ruler or of the statesman brings the recalcitrant facts themselves into a unity of purpose (*Zweckeinheit*) possible by virtue of their coordination. It is opposed to that |genius| of the artist or philosopher in its direction but is like their genius in its scope and grandeur" (6:230). Dilthey's argument for the scope and grandeur of the statesman is inescapably reminiscent of Bismarck, and the act of genius, that of national unification.[48] He concedes the power of the statesman, but we should retain the nuance: this power is comparable with the authority of poetic activity, which is certain. In another passage, Dilthey tends to efface the difference between poetic and political activity.

> This circle of experience, in which the poet operates, is no different from that out of which the philosopher or the politician creates. The youthful letters of Frederick the Great, like those of a statesman today, are full of elements likewise found in the soul of a great poet; and many thoughts of Schiller could be those of a political orator. [Given Dilthey's judgment on Schiller's poetry the distinction and priority of genuine poetry is ironically maintained.] A powerful life force (*Lebendigkeit*) of soul, energy of experiences of the heart and of the world, generalizing power and the power of inspiring conviction form the common maternal soil of intellectual achievement of very different kinds, among them, however, those of the poet. (6:128)

Dilthey's main point, however, appears to be his insistence on the greater *normality* of the poet, whom he wishes to free from the charge of passivity or pathology with which the Naturalist writers, especially, were regarded by the philistines of Berlin. This passage does not therefore jeopardize the special privilege of poetry. This distinction of priority has an exact counterpart in Dilthey's position against Treitschke in the debate in 1879 about the relative rank of free cultural activity and self-effacing activity in the service of the state. Dilthey spoke on behalf of free cultural activity.[49]

I return now to the metaphor of the poet-prince. Dilthey accords a special place to philological practice, which here serves as a subministry accessible to all other "Ministers of the Fine Arts" and indeed to the two princes. But without the influence of the imperial spirit, the kaiser, it is otherwise of doubtful utility. In this subministry the *Bildungsbürger*, like Dilthey himself, finds a place for his efforts to shape through poetics another *Zeitgeist*. He means to secure for philology an independent foundation on the "eternal" psychological laws of poetic activity, laws instrinsically favorable to *the individual subject*. Dilthey's own philological ventures, as Gadamer observes, are guided by an ideal of scientific rigor but at the same time exhibit—more decisively—individual tact which presupposes a moral (*seelisch*) culture and proves the survival of . . . the belief in individualism."[50]

Dilthey concludes the overture to his essay by detailing the effect of German Idealist aesthetics on philological practice. In this way he adumbrates the effect which his own aesthetics means to have. The central category of this aesthetics is that of feeling having access to its "own truth"; as such it is central to "the processes of creation, meta-morphosis of images, and composition" (6:119). German aesthetics everywhere "set into causal (*kausal*) relation the *Seelenzustand* (psychic condition, state of soul, mood, *état d'âme*) which produces a literary work and the form which is peculiar to it. This was grosso modo the step for-ward," writes Dilthey, "which defines . . . the view taken of works in this epoch. As a consequence the philology and criticism of this time may be characterized as aesthetic. Formal analysis according to the method of proceeding explanatively from a point within the inner life of the psy-che was thereafter applied to the manifold forms of European literature. . . . Thus there arose the great age of our German philology, criticism and aesthetics." It is impossible, Dilthey continues, to overestimate the productivity of this perspective, which nonetheless carried within it at all times the impulse toward its own abuse. The valuation of form as expressive of psychic force swiftly became an overvaluation of form as such, as in Schiller's "adoration of a domain of pure and ideal forms detached from reality. . . . The Romantic world of beautiful illusion set in" (6:122). But what, according to Dilthey, provokes this shift in valori-zation from "feeling" to "form" in the classic theorem of poetic activity? In this text both possibilities—the Classic and the Romantic—appear to be simultaneous.

      Christofer Zöckler speaks to Dilthey's critique of Romanti-cism when he writes: "Flight into the past is the expedient which offers itself increasingly to Dilthey because of the specific [repressive] devel-opment of the German Empire. Flight is indeed the partly latent ideo-logical transposition of the specific form of social 'praxis' of the culti-vated German liberal-conservative bourgeois (*Bildungsbürger*)."[51] But Dilthey's critique of Romanticism certainly establishes that his "flight" into the past is borne along on *understanding* the objectivations of the past. As such it is a highly meditated and selective kind of flight, based on an ideal of objective truth. This ideal is called by Dilthey "positive" and "objective to a special degree" and means to serve a philosophy of Objective Idealism and the Liberal ideology. Objective truth in history, for Dilthey, is to be found in the perspective of only that Objective Ide-alism which took root in Germany, "prepared for in the German move-ment, 'intimated' (*vorgefühlt*) by Goethe, and meant to be realized in the present."[52] This point emerges from a passage about Goethe from Dil-they's early writings: "In him poetry intimated what philosophy first suc-ceeded in representing conceptually many years later—the unity of life and the ideal; eternal identity; the realization of world-reason in his-tory."[53] Schiller's idealism is subjective, agonized, and voluntary, and represents a different possibility for "flight"—a possibility offered by the past and intolerable to Dilthey. Flight has its own scale of pragmatic implications.

Dilthey's stress on the inauthenticity of Romanticism belongs to a familiar critique, the terms of which actually owe more to Schiller than Dilthey realizes. Consult, for example, Schiller's critique of the Rousseauean idyll in *On Naive and Sentimental Poetry*. A version of this polemic was most recently conspicuous in the 1960s in a work like René Girard's *Deceit, Desire, and the Novel*.[54] Girard, too, identifies as "Romantic" the captivation by "metaphysical desire," the desire for an inhuman bliss which, as he points out, is covertly mediated by another text or another's desire, a mediation to which, however, the author (if not the hero) is blind.[55] This argument was resisted and interestingly inverted by Paul de Man, who declared the Romantic writer—Rousseau par excellence—to be entirely lucid about the impossibility of happiness, of a life of "beauty," under any circumstances, let alone by the lights of what Girard calls "desire according to the Other." Romantic alienation, for de Man, is not the mystification of the Romantic writer but a mystification which that writer—or writer's text—identifies as normative in and expectable from the social order of desire.[56] Along with this blindness, improperly alleged, de Man criticizes an alleged (and associated) romantic mystification about the value of the organic symbol.[57] Organicism means precisely the most literal version of Dilthey's formulation of "the German aesthetic": that there is a *Seelenzustand* which in each case produces a literary work as an agent causing and indeed reproducing itself within the form peculiar to it.[58] This relation, says de Man, is systematically recognized by Romantic writers, not as a correct description of poetic activity, but as an aberrant thesis. The aberration may indeed be constitutive. Although, in a phrase from Hölderlin's *Hyperion*, it is one of those "mere phenomena of the human spirit" (*blosse Phänomene des menschlichen Gemüts*),[59] it may still be inescapable, regardless of whether the belief is grasped as right or wrong.[60]

Dilthey seems to see this, over and above his polemic against a Romantic beatification of the beautiful. The bipolar formula associating mood with form allows and indeed encourages an arbitrary (*willkürlich*) and potentially endless reversal of priorities. If the causal theory carries in it the germ of an "unhealthy" overvaluation of the psychic particularity of the artist, it also carries in it the germ of a hypostasis of form. The point is that the devotion to form does not have to imply a rejection of the formula that sets form in the relation of effect to mood as its cause. It can arise reactively from within the formula as a reweighting of the neglected opposite pole of the correlation. The task of a more adequate poetics—the kind toward which Dilthey is aiming—is

to surpass the notion of a sheerly individual cause, a psychological entity creating "organically" an ideal verbal form, and at the same time to
eliminate the notion of an ideal, autonomous verbal form emptied of
the traces of an affect-charged individual psyche. The goal is not to for-
tify this or that position within the circle of strict cause and effect but
to get out of the circle in the right way. Romantic writers like Rousseau
and Hölderlin were thoroughly aware of the mutual involvement of ex-
pressivist and formalist errors. They are genuine precursors of Dilthey's
notion of a historical, text-like *Erlebnis* and its implicit articulation of
meaning, but it may be part of the voracious dependence of insight on
blindness that leads Dilthey to obscure his lights.

An early passage from Dilthey's diaries (1859) shows this direction of his transcendence of Idealist aesthetics. Dilthey notes within
"the Kantian-Fichtean" tradition the "distinct consciousness of the power,
over the mind, of categories, forms of thought, schemata." These of course
are not solely constitutive: the epistemological subject is constituted by
fundamental acts. "The ego is activity; each thought is to be regarded
as an element of this activity and not as something static. Every system
has to be explained as a movement of ideas." Zöckler comments, citing
Dilthey (in quotes):

> Idealism tends to refer the activity of individuals to these original actions.
> . . . It conceives of individual development on the pattern of the germ
> (*Keim*) "which shoots up out of itself from within" and which, from the
> outset, contains all determinative moments. This principle, however, is also
> the principle of the philological method which means to explain a text by
> a "genetic account of the circle of thoughts from certain inner begin-
> nings." The activity of the individual, however, who objectifies himself,
> among other ways, in texts, does not "shoot up out of itself from within.
> Rather, a coherent context of thought (*Gedankenzusammenhang*) takes form
> from . . . [the 'inner beginning,' the 'germ,' the 'crucial point' (*springender
> Punkt*)] according to psychological laws. It takes form in attaching itself to
> this point (*es bildet sich ihm an*). . . . A too exclusive role has been given to
> development from the interior outward." [61]

This is the germ of that crucial idea of *The Poetic Imagination*—
the "acquired context of the life of mind" (*erworbener Zusammenhang des
Seelenlebens*)—which is the concrete individual totality, the structured
history of one's *Erlebnisse*, the repository of what one knows of social and
historical life, the index of reality, and the mediator of all particular intentions (6:167). It is, along with *Erlebnis*, the most powerful of Dilthey's
historical categories intended to mediate and surpass as a third term
the specular oscillations of subject and object. The encompassing terms
often have the aura of a predominating subjectivity, for they tend to be

represented as "centers";[62] at the same time they allow for what Marxists call "the real comprehension of material practice."[63]

Dilthey's final argument against the overvaluing of beautiful fictions is more conventional within the tradition of anti-Romantic polemic. The psychological aesthetics of Kant, Schiller, and the Romantics is, he alleges, unhistorical. It cannot stabilize the oscillating valorization of inner and outer or introduce a progressive, dialectical moment—the category of history. Dilthey's critique does not speak against formalism on behalf of a theory of expression but on behalf of an altogether different account of the affective "cause" of form. In Gadamer's words: "In the expression (or objectivation: *Ausdruck*) the matter expressed (or objectified: *das Ausgedrückte*) is present in a different manner than is the cause (*Ursache*) in the effect. It is itself present in the expression and is understood when the expression is understood."[64] What is expressed is neither something inner nor something outer. "The aesthetic faculty," writes Dilthey, "raises the relation of inner and outer experienced in us to living energy and disseminates (*verbreitet*) it through that nature, too, which is dead to thought" (6:117). Despite the vitalist rhetoric, this vision has historical force. Whenever, in Dilthey, "human conditions are experienced (*erlebt*)"—even as "living energy"—we are dealing (as Habermas puts it), "not with human being but rather with the world, in which the historical-social life of man is expressed."[65] Aesthetic experience historicizes nature.

Where Dilthey still preserves a regressive causal logic (of *Ursache/Wirkung*) and hypostatizes "state of mind" as a source, he identifies the "cause" producing the form of the literary work as essentially feeling, yet feeling which is intelligible, historically intelligent—feeling saturated with value and discriminated life. Aesthetic feeling is bent on value. Thereafter, more insistently, and with important general implications for the historical sciences, he represents feeling as bent on meaning. "Dilthey," writes Makkreel, "increasingly regarded aesthetic feeling hermeneutically for the meaning it embodies."[66] But Dilthey is forever en route to abandoning the notion of a distinct psychic origin. This is shown, first, negatively: he gives shifting and contradictory accounts and valorizes arbitrarily different psychic entities—will, feeling, mood, value—as "originating" literature. Another account of the notion of the "cause" of literature comes closer to the movement of his thought. Whatever is termed a cause, as a distinct psychic origin, has to share the character of the "individual representation," which is non-self-identical, "metamorphic." "By the metamorphosis of individual representations," he writes, "I mean that the individual representation, the image, is not a constant atom of the life of mind, but rather a process emerging under changing conditions. The distribution of affective excitation in the individual image brings about heightened intensity, . . . displacement of parts. Thus representations do not change from without . . .; rather they are agents, processes. . . . With respect to this metamorphosis, the acquired context of the life of mind functions as a regulating apparatus." [67]

The "cause" is an agent in reciprocal play, the active element in a structure. The acquired context of psychic life, moreover, is itself an historical agent. "If now," writes Dilthey, "the task were given to us of conceptualizing states-of-mind which bring about the forms and are represented within them, only a psychology that showed us how to recognize the historical nature of man could help" (6:123). Heidegger remarks that

> what looks [in Dilthey] like disunity and an unsure, haphazard way of 'trying things out,' is an elemental restlessness, the one goal of which is to understand 'life' philosophically and to secure for this understanding a hermeneutical foundation in terms of 'life itself.' Everything centers in psychology, in which 'life' is to be understood in the historical context of its development and its effects, and understood as the *way* in which man as the possible *object* of the human sciences, and *especially* as the *root* of these sciences, *is*. Hermeneutics is the way this understanding enlightens itself. (BT, p. 450)

The object of this understanding is *Erlebnisse*. In Dilthey, historical life figures forth, is itself, the structure and context of experiences. *Erlebnis* individuates, organizes individuality: "Every individual *Erlebnis* occurs in relation to a self" (7:195). Literature, then, as the objectivation of a self, transcends contingent sensibility, and is accessible, finally, only to a "historical psychology" able to decipher the life-content (*Lebensgehalt*) of the individual expression. This means a science particularly alert to the social character and the governing "social function of literature" (6:236).

In profiling, at the conclusion of his essay, the social character of individuality, Dilthey returns to his starting point—that cultural crisis which has made Germany inhospitable to individual poetic activity.

The character of a historical epoch, he stresses, leaves its stamp on its literature quite as much as "on the business of state and the conduct of war" (6:230). As a literary text Dilthey's own essay is no exception. To a degree he has sought consciously to bring into his essay the widest possible awareness of the spirit of modernity. This spirit is itself the heightened consciousness of historicity. But there are ways in which Dilthey's consciousness of his own history does not coincide with or exhaust that history as it operates upon his work. The main element of this unconscious history is the magnification of the term of "power," of "might," that makes his work an aesthetics of force. His work is saturated with the midcentury Liberal ideology—"optimistic and peaceable and at the same time martial, rhetorical and violent."[68]

Dilthey is specifically aware of the radically changed political reality of modern Europe. The political seat of German Classicism was "idyllic Weimar"; the seats of post-Revolutionary European consciousness are London and Paris. London and Paris are the sources of unsettling new realities, a superconsciousness "in whose soul a new kind of poetry is circulating" (6:104). These cities have had their epic writers in Dickens and in Balzac and his heirs, but now "since we Germans have a capital, a new task has fallen to the German novel" (6:240).

The hallmark of that literature responsive to the super-consciousness of these cities is its expression of a "struggle" against "anarchy." "From all ages and from all peoples," writes Dilthey, "a motley crowd of forms presses in upon us and seems to dissolve every distinction among poetic genres and every rule. Especially from the East a primordial, formless literature inundates us. . . . In this anarchy the artist is abandoned by the rule, the critic is thrown back onto his personal feeling as the only remaining standard for determining value. The public dominates, the masses . . . make and break the name of the artist" (6:104).

Dilthey's equation of mass culture with anarchy is the standard position of the German bourgeoisie after 1871. Whereas in the reactionary period following the failed revolution of 1848 the bourgeoisie saw its enemy in the feudal classes, it afterward considered the masses of workers the chief threat to peace and order.[69] Dilthey does not escape projecting onto the masses a specter of "dark, brutal, dreadful" instability.[70]

The present-day democratic spirit—insistent and everywhere pervasive—penetrates art as it does "everything else around us." The modern writer cannot reanimate the aesthetic of an earlier century, when "natures who reckoned with what they *are*" (italics mine) could express their certitude in "a typifying (*repräsentative*) art ennobling subsistent beauty. Now our ideal lies not in the form but in the force which speaks to us in forms and movements" (6:105). In "forms and movements" aesthetic and political categories have become indistinguishable. The great artist must "wrestle" and "struggle" to know and shape this force.

A state beset by cultural anarchy is a state in crisis. Dilthey's text speaks in the rhetoric of violence that characterizes texts written in a time of crisis, a time habitual to Germany for all of Dilthey's life if we are to believe Droysen:

> Our spiritual life is deteriorating rapidly; its dignity, its idealism, its intellectual integrity are vanishing. . . . The exact sciences grow in popularity; establishments flourish whose pupils will one day form the independent upper middle class as farmers, industrialists, merchants, technicians, and so on; their education and outlook will concentrate wholly on material issues. At the same time the universities are declining. . . . At present all is instability, chaos, ferment, and disorder. The old values are finished, debased, rotten, beyond salvation, and the new ones are as yet unformed, aimless, confused, merely destructive. . . . We live in one of the great crises that lead from one epoch of history to the next.[71]

Droysen's essay was written in 1854; the sentiment underlies *The Poetic Imagination*. But there is in Dilthey's language a characteristically more fluid involvement of a figurative political rhetoric in a philosophical vocabulary. It bespeaks Dilthey's liberalism—his mediating spirit, his mood of hope, his offer of a constructive program. The thesis of the ultimately practical character of historical understanding in Dilthey is an articulation of hope in the political field. "It is one of the live tasks of contemporary philosophy," he writes, "to reconstitute the healthy relation between aesthetic thinking and art"—an art of force, of "gripping effects and upheavals" (6:104). The interplay of political and philosophical rhetoric defines the field of his struggle. The task of a poetics centers the general and urgent enterprise of the *Geisteswissenschaften* as the integration of cultural and political practice.[72]

The active and contemplative components of the artistic struggle do not exist simply divided between art, and thought about art. The historical spirit of movement and conflict pervades the historically aware consciousness in the very instant of its seizing hold of this spirit—and penetrates this consciousness in all its manifestations. Thus for all forms, the harmonious subject/object relation conjured up by the contemplative ideal exists only as the goal of a struggle, an action. "There is no human being and no thing" writes Dilthey,

> which could exist for me only as an object and not as a help or a hindrance, the goal of a striving or an involvement of the will, something of importance, making a claim on my consideration and inner closeness or else inspiring resistance, distance and strangeness. The life-connection, whether restricted to a given moment or long-lasting, turns these human

beings and objects for me into bearers of happiness, an expansion of my
existence, a heightening of my power; or in this connection they restrict
the free-play of my existence, they exercise pressure on me, they diminish
my power. (7:131)[73]

The destiny of struggle belongs even to the empirical scientific consciousness with which the new aesthetics wishes to ally itself, a
perturbed consciousness whose rush into pseudo-objectivity threatens
to increase division and estrangement.[74] "The spirit of scientific investigation goes into action vis-à-vis every object, penetrates every kind of
intellectual operation and excites the need to catch a genuine glimpse
of reality through every sort of husk or mask" (6:105). What Dilthey adumbrates is the degree to which science is itself in the grip of a particularly stark form of that *Variabilität* (6:108) which he paraphrases as the
"historical nature of man."[75] His own text, as a "scientific" tract, testifies to this perturbation mainly through its rhetoric: it is iconic with the
violence against which it speaks. Dilthey's epistemological theory of the
necessarily *active* imaginative reconstitution (*Nachbildung, Nacherleben*) of
the human object—seeking to overcome difference and delay—represents an attempt at once to acknowledge and to sublimate this restlessness.

But Dilthey speaks of course against violence and for its antithesis: for cohesiveness, conciliation, for the preservation of tradition.[76] His task will be to bend importunate, restless, divisive science
into the service of an intellectual-historical enterprise with normative
functions. Speaking of "empirical" methods, Dilthey writes: "The autonomous value of literature, the function which it has in society, can never
be demonstrated by those empirical methods [i.e., those without historical awareness]. If mind intended to confront its own creations only as
something objectively empirical, a self-estrangement of mind vis-à-vis
its own creations would set in" (6:125–26). Cognitive estrangement ex-
acerbates the historical process by which critical mind feels itself "thrown
back onto its personal feeling" (6:104), by which the practicing artist feels
himself isolated from traditional norms, yet captive of a "misology"—
the artist's hatred of reflection on art (6:105–106).

The function of aesthetic speculation has traditionally been
conservative. "In every productive period of literature, aesthetic reflection on the goal and technique of particular forms of artistic practice
essentially supported the development of a firm style and a coherent
tradition" (6:106). "Art persistently required a schooling of artists . . .
through aesthetic reflection." The great style of German Classical literature was sustained by the exercise of "the royal power" of the Weimar
poets Goethe and Schiller, "not without the terrorism of the *Xenien*," their

polemics in hexameter against Kotzebue, Iffland, and Nicolai. But this "royal power" is nowhere manifest now, and a better image for the struggle of aesthetic wills without cultural and political tradition is the definitive suppression of Kotzebue, not by diatribe but by the knife of a democrat assassin.

Philology figures in turn as the conservative Liberal wing of the Ministry of Aesthetics. "Its merit," writes Dilthey, "is to have made intelligible for the first time the coherence of the literature of a people both within itself and with respect to the life of the national spirit" (6:108). Penetrated by the historical consciousness, it now finds itself confronted only with historically conditioned and defined poetic practices. In this sense it is no more privileged than the general consciouness of a society entered "into an historical age," faced with a profusion of dead shapes from the past ("we are surrounded by the entire past") and the shapeless energies and violent effects of the present.

All forms of consciousness struggle for general law within a profusion of possibilities: it is precisely the troubled relation of historically limited and hence contingent forms with "the general laws of poetry which leads philology necessarily to the principles of poetics" (6:108). The historical consciousness grasps the historicity of the life of the mind, and the psychological consciousness asks: "Can we know how processes founded on the nature of man and hence operative everywhere produce these various groups of poetry, divided by peoples and ages? How is the self-sameness of our human essence, expressing itself in the uniformities [inhering in systems of culture] bound up with its variability, its historical character?" (6:108).

This is not the place to reproduce in detail Dilthey's "solution," his full contribution to a historical-psychological poetics. The reader who does not know German will find it in the books of Müller-Vollmer and Makkreel. What I have wanted to stress is the political and historical context of Dilthey's effort at a solution, his effort to find access and hold fast to a coherent human substance in an age of leveling, violence, and estranging science. He conceives his effort as a reciprocal illumination of psychology and history—a psychology of the "variable" literary object, a history of the permanent crisis of the spirit perpetuating the struggle of individuals for form.

Dilthey's practice is finally plainest in the rhetoric with which he identifies the matrix of poetic activity—the acquired context of the life of mind. This category belongs to the individual mind and is synchronic with it: "The acquired picture of reality in it regulates *our* understanding of the impression just occupying *our* consciousness; the acquired mode of weighing value distinctions in it determines the feeling of the moment; the acquired system of purposes of *our* will in it . . . governs the passions of the moment" (6:168) (italics mine). This category is also diachronic: it belongs to tradition. "Sensations leave traces behind; in [the order of] feeling and desire habits develop; gradually there arises in the unfolding life of mind, between the sensation and the motion, an *acquired context* of the life of mind" (6:167). As a diachronic category it covers, moreover, more than the individual history. Especially in the case of the "genius," "the acquired context of the life of mind . . . is determined by the coordination of the constituent elements of a [historical] period, and it therefore represents this coordination" (6:231).

The acquired context of the life of mind has, finally, the character of a *system*: "The *context or cohesion of events*: this is the most comprehensive state of things (*Tatbestand*) which befalls our mental experience" (6:167–168). This "state of things" includes the social world. "Society is our world. With the power of our entire being we experience sympathetically the interplay of social conditions, . . . the states and forces . . . constituting the social system" (1:36–37). The social world has a systematic character: "The coordination of the facts which constitute a [historical] period produces *reciprocal effects* and *affinities*, as a consequence of which this coordination can be compared with a system" (6:230).

The psychological context of the individual is therefore principally a social and historical index of reality. Precisely at this juncture, writes Dilthey,

> we can connect the historical with the psychological. We developed a psychological concept of the acquired context of the life of mind and related it to the activity of the writer. In the great man this acquired context represents, in the right, refined way, the existing structure of the coordinated facts [equally, "the historical spirit of the age," hence]: principles, value-distinctions and purposes. The genius then influences the processes which take place in consciousness. In this way the literary work becomes the mirror of the age. . . . Here the mystery is solved of how an age can become objective to itself and to us in the stories, actions and characters of its writers. The acquired context of the life of mind in a great man is causally conditioned and therefore represents the coordination of the elements of the life, the thought, the striving of an age. . . . [The essential coherence of a literary work] is always the breath of a historical age. (6:231)

Dilthey's call for a German genius who will produce the new German epic is therefore a call for the articulation (*Koordination*) of the facts of his age. Without such an act his age is not a historical period but a crisis. If we stress the social, synchronic, systematic character of that reality "represented in the genius," Dilthey is at the same time calling for a context of political institutions capable of regulating the facts (which are *forces*) of the new age. In the essay "Poetic Imagination and Madness," Dilthey terms the acquired context of the life of mind a giant "apparatus for order, restraint and regulation" (6:95). In this rhetoric, psychology, poetics, and politics are inseparable.

In envisioning, then, the new German epic, Dilthey is envisioning a psyche vast and orderly enough to represent the violent new reality—*and* he is projecting, as an allegory of a psychic ideal of coherence, a political ideal of coherence, which, in the present life of Germany, is altogether absent. That articulation of *Erlebnisse*, that "fusion of inner and outer" expressed by the genius in the literary work, is not a politically neutral substance but is categorically structured according to the norms of a political ideal.[77] Moreover, through the objectivations of genius, the acquired context of the life of mind literally enters the social world and becomes the instituted presence of a social-historical tradition hitherto absent. We grasp that the psychological category of the acquired context of the life of mind is conceived under the aegis of a time-bound political consciousness confronting Empire and anarchy without the intervention of a national-social tradition, without a mediating, consciously shaping context of political institutions. Renan's famous letter to Strauss in 1870 noted "the frightening thing about the German victory: Germany showed only force—blank, effective force—with no auspicious message."[78] Dilthey does not bring that message. But his psychological poetics of creative individuals testifies to the intensity with which he felt its absence.

We have seen that Dilthey roots the self in the acquired context of the life of mind, which comes to fullness in the genius. The subject can therefore be construed as a substantial self, whereupon art for Dilthey becomes its immediate expression or objectivation. There would be no provision, in so ostensibly naive a doctrine, for the future-oriented power of artistic creation to construct and disseminate a self. This is the view of the second wave of skeptical, poststructuralist readers of Dilthey.

Everything depends, however, on stressing the social, historical, and practical character of the artistic self and its expression. The acquired context of the life of mind is the representative of the historical world (6:231), causally determined by that world in the special circular character which Dilthey gives to causality. In turn the work of the genius gives a new coordination to the unarticulated life of the age; it constructs the unified "spirit" of an historical period. What is precisely a warrant for the freedom of the artistic self is the fact that Germany under Kaiser Wilhelm is without a "self," a cultural apparatus capable of regulating and ordering the life of the time. The artist's task is to express such an order in his work. What he thus expresses is a reality not yet constituted. It is not yet a visible precipitate of the age; it cannot yet have impinged on the artist's self as an institution. The artist's freedom is in the task laid on an incomplete self to supplement the incomplete reality of his time.

In this light Dilthey's political unconscious can be seen as torn by an absence corresponding to the functional impotence of the kaiser within the real text of politics—namely, culture. Perhaps one could call this absence in the cultural unconscious the "Name-of-the-Kaiser." What is crucial in this structure, however, is that this absence becomes for Dilthey the cause not of the artist's madness but of his freedom. The artist gains unparalleled scope—a wide potential for creation corresponding to the inordinate degree of inarticulateness of the Zeitgeist. He is asked to be the heroic mediator between a culture without center and an unborn epic.

Not curiously, within the culture which Dilthey accurately divines, the figure of Hölderlin will not stay banished to his place in history, to the Germany of the petty princes. It is thus more a tribute to Dilthey's own political and cultural acumen than to his critical sense of Hölderlin that his call for the German epic will be answered in subsequent years by the German epicizing of the figure of Hölderlin. To this reception of Hölderlin the mythic figure of Nietzsche decisively contributed—but that is a different story.

Paralipomena

1. The shift in Dilthey from an aesthetics of spectatorship (as in the Kantian tradition) to an aesthetics of production occurs as a valorization of personal force.

2. Dilthey intends to pacify by cultural knowledge and creation the violent crisis of his age, a predicament generated by an omnipresent "will to power" (7:170). Yet Dilthey relies for healing cultural activity on the element of individual power, "the mighty, heroic personality" (6:239).

3. The admiration for personal force penetrates Dilthey's own text as the violence and arbitrariness with which (when it adheres to the notion of "soul-caused" literary form) it assigns priority, alternately, to

such different terms as imagination, feeling, mood, will. In an age of violent will, the "dialectic" in a philosophy of self-assertion itself proceeds by the arbitrary assertion of priorities. Heinen concludes the impossibility of writing coherently about Dilthey: "No matter what one takes hold of as a starting point, as a beginning in Dilthey's philosophy, Dilthey always refers to its *a priori* connection with something else without which it could not exist."[79]

4. Dilthey's basic vision of the acquired context of the life of mind is of a powerful repository of forces "ordering, restraining and regulating" the immediate life indwelling the superior large individual. Outside him social reality is torn by chaos and anarchy. His task is to introduce into chaos this agent of order. This happens ideally when the work of art is projected actively into the social world. Then the acquired context of the life of mind becomes an instituted presence of national-social traditions. But this picture of creativity is disturbed by Dilthey's view that "the acquired context of the life of mind in a great man is causally conditioned."

5. Dilthey's glorification of the figure of the great and powerful individual has ambivalent implications. It can be read as inviting the strong leader or as passionately encouraging the cultivation of human talent pure and simple. This ambivalence exists through the whole of Dilthey's essay, generating parallel ambiguities: the act of poetic creation is a radical "metamorphosis" of life, but it is also a typifying of what is already at hand in the real. The exemplary new literature would speak of a heroic German essence, but it would also speak in the language of social realism. An empty politics of extravagant individuality shelters in the reality of social liberalism. In Lieber's words, "The individuality of any sort of human or historical structure is, according to Dilthey, nothing more than a 'singular' variation of the general structure."[80] Rodi, however, counters this reproach, which is founded on texts of the middle period (e.g., "Ideas on a Descriptive and Analytic Psychology" ["Ideen über eine beschreibende und zergliedernde Psychologie"]) with "a favorite thought of Dilthey's: to see the act of grasping the singular in history as dependent on a certain divinatory gift which . . . he basically conceded only to poets. . . . His definition of the poet-seer: 'By "seer" I understand the poet to the extent that he represents in a manner ungraspable to us—one that does not proceed according to the leading-strings of logic—man, individuation, the context which we call life—a context woven out of circumstances, human relations, personal depth, destiny.'"[81]

6. For Lukács, Dilthey contributed to the creation of *Lebensphilosophie* as the ideology of the imperialistic bourgeoisie: antisocialistic

historical relativism, nihilism, intuitionalism, irrationalism, fantasy, and mythification. Consider, on the other hand, Golo Mann's description of the German character in the years just after 1870:

> Germany produced industrial progress, military trumpet blasts and politics. If one looks at the picture from a distance without examining individual figures, one gains a fatally mixed impression: hard-boiled *Realpolitik* and oppressive piety, ostentatious theatrical poses, self-righteous nationalism combined with internal discord, and finally materialism, overwhelmed by the success of the natural sciences, but yet prepared suddenly to change into cheap mysticism.[82]

In no way does any element of Dilthey's "ideology" in *The Poetic Imagination* justify or further a single of these tendencies; yet it is this latter constellation that arises from the ideology of the imperialistic bourgeoisie!

7. The text of *The Poetic Imagination* enshrines the values of unity, harmony, and coherence in its view of the literary work. First, "living pulsations" in the creative will of the author survive without diminution in the work; they "saturate" the work (6:125). Second, the creative act is thoroughly penetrated by the acquired context of the life of mind, which is itself a "representation" of reality: the work of genius is an immediate expression of reality. Here Dilthey stipulates no distinction between culture and life. Third, this reality is communicated to the interior of the consumer-subject and is fully appropriated (Dilthey stresses the likeness too between the act of production and the act of reception). Would not the political implications of such notions sanctify the status quo and give comfort to the national ideal of uniformity by force—"blank effective force"?

On the other hand, the literary work speaks to the category of the self. Gadamer paraphrases Dilthey this way: "Historical consciousness is not so much self-effacement as a heightened possession of self."[83] For Dilthey it is the "highest function" of literature "to represent the dignity of the *person* in the midst of its determination" (6:238). *The Poetic Imagination* redefines philology as reflection on the laws producing geniuses. Literary activity requires a cultivation of tact which must collide with the crudely leveling thrust of the "machine factory" (1:3) of imperial Germany. Dilthey seeks to animate a past centering on the monumental individuality of Goethe: he makes German Idealism a *political* ideal. A perspective stressing the creativity of psychological individuals is implicitly socially emancipative.

8. What we remember of Dilthey is not his psychological aesthetics. His insights into the mechanisms of the imagination called

"association" and "fusion" and their potential correlation with the tropes of metonymy and metaphor are keen, but they have been absorbed into our conception of Freud. In general his poetics of continuity will not be attractive in the present critical climate, in which the formal elaboration of the literary work is grasped as a sequence of negations, as a beginning and not the issue of an origin. What precisely does survive in *The Poetic Imagination* is the embattled political tonality, the sense of a mind attempting to come to terms by cultural force with an oppressive and fallen social world concealing hidden "realities."

Postscript

"Our way of writing history, our classical way, which of course pretends to be authentic, I consider in fact to be like fiction. Like a dishonest fiction, because it hasn't the courage to admit it. Our historical knowledge is full of gaps, because we do not take from history anything but "paper currency," documents surfacing by chance and which were written tendentiously at the time. The writer, with his exact imagination, his vast power of representation, fills in the gaps. Not only does he reconstitute the political process, but he adds other elements not less historical, such as the development of food. . . .

"In asking [certain youth groups] to understand history as a succession of lived experiences, as a possibility of *developing* the imagination, as an invitation to exit from a present diminished by our rationalism, I hope thus to shape a little of the future."[84]

Günter Grass

CHAPTER THREE

Self and Subject
in Nietzsche
During the Axial Period[1]

To the memory of Walter Kaufmann

A philosopher must seek his way
to this right [to judge the value
of life] only from the most comprehensive—perhaps most disturbing
and destructive—experiences.[2]

Jetzt—
zwischen zwei Nichtse
eingekrümmt,
ein Fragezeichen,
ein müdes Rätsel—
ein Rätsel für Raubvögel . . .
—sie werden dich schon "lösen,"
sie hungern schon nach deiner "Lösung,"
sie flattern schon um dich, ihr Rätsel,
um dich, Gehenkter! . . .
O Zarathustra! . . .
Selbstkenner! . . .
Selbsthenker! . . .

—"Zwischen Raubvögeln"
    from the *Dionysos-Dithyramben* (2:1251)[3]

Nietzsche (1844–1900) and Dilthey (1833–1911) were contemporaries, but Nietzsche appears to have commented only once on Dilthey, and then critically. Nietzsche's comment occurs in a passage in *The Gay Science* (p. 301), in which he questions the belief that "the facts of consciousness" of the "inner world" can be the legitimate starting point for a critique of "knowledge." These are phrases unmistakably associated with Dilthey via his *Introduction to the Historical Sciences*.

Now Dilthey is the spokesman for the artistic self as a co-ordinator of the facts of the age and as therefore decidedly empirical. This self exists as a wealth of lived experience and articulates the possibility of historical experience for an entire age. Nietzsche, however, wrote early and negatively in *The Birth of Tragedy* of the artistic subject insofar as it is empirical: "We contend . . . that the subject, the willing individual that furthers his own egoistical ends, can be conceived of only as the antagonist, not as the origin of art. Insofar as the subject is the artist, however, he has already been released from his individual will and has become, as it were, the medium through which the one truly existent subject celebrates his release in appearance" (BW, p. 52). What distinguishes Dilthey from Nietzsche is the latter's insistence that such an art, the one true art, contributes nothing to the individual *Bildung* of the artist or the spectator. The ground from which this transpersonal self creates and with which it fuses, is prehistorical—the chaos of the so-called Dionysian will.

In his work after 1872 Nietzsche withdraws from this extravagant celebration of the artist. This withdrawal is commonly associated with Nietzsche's alleged destruction of the self. Certainly, the empirical self remains a dubious fiction, while the transpersonal self, as it is found in *The Birth of Tragedy*, figures more and more as mere "metaphysical comfort" (BW, p. 109). Is it correct to say, then, that Nietzsche abandons belief in a "creative self" and hence anticipates its deconstruction?

Discussing the "great climax of the Fall of Hyperion," Harold Bloom writes:

> The dialogue between Keats and Moneta concerns the problematic of poetic identity, which is an extreme form of the idea of an autonomous ego. Keats, in his speculation upon identity, is part of a very complex nineteenth-century questioning of the notion of a single, separate self, a questioning that culminated in the analytics of Nietzsche, Marx, and Freud, but which may be stronger in the poets even than it was in the great speculators. Is the poetic identity or autonomous ego only a reification? Emerson . . . certainly rejects any notion of a fixed poetic identity or of a single, confined human ego. Nietzsche, on more language-centered grounds,

did the same in denying what he called the unnecessary hypothesis of the human subject.[4]

This speculation is very stimulating and very dubious. Of course, given the uncertainty attending the use of such terms as "ego" (autonomous or dependent), "self" (single and separate or dual, plural, or implied), "identity" (poetic or prosaic), and "human subject" (hypothetical or real), it may be unreasonable to ask for too much single-mindedness, fixity, or limitation in such a discourse, especially as categories like singleness or fixity might themselves be derived from the notion of a determinate self. At the same time this obscurity should not make it easier to misunderstand writers who attempted to make careful distinctions between these categories.

Nietzsche is such a "speculator." But during his axial period (ca. 1882–1888) he never said that "the hypothesis of the human subject" was unnecessary. In fact what he said was that the fiction of the "ego," a term he generally identified with the "subject," had become "indispensable" (WP, p. 267). Furthermore, he did not so much consider the idea of the "autonomous ego" or "self" problematic as he considered problematic the relation of the self to the ego or subject. In *The Gay Science, Thus Spoke Zarathustra, Beyond Good and Evil, On the Genealogy of Morals*, and *The Will to Power*, Nietzsche did produce an answer to the question, What is the self? It is not a simple one, and so we shall have to follow several different tracks to find it.

The works of Nietzsche's axial period contain many propositions that appear plainly to deny the reality of the human subject. For example: "The 'subject' is not something given, it is something added and invented and projected behind what there is. . . . We can set up a word at the point at which our ignorance begins, . . . e.g. the word 'I'. . . . Through thought the ego is posited; but hitherto one believed . . . that in 'I think' there was something of immediate certainty, and that this 'I' was the given *cause* of thought. . . . However habitual and indispensable this fiction may have become by now—that in itself proves nothing against its imaginary origin" (WP, pp. 267–268). " 'The subject' is the fiction that many similar states in us are the effect of one substratum: but it is we who first created the 'similarity' of these states; our adjusting them and making them similar is the fact, not their similarity (—which ought rather to be denied—)" (WP, p. 269). "No subject 'atoms.' The sphere of a subject constantly growing or decreasing, the center of the system constantly shifting" (WP, p. 270).[5]

There are, however, propositions that affirm the reality of a self as plainly as these (besides the one above that speaks of "we"): "At the bottom of us, really 'deep down,' there is . . . some granite of spiritual *fatum*" (BW, p. 352). "Behind your thoughts and feelings, my brother, there stands a mighty ruler, an unknown sage—whose name is self" (PN, p. 146). "Whenever a cardinal problem is at stake, there speaks an unchangeable 'this is I' " (BW, p. 352). "We are unknown to ourselves, we men of knowledge—and with good reason. We have never sought ourselves—how could it happen that we should ever *find* ourselves. . . . Whatever else there is in life, so-called 'experiences'—which of us has sufficient earnestness for them?" (BW, p. 451). Here Nietzsche puts us on the track of our genuine, our "creative" selves (PN, p. 147). If we have missed ourselves, it is because we have not "had time" for, or "given our hearts" to, the venture, and not because the self is a deception (BW, p. 451). Nietzsche's quarrel in the context of these propositions is not with a theory of the self but with weak theories of the self, e.g., as pure spirit, as an indestructible monad, as the agent of introspection, and so forth (BW, pp. 193, 210, 213–214, 257 *et seq.*).

Faced with this contradiction it is tempting at first to "solve" it by adducing a familiar distinction. These propositions need not be incompatible. The first group, after all, speaks negatively of a certain "subject"—the ego—but not of a certain "being"—the self (BW, p. 451). It would not be difficult to find concepts in Nietzsche relying on this opposition and creating an apparently firm distinction of value within it. Thus, if Nietzsche attacks a superficial, merely instrumental, "herd" *ego* (GS, p. 299; BW, pp. 234, 399), he affirms a deep, creative, authentic self or *being* which founds (and eludes) the ego, a being linked to "the body" and to "the soul."[6] In addition to the polarities ("superficial"/"profound"; "instrumental"/"creative"; "herd"/"authentic"), a considerable number of parallel valuations can be adduced—everything necessary, it seems, to distinguish the ego from the genuine self.[7]

But the opposition of values belonging to the shallow self to those belonging to the deep self will not hold up for long. We find, in examining the range of Nietzsche's work, a persistent fluctuation. Typically, Nietzsche rejects a Platonic critique of the surface as deception, as mere seeming—affirming, by litotes, the value of the surface (BW, pp. 237, 241, 350 *et seq.*). He also speaks of intersubjective communication (herd behavior) as the chief refiner of self-consciousness and language. Under the pressure of the need to communicate, "consciousness . . . has developed subtlety." "The ultimate result is an excess of this strength and art of communication," whose "heirs are those who are called artists."[8] Moreover, if "consciousness . . . [is] at first at the furthest distance from the biological center of the individual, . . . [it] deepens and intensifies itself, and continually draws nearer to that center" (WP, p. 274). It becomes impossible, in the long run, to stabilize the predicates of the epiphenomenal self which Nietzsche allegedly attacks, and to oppose them to those of the deep self, which Nietzsche appears to affirm.

What may help in our perplexity is the fact that Nietzsche does not mean to assuage it on this point and says so explicitly at the outset of *Beyond Good and Evil* (BW, p. 199). His argument concerns the origin of our "will to truth" and turns on the surmise about what might underlie this will: a Who or a What?[9] The identical division pointed to above recurs here in the form of a question: Nietzsche hesitates to say whether the self is properly cast as an ego or a being. This problem is then immediately deepened; another problem has to be set up as primary, as preceding the question of the self. This is the question of the value of this will to truth (of the self). The question of the self pushes toward its own enabling structure. Who, when such a question is asked, asks? The self? Which self? With what authority? Or does the question pose itself? "The problem of the value of truth," writes Nietzsche, "came before [was confronted by] us—or was it we who came before [were confronted by] the problem? Who of us is Oedipus here? Who the Sphinx? It is a rendezvous, it seems, of questions and question marks."[10] Can the self be, finally, only this very question that comes *as if* to provoke an answer, to dispel an illusion, or to fill in a void—but remains inexpungibly "the problem we *are*" (BW, p. 352)? For "the genuine philosopher . . . constantly risks himself" (BW, p. 315).

This passage from *Beyond Good and Evil* might be clarified in the light of the introduction to Heidegger's *Being and Time*—"The Formal Structure of the Question of Being."[11] To make the comparison fitting, one substitution is necessary. This is done by replacing the term "the value of the will to truth" in the passage from *Beyond Good and Evil* with the term "our being" (*unser Sein*), which occupies an equivalent position in the argument of the first part of the "Preface" to *On the Genealogy of Morals* (2:763). Here Nietzsche's formulation reads:

> As one divinely preoccupied and immersed in himself into whose ear the bell has just boomed with all its strength the twelve beats of noon suddenly starts up and asks himself: "what really was that which just struck?" so we sometimes rub our ears *afterward* and ask, utterly surprised and disconcerted, "what really was that which we have just experienced?" and moreover: "who *are* we really?" and, afterward as aforesaid, count the twelve trembling bell-strokes of our experience, our life, our *being*—and alas! miscount them.—So we are necessarily strangers to ourselves. (BW, p. 451)

This passage also turns on the question of the value of the will to truth or self-knowledge,[12] and it links this question to the being of the self that evades it.

Now the key trope in both Nietzsche passages, making the substitution possible, is the metonymic reversal of questioner and question in "a rendezvous of questions and question marks." In the passage from the *Genealogy* too it is not a conscious ego that sovereignly poses the question of its will to truth. Instead the ego, "utterly surprised and disconcerted," is assailed by the question of its being. Here Nietzsche anticipates—and "corrects" Heidegger's description in *Being and Time* of human existence (*Dasein*) as questioning-being.

Nietzsche's formulation of the problem of the self was "we came before [were put into question by] the question of the value of truth"—or, by substitution, "we come before [are put into question by] the question of our being." Here now is Heidegger: "To work out the question of Being means to make a being—he who questions—perspicuous in his Being. Asking the question, as a mode of *being* of a being, is itself essentially determined by what is asked about in it—Being. This being which we ourselves in each case are and which includes inquiry among the possibilities of its Being we formulate terminologically as *Dasein*. The explicit and lucid formulation of the question of the meaning of Being requires a prior suitable explication of a being (*Dasein*) with regard to its Being."[13]

For both Nietzsche and Heidegger a fundamental mode of human being is constituted by a question. This question is inevitable. If man expressly formulates it, he does not invent it; he is the occasion of that question. Man questions explicitly *because* the question of being is a constitutive mode of his being. For Heidegger, "The asking (putting as a question) of this question is . . . *a mode of being* of a being" (*Das Fragen dieser Frage ist . . . Seinsmodus eines Seienden*).[14] Through that question a certain mode of being comes to light.

The difference between these two writers, however, is crucial. The difference turns on the subject matter of the question which constitutes the questioner, a question "itself essentially determined by what is asked about in it." For Heidegger the question is the meaning of Being; for Nietzsche, the question is of *our* being—the self. That man is asked the question of his being means for Nietzsche neither more nor less than that the self exists as the question of its being and to this extent is self-determined.[15]

In Nietzsche, the self is constituted not by the question of the meaning of Being but by the question of its being. This is also what Zarathustra says in the "speech" called "On the Afterworldly": "All Being is hard to prove and hard to induce to speak" (*Schwer zu beweisen ist alles*

Sein und schwer zum Reden zu bringen) (2:298; PN, p. 144). Nietzsche turns the question to one proposed on behalf of the ego: "Indeed, the ego (*dies Ich*) and the ego's contradiction and confusion still speak most honestly of its being—this creating, willing, valuing ego, which is the measure and value of things." And this most honest being, the ego, speaks of the body and still wants the body, even when it poetizes and raves and flutters with broken wings. It learns to speak ever more honestly, this ego: and the more it learns, the more words and honors it finds for body and earth" (PN, p. 144). But we must be wary of such praise of the ego. Zarathustra's speech is so antimetaphysical in its thrust, so bent on speaking on behalf of man and not his gods, so violent in closing off any access to truth and being that leads away from man, the body, and the earth, that in its urgency to anchor the human ego it forgets that in its being, the ego is a question.

Nietzsche does not forget for long. Whatever claims he makes for a "most honest" being that "speaks of the meaning of the earth," he soon relativizes in irony or else contradicts in the course of an allegorical narrative (PN, p. 145). The next speech of Zarathustra, "On the Despisers of the Body," takes from the earlier speech any suggestion of finality. It introduces another being, the "ego's ruler" (*des Ichs Beherrscher*)— the self (*das Selbst*) (2:300). The status of the ego is made fully problematic: it literally becomes a question; for the purpose of even the ego of Zarathustra, Nietzsche's fullest fiction, is to *break*, to *shatter*—"Who am I?" says Zarathustra. "I await the worthier one; I am not worthy even of being broken by it" (PN, p. 258). Zarathustra's speech on behalf of the self is worth quoting.

> But the awakened and knowing say: body am I entirely, and nothing else; and soul is only a word for something about the body.
> The body is a great reason, a plurality with one sense, a war and a peace, a herd and a shepherd. An instrument of your body is also your little reason, my brother, which you call "spirit"—a little instrument and toy of your great reason.
> "I," you say, and are proud of the word. But greater is that in which you do not wish to have faith—your body and its great reason: that does not say "I," but does "I."
> What the sense feels, what the spirit knows, never has an end in itself. But sense and spirit would persuade you that they are the end of all things: that is how vain they are. Instruments and toys are sense and spirit: behind them still lies the self. The self also seeks with the eyes of the senses; it also listens with the ears of the spirit. Always the self listens and seeks: it compares, overpowers, conquers, destroys. It controls, and it is in control of the ego too.

Behind your thoughts and feelings, my brother, there stands a mighty ruler, an unknown sage—whose name is self. In your body he dwells; he is your body.

There is more reason in your body than in your best wisdom. And who knows why your body needs precisely your best wisdom?

Your self laughs at your ego and at its bold leaps. "What are these leaps and flights of thought to me?" it says to itself. "A detour to my end. I am the leading strings of the ego and the prompter of its concepts."

The self says to the ego, "Feel pain here!" Then the ego suffers and thinks how it might suffer no more—and that is why it is *made* to think.

The self says to the ego, "Feel pleasure here!" Then the ego is pleased and thinks how it might often be pleased again—and that is why it is *made* to think.

I want to speak to the despisers of the body. It is their respect that begets their contempt. What is it that created respect and contempt and worth and will? The creative self created respect and contempt; it created pleasure and pain. The creative body created the spirit as a hand for its will.

Even in your folly and contempt, you despisers of the body, you serve your self. I say unto you: your self itself wants to die and turns away from life. It is no longer capable of what it would do above all else: to create beyond itself. That is what it would do above all else, that is its fervent wish.

But now it is too late for it to do this: so your self wants to go under. O despisers of the body. Your self wants to go under, and that is why you have become despisers of the body! For you are no longer able to create beyond yourselves. (PN, pp. 146–147)

However, in copying out Nietzsche's text on the creative self that rules the ego, I appear to have returned to the beginning of my argument. How could there be a plainer statement on behalf of a substantial self anchored in the body, a deep self not to be confused with the epiphenomenal ego? Speaking in a Heideggerian manner, one could say, "Indeed something like a priority of the bodily self has announced itself."[16]

But this would be a mystification. The meaning of Nietzsche's celebration of the body is severely limited by context. Here in *Zarathustra* it frames Nietzsche's polemic against the "afterworldly" who figure as "despisers of the body." For the text speaks less on behalf of the body than it does against those "who are angry with life." It begins, "I want to speak to the despisers of the body," and concludes, "I shall not go your way, o despisers of the body! You are no bridge to the overman!" When the term of self is introduced, it is as a necessary supplement to the body, a "name" that confers prestige on the body: "A mighty ruler

. . . whose name is self . . . is your body." And when the body is ana-
tomized for exact celebration, Nietzsche simply uses for this task the very
words of the metaphysical tradition which, elsewhere, he is at work venting
of their meaning: "reason,"[17] "sense" (or "meaning"—"mit *einem* Sinne"
[2:300]), and "society" in the pejorative term "herd," viz., "the body is a
great reason, a plurality with one sense, a war and a peace, a herd and
a shepherd."[18]

This text is important, but it does not make a decisive contribution to Nietzsche's egology: it does not sustain its authority. As soon
as the self has been defined as the body, the body is in turn translated
back into the key words of the metaphysical tradition. This is familiar as
the strategy—and the pitfall—of Nietzsche's argument at the outset of
Beyond Good and Evil on behalf of the "will to truth." As that argument
advances a little past the first aphorism, and Nietzsche comes down from
the mystified heights of dogmatic metaphysics, he has no place to land
but on the body: "Most of the conscious thinking of a philosopher is
secretly guided and forced into certain channels by his instincts" (BW,
p. 201). But the body quickly imposes on Nietzsche a notion of plurality—"instincts" in the sentence above, and afterward "drives." For example: "I do not believe that a 'drive to knowledge' is the father of philosophy; but rather that another drive has, here as elsewhere, employed
understanding (and misunderstanding) as a mere instrument. But anyone who considers the basic drives of man to see to what extent they
may have been at play just here as *inspiring* spirits . . . will find that all
of them have done philosophy at some time—and that every single one
of them would like only too well to represent just *itself* as the ultimate
purpose of existence and the legitimate *master* of all the other drives. For
every drive wants to be master—and it attempts to philosophize in that
spirit" (BW, pp. 203–204).

The "self," which in Zarathustra is "that mighty ruler . . . the
body," still had to search for itself, it appears, in *Beyond Good and Evil*, in
the master drive. This argument, however, is plainly regressive. Its mastery could be explained by virtue of its superiority in possessing a decisive attribute, but what could this one attribute be? So Nietzsche
promptly revises his argument: "[The philosopher's] morality bears decided and decisive witness to . . . what *order of rank* the innermost drives
of his nature stand in relation to each other" (BW, p. 204; italics mine).
The master drive has become an "order," a "structure"—and not a substantial term—and yet, at the same time, this instinctual order of rank
is supposed to define "*who [the philosopher] is*" (BW, p. 204). As the answer
to the question of the self darts from the aporia of the Who/What to the
seeming unity of instinctual life—to the body—that life splits into an

agon: it is metaphorized, displaced, disseminated in social strife and then swiftly reassembled into the Who of the personal subject of the mischievous "subject and ego superstition" (BW, p. 192). The question of whether the self is to be cast as a Who or a What is not resolved. At whatever point attributes of personality are dissolved, and the surviving agent termed an unknown structure or being, the What is dispersed, pluralized, but then also regathered into a Who, a cryptic personality. The problem of whether the self is properly understood as like an ego (Who) or a being (What) remains unresolved.

The fact that in these texts the self is linked to the body is not as such an argument on behalf of a substantial self. The "move," in Zarathustra, is based on an act of vehement opposition to a traditional metaphysical-religious rhetoric exalting subject, soul, or ego. The argument against the body despisers knows no better revenge than to adopt for its party some of the etiolated key words of the adversary position. Nietzsche's tactic is to perform one more "herd-moral" inversion on the "original" herd-moral inversion of strong values by dogmatic philosophy. If there has to be a rhetoric of "spirit"—of reason and meaning—then these terms can be reconquered for the body. In the couple "a herd and a shepherd" Nietzsche makes a precise allusion having a self-reflexive function: it names the procedure of reinverting inverted values. This procedure is also plain in the phrase from *Beyond Good and Evil* cited above (BW, p. 204). Considering that "the way is open for new versions of and refinements of the soul-hypothesis," Nietzsche offers one such new "scientific" hypothesis: "soul as social structure of the drives and affects" (BW, p. 210). He inverts the terms of the original catastrophic frustration of instinct producing "the *internalization* of man" ("thus it was that man first developed what was later called his 'soul' "), and he draws into the soul the currents of bodily life (BW, p. 520).

The procedure, however, of reasoning by the trope of litotes—viz., the soul is not nonbody—never, for obvious reasons, finds firm ground. The strategy which informs it is to declare some term *not* the negation of another term to which it is conventionally opposed. But this strategy can be implacably leveled against itself. Indeed this is what Nietzsche does again and again when, with a sort of throwaway gesture, he unsettles the achievement of one text with another. For example, the phrase from *Zarathustra* "a plurality with one sense" (PN, p. 146) is replaced in *The Will to Power* by an asymmetrical polyvalent term for the self: "no subject 'atoms' . . . the center of the system constantly shifting" (WP, p. 270). Or, in an aphorism from *Beyond Good and Evil*, just following the definition of the soul as a "social structure of the drives and affects," Nietzsche amusingly redefines the *body* as "a social structure composed of many souls" (BW, p. 216). Typically, at this point of irony, circularity, and dispersion of meaning, Nietzsche again arbitrarily asserts a center, a Who: "the complex state of delight of the person exercising volition . . . [includes] his feelings of delight as commander[!]" (BW, p. 216). This Who can be further dispersed, and Nietzsche implies that the process is interminable. It is the ebb and flow of the world, as in the triumphant account concluding *The Will to Power:*" a sea of forces flowing and rushing together, eternally changing, eternally flooding back . . . , out of the simplest forms striving toward the most complex. . . , most self-contradictory, and then again returning home to the simple out of this abundance, out of the play of contradictions back to the joy of concord" (WP, p. 550).

Is it this "sea of forces" which returns us now to the intact bodily self that, speaking with Heidegger, "announced itself" with apparent priority in Zarathustra's speeches? This is not a genuine conclusion. If such a self announces itself in this account of Nietzsche's reflections, it is only because I linked it to a sequence illustrating the point that for Nietzsche, unlike Heidegger, "the belly of being does not speak to humans at all, except as a human" (PN, p. 144).

We should not leave this *Zarathustra* passage, however, without marking out a positive result. The passage asserts the priority of the self over the ego (however readily it can be shown that these terms do not point to exclusive groups of attributes). This is a distinction about names which Nietzsche maintains throughout his work.[19] Occasionally he uses the term ego as an equivalent of self when he speaks on behalf of the self—when, for example, he writes of the herd's suspiciousness of ego: "The delight in the herd is more ancient than the delight in the ego; and as long as the good conscience is identified with the herd, only the bad conscience says: I" (PN, pp. 171–172). When he wishes to discredit belief in the subject, however, he will speak not against the self but rather against the ego, as in "the soul superstition which, in the form of the subject and ego superstition, has not even yet ceased to do mischief" (BW, p. 192). The name "self" enjoys special protection—and has indeed more than a nominal privilege, since, as Wittgenstein said, entities *are* sublimated names.[20] The "self" points to something irreducible even if its difference from the signified of the "ego" cannot be defined. But "is it not sufficient to assume *degrees* of apparentness?" (BW, p. 236)

Reprise

In Nietzsche the question of the self, it appears, cannot be answered directly—apart, that is, from the question about the question(er) of the self. The question of the self is itself insistently problematic. One kind of answer is the one, perhaps, we want to have but which, according to Nietzsche, we cannot have or even hope for. Such an answer would be substantive; it would, for example, equate the self with a unified body. This would be the outcome of the supposition that the questioner of the self is the self which the question refers to (as its predicate nominative) and that this questioner is a self-identical substance. Such an answer could identify the substantial identity of the questioner, as, say, the body, certain drives, a highest value. (But even "the body |has| despaired of the body" |PN, p. 143|.)

We are no closer to a solution even when the thesis of the substantial identity of questioner and nominative is widened to include duality and contradiction. The questioner-self might then be marked "deep" or "authentic" in opposition to a "superficial" or "instrumental" ego not earnestly involved in the questioning, but this distinction does not hold. Indeed the entire question may be regarded—as Nietzsche sometimes regards it—as a weak question in the sense that his essays on slave morality make clear. The very asking of the question marks "the slowly arising democratic order of things: the originally noble and rare urge to ascribe value to oneself on one's own . . . |is| actually encouraged more and more" (BW, p. 399). "But just this need *for* what is noble is fundamentally different from the needs of the noble soul itself and actually the eloquent and dangerous mark of its lack" (BW, p. 418). " 'Truly high respect one can have only for those who do not *seek* themselves' " (thus Nietzsche cites Goethe) (BW, p. 405).

This lack in the slave type provokes the weak answer to the question, the weak theory of the self; it validates the slave, who invents the self as "a neutral substratum . . . *free* to express strength or not to do so, . . . the little changeling. . . , the neutral, independent 'subject' (*das indifferente, wahlfreie 'Subjekt'*)" (2:791; BW, pp. 481–482). This theory pretends to reflect a meritorious attitude of scientific objectivity. In fact it is interesting for the weak to declare the self free, "just as if the weakness of the weak |could be| . . . a voluntary achievement, willed, chosen, a *deed*." To perceive, now, "the sublime self-deception that interprets weakness as freedom" is to advance, on behalf of the master, a strong, demystified theory of the weak self as part of a theory of the strong self. This perception divides the substance of the weak questioner along the lines of his own dissimulation.

The weak theory of the self inclines to another form of the question, presupposing "the concept of 'immediate knowledge' " and tending to produce the speciously definite self-knowledge which Nietzsche calls *Selbst-Erkenntnis* (2:748; BW, pp. 414–415). "There must be a kind of aversion in me," he writes, "to believing anything definite about myself"

(BW, p. 415). "To become what one is, one must not have the faintest notion *what* one is" (BW, p. 710). (Even this invoked ignorance, of course, follows a repetition of the question of the self, is another answer.)

No matter how we conceive the value of the question of the self, however, the distinction between noble and weak forms of the question cannot be maintained on the basis of a firm polarity of attributes distinguishing a more authentic questioner from a less authentic questioner. (Recall, too, Nietzsche's hostility to polarities).[21] Nietzsche's deconstruction of this difference is persistent. In his account in *The Gay Science* of the refinement of consciousness, the furthering factor is intersubjective communicative utility (GS, p. 298). This instrumental effect operates even when, for example, consciousness puts into question its own usefulness to life.[22] The instrumental ego might suppose that by thinking instrumentality, it subverts the intersubjective intent and thus grows deep. Here it is deluded.

True, "for us the falseness of a judgment is . . . not necessarily an objection to a judgment." Indeed "we are fundamentally inclined to claim that the falsest judgments . . . are the most indispensable to us [as 'life-promoting, life-preserving, species-preserving']" (BW, p. 201). Thus even if the ego's delusory judgment were true, the ego would acquire depth only at the cost of debilitating life; in this sense it would be false. As a false judgment, however, it continues to act as a species-preserving instrument; thus it promotes life and in this sense is true.

Finally, however, "even what is here called 'utility' is ultimately also a mere belief, something imaginary, and perhaps precisely the most calamitous stupidity of which we shall perish some day" (GS, p. 300). Utility—whether to the herd or to life—becomes a predicate assignable neither exclusively to the shallow nor to the deep side of the ego and thus unsettles the polarity.

The crucial articulation in Nietzsche's chain of questions is its link to a different level of reflexiveness. The question of the self no longer reads reflexively as the question of the character of the self who questions. The personality, integrity, steadfastness, etc., of the self who questions is put into question in the question. The personal attributes of the self dissolve under the force of Nietzsche's surmise about "the perspective character of existence": "[Is not] all existence essentially actively engaged in *interpretation* [?]" "One may not ask: 'Who then interprets.' "[23] The question of the self continues to reflect itself as the question of its origin but does so as the rhetorical question, *What* (not Who) is the self?[24] As such it can provoke no answer except whatever (not whoever) is the provenience of the question of the self. In a word, the self tends to become the question which asks itself.

In this case the substantial self proves marginal to the chain, as only a spent fiction having enabled the chain to generate new links. The chain advances as a *rhetorical* movement, or what may at least initially be called a rhetorical movement. For if we term it thus, we still understand on the model of a certain symmetry and homology the self-reflexiveness even of the question that is self-positing. This is the very model of the self-reflexiveness that we ascribed to the question that poses an answer in terms of the substantial properties of the questioning self. Just as we posited the meaning of the self—in the question, Who is the self?—as the substance of the questioner, the Who, here too we are positing the meaning of the self—in the question, What is the self?—as the "substance" of the questioner, the What—namely, as language itself. The interrogative sentence arises within questioning language. The answer to the question, What is the self? is the anonymous language of the very question.

Is there not, however, a model of self-reflexiveness other than the model of homology and symmetry? The question is, What is the self, such that the question of the self could arise without a speaker? One answer is: that event in language which produces the question. The self is the articulate energy of language which provokes the question of the self; it is questioning-language.

But if instead we break with this model, as Nietzsche does, we ask in a renewed way about this rhetorical fold. That event in language which asks, What is the self? need not be self-referential on the model of the self-reference of the name "self." That is, it need not be constituted as only the answer "*This very question* of the self." The verbal question can arise as the asymmetrical trace of a questioning something and still be self-reflexive—self-mirroring *and* self-skewing, setting its origin, a being itself mirrorlike, *en abîme*.[25] For the verbal question is mirrorlike: "The human intellect cannot avoid seeing itself in its own perspectives, and *only* in these. We cannot look around our own corner" (GS, p. 336). The self to which the question alludes is also mirrorlike: "And do you know what 'the world' is to me? Shall I show it to you in my mirror?" (WP, p. 549–550). "The whole of life would be possible without, as it were, seeing itself in a mirror" (GS, p. 297). The self is a mirror in the sense of having always to face away from itself, to picture something other than itself, and to introduce the subtle skew of secondary representation. The question of the self, therefore, mirrors something itself mirrorlike (the self) of which it is but part but which is only partly like the question itself—in the manner of an indexical and not an iconic sign, that is, as an effect of the self and not as its double.[26]

The name "self," then, need not be a true name at all, in the sense of its failure to designate a definite being with the identity conditions governing all entities. It may name neither a speaking subject nor a referent nor a content of thought, while mediating a discourse whose subject is an irreducible being.[27] This being is not Being; neither is it language without a maker. Nietzsche does not fabulate language as arising without an agent: nomination is the enterprise of the will to power; the genealogy of questions is a genealogy of morals and hence a semiotics of the self (PN, p. 501; BW, p. 203). The question of the event which produces the question of the self is the question of the will to power. "For Nietzsche, the will to power and the self have the same structure."[28] This being may withdraw in leaving the trace of the rhetorical question and produce (what one recent writer calls) "originary bewilderment." "Thus," writes Harold Alderman, "does Nietzsche make philosophy . . . whole by asking the philosopher to repeat the originary experience of bewilderment out of which thought is born."[29] The self would be an incommensurable being precisely in provoking a continuous withdrawal from itself. This falling away generates in language—or elsewhere—the question of, or openness toward, whatever the self has taken itself to be.

In introducing, however, such terms cognate with bewilderment as "openness," "wonder," "unansweredness," "questioning-being," we should not fail to stress that all this has an antithetical air. Nietzsche repeatedly asserts, as in *Beyond Good and Evil*, that the strong self, the "noble human being," possesses "some fundamental certainty . . . about itself, something that cannot be sought, nor found, nor perhaps lost."[30] "The noble soul accepts this fact of its egoism without any question mark" (BW, p. 405). "At the bottom of us, really 'deep down,' there is . . . some granite of spiritual *fatum*, of predetermined decision and answer to predetermined selected questions" (BW, p. 352). If we are tempted to construe this nobility as a being that does not put itself into question, we will of course be producing an antinomy: What has happened to the self that is the question of itself?

Even the noble self thus self-possessed exists as a question—as a fate that always needs to surpass itself, always requires, like an answer, another mode of its being. It sustains an opennesss to being, an unansweredness, with athletic poise, not needing and disinclined to ask the question of the self explicitly, yet conscious of the self as an affect.[31]

In *The Will to Power* Nietzsche describes the subject purely and simply in qualities that can be accommodated by the noble soul: "No 'substance,' rather something that in itself strives after greater strength, and that wants to 'preserve' itself only indirectly (it wants to surpass itself)" (WP, p. 270). The self is the question of the being whose trace is the explicit question but which otherwise comes to light.

The formula of the self "that wants to 'preserve' itself only indirectly (it wants to surpass itself)" fulfills the requirements of questioning-being. "We see ['certain solutions'] only as steps to self-knowledge" (BW, p. 352). All the experience of such a self aims to preserve itself as a question while appropriating the virtual answers it calls the world.

Mastery as an Aesthetic State

Questions are viable as they are legitimate, i.e., able to provoke answers. The self lives only as it provokes answers full of "significance and use" to its concerns (GS, p. 224). The masterful self sustains itself as a question even while failing to ask the explicit question of the self. It does so by continually performing the acts of interpretation which bring it the answers it calls experience. "The spirit's power [is] retouching and falsifying the whole ['of "the external world" '] to suit itself. Its intent in all this is to incorporate new 'experiences'" (BW, p. 350). "Whatever exists, having somehow come into being, is again and again reinterpreted to new ends, taken over, transformed and redirected by some power superior to it; all events in the organic world are a subduing, a *becoming master*, and all subduing and becoming master involves a fresh interpretation, an adaptation through which any previous 'meaning' and 'purpose' are necessarily obscured or even obliterated" (BW, p. 513).
Nietzsche does not say, however, that mastery can be measured according to the degree of felt disparity that must be overcome by my interpreting something to my usage "worlds apart [from] the cause of [its] origin" (BW, p. 513). Mastery is not principally in the degree of recalcitrance overcome by the self in its commerce with contingencies."[32] In discussing whole cultures Nietzsche's early text "Of the Use and Disadvantage of History for Life" criticizes the dissolution of societies into warring "inwardness and convention." "That people to whom one attributes culture," he writes, "ought at least to be a living unity and not miserably divided into something internal and external—content and form" (1:233–234). Nietzsche's early argument against vehement "self-control" or "self-mastery" (*Selbstbeherrschung*) (2:180) attacks a type of negating interpretation that issues from the fortress of the self:

Self-control—Those moralists who command man first of all and above all to gain control of himself thus afflict him with a peculiar disease; namely, a constant irritability in the face of all natural stirrings and inclinations—

. . . Whatever may henceforth push, pull, attract, or impel such an irritable person from inside or outside, it will always seem to him as if his self-
control were endangered. No longer may he entrust himself to any instinct or free wingbeat; he stands in a fixed position with a gesture that
wards off, armed against himself, with sharp and mistrustful eyes—the
eternal guardian of his castle, since he has turned himself into a castle.
Of course, he can achieve *greatness* this way. But he has certainly become
insufferable for others, difficult for himself, and impoverished and cut off
from the most beautiful fortuities of his soul. Also from all further *instruction*. For one must be able to lose oneself occasionally if one wants to
learn something from things different from oneself.[33]

Self-control is aggression turned inward from the fear of self-
loss. Its value increases when the danger of self-loss is already overwhelming. Then it exerts a counterpoising force upon a being already
conflicted to an unbearable extent, assailed by an abundance of internalized world and excessive fortuities:

> In an age of disintegration that mixes races indiscriminately,
> human beings have in their bodies the heritage of multiple origins, that
> is, opposite, and often not merely opposite, drives and value standards
> that fight each other and rarely permit each other any rest. Such human
> beings of late cultures and refracted lights will on the average be weaker
> human beings; their most profound desire is that the war they *are* should
> come to an end. Happiness appears to them, in agreement with a tran-
> quilizing (for example, Epicurean or Christian) medicine and way of thought,
> pre-eminently as the happiness of resting, of not being disturbed, of sa-
> tiety, of finally attained unity, as a "sabbath of sabbaths," to speak with
> the holy rhetorician Augustine who was himself such a human being.
> But when the opposition and war in such a nature have the
> effect of one more charm and incentive of life—and if, moreover, in ad-
> dition to his powerful and irreconcilable drives, a real mastery and sub-
> tlety in waging war against oneself, in other words, self-control, self-out-
> witting, has been inherited or cultivated, too—then those magical, incom-
> prehensible, and unfathomable ones arise, those enigmatic men predes-
> tined for victory and *seduction*, whose most beautiful expression is found
> in Alcibiades and Caesar . . . and among artists perhaps Leonardo da Vinci.
> (BW, pp. 301–302)

The function of interpretation and mastery is conciliatory,
aiming to create an aesthetic mode of existence in which the world may
appear as already interpreted, already mastered. Conciliatory passages
like these are by no means confined to the early work: they are fundamental and recurrent, and they mitigate both the popular and the eso-
teric view of the Nietzschean self as posited by an act of arbitrary violence. The providential mood of the Sanctus Januarius passages of *The*

Gay Science strikes this basic note: an experience of the harmonious copresence of sign and meaning:

> There is a certain high point in life; once we have reached that, we are, for all our freedom, once more in the greatest danger of spiritual unfreedom, and no matter how much we have faced up to the beautiful chaos of existence and denied it all providential reason and goodness, we still have to pass our hardest test. For it is only now that the idea of a personal providence confronts us with the most penetrating force, and the best advocate, the evidence of our eyes, speaks for it—now that we can see how palpably always everything that happens to us turns out for the best. Every day and every hour, life seems to have no other wish than to prove this proposition again and again. Whatever it is, bad weather or good, the loss of a friend, sickness, slander, the failure of some letter to arrive, the spraining of an ankle, a glance into a shop, a counter-argument, the opening of a book, a dream, a fraud—either immediately or very soon after it proves to be something that 'must not be missing'; it has a profound significance and use precisely for us. . . .
>
> I think that . . . we should . . . rest content with the supposition that our own practical and theoretical skill in interpreting and arranging events has now reached its high point. Nor should we conceive too high an opinion of this dexterity of our wisdom when at times we are excessively surprised by the wonderful harmony created by the playing of our instrument—a harmony that sounds too good for us to dare to give the credit to ourselves. Indeed, now and then someone plays with us—good old chance; now and then chance guides our hand, and the wisest providence could not think up a more beautiful music than that which our foolish hand produces then. (GS, pp. 223–224)

No discounting of course the restless sly play of interpretations upon this moment that seemed to require none (being of "immediately . . . profound significance"). Is this meaning produced by invisibly rapid dexterous movements of interpretive skill, or chance, or providence? But this text's claim to unitive experience cannot be so rapidly deconstructed, especially in light of Nietzsche's astonishing account of his inspired moods while writing *Zarathustra*:

> Has anyone at the end of the nineteenth century a clear idea of what poets of strong ages have called *inspiration*? If not, I will describe it.—If one had the slightest residue of superstition left in one's system, one could hardly reject altogether the idea that one is merely incarnation, merely mouthpiece, merely a medium of overpowering forces. The concept of revelation—in the sense that suddenly, with indescribable certainty and subtlety, something becomes *visible*, audible, something that shakes one to the last depths and throws one down—that merely describes the facts. One hears, one does not seek; one accepts, one does not ask who gives;

like lightning, a thought flashes up, with necessity, without hesitation regarding its form—I never had any choice. . . .
     Everything happens involuntarily in the highest degree but as
in a gale of a feeling of freedom, of absoluteness, of power, of divinity.—
The involuntariness of image and metaphor is strangest of all: one no longer
has any notion of what is an image or a metaphor: everything offers itself
as the nearest, most obvious, simplest expression. It actually seems, to
allude to something Zarathustra says, as if the things themselves approached and offered themselves as metaphors. ("Here all things come
caressingly to your discourse and flatter you; for they want to ride on your
back. On every metaphor you ride to every truth. . . . Here the words and
word-shrines of all being open up before you; here all being wishes to
become word, all becoming wishes to learn from you how to speak". (BW,
pp. 756–757; PN, 295–296)

     For Nietzsche the world is a text, its component signs re-
quiring interpretation.[34] But seen with great health, the world's signs are
more than signs: they are vehicles of the things they name that ride upon
their backs (as the things that would ride on Zarathustra's back, and he
too upon *their* vehicles to every truth). Active interpretation is at an ebb.
Things offer themselves astride their own names. They too are metaphors, they carry themselves and their meanings over into the discourse
of the inspired self. The ability to see the world of things in a figurative
text is a function of poetic rapture. *Then* only: "It . . . happened—and
verily, it happened for the first time—that his word pronounced *selfishness* blessed, the wholesome, healthy selfishness that wells from a powerful soul—from a powerful soul to which belongs the high body, beautiful, triumphant, refreshing, *around which everything becomes a mirror*"
(*Zarathustra*) (PN, p. 302; second italics mine). The soul for which all things
are mirrors already possesses these things in its discourse.
     Nietzsche's phrase for this blessed selfishness is "selige
Selbstsucht." Readers of German will smile—or wince—since "selige
Sehnsucht" (blessed longing) is the title of a notorious lyric of Goethe
concluding "The Book of the Singer" of the *West-Easterly Divan* (*Westöst-
licher Divan*). Goethe's poem, like Nietzsche's, speaks of a highly sexualized kind of extinction, playing on the sexual meaning of dying; a self
dies (in orgasm) to become himself again—"stirbt und wird"—but he
becomes himself through an other—his lover, his candle flame and his
grave. Nietzsche's emulation of this poem is remarkable in substituting
for the medium of this resurrection not another human being but another mode of self. Suppose the ego is whatever the self has taken itself
to be (*Satzung*) and the self is the openness from which this particular
being has sprung (*Setzung*).[35] Then the love which Nietzsche celebrates

is that of the ego for the self or soul, "around which everything becomes a mirror." [36]

In an important sense Zarathustra, even more than *Ecce Homo*, is Nietzsche's book of the self; it is nothing but a book of the self, of a higher selfishness. "The Wanderer" (part 3, section 1) reads:

> And whatever may yet come to me as destiny and experience will include some wandering and mountain climbing: in the end, one experiences only oneself. The time is gone when mere accidents could still happen to me; and what could still come to me now that was not mine already? What returns, what finally comes home to me, is my own self and what of myself has long been in strange lands and scattered among all things and accidents. And one further thing I know: I stand before my final peak now and before that which has been saved up for me the longest. Alas, now I must face my hardest path! Alas, I have begun my loneliest walk! But whoever is of my kind cannot escape such an hour—the hour which says to him: "Only now are you going your way to greatness" (PN, p. 264) [37]

The phrase "You are going your way to greatness" is repeated twice. Zarathustra merits the charge of self-consecration to a degree that would have alarmed even Wordsworth. [38]

The question of the self must live as an openness, an unansweredness to being, yet it must bend the world into virtual answers in order to preserve itself as a question. The self is an interpreting being (*ein auslegendes Dasein*, 2:249) that needs to interpret in order for that interpretation to interpret the self (GS, p. 336). Only in finding answers can it find the occasion to reformulate itself and to produce a new "articulation of self-consciousness." [39] The mood of the fullest answer, which thus fully identifies but does not close the question, is inspiration, and not the vacuity of nostalgia or the agitation of coerciveness: "Learning to *see* . . . is almost what, unphilosophically speaking, is called a strong will: the essential feature is precisely *not* to 'will'—*to be able* to suspend decision" (PN, p. 511). The semiotic paraphrase of inspiration—the rapture of the historical sense—is the convergence of figure and thing.

Conclusion

This discussion about what is alive in Nietzsche's reflections on the self gains cogency from the background of recent discussion about the death of the self in Nietzsche. [40] Debate on this matter has been foreclosed chiefly by the general appeal—in our literary climate—of attacks upon the "subject" (the loss of self has functioned productively as a heuristic term in treatments of Rousseau and Freud). Furthermore, *The Will to Power*, which speaks against the subject, has, following Heidegger's practice in his Nietzsche book, been revalorized as part of a general appreciation of marginal, unspoken, and fragmentary texts. Finally, for contemporary readers, *Zarathustra* has proved hard to take. The result is that the destructive commentary in *The Will to Power* on certain cognate forms of the self has been taken as extending to the self.

Without reading *Zarathustra*, however, it cannot be understood that ego and subject are not the self. And when *Zarathustra* goes unread, what a woeful flattening out of "the Dionysian drama of 'The Destiny of the Soul'" ensues (BW, p. 458).

The claim, furthermore, that Nietzsche speaks the self to death is untenable for a number of reasons. One of these emerges from taking an indirect route and putting into question the seemingly powerful argument that the preponderance of irony in Nietzsche determines the loss of the self.

Certainly it is not easy to write about Nietzsche's irony with an assumption of authority: his texts are repercussive. Ernst Behler (while not commenting on the question of the self) has made a helpful preparatory classification of Nietzsche's tonalities and types of irony.[41] It is still a daunting task to find the uniform principle or principles generating this diversity.

The first remarkable fact about irony in Nietzsche is the rarity of this word in his work, despite its apparent saturation by ironic themes and moods. This may be a telling suppression or not: if so, then one can speculate (as does Behler) that the word is suppressed because of its association with a Romantic philosophical tradition including especially Fichte, Hegel, and Friedrich Schlegel. The first two names are almost always polemical targets for Nietzsche; on the other hand, he seems not to have read Schlegel and nowhere mentions him, despite their astonishing similarities in tone, rhetoric, and philosophical thrust. But the association with Romantic literary practice of the word "irony" (like, incidentally, the word "mood" [*Stimmung*], with which Nietzsche happens also to associate the word "irony") probably determines the omission.

Without a decisive intertextual line leading from Nietzsche to earlier theorists of irony, and without more than occasional mention of the word, interpreting Nietzsche's irony is then itself a matter for irony in the modern sense: i.e., free play. Behler speaks of at least five strains in Nietzsche's writing which can come under the head of irony. First is Nietzsche's theory of the necessity for elliptical communication (in effect Nietzsche translates the trope of irony [Latin: *dissimulatio*] as "mask"). Next is his sense of the innumerable strata and therefore the groundlessness of personal identity, provoking a certain artistry of pose and feeling. Finally, Behler identifies Nietzsche's "romantic" irony (an endless, self-reflexive play of antithetical positions), his sense of the "tragic" obligation of affirming inescapable suffering, and his sense of the world-historical irony of the individual blind, because of his particular interests, to the exigencies of nature and history. Nietzsche implies many other types. What is immediately valuable about this table of categories is the cumulative effect it makes. Indeed Nietzsche's work, despite his frequntly asseverated distaste for ironic (read, "decadent") attitudes in others, lends itself uniformly to one or another category of ironic subject matter, so that the work, it appears, can be called panironic.

The current discussion about the ubiquitousness of Nietzsche's irony, however, goes beyond describing the various types of intended irony. Not only does Nietzsche conceptualize irony but he does so uncontrollably, it is said, even while knowing it. In this case he heralds more than the death of God ("our most enduring lie") (GS, p. 283); he also heralds the death of the little god—the human self. This death is a corollary of the unrelenting irony in which his texts engage us. These views on Nietzsche, if they are true, mutually sustain each other. In the absence of an organized intentional subject capable of acts of exact projection (an absence afflicting Nietzsche himself), texts cannot have a stable meaning (*Meinen*). Their various meanings or illusory feints at meaning subvert one another, more radically even than meanings deliberately projected as unstable, infinite irony. If Nietzsche saw better than any other writer the merely fictive character of the self, then he would have to be considered the most thoroughgoing of ironists. The converse of this hypothesis is also true.

Despite this flux, Nietzsche's writing might still be shown to possess a residual coherence in the patterned recurrence of distinctive metaphors, moves, or fictions. These might indeed turn out to be the familiar tropes of originary states, causes and effects, personal types, epochs, cultures, and worlds. One could construct chains of such metaphysical tokens in the effort to escape the panironical position. But in so doing one would be choosing to forget that in other places Nietzsche exposes these patterns as fraudulent—as the counterfeits, the "errors" of reason.[42]

However solid and plausible such figurative constructions may seem, they cannot stand for long against the thrusts of Nietzsche's irony. One cannot ignore Nietzsche's instruction on rhetoric: First, only in certain inspired states which we must take on faith do metaphors literally bear the burden of things.[43] But without the presence of signified things—contents of thought—or of things to sustain the analogy, it is impossible truly to connect metaphorical figures of thought. Second, all metaphors have a genealogy, a prehistory; it is a "question of origins" (BW, p. 453 *et seq.*). As "semiotically compressed processes" they carry along, not things, but a textual history of the accommodations to which other metaphysicians have submitted them.[44] Nietzsche's text is only a moment in sign chains crisscrossing the greater text of European writing;[45] they have no author.[46] Finally, much the most stubborn obstacle to the stabilizing of Nietzsche's metaphors is his critique internal to metaphor. The efficacity, the intelligibility, of metaphor itself depends on the reduction of the strange (sign) to the familiar (meaning). "All thought, judgment, perception, considered as comparison," Nietzsche writes, "has as its precondition a *positing* of equality, and earlier still a '*making* equal'" (WP, pp. 273–274). What, however, is the validity of such equality? Apart from its usefulness for life, it is, in Nietzsche's phrase, a "fiction of logic" (BW, p. 202). Metaphorical comparisons, where a human sense is involved, means "measuring reality against the purely invented world of the unconditional and self-identical. . . , a constant falsification of the world by means of numbers" (BW, p. 202). The possibility of making comparisons is sustained by the myth of integral being. Not only (so this deconstruction proceeds) must we dispense, therefore, with the subject that integrates being on the strength of its own self-presence, but it would appear that nothing whatsoever of this subject remains to be salvaged. To reduce the self to a mere metaphor is in fact to make it the epiphenomenon of a self, dependent on some other self for the act of equalization without which it could not come into existence. This other self would itself be subject to another such deconstruction and so on . . . The self—like all philosophy—is annihilated, lowered into "an abysmally deep ground" (BW, p. 419). And in the absence of a unitive self, writing becomes a boundless flux of fragmentary metaphors. The momentary victory of a metaphorical meaning comes from the mere assertion of an interpretive will blind to the irony of its inflicting upon a text an authenticity which the text cannot own.

There is of course a good deal in this argument that finds support in Nietzsche, but also a good deal that is contradicted. The extreme familiarity of the case (under the head of deconstruction)—the fact that this demonstration of "wild" irony has been applied persuasively to Rousseau and Freud, to Romantic writers, and to the "modern scriptor"—might in fact give one pause. How enfeebling if Nietzsche wrote with the same intention as every other modern writer and his distinction were at best only his centrality within the modern tradition, that is, his special tenacity and vigilance in contributing to the dissolution of man! This is exactly the surmise that one might welcome as a provocation to read Nietzsche from beginning to end to see if the story is not differently nuanced.

Indeed the story is different. Not only does Nietzsche's discussion of the self implicitly speak against a panironic reading, but his explicit remarks on irony reinforce this argument. On a closer view the notion of a panironic text proves a misleading, an unintelligible idea: it hides the fact that irony can take place only through punctual abrogations of irony. Something must be taken seriously for its ironical sublimation to matter. The movement of irony has to occur within a frame of rule-directed activity. The rules themselves cannot be ironical, or else irony could not be distinguished from chaos. Yet Nietzsche holds that irony is not chaos but rather a relation between form and chaos:

> The total character of the world . . . is in all eternity chaos—in the sense not of a lack of necessity but of a lack of order, arrangement, form, beauty, wisdom, and whatever other names there are for our aesthetic anthropomorphisms. . . . Judged from the point of view of our reason, unsuccessful attempts are by all odds the rule, the exceptions are not the secret aim. . . . None of our aesthetic and moral judgments apply to it. . . , it does not observe any laws either. (GS, 168)

"Pure" irony, like "an eye turned in no particular direction," would be indiscernible from blind chaos (BW, p. 555); its chaos is not that of Dionysus but that of "lascivious ascetic discord that loves to turn reason against reason." In pure irony a frenzy of asceticism turns on the universe in which neither "heartlessness and unreason [n]or their opposite" prevails (GS, p. 168). This idea clearly does not have a solitary rule in Nietzsche: it figures in fact as the negative pendant of a "godlike feeling . . .—humaneness." Here "the historical sense" has turned to the human past and "manage[d] to experience the history of humanity as a whole as *his own* history. . . . If one *could* endure . . . the losses, hopes, conquests, and the victories of humanity; if one could finally contain all this in one soul and crowd it into a single feeling—this would surely have to result in a happiness that humanity has not known so far: the happiness of a god full of power and love" (GS, p. 268). This unborn Faust of the historical sense conjures an ideal of the full self that endures the separate frenzies of Socrates and Dionysus.

Without now adding much discussion to this point, or indeed in further sentimentalizing it, I should like to state its direction apodictically. Nietzschean irony does indeed devalue the category of the ego—the so-called personal subject—as the agent or object of reflective cognition. "A thought comes when 'it' wishes," he writes, "and not when 'I' wish, so that it is a falsification of the facts of the case to say that the subject 'I' is the condition of the predicate 'think.' It thinks; but that this 'it' is precisely the famous old 'ego' is, to put it mildly, only a supposition, an assertion." A supposition which, moreover, is not harmless and needs to be unmasked by another movement of ironic consciousness as an apology for "the weakness of the weak" (BW, p. 214). Nietzsche's irony, on the other hand, does not discredit the self an an "organization" of ironical practice. I say "organization" and mean with this word to defer the self's irony. The self, while it has a questionable structure, can evidently speak ironically or not. Ironic practice in language is therefore not wild, not uncontrolled, because it is not the invariable symptom of a self.

Indeed the terms self and irony are more often than not oppositional, with self dominant. It is the virtual absence of self in the "decadent" which issues into uncontrollable ironical expression. This irony is pejorative, privative in a sense exactly contrary to the sense in which the link of self and irony is asserted by "wild" readers. The strong self neither perceives nor furthers its dissolution in irony. For Nietzsche, irony as often marks fatigue, a superfoetation of the historical sense, of the sense of possibility stifling action; irony is Socratic lassitude; only the obliterated self speaks ironically. On the other hand, a strong spirit of determinate irony speaks against all the unselfing tendencies of religion and culture. The "noble" personality has "faith in [it]self, pride in [it]self, a fundamental hostility and *irony* against 'selflessness' " (BW, p. 395; italics mine). Ironical practice in Nietzsche is consistent with a strong self grasped as an "abysmal" mirrorlike structure of questioning-being reflecting itself—but not entirely or necessarily—in the explicit question of the self. When such a self does pose the explicit question of itself, it does so with a certain irony: "A matter that becomes clear ceases to concern us.—What was on the mind of that god who counseled: 'Know thyself!' Did he mean: 'Cease to concern yourself! Become objective!—And Socrates?—And 'scientific' men?—" (BW, p. 271). The question of the self is posed in order to put a stop to reflexive cognition. Though this may be an ironical state of affairs, the question of the self is not posed ironically. Unless an answer is forthcoming there can be no meaning to the word "objective."

In writing directly on Nietzschean irony one should not pretend to a certainty which this topic cannot allow. Heidegger (and Derrida) are right in marking Nietzsche's "transformation of the very value of hierarchy itself"—the category which enables a conventional account of irony as a play of distinct positive and negative moments.[47] If irony functions beyond hierarchy it cannot be conceptualized, but neither does this fact prove its universal diffusion.

Another Route

There may be another way, also indirect, of doing justice to Nietzsche's organization of ironies. This path leads back to the crucial point in the argument for wild irony—Nietzsche's alleged dissolution of the self as a fiction or metaphor whose intelligibility is itself dependent on a fiction of logic.

The argument for wild irony attaches itself to Nietzsche's statement that the subject as a fiction added to an act or event, an imputation (something shoved under as a support), a supplementary metaphor of origin. For example, we are inclined to add a fiction, an underpinning, or a conceptual supplement, say, to a lightning flash, saying "lightning" caused the lightning flash, and lightning is the "subject" of this event (BW, p. 481). *"The mistake lies in the fictitious insertion of a subject."* [48] This mistake is characteristic of "first" thinking, which is less like thought than the production of fetishes.

Nietzsche, however, has more to say on the subject of first thinking than to detect its skew, its poverty at the origin. He also writes about first thinking as normative, as thinking as such. A crucial aphorism in the *Genealogy* describes all thought as springing out of a basic measuring of the self against another self, out of a fixing of interpersonal relation—of subordination, or indebtedness, etc. Thought is essentially a "setting prices, determining values, contriving equivalences" (BW, p. 506); thought doubles perceived likeness and makes metaphors. But this action, however described, flows out of or along with what Nietzsche calls "this *Selbstgefühl*" (2:811)—"pride" but also "self-consciousness," "sentiment of self" (BW, p. 506). The self is not a fiction or an underpinning or a concept subsequently added to the essential act of thought marking difference and likeness.

A sense of self is inexpungibly present at the event of thought. To say that the self is (only) a metaphor and therefore the product of an act of likening, of equalizing, is to reverse the priorities established in the *Genealogy*. The self precedes, it is not itself the product of a primary act of making metaphors and comparisons. [49]

In many other passages rarely encountered in the "new Nietzsche," Nietzsche gives primacy to a movement of self-constitution and locates a self at the origin of society. [50]

The "blond beasts exemplify that terrible artists' egoism that . . . knows *itself* justified to all eternity in its 'work.' " Their work is nothing less than the creation of the "state"—"an instinctive creation and imposition of forms; they are the most involuntary, unconscious artists there are—wherever they appear something new soon arises, a ruling structure that *lives*, in which parts and functions are delimited and coordinated, in which nothing whatever finds a place that has not first been assigned a 'meaning' in relation to the whole" (BW, pp. 522–523; first italics mine). We are not, in talking about unconscious artists, impoverishing or eliminating their egoism, their sense of self, since "consciousness does not really belong to man's individual existence but rather to his social or herd nature" (GS, p. 299). "Egoism," meanwhile, "belongs to the nature of a noble soul": it is a species of self-magnification (BW, p. 405). This, then, "is how the 'state' began on earth." Social organization is secondary to an original state of affairs, consisting, on the one hand, of the strong self—"he who can command, he who is by nature 'master' "—and, on the other, of an "unchecked and shapeless populace" (BW, p. 522).

Consider, again, the primacy awarded to the self as Nietzsche describes that "noble soul [which] accepts this fact of its egoism without any question mark: . . . perhaps it admits under certain circumstances . . . that there are some who have rights equal to its own; as soon as this matter of rank is settled it moves among these equals with their equal privileges, showing the same sureness of modesty and delicate reverence that characterize *its relations with itself*" (BW, p. 405; italics mine).

Finally, in the celebrated creation in *Beyond Good and Evil* of the noble type, the self is constituted by an initial act of reflection. "The noble type of man experiences *itself* as determining values." The self arises within a feeling (the *Selbstgefühl* of the account of "thought as such" in the *Genealogy*). "Everything it knows as part of *itself* it honors; such a morality is *self*-glorification. In the foreground there is the feeling of fullness, of power that seeks to overflow, the happiness of high tension, the consciousness of wealth that would give and bestow. . . . The noble human being honors *himself* as one who is powerful" (italics mine). The value system organized on the polarity good/bad originates with an act of self-magnification. The "good" has both logical and temporal primacy over the "bad." Bad is discovered in the master's feeling of "contempt" which he attaches to beings (*die Wesen*, 2:730) perceived as "cowardly, anxious, . . . petty" and also to "the suspicious with their unfree glances" (BW, pp. 394–395; italics mine).

The initial founding act that discovers the good is presocial.

Nothing in this account of the discovery of the good seems to require a social situation. The act of perceiving (properly, performing) the negation of the mood of abundance is of course secondary; this is the act which creates social distinction and hence constitutes a society. This act occurs simultaneously as the felt "pathos of distance" (BW. p. 391). The distance between social classes is the expression of an inner division—the scene of the conversion of self-abundance into contempt.

The self is conceived in advance of a social situation; the self is not of social provenance. Since evaluative acts are self-reflexive, i.e., arising directly or indirectly from a centering on qualities of the self, social beings and acts too are to be judged with respect to a presocial self.

This last argument for a self preceding society is clearly the product, however, of only a certain foreground—what Nietzsche calls "a frog perspective" (BW, p. 200). This perspective, while legitimate, is joined in the *Genealogy* to a quite different one, which turns things around and reverses the flow of the argument.

The section of the *Genealogy* dealing with the *Selbstgefühl* of first thinking simplifies the story of originary thought. It also ignores the complication of its having situated this moment in a rudimentary system of interpersonal exchange—in society. It might be possible to sidestep this difficulty by citing the letter of the text: "Buying and selling," writes Nietzsche, "together with their psychological appurtenances, are older even than the beginnings of any kind of social forms of organization and alliances" (BW, p. 506). The kinds of comparison Nietzsche has discussed strictly speaking precede social forms. Nonetheless "the custom of comparing, measuring and calculating" exerts itself on "power against power"—the first man to think and hence to experience a *Selbstgefühl* does so in a social matrix, *primus inter pares imparesque*.

Now, we will wonder, where at the beginning is the Other? In what way does it affect, in what way is it excluded from the self? The question is inevitable. Earlier we cited a phrase from *Beyond Good and Evil*: "the soul as social structure of the drives and affects" (BW, p. 210). In an unpublished note Nietzsche writes, "The ego is a plurality of forces—each one like a person (*personen-artigen Kräfte*)."[51] Such passages employing social metaphors for the self are abundant and compelling. In Zarathustra's speech on the self, the self figures *ab initio* at once as ruler and ruled ("shepherd and herd") (PN, p. 146). The Other is actively "inside" the self before the self has encountered other persons, in which matrix it discovers itself.

We saw further that "the ruling group" of masters discovers the good on the basis of "exalted, proud states of the soul." But Nietzsche also describes this moment in nonpositive terms. "The moral discrimination of values," he writes, "has originated . . . among a ruling group whose consciousness of its difference from the ruled group was accompanied by delight" (BW, p. 394). Here "delight" figures not as a synonym for the strong mood of self-glorification on which the good is founded. It is instead an epiphenomenal consciousness supplementary to what is basic—a "consciousness of its difference from the ruled group." Further on Nietzsche adds, "When the ruling group determines what is 'good,' the exalted, proud states of the soul are experienced as conferring distinction and determining the order of rank. . . . The noble human being separates from himself those in whom the opposite of such exalted, proud states finds expression" (BW, p. 394).

This account speaks not of an experience of self but of a consciousness of difference, of states of mind which confer distinction and determine the order of rank, of an act of separation from what is opposite. These categories will make post-Saussurean readers think of the diacritical categories constituting a language without positive terms. "From the structuralist point of view" (as Gerald Bruns puts it), "the sign is a negative entity: its being lies in what it is not, that is, in the systematic way in which it signifies its opposition to other words in the language." [52] The noble type has no more an abundant experience of the bedrock meaning of the self than does the reader solely by virtue of reading these words. Whatever sense the reader can make of such experiences depends on his power—better, the power of his language—to discriminate these signs from their opposite numbers (not "cowardly," not "anxious," not "petty"). Equally, the noble type has an experience of difference, distinction, separation, and opposition from what is not the self. This elides an immediate experience of the self, since the former experience can arrive at the self only after a putative immediacy has been awarded to what is Other, then the negation of this Other performed and perceived. This state of affairs puts the self precisely in the relation toward itself of a language-user, not a being capable of "immediate experience of the inner life"—an interpreter, not a reader of the "basic text of *homo natura*" (*der Grundtext homo natura*, 2:696) (BW, p. 351).

We see that this account is diametrically opposed to the account of the origin of the self earlier unfolded from this aphorism. The revelatory, disclosive act of valuation is performed not on the self but on the other as the occasion of an experience of difference. The noble type, the author of the moral polarity good/bad, is revealed to be no less reactive than its posited opposite, the slave type, the author of the moral polarity good/evil. Even before the noble self has been constituted, it contains a trace of the Other as the derivative of the other person (the slave) encountered in an interpersonal exchange. The noble type would himself bear the marks of the internal aggressiveness which Nietzsche paraphrases as the property of the reactive slave type—*ressentiment* (and which Lacan has identified as a residue of the mirror phase).

We find ourselves in the interpretive situation which all readers of Nietzsche sooner or later encounter and which makes inevitable such words as aporia and irony. Nietzsche inscribes into his genetic fictions of polar valuations everything the reader needs in order to produce the topsy-turvy account, in which polar terms leap incessantly across the bar of their division. If the polarity is founded, as inevitably in such accounts, on an attribution of firstness to the dominant term, it soon emerges that that firstness is in fact based on its difference, distinction, opposition to what is secondary.

Is there any way to arrest this circulation of ostensible priorities? What seems to be insufficiently appreciated is that the act of arrest is a precise metaphor for the critical act. Not all criticism is required to exhaust itself in ferreting out antitheses. A criticism more faithful to a Nietzschean sense arrests the flux of meaning by an act undeniably arbitrary but not yet violent. Criticism draws sharp boundary lines against points remote from the target center where the author in the text has aimed his emphasis.[53] "It was Nietzsche," wrote Thomas Mann, "who recalled the use of the bow beside the lyre as an Apollonian instrument; he taught us how to score hits, and indeed fatal hits at that" (BU, p. 56). Nietzsche is one case, Kafka another. Nietzsche makes distinctions in order (if only momentarily) to unify them in one will. Kafka dissolves every "arrest" into a violence as empty of authority as a grimace on the face of a dreamer.

We faced a similar problem earlier when we explored the impossibility of distinguishing in an altogether rigorous way the properties of the ego from the self. Nonetheless the critic must show Nietzsche giving primacy to the self over the ego. For the self, unlike the ego, never designates the hypostasis of the subject or object within the closure of so-called "self-knowledge" (*Selbst-Erkenntnis*).[54] The primacy of the self can be eroded by antithetical arguments produced from different standpoints, but the self remains indispensable, an insistently productive perspective within Nietzsche's system. The self promotes discourse in various registers—the nexus between key concepts, metaphors, and narrative situations. It articulates the field of metaphysics: the self, as a being that has to become what it is, distingishes being from becoming. It articulates the field of metapsychology, allowing for the distinctions between depth/surface, authentic/herd, etc. It allows for distinctions in psychological kinetics—or, put more grandly, in the "Dionysian drama of 'the Destiny of the Soul'" (BW, p. 458)—viz., "The great tragedian,

. . . like every other artist, arrives at the ultimate pinnacle of his greatness only when he comes to see himself and his art beneath him."[55] Finally the self allows for distinctions which articulate the social field. The self is a synonym for the noble type, the master, which "has some fundamental certainty . . . about itself, something that cannot be sought, nor found, nor perhaps lost" (BW, p. 458). It therefore enables the master to stand apart from the slave.

In the social field the self has primacy over the Other encountered in interpersonal exchange, even granting the impossibility of maintaining a strict distinction—the Other is always already in the self. Still this difficulty can be grasped intelligibly. In Giesz's words: " 'The self' cannot be spoken of as something-at-hand in the world (*vorhandenes Weltding*), since it is always already a *relation to itself*. This circumstance first makes it possible to reach for social analogies for the strivings of human inwardness."[56] The social metaphor is irresistible because the concept of the self involves self-overcoming, a relation of mastery. The will to power is informed by an entire organization of wills—a social organization with a history and a prehistory beset by a struggle for mastery. The enigma still exists, the uncertainty has not disappeared, of the appositeness of mastery for relations internal to a self that has yet to establish its mastery over another. But here we stop. This sort of circularity has an indefatigable power to engage, tease, perplex, exhaust, and engage again.

For the self-conscious writer of fiction, whose first business is his rhetoric—his figures of speech including figures of argument—the discussion about the self- or non-self-origination of valuable features (language, reason, personality) will serve to point a story. He thinks that as a problem of origins, it is unanswerable, and it does not presuppose or produce for him the disputatious analytical attitude. Instead it is a rhetorical figure which can be located strategically and manipulated for effect, to produce more rhetoric, but it has no other truth. Here this crucial foundational argument has become a trope. This is not the case for Nietzsche, although it is for Kafka. Consider Kafka's "Report to an Academy," the story of an ape's account of how it has emerged as a man. "Today I can see it clearly: without the most profound inward calm I could never have found my way out. And indeed perhaps I owe all that I have become to the calm that settled within me after my first few days in the ship. And again for that calmness it was the ship's crew I had to thank."[57] But the philosopher's and critic's first concern is different. It is not, for Nietzsche, the founding figures of rhetoric. The primal act of the human world is the arrest that individuates "the will as the most originary form of appearance, encompassing all becoming."[58] Nietzsche repeats this act when he asks the question, "And what created . . . value and will?" and answers, "the creative self" (PN, p. 147).

Summary

The self in Nietzsche is not a simple or vacuous fiction, and it is not urgently in need of deconstruction. For the "fiction" of the "self" we can now write, simply, the self, since truth—i.e., words without actual or virtual quotation marks—is in each case fictions or metaphors that are not simple, vacuous, or urgently in need of deconstruction. In Nietzsche's hands the self is a generative word, a generative concept: "Individual philosophical concepts . . . grow up in connection and relationship with each other. . . ; they belong . . . to a system. . . . Something within them leads . . . them in a definite order, one after the other—[namely] the innate systematic structure and relationship of their concepts. Their thinking is in fact far less a discovery than a recognition, a remembering, a return and a homecoming to a remote, primordial and inclusive household of the soul, out of which those concepts grew originally" (BW, p. 217).

"Self" is the name of such a concept, whose different aspects are also named by such terms as "will to power," "ego," "mastery." Equally, in such names different concepts ("processes") are semiotically concentrated (BW, p. 516), and each prompts and informs a potentially endless reflection on its implications, an endless unpacking. The power of the concept self is not sheerly linguistic. The word "self" does not produce infinite reflection by virtue alone of the history of its textual juxtapositions. This history of the word articulates a reflection urged by experience. There is always abundant experience of the will demanding and forcing writing on the subject of the self. "The will to power interprets. . . : it defines, limits, determines degrees, variations of power. Mere variations of power could not feel themselves to be such: there must be present something that wants to grow and interprets the value of whatever else wants to grow" (WP, p. 342). Indeed apart from such upheavals of the will, such "extreme states," "the milder, more middling and indeed the lower levels in perpetual play weave the texture of our character and our fate." By assuming "that really words exist only for superlative degrees of [inner] events and drives . . . we misread ourselves in this apparently clearest letter-script of our self (Buchstabenschrift unseres Selbsts)" (1:1090). This texture, torn by the abrupt intermittences of the will, forces an endless writing.

What movements in this Book of the Self recur? I hold to just three.

1. *Unity*. The strong self is one thing—not at once itself and something else. Like the biological cell, it is not strictly speaking "a separate entity. . . . The marks of identity, distinguishing self from non-self, have long since been blurred." Nonetheless, it is informed by "mechanisms for preserving individuality," for "the discrimination between self and non-self," which are able to generate "precise unequivocal directions about . . . how to establish that one is, beyond argument, one's self."[59] The self "desires to 'preserve' itself only indirectly," because it is not a separate entity but a relation of self-surpassing (WP, p. 270). Yet it keeps "a fundamental certainty about itself," without which indeed no violence to itself would not be acceptable (BW, p. 418).

2. *Responsibility*. This concept of individuality secures a certain truth in resisting the contrary position, which is seductive, namely, the self as sheerly other: "What indeed *does* man know about himself?"[60] "We are unknown to ourselves, we men of knowledge" (BW, p. 451). For the self as individual is responsible; it cannot be that at the moment that I acted, I was elsewhere—my other self prevailing—and that therefore the action is another's. "For what is freedom? That one has the will to assume responsibility for oneself" (PN, p. 452). The self as individual cannot be another self, however desirable it is to be that other self. "The weak-willed . . . seek to *lay the blame for themselves somewhere else*."[61] This moment contains Nietzsche's critique of "renunciation" in which the self cannot invent itself as more severe, more ascetic, than it *is*.

Certain of himself, Nietzsche can make use of another self, other selves: " 'objectivity' . . . as the ability to *control* one's Pro and Con and to dispose of them, so that one knows how to employ a *variety* of perspectives and affective interpretations in the service of knowledge" (BW, p. 555). But the self is not its mask. "The ugliest man [is he] who has to decorate himself (historical sense) and always seeks a new garment." "There is a sort of actor's art of temporarily assuming an alien soul. . . . At the same time a sign of weakness and lack of unity . . . etc. Romanticism."[62] Nietzsche cannot become a single authorial self, either, and guarantee consistency. His resolution in *Das Philosophenbuch* "to write . . . in an impersonal and cold manner" registers this insight: "Avoid all mention of 'us' and 'we' and 'I.' "[63] Nietzsche perceives (and enacts) the fact that the yield can be great short of *becoming* this second self.

While still young, Nietzsche wrote that if the social man is devoured by others, the solitary devours himself. This state of affairs has an exact epistemological correlative. The self in solitude would double itself in creating an interpreter of itself, yet succeeds in projecting that second self as a genuine center of thought, of reflection, and of literary activity (supposing this were possible) only at the instant it ceases to be itself. What is not the case cannot be invented as the case. The invention cannot adequately read the self. As interpreter it is only a certain mask of a mode of its being.[64] The self is most transparent as a state of exorbitant "freedom"—acutely unsettled, torn by inquiries—but unidentifiable; it cannot be situated, since it exists as a function of devouring and incorporating its successive witnesses.

3. *Passion.* In *The Middle Years* Henry James has the character Dencombe say " 'A second chance—*that's* the delusion. There never was to be but one. We work in the dark—we do what we can—we give what we have. Our doubt is our passion and our passion is our task. The rest is the madness of art.' "[65] Nietzsche specifies this madness. "That hidden and masterful something for which we long do not have a name, until finally it proves itself to be our task—this tyrant in us wreaks horrible revenge for every attempt we make to dodge or escape it, for every premature resignation, for every acceptance of equality with those among whom we do not belong, for every activity, however respectable, which distracts us from our main cause—indeed for every virtue which would protect us from the hardness of our inmost responsibility" (PN, p. 677). And where should we find named this task, this self of Nietzsche? It is revealed *and* turned back on itself in *Beyond Good and Evil:*

> To translate man back into nature; to become master over the many vain and overly enthusiastic interpretations and connotations that have so far been scrawled and painted over that eternal basic text of *homo natura*: to see to it that man henceforth stands before man as even today, hardened in the discipline of science, he stands before the *rest* of nature, with intrepid Oedipus eyes and sealed Odysseus ears, deaf to the siren songs of old metaphysical bird catchers who have been piping at him all too long, "you are more, you are higher, you are of a different origin!"— that may be a strange and insane task, but it is a *task*—who would deny that? Why did we choose this insane task? Or, putting it differently: "why have knowledge at all?" (BW, pp. 351–352)

Here our circle closes.

CHAPTER FOUR

Mann as a Reader of Nietzsche

Irony is no joke.[1]
—Schlegel

Toward the end of his life, in 1952, Thomas Mann (1875–1955) wrote to Hermann Weigand this triumphant sentence: "Even in these times it is possible for a man to construct out of his life and work a culture, a small cosmos, in which everything is interrelated, which, despite all diversity, forms a complete personal whole, and which stands more or less on an equal footing with the great life-syntheses of earlier ages."[2] According to Harold Bloom in *The Anxiety of Influence*, however, time has darkened such confidence; the influence that flows inexorably from the great life syntheses of earlier ages "has been more of a blight than a blessing, from the Enlightenment until this moment [1973]."[3] But Mann does not speak of influence as a blight. Along with Goethe and Nietzsche, he is a great denier of influence. This phrase intends to make the point directly. It does not mean what Bloom means by it—that Mann is a great denier of the anxiety of influence (AI, p. 56).

Mann never tired of affirming his place in German intellectual and literary history—"the great tradition of Germanism" (*das grosse Deutschtum*) from Luther to Bismarck and Nietzsche" (L, p. 97). "What I owe to the German tradition of thought," he wrote, "and how deeply rooted I am in that tradition, is perfectly clear" (L, p. 184). This is a direct and confident acknowledgment, and it gives strength, especially to the act of writing fiction. Criticized for the lack of "creative imagination" in his early work, Mann replied: "I say that very great writers did not invent anything in their whole lives, but merely poured their souls into traditional materials and reshaped them" (L, p. 49). For Bloom "the genius is *strong*. . . . His strength exhausts . . . those who come in his wake. . . . He *floods* them" (AI, p. 51). In Mann, however, the water imagery is different. No genius so much floods "traditional materials" that these materials founder. They take, and take in such a fashion as always to be more, not less, receptive to the soul flood of the strong writer who comes to try them again. What the writer finds before him has been shaped by his precursors, is their labor, not his; and this relation is precisely the *gift* relation, that of the *Glücksfall* and *Glücksfund* ("the good fortune" and perhaps also "the fortunate fall" of tradition, and the "lucky find" of the great artist): such was Schopenhauer's philosophy for Wagner.[4] When Mann conceives of his relation to Nietzsche's thought, it is indeed as Nietzsche's *gift*—possibly to him. Mann writes: "I've often felt that Nietzsche's philosophy might be able to become the good fortune and the lucky find of a great writer [*Dichter*]. . . , the source of the loftiest, most erotic and slyest irony playing between life and mind. . . . Unlike Schopenhauer, Nietzsche has not found or not yet found his artist" (BU, p. 84). But it is hard to believe that Mann at this moment was not unanxiously supposing that the project of completing Nietzsche would be his and no one else's. Indeed the next sentence of this text—it is from *Reflections of a Nonpolitical Man* (*Betrachtungen eines Unpolitischen*), 1918—speaks of Mann's intellectual gratitude to Nietzsche for a principle wholly cognate with Nietzsche's irony, as Mann understood it: "just this: the idea of life" (BU, p. 84). (For Mann the ideas of irony and life are related.)

If this is so, how then can Harold Bloom, having conceived of Mann as a great denier of influence, go on to describe Mann as "a great sufferer from the anxiety of influence and one of the great theorists of that anxiety" (AI, p. 52). The text he quotes as evidence (Mann's essay *Freud and the Future*) speaks precisely of the plausibility of a *Bildung*, of a full unfolding of personal energies. And the "happiest element" in this process is just this "powerful influence of admiration and love, this childish identification with a father-image elected out of profound affinity."[5] Mann speaks on behalf of the happy bond between ephebe and precursor, which Bloom acknowledges, except, Bloom writes, in this passage everything that "matters most—the inescapable melancholy, the anxiety that makes misprision inevitable" is missing (AI, p. 54). Everything, that is, that Bloom thinks matters most is missing from what Mann actually says.

Now it is beyond dispute that Mann may have misunderstood his "father-image" Goethe (to whom the above passage alludes) and misunderstood the crucial figure of Nietzsche. It comes as no surprise that even readers as perspicacious as Mann can have misunderstood the texts of precisely those predecessors whom they value most. Bloom's point, more than this, is that the inevitable misprision—of the kind we may expect to find between Mann and Nietzsche—is grounded in melancholy and anxiety; that the way Mann testifies to the shadow laid on him is *to read himself into his precursor*; and that this kind of projection occurs exactly as does Mann's misinterpretation of Goethe, which was "to read precisely his own parodistic genius, his own kind of loving irony, into his precursor" (AI, p. 54). This is how I complete Bloom's hypothesis; it is at least consistent with his puzzling statement that Nietzsche is "a poet who is desperately afraid of irony" (AI, p. 55).[6] Mann's way of swerving from Nietzsche would be to supply him with a kind of irony called "loving irony," where in fact there was in Nietzsche desperate fear of irony. Mann would thus save himself from foundering in his own anxiety by shrinking Nietzsche's soul-destroying irony to a loving irony on behalf of life, with which he could connect.

Now there is certainly some truth in this last idea. At *one point in his life* Mann did indeed read into Nietzsche a kind of loving irony. But the point holds only as it figures in a fluctuating history of texts in which Mann reads Nietzsche. There is a diachrony in this reading relation which rebuts the Bloomian mode of reasoning from the synchronic trope of unconscious reversal. It is misleading to argue that "the great deniers of influence—Goethe, Nietzsche, Mann . . . are enormous fields of the anxiety of influence," meaning whatever these writers say can be freely reversed to mean the opposite (AI, p. 56). If Bloom then argues tendentiously that Nietzsche was afraid of irony, and Mann anxious about Nietzsche—Mann's anxiety thus being inspired by his timid precursor—then, by Bloom's mode, such assertions about Mann and Nietzsche cannot be wrong, since these propositions also operate at another level, where they too serve as fields for wholly opposite propositions. Undoubtedly, however, Bloom's argument is strong and therefore in one sense right: he employs the terms that any other good argument about this subject would have to employ. His most cogent formulation emerges from the appropriate modification of his remark about Mann and Goethe, namely, that Mann's swerve away from Goethe represents the "ironic denial that any swerve is necessary" (AI, p. 54).

I begin by asking whether there is indeed irony in Mann's denial, in the *Reflections of a Nonpolitical Man*, that any swerve from Nietzsche is necessary, and further, What consciousness of irony generally informs Mann's misprision of Nietzsche?

When Mann, from his American exile, wrote, "Where I am, there is German culture,"[7] he meant by the word "culture," to a degree remarkable for a novelist, the German philosophical tradition. This had also been the case on a comparable occasion thirty years before. In 1918, occupying an adversary position with respect to a large body of German intellectuals, Mann completed writing a spiritual autobiography, his *Reflections of a Nonpolitical Man*. There too Mann defined his tradition within the German past as mainly a philosophical one. "The three names which I have to set down when I ask myself about the foundations of my intellectual and artistic development—these names for a triple constellation of eternally connected spirits—[are] Schopenhauer, Nietzsche, and Wagner" (BU, pp. 71–72). For Mann these figures in their succession constitute an objective historical and textual development: "Their destinies as creators and dominators are profoundly and inseparably linked"(BU, p. 79). But they are linked in another way: "The three of them are one. The reverent disciple, for whom their mighty careers represent a culture, could wish to speak of them all simultaneously, so difficult does it seem to him to keep separate what he owes to each individually" (BU, p. 79). The interiorization of the objective historical interconnectedness of these thinkers might be accomplished—but only with difficulty, a difficulty whose other side would be the right to proceed arbitrarily, as if indeed the three of them were one.

The lifelong process by which Mann attempted to assimilate the work and personality of Nietzsche is important in a specific sense. "The experience of Nietzsche's criticism of culture and his stylistic artistry," wrote Mann, "is of the first order of importance in . . . my life."[8] This process is important too because it illustrates in a decisive way the equivalence which allows Mann to exchange elements of his political, artistic, and critical activity.

The Mann-Nietzsche nexus is prominent in at least four non-fictional works. They are the "Preface" and the chapter "Introspection" in *Reflections of a Nonpolitical Man*; Mann's speech in 1924 on the occasion of a musical evening honoring Nietzsche;[9] *A Sketch of My Life* (*Lebensabriß*), 1930, Mann's obligatory autobiography composed shortly after receiving the Nobel Prize for literature in 1929;[10] and finally the essay "Nietzsche's Philosophy in the Light of Contemporary Events" (1947), Mann's revaluation of Nietzsche after the Second World War.[11] Furthermore, there are Mann's *Letters* (1971), which abound in references to Nietzsche and, of central importance, the novel *Doctor Faustus* (1948), which Mann called "basically a Nietzsche-novel," although the hero shares only certain traits with Nietzsche and others with Hugo Wolf and Mann himself (L, p. 490).

The change in Mann's attitude toward Nietzsche emerges most sharply from the contrast between his earliest and his latest essay, both written under the pressure of world wars. In the first, Nietzsche is an "educator," whom Mann praises for his remarkable precision (BU, p. 88). In the second, Nietzsche is said specifically to be "untouched by any sense of pedagogic responsibility," and a good deal of his work is judged an intolerable romanticizing of evil.[12] The pattern appears to be one of sheer reversal, and since "Nietzsche's Philosophy in the Light of Contemporary Events" has been widely read, this trope of reversal has been accepted as the dominant figure for Mann's relation to Nietzsche. This scheme, however, is too simple. Part of the obstacle to understanding is the peculiar density of the early work, the *Reflections*, which until 1982 had not been translated into English.[13] It may be most useful, then, to focus on the earlier works, the texts of 1918 and 1924. The patterns which these texts reveal are pertinent to the later works and modify their sense.

Mann prefaces his *Reflections of a Nonpolitical Man* with "a musical prelude" connecting the motifs of the main text. The phrase is important since the theme of music recurs in Mann's readings of Nietzsche. The motifs which Mann connects "musically" create the perspective in which he will always read Nietzsche.

Reflections is, says Mann, at once more and less than a book. The reason for its hyperbole and its ellipsis, for its overshooting and its falling short of the mark, is that it has no basis, and as a result it has no subject or at any rate no subject matter over which the author could exercise a definite control (BU, p. 1).[14] It has neither basis nor subject because it was written during a period, the war years, which offered the artist no support and no substance—a time Mann describes as an

> agitation of everything stable, a shattering of all cultural foundations, a tumult of thought absolutely fatal to any sort of creative work; the naked impossibility of *creating* anything on the ground of a *Being*: the dissolution and making problematic of this Being itself by the age and its crisis; the necessity of grasping, clarifying, and *defending* this Being put into question, put under stress, no longer standing firm, no longer something unconscious, something to be taken for granted; . . . the ineluctable necessity, therefore, of a revision of all the foundations of the artistic mode itself, its self-investigation and self-affirmation without which its praxis, its effect, its serene realization—all making and doing—seems henceforth a sheer impossibility. (BU, p. 4)

How is such a work to be described? or led up to? Its subject is the absence of the foundation on which works are made, the very impossibility of its existence as a work. The problem for Mann is, let us note, the outcome of a quite particular age and its crisis; in this sense the problem is unlike any other. And for this reason, for the peculiarity of the predicament from which it emerges, the text has to be given a special name. It cannot be called "the fruit of these years [of speculation]. . . . I'd do better instead to speak of a residue, a remainder" (Mann's word is *Rückstand*, which also means the arrears of a debt, so that the word has overtones of shortcoming and indebtedness). It must be termed "a deposit, or better, a trace (*Spur*) and indeed the trace of pain"—thus (and here Mann needs a sheer neologism) "the *Bleibsel* [something like the "leavings"] of these years," an entity without real duration (BU, p. 1).

What seems remarkable about this attempt to define a writing of crisis is the nonsubjective character of its terms. A residue, a remainder, an arrears, a deposit, leavings, a trace are not the products of an intentional consciousness. They do not belong to the logocentric vocabulary of "meaning," "expression," "form." Neither are they the products, or certainly not the valorized products, of organic nature. They are Mann's terms (a half-century before Derrida) to describe a writing that arises in the felt absence of a personal center, a sustaining ground.

Yet, unlike Derrida's, this writing has to arise, for Mann, from a quite particular predicament in which writing finds itself. This is not the predicament of any writing responsive to time, to the form of time as such—to mutation, deferment, noncoincidence, finitude. Mann describes, with an imagery of impersonal process, writing that must respond to an obscure disaster that has caused a time peculiarly without objective character. This time cannot be structured in and through events (nothing eventuates). To be conceived, it would have to be produced by a subjectivity, but the subject is itself lost in this dissolution. The predicament which Mann describes would appear to be a special case of what, for Derrida, is the general case.

Under such circumstances writing is sheerly "experimental," "nebulous," "a groping" (BU, p. 2). Now for Mann, any sort of writing is as such problematic. "Writing itself always appeared to me as the product and expression of a problematic of the Here and yet There, the Yes and No, the two souls in one breast, the bad richness of inner conflicts, antitheses, and contradictions. Why or whence such a thing as writing at all if it is not the intellectual and moral concern for a problematic self?" (BU, p. 12) This is the normal condition of writing, of the writing which could produce a work of art. But (as is clear from the context of this passage) this condition is founded on a time sufficiently consistent in itself, endowed with a center or centers, a culture, and a "genuine itinerary" (BU, p. 12), so that something like a self, however problematic, could come into being as its opposition, could cohere—says Mann—even as the spirit of doubt, as the questionable figure among the retinue of knights in the service of the *Zeitgeist* (BU, p. 12). The product of such a problematic writer might very well appear to have the form of an organic product, the sweetness and solidity of a fruit, all the while it would dissolve in the mouth into the emptiness of an unkept promise. But the work at hand, the *Reflections*, is not even such a specious product. If it were, it would be possible to grasp its underlying idea as "organic and forever present." But this is an impossible task, for "it is only with the wavering mood of such (an idea) that the whole is saturated" (BU, p. 2).

      This emptiness is different from the lack of outcome in a structured clash of antithetical intentions, for it is not the issue of even a conflicted self. Its emptiness is different from even the dispersive negativity everywhere in writing which writing could perhaps identify. It is instead the residue of a crisis, an unnameable *Mittelding*, in which writing survives as a trace, the mark of a nameless pain, a shortcoming.

      Are then these *Reflections*—to come directly to the point—free play, the movement of difference, oriented entirely to a future and offered to an active interpretation?

      Yes and no. A problem or confusion here assails us: Mann has actually italicized it for us. The impossible goal of this work was described as one not only of articulating the loss, the absence of Being, of all cultural foundation—of playing the game in the absence of a reassuring order—but of *defending that Being in its absence*. This is something quite different. As a work of defense it becomes in principle no different from the productions of the Defenders of the Age whom Mann dismisses as mere "literati." The task of the genuine German writer, according to Mann's own account, may be, perhaps, to *portray* the Defender of the Age or indeed of past ages, but at no cost can it seek to *defend* him and his practical interest.

      To appear as the defender of a vanished principle would be to reduce the reality of a crisis—of a time without form—into the pseudo-dialectic of an apparent crisis, concealing an authentic, if recalcitrant, temporality. This strategy anticipates, if you like, Heidegger's in *Being and Time*. It is finally to substitute morality and polemic for *irony*, for let us now name in the most direct way with "irony" what Mann has right along meant by writing in a condition of greatest uncertainty. To defend a principle is to break off the lesser irony which is the subject of writing normatively—what Mann called "the bad richness of inner conflicts, antitheses, and contradictions." It is to break off too the greater irony of form and subject which allegedly saturates this work, the work without substance and support. It is finally to substitute for the linguistic or indeed the ontological category of irony the intersubjective or social category of polemic, to substitute for the work without foundation that literature of wishful thinking which aims at the persuasion of others, at society, and which coming from a German pen is a product (in Mann's word) of "alienation." For "never will [the German] understand under the head of Life—Society, never subordinate to the social problem, the moral, the inner experience. We are not a people for society and no treasure trove for parlor psychologists. The self and the world are the objects of our thinking and poetizing, not the role which a self sees itself as playing in society" (BU, pp. 27–28).

Mann perceives, however, if without anguish, how his book is a polemic finally written in defense of troubled values, of conservative values, the values of the nineteenth century, and how polemic undermines precisely the sort of thinking and writing about the self and the world which he argues to be genuine. His tract becomes one more blinded effort to will into being a more desirable state of affairs, of a piece with the journalism of the party of progress—England and France—and a residue, finally, of the age in a far more negative sense than he at first intended. Here is the surprising conclusion to this preface:

> But why this extraordinary effort? . . . You don't worry to this extent about something you don't *have* to worry about, something which is of no concern to you because you know nothing about it, and you have nothing of it in yourself, *in your own blood.* I said, Germany has enemies within its own walls, in a word, the allies and proponents of world-democracy. Is this to be repeated in a narrower compass, and am I to harbor within me, in my own conservative inwardness, elements which further the "progress," the progress of Germany? Could it be that my being . . . and my effect do not in any way correspond precisely to what I think and what I mean to say: and that I myself with a portion of my being am . . . destined to further Germany's progress toward that condition which in these pages is named with the quite inauthentic name of "Democracy" . . . ? And what sort of part of myself, then, would that be? Perhaps the *literary*? For literature— let us say once more what we know!—literature is in its innermost basis democratic and civilizing; better: it is *the same thing* as democracy and civilization. And my writing then would be that which makes me for my part advance the "progress" of Germany—advance it *because* I challenge it in the name of conservatism? (BU, p. 32)

This argument lyrically brings together Rousseau ("Reader, judge me!") and Nietzsche, whom Mann will consider the prime case of the unwitting literatus who furthers "democracy" as he attacks it. It does so while registering plainly enough the personal impulse behind this work. Mann writes of his "own conservative inwardness," the "conservative challenge" which this book intends. This is all a far cry from the work which arises from the "dissolution of . . . Being itself," as the trace of a nameless pain. The character of the turnabout is caught quite precisely in terms of irony. If at the outset Mann described this book as the product of the greatest lucidity *and* the greatest uncertainty, a condition we called irony, the ironical character he now perceives in this work is only that of the banal surmise touching efficient communication: "Could it be that my being . . . and my effect do not in any way correspond precisely to what I think and what I mean to say?" The surmise is cast as an appeal to the reader for confirmation of the integrity of a subject irritated to the point of losing control. A crisis of an epochal character has lapsed into a banal quarrel within a subject. The writing of the literatus, we recall, was described as the expression of the problematic of a divided sensibility. Now at the end of the *Reflections*, Mann decisively describes *this* work too as the "representation of a division and conflict within a subjectivity" (BU, p. 33).

A singular epochal crisis, then, said to be ineffable, has been reformulated in terms at once flaccidly general and dramatically personal. First, the predicament of writing without foundation at a certain historical juncture becomes a negative feature of writing in general. Because of its irresponsible, rhetorical, and hence democratizing character, writing can never defend or reinstitute a practical (conservative) principle. This general motive plays the minor role in the argument. The predicament, however, is also formulated in the most particular terms, and this is the major motive of the shift. The epochal crisis becomes a conflict between portions of the self of Thomas Mann—his character as a conservative politician and as a literatus. Mann's initial insight has shifted into two different registers of duplicity. The first would incapacitate all writing seeking a determinate effect on the world. The second makes all writing the spectacular illustration of a personal confusion.

When a shift of such proportions occurs, it is not likely to occur harmlessly. It will leave marks, revealing the perturbation in the consciousness that allows it. These marks are evident in Mann's rhetoric, which acts to defend the legitimacy of his "move" in three different ways at once. First, this reversal of perspective is softened as only a surmise. Second, it can be affirmed only naively. Finally, it is aestheticized, musicalized. This is crucial. At the moment when this reversal occurs most decisively, when the irony of pure writing has descended to polemic, Mann attributes to his prologue a musical character. This initial essay in self-division becomes a musical prelude. As such a prelude, announcing such themes, it therefore heralds a text, says Mann, that is neither a "book" nor a "work of art" but something quite different: "almost a *Dichtung*." The question of the reversal in Mann's argument can therefore be stated as the question of the meaning for him of *Dichtung*. The fall of irony into polemic is "poetry."

This sort of *Dichtung* first has to be distinguished from a book and a work of art. It is neither. As such, this text is brought back into proximity with that absolute writing fraught with irony, without foundation, structure, or centered time—without a history. For such writing was also opposed earlier to the book, the work of art, and to literature. *Dichtung* is thus defined as irony to which something else has been added. What was before a nebulous groping toward a trace of pain is musically extended; the formless residue of a crisis becomes a poem.

Each of these types of writing can be clarified in terms of its ironic dimension. First, *Dichtung*, a work of thoroughgoing irony, exhibits irony of subject matter and form, yet is musical. Second, the work of art (*Kunstwerk*)—equally, the book—is the "fruit" of artistic labor, exhibiting finite irony of subject matter and pseudo-immediateness, apparent naturalness, of form. Finally, there is mere "literature," marked by pseudo-immediateness, naturalness of subject matter ("life"), and unintentional irony of form (fashion, the mode). These distinctions help to understand music functionally. Historical life has been arrested by a crisis. The public sign of this crisis is the hegemony of literature—all-civilizing and, at the same time, all-leveling, irresponsible, and destructive. Literature is unwittingly ironical and heightens a consciousness of irony. It is a rhetoric that speaks in the accents of personality all the time it issues from an empty self. And it is that historical and cultural action which, while urging action, actually suspends it. The literatus may advocate practical imperatives, but his rhetoric produces the opposite effect: the loss of reality. His unwitting irony reduces the personal self to a verbal movement, but as it veers toward angry polemic, it uncovers a self in the rifts of its confusion.

Suppose, however, one wrote, faithful to even the clearest consciousness of irony? What would be the gain? The freest writing appears to be peculiarly vulnerable to a degradation. Thus music supplements irony's dangerous tendency to rant, mollifies its dying fall into a language of need. The crash of irony into polemic becomes melodic.[15]

Here we have an early version of Mann's life-long attribution to music of a radically personal meaning. The musical character of the *Reflections* designates the kind of writing that shall, must, be his. This association is sharpest in Mann's reading of Nietzsche as one who was personally constituted by music and then significantly depersonalized through his renunciation of (Wagner's) music. The attachment to music, or its decisive renunciation, constitutes or annihilates a self.

The musical character of writing is thus meant to arrest its betrayal by destructive polemic. The fall into polemic is bound up too with an expiatory intent that means to pardon it. For if from the start Mann spoke of writing as "trace," he also spoke of it as "guilt" (a *Rückstand*, an arrears), guilty of what one might conceivably call (with Derrida) "broken immediacy."[16] This is a guilt which has to press toward its own abolition. The negativity of the project proposed at the outset cannot be endured. Its trace must become the trace not of sorrow but of anger; it aims at *recovery* of the hospitable atmosphere of the nineteenth century and the "moral and intellectual foundations" of Mann's artistic practice (BU, p. 13). The *Reflections*, Mann perceives, is therefore in the end confessional, mimetic of a need, "not unworthy of being known by readers today and those afterwards, if only because it is a symptom of the age" (BU, p. 10). "Intellectual excitedness," "the eagerness to speak of everything at once," in this context is not a negative term. If it earlier characterized Mann's indebtedness to Schopenhauer, Wagner, and Nietzsche, it now characterizes his indebtedness to his age and therefore suggests not estrangement but a maximum of responsiveness, however needy. This confessional mode calls forth, almost automatically, an extended reference to Rousseau, to the justification in Rousseau's precedent. Rousseau, says Mann, set a negative standard in the uninhibitedness of his disclosures which pardons in advance the confessions of the solitary—"the publicly solitary"—writer who comes after him.

The description of Mann's own project, his interpretation of his reading of the war years, fairly cries out now for this pendant, this sentence of Derrida's, which in other contexts has become familiar. "Turned towards the lost or impossible presence of the absent origin, this . . . thematic of broken immediacy . . . is the saddened, *negative*, nostalgic, guilty, Rousseauistic side of the thinking of play whose other side would be the Nietzschean *affirmation*, that is, the joyous affirmation of the play of the world . . . without truth and without origin, which is offered to an active interpretation." Derrida explains: "The one seeks to decipher, dreams of deciphering a truth or an origin which escapes play and the order of the sign, and which lives the necessity of interpretation as an exile. The other, which is no longer turned toward the origin, affirms play and tries to pass beyond man and humanism, the name of man being the name of that being who, throughout the history of metaphysics . . . has dreamed of full presence, the reassuring foundation, the origin and end of play."[17] Nietzsche, writes Derrida, showed the way to the second interpretation of interpretation: interpretation as irony.

Intermittently, Nietzsche does so for Mann as well by showing him the way to that Dichtung which is the irony of form and of substance but which Mann cannot, will not, sustain. A radical oscillation between irony or play and the literature of personality and persuasion—the "end of the game"—informs the whole of the Reflections.

Both Mann and Derrida use Rousseau to misunderstand him; both discredit him in order to valorize Nietzschean irony, while ignoring, mistakenly, the category of the self. For Derrida, Rousseau represents nostalgia for a lost presence, but this description is nullified in fact by the Rousseau of the Fifth Promenade. He knows a fullness of free play which, if it is to express itself, can do so only by the metaphor of the divine. Rousseau says he "plays" with his own consciousness "comme Dieu";[18] "presence" goes with "another sort of joy," for which there is not yet a word.[19] Not a word, perhaps, until Nietzsche in Ecce Homo, as Mann suggests, would give an account of rapture, of inspiration, which is the fullness of creativity and not of divine presence. Both Mann and Derrida valorize Nietzsche and misunderstand Rousseau. For Mann, Rousseau is part of the eighteenth century, a foil for the being linked to Nietzsche and the nineteenth century which Mann wishes to recover. And though Mann needs Rousseau as a precedent for a confessional work, he protects himself against the dangers of his own honesty by attacking Rousseau as shameless and misguided. Rousseau was in error: he supposed that his example of frankness would never inspire a rival, yet the confessional mode became an inveterate feature of nineteenth century discourse. Rousseau does not figure interestingly in Mann's text because Mann has adopted the formidable German tradition of the misinterpretation of Rousseau, begun by Wieland, canonized by Schiller in On Naive and Sentimental Poetry, and adopted by Nietzsche. In Schiller Rousseau figures as divided and as dissolute: his intellect leads him to the destructive violence of his political writings; his sensibility, to the idyll, with its nostalgia and craving for physical complacency.[20] Mann denies to Rousseau the strength he reserves for Nietzsche as someone in whom the tendencies of his age came to a full head and who swerved inwardly and attacked them. That is because in Mann's narrative, the eighteenth century, as the century of Anglo-French progress, must be kept shallow and opaque; this way, the nineteenth century, with its melancholy, its sense of human limitation, and its loathing of knowledge—in a word, its irony—can figure more sharply against it.

If Mann seizes on Rousseau's representation of a divided self to justify the confessional impulse in himself, it is with hostility and distaste. Rousseau's alleged nostalgia for originary immediacy became for Rousseau every man's right to simplicity and hence to happiness: Rousseau's pathos fathers "democracy." Within the economy of the *Reflections* Mann's hostility can be seen as the product of bad faith, as the embarrassment accompanying his lapse into personality. Rousseau has for Mann an indispensably exemplary character. But their relation is characterized by a distaste of influence, a horror of contamination. The relation with Nietzsche affirms influence: Nietzsche is a source of strong identification. "Nietzsche's criticism of the previous century," Mann writes, "never seemed more grandly cogent than in the perspective of the present moment" (BU, p. 15).

Mann's discussion of Nietzsche differs immediately from his discussion of Rousseau in substituting an expository for a polemical tone. Nietzsche's insight, says Mann, is to grasp mind and art as deficient modes, as products of the decadence of life, as biological inadequacy. This is the essential skepticism of the nineteenth century which Nietzsche brought to a head and which is Mann's artistic life breath. But the nuance which the idea received from Nietzsche has not yet been fully appreciated. Nietzsche grasps that the perception by mind of its own compensatory nature—its character as a supplement to insulted life and its longing for health through self-sacrifice—"completes" a process which Mann calls the loosening of the "domination of ideals" (BU, p. 14). Nietzsche also sees that this process is not simple but complex and heterogenous. The perception of the variously antithetical structure of the "mind's submission to life" might be the source of works of art different in principle from those which have originated from a simple reading of Nietzsche. This is the nuance which Mann just barely discovers in Nietzsche. The question is whether he will be faithful to this insight.

Of these simpler, impatient products of irony we may say that they correspond entirely to what Derrida indicts as the dominant mode of interpretation. They speak on behalf of life, presence, the origin, center, and the end of the game—in Mann's words "an enthusiastic, erotically intoxicated submission to Power" (BU, p. 17). In this sort of writing, however, there is also a sentimental, aesthetic submission. At its extreme it becomes "that aestheticism of ruthlessness, of the Renaissance, that frenzied cult of Power, Beauty, and Life to which for a while a certain order of poetry succumbed" [read d'Annunzio and Stefan George] (BU, p. 17). Another kind of poetry, however, could arise from the perception of the heterogenous play of substitutions beginning with mind— the irony of mind that in seeking life by its calculated sacrifice seeks it all on the mind's terms. What then emerges, however, as the crux of Mann's *Dichtung*, of the entire web of antitheses and reversals at the point it might flow into generosity is the point at which Mann constructs . . . *himself*, himself as subject. This other possibility of the interpretation of Nietzsche, this "find for the artist," is the *personal* principle of Thomas Mann. In speaking of irony, Mann writes: "I speak of my case. In my case the experience of the self-negation of spirit on behalf of life became irony" (BU, p. 17).

But how, one asks, can a heteronomous movement of self-overcoming amount to a personal attitude? The task of converting a movement of ironies into a moral center could not be accomplished without a thoroughgoing substitution in kind. For the openness of irony, for the freedom of forever passing beyond the assertion and its contradiction, there would have to be "the *substitution* of *given* and *existing, present* pieces" (Derrida).[21] This substitution is not sanctioned by Nietzsche; it is Mann's special modulation. Irony becomes, writes Mann, "a moral attitude, for which I do not know any other paraphrase or definition than this: irony is the self-negation, the self-betrayal of spirit on behalf of Life, whereby, by 'Life,' quite as in the case of Renaissance Aestheticism, I understand—in another gentler and slyer nuance of feeling—the charm, the happiness, the strength, the grace, the pleasant normality of a lack of wit (*Geistlosigkeit*), unwittiness (*Ungeistigkeit*)" (BU, p. 18). This odd domestication of the history of irony in German letters, which yields us the dazzling list of Goethe, Fichte, Schlegel, Hegel, Kleist, Kierkegaard, and of course Nietzsche, this tapering down of irony to a free play—*but. . . , to a sure* irony—is, at this stage of the game, what is meant by the humanism of Thomas Mann.[22]

Mann notes, true, that even domestic irony has an elastic, aggressive component provoking movement. "The self-negation of the spirit can never be wholly serious, wholly complete. Irony *courts*, if surreptitiously, it seeks to win things for the spirit, if even without hope." It is not animal, but intellectual, not gloomy, but witty. Yet "it is above all a *personal* ethos through and through" (BU, p. 18). Nietzsche functions as the find for a philosophical style and a personal existence, a style that shall be faithful to irony and free play and yet suspend irony, modify it to a quite particular case of limited antithesis—that of the witty outsider and the unwitty Bürger—and this way yield a personal identity. All Mann's interpretive energy, in this book, as it is applied to Nietzsche, flows into the same pattern. He celebrates the free play and the irony he finds there, only at once to draw back from its nonmorality or immorality. He claims irony as his principle, but irony packed into "*given* and *existing, present* pieces." The substitution is one of nature or pseudo-immediacy (the unwitty or witless Bürger) for the term of life in Nietzsche's ironic spiral.

We are now in a position to see most clearly what Mann meant in describing his introductory essay as a musical prelude. This prelude to the *Reflections* has a movement of winding down. The movement begins in pure writing (irony of form and subject). It alludes to the *Kunstwerk*, with its pseudonaturalism of form and its finite irony of subject matter (as, for example, in the opposition between the artist and the *Bürger*). It alludes to the book, the fruit of a personal exertion and the expression of an ethos. It goes through these stages before descending to literary polemic, the express urge to overcome irony. For irony is, after all, "weak-willed and fatalistic and far from putting itself seriously into the service of the social desideratum, the ideals" (BU, p. 18). We grasp better now the meaning of music in a piece which describes this fall as musical. Music is a "solicitation of Life—charming, unwitty, graceful"; never mind that the conceptual equivalent of music has turned out to be the lapse of free play into self-defense.

This definition of music is fiercely at odds with the definition which music is explicitly given later in the essay, in Nietzsche's strong differentiation of music from politics and morality. There music means for Nietzsche German "depth." It means a certain return of the same, and, as in the figure at the close of *The Birth of Tragedy* of a Socrates who practices music, it is a compressed spiral of reflection, a point by point narration of ironies, a laying out of ironies in time. But in the "Prelude" Mann tempers and temporizes: music means an expression of *Gemüt*, something soulful, not of the order of thought, and therefore unaggressive. Music is the fall of irony into the sweetness of bourgeois life, the song of bad faith pretending to be life.

We have seen Mann split Nietzsche's conception of life into two parts. One is linked to language serving the aestheticism, force, and cruelty of the strong self; the other, called irony by Mann, seeks (for him) conciliation between the order of mind and the pleasant normality of the unwitting, the unwitty. This is irony as a condition of mind doing well in social life. But the figure of Nietzsche who emerges through this work does not offer the same example of a reconciliation, of a unity, except in rare raptures, and for higher stakes. Music for Nietzsche is not the agent of easy connections. There is a tension in music too, which we will feel on advancing into the body of the *Reflections*.

In the *Reflections* Mann sees Nietzsche as chiefly a critic of the German character and probably has in mind Nietzsche's criticism of Schopenhauer and Wagner. The acuteness of Nietzsche's pronouncements on "the German question" suggests the passion of his concern.

The word "passion" is key. For Mann it means not blind love, but love frustrated by doubt, a mixture of love and criticism. As scathing as Nietzsche is toward the Germans, nowhere in this polemic, Mann declares, can one find the asperity with which he speaks of other subjects: the English character, for example—English utilitarianism and English unmusicalness. (If Nietzsche also criticizes France, he is somewhat less cruel, for the French were only the soldiers, and the sacrifices, of English ideas.) The point is that Nietzsche's criticism of Germany is native and complex and has nothing in common with the moralizing of Entente democrats. The phenomenon of Nietzsche makes Germany interesting. Nietzsche educated the young Mann into a kind of "psychologically oriented patriotism," an intellectual love of the nation that inspires passionate criticism.

German self-criticism is special for its source and its goal. Nietzsche's own anti-Germanism arises within a highly developed "European" tradition to which Goethe, Schopenhauer, and Wagner belong. It was the "moral mood" of Schopenhauer and Wagner which attuned Mann to Nietzsche's moralism, his fundamentally German resistance to decadence. Mann notes: "I well remember the smile, or was it the laugh, which I had to suppress, when one day Parisian *literati*, whom I sounded out on Nietzsche, gave me to understand that basically he had been nothing more than a good reader of the French moralists and aphorists. If at least they had mentioned Pascal . . . ." (BU, p. 82). French blindness illuminates Nietzsche's essentially German character. "What could be more German than his contempt for the 'modern ideas,' 'the ideas of the eighteenth century'. . . , [more German] than 'that deep disgust' with which the German spirit itself rose up against the English-French world of ideas. . . . One sees how well Nietzsche understood Dostoevsky on the *recalcitrant* role of the German character in European intellectual history. . . . [That] 'deep disgust'. . . . There it is, the origin of this war, the German war against Western 'civilization'!" (BU, p. 83). Mann legitimizes the First World War on grounds provided by Nietzsche.

Nietzsche is arch-German in the degree to which he opposed the radicalism of the Western democracies. Or to put the matter positively: Germany, because of its anti-radicalism and its "unliterariness," emerges as the "people of life." "The *concept of life*—it is this most German, most Goethean, and in the highest religious sense conservative idea that Nietzsche imbued with new feeling, clothed in a new beauty, force, and sacred innocence, elevated to the highest rank and brought to spiritual dominance" (BU, p. 84). Nietzsche's critique of decadence always speaks in the name of this ideal. This moment seems to Mann— for one moment—to be a unique origin; for until Nietzsche, the bold temper of modern criticism had been inspired only by aestheticism. Nietzsche is the first to put moral ideals, indeed truth itself, into question by asking the value of truth for life.

"Or did he perhaps only give beauty a new . . . name—that of life? And was, then, his rebellion against morality more the rebellion of an artist . . . than of a genuinely philosophical spirit?" (BU, p. 84). This surmise makes Nietzsche a good deal more accessible to Mann and prompts him to ask, rightly, whether Nietzsche could not then serve the great writer "as the source of a loftiest, erotically most cunning *irony* playing between life and mind?" (BU, p. 84). If, on the other hand, Nietzsche's criticism is finally aesthetic in its inspiration, it cannot function as a critical idea. It may serve as a trope for the philosophical artist who comes after him, but it allows for, indeed sooner or later cries out for, moral use—for the correction of ethics and the uncovering of more life. As a moral artist, Mann may therefore rewrite Nietzsche's irony, all the while being conscious of his debt to him for the value finally at stake—"the idea of life . . .—an anti-radical, anti-nihilistic, anti-literary, a most conservative, a German idea . . . and yet . . ." (BU, pp. 84–85).

There still remains the important distinction between Nietzsche's doctrine and the way in which he taught it. For if his doctrine is German, his style is not. Nietzsche's language is that of the European intellectual, the type of the worldly prose writer, the feuilletonist whom, precisely, France and England excel at producing. His all-probing, all-dissolving style taught the whole of Europe, Germany included, how to write, how to criticize, how to be radical. Nietzsche's paradoxical importance for Germany has turned not on his producing the new man of whom he spoke but the new man who would speak like him. "He influenced the intellectual life of Germany . . . at least, at the very least, as strongly as a prose-writer working in the European mold as through his 'militarism' and his philosophical idea of 'power'; and his 'progressive,' civilizing effect consists in an enormous strengthening, encouraging, and sharpening of the institution of the writer (*Schriftstellertum*), of the literary critical spirit, and of radicalism in Germany" (BU, p. 87). Nietzsche's style cultivates an attitude of emulation of the dubious progressive spirit of the Entente. His example could not, should not, inspire German writing even if it explains Mann's own captivation by the civilized style.

This first essay on Nietzsche is full of unwitting paradoxes. Mann defines Nietzsche's arch-Germanness by the force of his attack on the German character, but this character Mann defines also as "an extremely peculiar *European* element provoking passionate criticism" (BU, p. 78; italics mine). Nietzsche's attack proceeds in the name of the ideal

of life—whence his educative effect. But his main educative effect occurs through the medium of his style, which has heightened the presence of a life-eroding European element in Germany. This mutual resorption of opposites recurs. Mann opposes the term of life to mind, to
radicalism, and to truth, and each of these latter terms to one another.
Music is opposed to the critical spirit, yet is an element of Nietzsche's
feuilleton style.

What Mann assimilates of Nietzsche's irony at this point in
his development is a restless narrative manner, more disturbed than his
source. His reading of Nietzsche occurs as an unsteady appropriation of
his model, an irritated mimesis, not a "style" and not a "criticism of
culture" (see p. 132).

Mann's second Nietzsche essay, "Nietzsche and Music" (*Vorspruch zu einer musikalischen Nietzsche-Feier*), 1924, was delivered as a preface
to a musical evening honoring Nietzsche. The German title of this piece
offers an immediately instructive contrast with the conclusion of the
preface to *Reflections of a Nonpolitical Man*. That preface was called at its
end a musical prelude (*Vorspiel*) to a work in prose (*Dichtung*) and centered on Mann's debt to Nietzsche. The text before us now is a rhetorical preface (*Vorspruch*) to a musical occasion celebrating Nietzsche, and
we will see that it reformulates that debt entirely. We are witnessing
something like the progressive musicalization of Nietzsche, a continually intensified association of the figure of Nietzsche with ideas about
music, quite apart from Nietzsche's actual relation to music.

The key importance of this new essay is that it postdates
Mann's political and moral turn to the cause of the German republic.
And if, as he would later write, "philosophy is no cold abstraction but
experience, suffering and sacrificial deed for humanity,"[23] then Mann,
who suffered for his republican views, has the right to be taken as the
more accurate philosopher. When he now calls Nietzsche an "educative
spirit,"[24] he no longer repeats the paradox of the *Reflections*. There education meant simultaneously education away from Europe and unwittingly toward it. Here education means one thing only—the intentional
turn toward Europe, the willed German overcoming of the German past.

The decision to honor Nietzsche with music and not with
speeches is therefore crucial. To do so "is to acknowledge what he means
to us today—in what sense, precisely now, in this moment [of destiny]
for Germany and Europe, we feel him to be our moral master" (NM, p.
140). It is in Nietzsche's relation to German music that Mann's audience

must find a moral example. For Nietzsche abandoned German music, though not lightheartedly, since he loved music as no one else; indeed "his language is itself music" (NM, p. 142).

If we recall Mann's covert sense of music in the *Reflections* as the dying fall of irony into un-self-conscious life, then Nietzsche's renunciation of a music with which he fully identified his style should indeed suggest Nietzsche's decision to renounce aestheticism and the seductions of Dionysus in his earliest work (written under the spell of Wagner) for the gay science of mind, for irony, and for an open future.

The identification of style and music would further suggest that everything realized in Nietzsche under the head of life is finally an effect of style, of rhetoric—the music of Nietzsche's language.

Of course Nietzsche also saw the future as the necessity of a renascence: a moral hermeneutic is irresistible. Even here, however, the life for which Nietzsche hoped can hardly be linked to the life which, for Mann, irony courts—unintellectual, marked by a graceful absence of thought. Nietzsche's renunciation of music would have to mean, surely, a renunciation of any conception of life not flooded by will and intelligence. And if, for Nietzsche, irony is par excellence (as in Socrates) the trope of intelligence, then Nietzsche's renunciation of music implies a renunciation of a conception of music in the service of any life but the life of the mind.

This reading, however, appears to ask too much. Its first assumption is that Mann's (unconscious) sense of music from the *Reflections*, as the trajectory from irony to unself-consciousness, is indeed being carried over into this work. The second is that Mann is willing to register, indeed cultivate, Nietzsche's heterogenous irony. In fact a host of readings of Mann's essay comes into view, all of which suggest the opposite—Mann's suppression of the theme of irony. One implication is then the extent to which Mann's reading of Nietzsche in this text is imposed on him by Ernst Bertram's *Nietzsche: An Essay in Mythology* (*Nietzsche: Versuch einer Mythologie*), a work whose power Mann acknowledged.[25]

Mann's account of Nietzsche's renunciation of German music is without irony; it is rather a dialectic consisting of one step. Mann stresses that when, for the sake of the future, Nietzsche abandoned German music, he sacrificed something of immense personal value. In the *Reflections* too Mann had attributed a certain musicality to Nietzsche's language, but only as one among various qualities defining it as intellectual speech—the agile instrument of the European critical voice. To continue to conceive of Nietzsche's language in this way would make his repudiation of the German musical character an inevitable and possibly painless part of his development—*away* from the *Zeitgeist*. But to see Nietzsche's style, instead, as virtually fusing music and criticism is to conjure him as a martyr. In the *Reflections* Mann had cited Nietzsche's magnificent line from the second preface to *The Birth of Tragedy* about the soul of the author of that book: "Sie hätte *singen* sollen, diese 'neue Seele'—und nicht reden." ("It should have sung, this 'new soul'—and not spoken.") To be precise, Mann had cited the line in the transposition it undergoes in a poem on Nietzsche by Stefan George (BU, p. 85). Mann had then gone on to comment that George (and presumably Nietzsche) had missed the point. Nietzsche's voice was quintessentially one that never did sing. It spoke, in prose, and because it did, its effect had been deleterious—radical. Now, however, in 1924, "the phenomenon we know as Nietzsche reveals at the level of personal genius the peculiar affinity and inner unity of criticism and music" (NM, p. 142). A renunciation of music thus implies a fundamental change, a metamorphosis, and the passage into a wholly new discourse, an open future.

At this point, however, the "conservative" movement occurs with which we have already become familiar. Mann undertakes to mollify the most radical implications of a loss of this "inner unity." The unity is divided back into two; the terms of music and criticism are detached. The renunciation of music does not have to imply the renunciation of the critical spirit, the European spirit. The opposite is also true. The renunciation separates, profiles, and sharpens criticism and enables it to survive. "The ruling spirit" of Nietzsche is "strong," in fact, strongest, "in enlightenment" (NM, p. 142). Indeed what survives through him is not only criticism as such, the spirit of the modern European mind, but the entire logocentric discourse of which criticism is part. Nietzsche may be made the exponent of more than the familiar category of criticism. He can shore up the entire conservative metaphysical system of binary oppositions to which this category alludes. The change brought about in Nietzsche by his renunciation of music can therefore be assimilated to a "given existing piece"—the European intellectual status quo. The change is not a metamorphosis but a swing back to a binary possibility always at hand in his earlier work.

The spirit of criticism, writes Mann now, could never have been linked univocally to music; for this link is after all one of passion, and passion includes the crisis of doubt. Doubt about what? Nietzsche's doubt about music arose from his identifying music with the romantic spirit and his identifying the romantic spirit with Germany. His fate would be always to oppose this powerful complex.

In Nietzsche's case, to oppose Germany meant to overcome himself, for, like Wagner, he too was a late-born son of German romanticism. "But Wagner was a mighty and fortunate self-realizing self-glorifier, whereas Nietzsche was a revolutionary bent on self-overcoming; thus Wagner, however glorious and infinitely fascinating, was the end of an epoch—whereas Nietzsche has become seer and leader into a new future for mankind" (NM, pp. 143–144). The crux of Nietzsche's renunciation of music is his self-overcoming, the renunciation of his person. For what? For *criticism*—truly?

In the *Reflections* Nietzsche was seen as attacking German philistinism in an intellectual style which ushers in a future itself philistine. Here, Nietzsche renounces the priority of music—the musical character of his language and the musical character of his person—to become, by virtue of his sacrifice, the prophet of the new Europe. "For the romantic is the song of nostalgia for the past—it is the beguiling song of death; and the phenomenon of Richard Wagner, which Nietzsche so dearly loved and which his ruling spirit had to overcome, was no other than the paradoxical and eternally interesting phenomenon of the world-conquering obsession with death" (NM, p. 144). And he who "conquers death"? Such a figure requires the allegory of religious language.

Mann calls Nietzsche "the truest son [of romanticism] . . . who, for us all, in his self-overcoming, consumed his life and died—on his lips the new word which as yet he barely knew how to speak, which we too as yet barely know how to stammer, the prophetic word of friendship with life and the future"(NM, p. 145). He did betray Wagner, he became a Judas; but because he did so, "today everything that believes in the future swears by his name, and he has become the evangelist of a new covenant between man and the earth" (NM, p. 145).

Mann finds religious-allegorical support in the figure of a dying-into-life for the dream of a rewarding renunciation, for a collapse of value ultimately painless, since it will somehow issue into greater value. In the prelude to the *Reflections* the collapse of Mann's own rigorous irony into personality and polemic was tempered as "music," as an accession to "life." This reassuring model was obtained by an identification with Nietzschean irony but also by a diminishing of the force of that "gift": Nietzsche's irony comes out on the side of un-self-conscious life.

In the essay of 1924 Mann resolves his intellectual exigencies with another gift from Nietzsche, another aspect of the Nietzschean myth. In reading passionately and sympathetically Nietzsche's renunciation of music, Mann perceives the implications of this renunication— the loss of personality, of selfhood, of life as that necessary evasion of irony that would somehow be charming. What survives this renunciation can only be a certain ironical and critical intelligence, hardly able "to put itself into the service of the social desideratum, the ideals." But Mann cannot finally bear it this way. The critical factor that survives must be swiftly masked in religious allegory, whence it figures as the spirit of "friendship with life." The strict allegorical meaning of this new covenant is European republicanism: Mann finds a way of keeping himself intact as a disciple of Nietzsche at the same time that he sustains his new democratic position, and he subsumes both terms under a religious allegory. If in the first book the religion of conservatism appears as music, in the second essay the renunciation of music appears as religion.

Thus Mann keeps reinterpreting his source to foreclose irony; for irony inhibits action, destroys the political body. We must beware, however, of implying that it is simply Mann's practical life, his need for self-justification at the order of public life, that inspires his use of intellectual history. The line that links his life and his art is less direct. In a letter to Ernst Fischer (May 25, 1926), Mann notes that Nietzsche's transcendence of romanticism is a constitutive feature of his *own* work, indeed the guarantor of its merit. "There is another element that links me with modernity and alone gives my work some validity on the intellectual plane: my experience with romanticism's self-transcendence in Nietzsche. What you feel to be fascinating . . . in my works is a distortion by the critical spirit of fundamental instincts: namely, irony" (L, p. 152). In the *Reflections*, we recall, Mann was shown suffering the loss of foundation, experiencing the conditions of the production of irony, and perceiving too that Nietzsche's great gift to such a writer would be this irony. He asserted these truths explicitly, but implicitly distorted Nietzsche's irony to make it generate, musically, the value of happy unself-conscious life.

In the essay of 1924 Mann came to Nietzsche after undergoing a painful political reversal. There he asserted Nietzsche's great gift to be the example of his renunciation of music. However, he does not make this renunciation generate the value which, on the basis of his explicit argument, it should, namely, the critical spirit, the "distortion of instincts," irony. This value remains implicit. Mann concludes explicitly on behalf of "a friendship with life"—with personality, polemic, and the democratic pathos of European republicanism.

Now, finally, in 1926, Nietzsche's renunciation of Romantic music is turned around once again explicitly to inspire—the spirit of irony!

It thus appears that Mann *systematically* misunderstands Nietzsche. His work is ruled by the peculiar irony of the orderly mutation of implicit into explicit over time: the diachrony of blindness and insight. For the moment I shall only indicate the problem, meanwhile compounding it by noting that where the Nietzsche text requiring interpretation is a fiction, as the novel *Doctor Faustus* to follow, the process of

comprehension is delayed by still one later stage. The distinction between implicit and explicit truth in the novel emerges only in those subsequent works of interpretation which are the novel's paraphrase.

Certainly one conclusion, however, which this preparatory
analysis allows us to reach is the impossibility of establishing the priority in which "texts" stand in Mann's personal and artistic cosmos. No
single factor governs essentially—neither his understanding of tradition,
his novelistic practice, nor his moral and political life. His own reluctance to assign a priority comes through plainly enough in his allusion
to Nietzsche in A *Sketch of my Life* (1930, 1960). Here Mann recalls the
"great and decisive" experience of reading Nietzsche and Schopenhauer,
but notes too that such experiences, if they are to be formative, presuppose a nature capable of being thus formed; and he will not undertake
"to investigate . . . what sort of modification, what sort of transmutation the art and ethos of Nietzsche suffered in [my] case."[26] We may see
here the resurgence of the Rousseauistic confessional moment of the
preface to the *Reflections*: in a matter calling for interpretation as delicate
as this, "Reader, judge me!" We may wonder whether such a move is
not made in bad faith too since the author in other places has no hesitation in offering interpretations at least potentially self-justificatory. Is
it that the "transmutation" which Nietzsche suffered "in his case" was
all too deliberately intended to be self-serving? Mann then goes on to
remark the historicity of his experience of Nietzsche, distributed in various phases over a number of years. We must ask a little further about
the rule of this transformation.

How shall we read the script between the lines? In *Reflections*
we have a Nietzsche fragmented into several Nietzsches: first, the cult
philosopher of life-in-a-self-glorifying vein, life as beauty and force; second, the exoteric philosopher of life who, according to Mann, recom-
mends irony, "healthy irony," on behalf of an assimilation of normality;
third, the arch-example of "literature," the advocate, however unwitting,
of pan-European literacy. In sum we have a torn Nietzsche whose future
is indeterminable. In 1924, in "Nietzsche and Music," we have a unified
Nietzsche, Nietzsche unified by a decisive act of renunciation: he renounced music on behalf of life, a European future.[27] The new Nietzsche
surrenders a musical mood of totality for the culture of logic and friendship; he turns away from his native North and East to the South and
West; or, as Mann accents the turn for his own position, he turns to
Europe, to the German Republic. What is the meaning of the line which
differentiates the two positions?

The line cannot be an increasing approximation to Nietzsche's case. One needs to know very little about Nietzsche to recognize the aberration in Mann's first position. The split which Mann defines between Nietzsche's aesthetically organized life and another sort of life—natively graceful and well-constituted—is an enfeebling distortion; it reproduces the problematic of *Tonio Kröger* but not that of the *Genealogy of Morals*, where the key division is not between art and life but between slave morality and life. One sees too the aberration in Mann's second position, in his account of Nietzsche's alleged renunciation of music. It takes only a glance into *The Case of Wagner* to note that Nietzsche did not renounce music but renounced Wagner on behalf of a music which Bizet suggested, a music full of *limpidézza*. Nietzsche dreamed of Socrates and music.

The line is not therefore a greater approximation to the case of Nietzsche. Is the line produced by the principle which Mann perhaps annexed—the loftiest, most erotic, and slyest irony? Do the two readings stand in this sort of ironical relation? An answer here will depend on how we understand such irony. One could proceed by using the distinction which Mann himself introduces in his final essay on Nietzsche, "Nietzsche's Philosophy in the Light of Contemporary Events," when he speaks of Zarathustra as "this faceless and formless monster . . . , with the rose crown of laughter on his unrecognizable head . . . ; Zarathustra . . . is not a creation, he is rhetorical, impassioned linguistic wit." This, for Mann, disfigured being (*Unfigur*) is a figure of speech and not the representation of a self.[28]

Such rhetoric is ironical in the sense that it functions not only as language but also as "passion," and hence as "creation"; it functions as a linguistic figure in suspending the referential illusion it accomplishes. A language governed by this double intention might introduce doubt into the degree of control exercised by the subject behind it. As Barthes writes, "When the writer is working with an irony impregnated with uncertainty . . . , *one never knows* if there is a subject behind his language."[29] De Man makes this point directly: "Irony . . . puts the notion of the self in question: irony is a purely linguistic trope; in Nietzsche we are dealing with a radically ironic rhetorical mode."[30] This formulation is useful in constituting an extreme position, which does not, however, describe Mann's relation to his own texts on Nietzsche nor, we might recall, Nietzsche's relation to his own texts either.

De Man is right about Nietzsche only if the phrase "to put the self in question" is taken in the literal sense developed in the previous chapter. To put the self in question is not to dissolve it but precisely to intensify its character as an openness to being. Irony is the constitutive character of a self mirroring, in interminable interpretive activity, its native openness; irony puts this questioning into practice. Indeed Nietzsche defines noble morality as "faith in oneself, pride in oneself, a fundamental hostility and *irony against 'selflessness'*" (BW, p. 395; italics mine). Therefore the self in Nietzsche cannot be reduced to a rhetorical mode of being.

And of course Mann never thought it could be, although his description in the *Reflections* of a crisis in Being and the artistic mode (shaped by his consciousness of Nietzsche) leads to a position on absolute irony, free play, pure rhetoric, and the illusory subject congruent with views of Barthes, de Man, and Derrida. And certainly it can be argued that to imply the irony of Nietzsche's rhetorical suspension of reference—one perhaps suggesting the "death of the author"—is a good deal more daringly incisive than to seize on Nietzsche's irony as the life artistry of a substantial ego. The point seems clear, however, that in reading Mann on Nietzsche, we are dealing not with a self-consciously "radical ironic rhetorical mode" but rather with something closer to *skepticism*, which is the attitude of a subject. And Mann's uses of Nietzsche, as well as his apparent imperviousness to the anxiety of influence, could stem from his reluctance (or inability) to take Nietzsche or his philosophical sources seriously, to open his language to their truth. This surmise is not meant to be harsh: it responds to Mann's own (amazing) admission: "I took nothing literally from Nietzsche; I believed him hardly at all."[31]

In the polemical work *Die Welt ohne Transzendenz*, Hans Egon Holthusen identifies Mann as "skeptical, without convictions, ambivalent" and asks, "Where in Mann's world—this world without feeling, without a genuine conception of truth, without transcendence, without yes and no—where is the archimedean point?" He answers: "It lies in the person of the writer himself. It lies at the place where he happens to be standing, the place which—through [the exigencies of] the writer's existence—he himself represents (*die Stelle, die er selbst darstellt*)."[32] And language in the service of personal representation is not ironical.

Now the point is not that one is able to assert a plain superiority of irony, which is consistent with philosophy, over self-representation, the self-love in Mann's formulation "loving irony." Nothing stands in the way of inverting Holthusen's priorities and declaring that in a world indeed genuinely without a conception of truth, without transcendence, without an archimedean point, Mann shapes and occupies, a half century before structuralism, a position of fearless lucidity: he perceives that his work originates only with the arbitrary act of "taking himself seriously" or, in Holthusen's geometric code, with his assigning himself, through the exigencies of the writer's career, his place and his position, in an act of self-representation. Mann did write after all that "the artist's nature consists not in judging or pointing directions but in being, doing, expressing states of mind: only in doing this is he *significant*."[33] "What is a poet? He whose life is symbolic."[34]

Mann's different readings of Nietzsche—in 1918 of Nietzsche fragmented; in 1924 of Nietzsche unified by an act of renunciation—are significant doublings of Mann's own state of mind. The point as it applies to the second reading of Nietzsche admits of absolute proof. Shortly after writing this speech, he wrote a letter to the conservative composer Hans Pfitzer. Here Mann repeats word for word the language with which he distinguishes the self-consummator Wagner from the self-conquerer Nietzsche. And in what context? To create a perspective in which Pfitzner, the latter-day Romantic composer, can grasp that posterity will not support his case against the alleged Judas, *the republican Thomas Mann* (L, p. 145).

Despite this argument *for* skepticism, one is inclined to resist interpretation which is personal representation and turn away from the reader who interprets only in order to affirm himself. One asks from Mann that in identifying Nietzsche's irony and even in appropriating it that he preserve its character: that he relinquish his self-interest for a language of faithful interpretation. But has this demand any basis? In a contribution to this problem, apropos of the question of the subject, Eugenio Donato showed that the momentary fixing of a text in the act of interpretation is dependent always on reestablishing that very subject whose disruption provoked the interpretation. He quoted Foucault: "Interpretation will henceforth always be an interpretation by the 'who.' One does not interpret that which is in a signified but in the last analysis the one 'who' has laid down the interpretation. The principle of interpretation is nothing but the interpreter himself."[35] But this place which fuses interpreter and subject is not a place where we can rest either; even this highly advanced formulation of Foucault's recovers as single the category of the subject—the subject of "the interpreter himself." What is the meaning of "the interpreter himself"? Certainly this is not one thing, or it is one thing only at a level of obscure simplicity before it is itself interpreted.

It seems to me that an interpreter comes into being only through an act of reading that achieves the recognition of the difference between text and self-interest. This difference itself derives from what Derrida calls the difference between the two interpretations of interpretation. (The distinction does not of course begin with Derrida. Benjamin's *The Origin of German Tragic Drama* might function as an equally strong modern occasion.)[36] The difference is in the stance toward allegory and that toward symbol—between, on the one hand, the interminable, disinterested reading, by Benjamin's brooding *Grübler*, of the object without transcendental significance, which Benjamin calls allegory as script; and on the other hand, the appropriative, desymbolizing decipherment. But what Derrida says very well is that these two interpretations of interpretation are "absolutely irreconcilable . . . even if we live them simultaneously and reconcile them in an obscure economy. . . . These two interpretations must acknowledge and accentuate their difference and define their irreducibility. We must [moreover] try to conceive of the common ground and the 'difference' of this irreducible difference." [37]

This second order of intimacy and difference informing the difference between symbolic and allegorical reading would have to include what could be accounted an active will to concealment masking the difference existing at the first order. It would have to include the historical lag in the emergence for the subject (with any degree of clarity) of the first order of irreducible difference between these interpretive modes.

The difference is at hand, however, in a plain and unreduced form, whenever we make the distinction between truth and self-interest; whenever we ask, as Holthusen asks Mann, what advantage, what *parti pris*, is animating the position which he asserts through Nietzsche; and whenever we show the advantageousness to Mann's empirical person of his readings.

We come to the same point by asking the most cogent form of the question: what interest compels Mann to mask the difference for him between grasping Nietzsche's irony as pervasive, as informing even life with a play of perspectives and fictions punctuated by the will; and reading Nietzsche's irony, on the other hand, as the smiling self-betrayal of the ironic intelligence, whether from love for the German bourgeois or the search for personal integrity through renunciation? If Mann had annexed Nietzsche's irony in the spirit with which, according to Mann, it operates in *Zarathustra*—namely, as a linguistic figure—he could in principle have accepted the substitution of one of his positions for another, since no position has finality. The (life-)line connecting his texts on Nietzsche would then be the line of a certain irony, an intertextual figure. But we see that Mann, given his empirical interests at the time, could not have supported this substitution of positions, could not have read Nietzsche in 1918 as a Judas, or Nietzsche in 1924 as the source of the "conservative idea of life," or—we can now add—could he have *failed* to describe Nietzsche's later ideas as atrocities and drunken messages of power, violence, and cruelty while writing from California in 1946.

We are not requiring Mann to identify Nietzsche's irony, to

annex Nietzsche's irony and repeat it. We do not cry out, at the disappearance of the personal subject, "o beneficent loss!"[38] We do, however, insist of Mann that he not say he has suffered Nietzsche with a *loving irony*, for all the love in this phrase is the subject's love of (a) position.

Another way of describing Mann as a reader is to suggest that his imperviousness to the anxiety of influence is the function less of scathing insight, and defense, than of an intensely imagined security sheltering against contact with whatever might alienate him from his fated course. Hence it becomes misleading to describe Mann's obscurantist reading of Nietzsche after the Second World War as a reversal of his attitude toward Nietzsche just after the First World War. In fact his relation to Nietzsche always remains constant. Within this relation Mann never reads Nietzsche except to discover in him a rhetoric for affirming attractively his own position.[39] But there is another and more interesting sort of irony in this matter.

Each of Mann's essays opens with a premise which accurately reflects Nietzsche's predicament and Mann's own. In the course of the essay Mann draws a conclusion about Nietzsche inaccurate to the premise yet justifying the position which Mann wishfully adopts. What is ironical is that the conclusion which Mann draws in each of his subsequent essays on Nietzsche—invariably a retreat from the premise of *that* essay—is far more faithful to the premise of the preceding essay, is *its* logical conclusion.

Mann's "friendship with civilization" in 1924 and his polemical advocacy of an alliance with Anglo-French values could reasonably have proceeded from his rejection in 1918 of Nietzsche's groundless irony. Instead Mann chose to defend happy, graceful, unwitty life. Equally, Nietzsche's renunciation of music, which Mann addressed in 1924, could have led to an affirmation of the critical element of irony. Instead it led Mann to assert political sociability. This very value of irony, however, surfaces in the 1926 correspondence with Ernst Fischer. Finally, we could doubt the logic of Mann's justifying the war against Nazism in 1935 on the grounds of Nietzsche's romanticizing of evil. If Mann had to go to war with Germany, then he could have found his *casus belli* in the defense of the innocent, naive, charming life he recommended in 1918. The circle is full (see figure 2).

Mann finds in Nietzsche the wisdom explicitly accurate to his premise always contained in one later text. The argument that then explicitly appears is implicit in the preceding text. Each statement recurs in this double register. Hence, the reversal in the specific content of Mann's reading of Nietzsche from historical period to historical period has not only a diachronic but also a synchronic component: the later

	1918	1924	1926	1945
Year				
Text	*Reflections of a Nonpolitical Man*	"Preface to a Musical Evening Honoring Nietzsche"	Letter to Ernst Fischer	"Nietzsche's Philosophy in the Light of Contemporary Events"
Premise	World War I: a crisis of values, of foundation	Nietzsche's renunciation of Wagner's music	Nietzsche's renunciation of Wagner's music	World War II: Germany's mad adventure
Legitimate (logical) conclusion: implicit	1. Thoroughgoing irony 2. Civility, solidarity, friendship with the future	Irony, writing in the late Nietzschean manner	Nietzsche's hatred of Christianity; Nietzsche's histrionic martyrdom devoid of pedagogical responsibility	Nietzsche's hatred of German militarism, 1. anti-Semitism, 2. ressentiment 3.
Actual (ideological) conclusion: explicit	[Life]: happy, graceful, charming	Criticism, solidarity, friendship with the future	Irony, writing in the late Nietzschean manner	Nietzsche devoid of pedagogical responsibility

Figure 2

reading profiles as explicit what is already implicit in the previous reading.

Suppose now that the series of Mann's readings of Nietzsche is indeed generated by a principle of consecutive reversal, so that the position implicit in a reading is explicitly proclaimed in the very next reading. This description of the series leaves out another important principle: the explicit reading thus produced in each case fits Mann's practical interests in the historical reality that he perceives. This situation indeed underscores the "unity" of life and work of which Mann boasted in his letter to Hermann Weigand, an achievement which readers of Mann are inclined to regard with awe as an unparalleled feat of will, effort, and culture. But the curiously automatic character of the fit of Mann's misreading with the practical necessity for an ideological stance gives one pause.

Mann's readings are powerful readings, full of value for life because of their efficacious fit; however, the fit is produced by the automatic operation of a principle of reversal. It is one of the better ironies of this situation that Nietzsche who spoke unremittingly of the usefulness to life of lies (of misreadings and special perspectives) should be the occasion of this demonstration. Or should we conclude even more suspiciously?

We have seen Mann read Nietzsche four times, each time producing—from premises logically leading to a certain position—positions contrary to that logic, and then using these latter positions explicitly to justify a historical stance. First, he reads Nietzsche to justify the war against Europe; second, to justify friendship with Europe; next, to justify literary irony; finally, to justify support of the war against Germany. In each instance (after the first) the position arrived at would appear to be politically "correct," yet it is obtained by an application, to a historical situation, of the position suppressed in the preceding reading. What then for Mann is the status of the historical reality? Does it guide his conclusion, or is it not rather a fiction constructed to accommodate ideological writing already inscribed? Then the fit is only the inevitable fit of tautologies, of positions implicitly elaborated and now repeated in order to address an uncomprehended but reconstructed reality. Mann's survival and success within this vacuum would then be the result of luck, reputation, and a persistent will to imitate himself.

Indeed it may be this latter theme which is profiled and reflected in *Doctor Faustus*. What is enacted here in Zeitblom's friendship for Adrian Leverkühn is less the theme of Nietzsche than the theme of taking from Nietzsche without comprehension. If such taking seems like a genuine exchange—producing, for Zeitblom, thought and writing and intellectual survival—then there is an ironical lesson here about how to appropriate without blame: Cite one's source with reverence, read him wrong, read him wrong again, and make up the historical reality which the newer fiction will fit. But to see this as an act of "love," even part of a "loving irony," can hardly be called ironical. Mann wrote that he was not a great man but only stood on a playful footing with greatness. This shows that it is not only the genius who (as Rivarol wrote) "throttles the precursors whom he plunders."[40]

One practical result of this discussion would be a way of reading *Doctor Faustus* as a Nietzsche novel, namely, as a novel enacting and reflecting the successive modes of Mann's understanding of Nietzsche as they shape Mann's sense of his own fate. The various stages of Mann's relation to Nietzsche can be summarized as, first, the *Imitation* of a style— recall the Nietzschean tone of the *Reflections* of 1919; second, the *Identification* with a life—Mann's turn to Europe and the League of Nations in 1924; third, the *Repudiation* of the life and the style as an instruction in evil—Mann's essay on Nietzsche in the aftermath of World War II in 1945; and fourth, the *Commemoration*, a gesture of critical sympathy recalling the previous relations—the adventure of *Doctor Faustus*. These modes— Imitation, Identification, Repudiation, Commemoration—would also seem to constitute the general phases of a *Bildung* in its orientation toward the father figure. Thus, Nietzsche's style is imitated in Adrian Leverkühn's language, and his life is identified with in Leverkühn's biography. At the end of the novel Zeitblom repudiates Adrian following Zeitblom's pious commemoration of his friend. This analysis confirms that Nietzsche as the object of an intellectual and critical relation is second for Mann to Nietzsche as a figure inviting representation: "I took nothing literally [from Nietzsche]; I believed him hardly at all." Mann is a master of the *art* of reading Nietzsche.

CHAPTER FIVE

The Author Survives on the Margin of His Breaks: Kafka's Narrative Perspective

The interdependence of Mann's art and life and politics, a "small cosmos" in which each factor seeks and yields primacy, lends to Mann's work a certain aura of secular abundance. In Kafka's world (1883–1924) this abundance is severely reduced, as a function of the rigor with which art asserts its precedence. The critical reception given Kafka, shaped by the essays of Maurice Blanchot, has stressed the intensity and single-mindedness of Kafka's devotion to literature, indeed the degree to which he considered his being entirely literature, *Schriftstellersein*.[1] Kafka wrote to his fiancée that everything essential in him belonged to writing: "It is not that I am interested in literature, I am made up of literature. I am nothing else and can be nothing else."[2] This claim is more radical than even Hölderlin's unconscious claim about literature. Hölderlin means to survive as himself in his poetry. Kafka does not say he means to survive as himself in literature but that he *is* literature. Between his self and his writing there must be no margin of difference.

So extreme a statement, in being addressed to Felice Bauer, may be read as a device to have her lower her expectations. Yet in more meditative moments, in his notebooks and diaries, when Kafka had nothing to gain by exaggerating the claim, he insisted that he was only literature.

If Kafka, the man, embodies literature, if, indeed literature inscribes Kafka, then it would seem, in a strict sense, that no such thing as Kafka's self exists. If the self were indeed nothing else than literature, there could be no way of distinguishing it from what, for the writer, is his outlying source, goal, or adversary, namely—literature. There would be no subject tenuously dominant over a body of texts.

Surely the quest for Kafka's self is especially badly served by Kafka's fiction, and no reader would persist in looking for it there were it not for his desperation. Kafka's unyielding narrators offer faceless protagonists in unplaceable locales, speaking a rhetoric that baffles understanding. No Kafkan self survives, it seems, either outside Kafka's texts or within them—not even a self stripped of its substantial properties and described, à la Lacan, as a locus of functions and relations, or described by Paul de Man as "the center [which in a text] produces the affirmation," if even one so negatively ironical as "the insignificance of the human subject."[3] No diagram of the authorial self can be drawn *in* Kafka's works, and there appears to be no structure or even inventory of intentions, other than the will to write, outside his texts to which one could refer in order to clarify obscurities inside them. The phenomenon of Kafka appears to illustrate par excellence "the death of the Author." This phrase is the title of a striking essay by Roland Barthes.[4] But how accurately in fact does it fit the case of Kafka?

To get a good grip on Barthes' essay one must keep in mind the notorious difficulty, in Kafka's novels, of locating an authorial voice explicitly designing and evaluating the action. Barthes' first point therefore seems correct. "[Writing] is the destruction of every voice, of every point of origin (*de toute voix, de toute origine*)." Writing is this destruction—or else it is the invention of an uncanny voice in which various voices without a specific origin mix indistinguishably. "Writing is that neutral, composite, oblique space where our subject slips away, the negative where all identity is lost, starting with the very identity of the body writing."[5]

No author survives outside this space to lament his own extinction—when even to be a lament in the mouth of the lover is splendid. "The modern scriptor is born simultaneously with the text, is in no way equipped with a being preceding or exceeding the writing. . . . The hand, cut off from any voice, borne by a pure gesture of inscription (and not of expression), traces a field without origin—or which, at least, has no other origin than language itself, language which ceaselessly calls into question all origins."[6]

The birth of the *scriptor*, of that writer "born simultaneously with the text," entails the death of the author. The scriptor does not strive to speak: he is out of earshot of every voice. If the goal of interpretation had ever been to catch the inflections of the *voice* of the author, that goal would now be intrusive, even obscene.[7] The scriptor *writes*. "Linguistically, the author is never anything more than the instance writing, just as I is nothing other than the instance saying I: language knows a 'subject' not a 'person'; and this subject, empty outside of the very enunciation which defines it, suffices to make language 'hold together' ['work': *'tenir'*], that is to say, to exhaust it [language]."[8] The scriptor is the sum of purely grammatical subjects (stripped of personal properties) which makes language "work"—to the point of exhaustion.

This is not of course a very vital picture, etiolated to a degree, especially if one comes to Kafka from Dilthey and Nietzsche. We have on the one side, the death of the Author, and on the other, language worked to exhaustion. Rhetoric of this kind, within the discourse on poetics, marks the temper of modernism. How well, however, does Barthes' analysis of "the modern scriptor" actually answer to the case of Kafka's *Schriftstellersein*? In fact, Kafka's account of the writing self is more complicated.

Here is a key passage from Kafka's diary:

> I have never understood how it is possible for almost anyone who writes to objectify his sufferings in the very midst of suffering them; thus I, for example, in the midst of my unhappiness—my head, say, still on fire with unhappiness—sit down and write to someone: I am unhappy. Yes, I can even go beyond that and with the various flourishes I might have talent for, all of which seem to have nothing to do with my unhappiness, ring simple, or contrapuntal or a whole orchestration of changes on my theme. And it is not a lie, and it does not still my pain, it is simply a merciful surplus of strength (*Überschuß der Kräfte*) at a moment when suffering has raked me to the bottom of my being and plainly exhausted all my strength. But then what kind of strength is it?[9]

The point of exhaustion here is not the hypothetical end state of a play of language but the extremity of the suffering author.

This passage is a tour de force, a marvel of compression, packing together the leading aesthetic positions of the last hundred years. The first position involves the "deep" experiences of the writer, which the literary act, it is said, aims to objectify and communicate. It is the position associated (often in too simple a form) with Dilthey.[10] This position is equal to some of the facts of Kafka's case, since Kafka, suffering, can after all "write to someone: I am unhappy." Nonetheless, as he says, its mechanism is by no means clear. "I have never understood," he writes, "how it is possible." The position is completely untrue, however, if it is understood in the ordinary way as promising cure. There is in this "objectification" no therapeutic effect, even if the effect is expected along lines put as tactfully as the following: "The act of verbalization makes possible critical appraisal. If one can talk about an emotion, one is, at least at that moment, no longer possessed by it."[11] But what does "possession" mean? For Kafka it is produced precisely whenever there is talk, since ordinary language speaks of property and possession. "Corresponding as it does to the world of appearances, it is concerned only with property and its relations."[12] "Verbalization," "objectification," does not expropriate possession, "does not," says Kafka, "still my pain"—which is precisely the pain of being possessed.

Kafka identifies a second position on the way to surpassing it: it is the aesthetic position par excellence, and it does share features of Barthes' mortuary view of the Author. Kafka explains: On the simple communicatively oriented sentence "I am unhappy," he is able to ring a whole orchestration of plain and contrapuntal changes. These flourishes are "not lies"; they appear to be the product of a demystified literary awareness, since Kafka perceives that "they have nothing to do with [his] unhappiness." Undoubtedly they are beautiful: as part of an aesthetic theory, these flourishes answer to the case. And yet if they are not examined as to their source, they are, in one important way, empty, for "they do not still my pain." And they add nothing in the way of an answer to the question they provoke: what kind of merciful surplus of strength gives rise to them? What is this strength?

Almost the same phrase as Kafka's appears in a key passage in Nietzsche's *Ecce Homo* to describe his state of mind while composing *The Birth of Tragedy*. There he wrote, "A surplus of strength (*ein Überschuß von Kraft*)" is a condition of that courage required to comprehend a fundamental truth. "This ultimate, most joyous, most wantonly extravagant Yes to life represents not only the highest insight but also the *deepest*. . . . Nothing in existence may be subtracted, nothing is indispensable— those aspects of existence which Christians and other nihilists repudiate are actually on an infinitely higher level in the order of rank among values than that which the instinct of decadence could approve and call good" (BW, p. 728). For Nietzsche a surplus of strength inspires with sympathetic joy the act of understanding the joyous affirmation of life as the deepest insight. For Kafka a surplus of strength inspires the production of fictions (of "flourishes"), taking their career apart from life and unable to modulate his *Grundstimmung*, his unhappiness. This moment is one of Kafka's fundamental deafness to a Nietzschean strain of fin-de-siècle aesthetic vitalism.

Kafka's text forces the conclusion that his *writing* is the response to the unanswered, perhaps unanswerable question of the nature of his surplus, his excess. He points to a "modern" aesthetic. How well does Barthes' surmise respond to it?

There would be more than one problem in coming to terms with this diary passage through the perspective of "the death of the Author." The question again is, Does the act of writing, as performed especially by a modern writer of advanced literary awareness, mean anything more than "the instance writing"? Or does Kafka's pen, in tracing the word "I," produce only the graphic trace of the scriptor and refer only to a grammatical subject?

Kafka says exactly the opposite. He says that when he writes "I" in the sentence "I am unhappy," the I to which he refers is not the instance writing—the scriptor—but the man who suffers. Furthermore, the act of writing the sentence "I am unhappy" immediately generates another agent of the self—the "ringer of changes." This second self arises in "exceeding" a simpler mode of the I, which had failed to cure itself in the simple sentence "I am unhappy." The new agent, the ringer of changes, exhibits attributes of selfhood such as centrality, articulateness, and generativity. As a center, it sustains and varies the theme of suffering, and generates a work of art. We could call this second mode of the self a surplus-subject. Unlike the empirical subject constituted by Thomas Mann's irony, Kafka's subject is a poetic self.

The surplus-subject surpasses the scriptor-subject, since (citing Barthes) the scriptor-subject is "empty outside of the very enunciation which defines it," whereas for Kafka the surplus-subject is *more* than any enunciation which would define it. This subject is precisely, therefore, inexhaustible. It is inexhaustible in the very sense that we see surplus *enacted* in this passage. The surplus is not in suffering, nor is it in the objectification of this suffering in the sentence "I am unhappy." It is not in the flourishes which can be rung on this theme, nor is it quite in the strength with which these changes are rung. It exceeds even the strength with which the strengthened self turns upon itself to ask, "But then what kind of strength is it?" This sentence asks about an origin but does not in asking erase the origin, for the sentence originates "in the midst of" the suffering of the man who suffers, in the *man* who is its *author*.

The word "man" of course will sound odd in the recent discourse which has seen man too fall into disfavor if not indeed into disuse. "It is a source of profound relief," writes Foucault, "to think that man is only a recent invention, a figure not yet two centuries old, a new fold in our knowledge, and that he will disappear again as soon as that knowledge has discovered a new form." [13] Without lending support to this desideratum, Manfred Frank has suggested the word "Subjektivität" as an encyclopaedic word—at once including and surpassing self—for the phenomena and functions which Kafka designates with "I" and "suffering" and "surplus" and "my being." This word, by dint of its long history of uses in German Idealism, by Hegel and Schelling especially, and then by Kierkegaard, can have dimensions of intellectuality and irony missing from the English translation. A fair English translation of "Subjektivität" might be "the inner life of the mind." But this phrase is bulky and archaic.

Julia Kristeva favors the self-word "subject." "Far from being an epistemological perversion," she writes, "a certain subject is present from the moment that there is the consciousness of a meaning." [14] Her term of course is "a certain subject"—plain "subject" is too unguarded. But even if "a certain subject" is admissible, its full expansion into "une certaine subjectivité" would be felt today, certainly in France, as very naive.

In finally deciding to call the entire field of individual and superindividual elements of Kafka's writing about the self "man," I adopt a solution resembling the one hit upon by Kenneth Burke. He recalls, in a similar case, the difficulty of finding an adequate term to translate into English the German word *Geist*.

> Once, when I was translating a German biography, I found the word particularly bothersome. We were told that the character's *Geist* did this, the character's *Geist* did that, the character's *Geist* did the other, and so on. Did his spirit do it? Did his mind do it? Did his wit do it, or his essence, or disposition, or demon? I tried all sorts of synonyms, and none seemed quite natural in English. Then of a sudden, a breakthrough; whereupon, lo! I translated simply: "He did it." [15]

Kafka of course makes Burke's questions problematic when he asks, "But what kind of strength is [this merciful surplus]"? For this question aims at something general, even if it is asked by a suffering man: this would seem to be, for Kafka, the literary situation par excellence. The question which the writer asks is not exhaustible, because the answer it produces is never more than figurative. Elsewhere, when Kafka is carried away by the surplus, by *Schriftstellersein*, he will couch his answer in the language of another text, in Faustian language: "Writing is the reward," he writes, "for service to the devil." [16] In this way—figuratively, allusively—is literature made from suffering. Writing heightens inexhaustibly, but does not still, the pain. "Art for the artist," said Kafka, "is only suffering, through which he releases himself for further suffering." [17]

Yet literature is not alone "the negative where all identity is lost." The "modern scriptor" (if Kafka may speak for him) is supplied precisely "with a being who precedes and exceeds the writing." That being which precedes his writing is suffering; the being which exceeds his writing is the surplus—a strength whose relation to suffering is the question which literature asks. Writing is not only "the oblique space where our subject slips away." It generates, at the cut it makes, a second oblique space, in which an excessive subject raises the question, What kind of surplus is this? This space bears traces of another self or selves, capable of objectifying or enlarging but not of destroying the truth of what that first oblique asserts: "A man is unhappy."

One important feature of Kafka's critique of Barthes (or of Kafka's own view, when he wrote to Felice Bauer) is that it denies the implication of fusion. It denies that the writer's self, even as an "instance," could vanish into the inscription, be identical with the inscription. The inscription, in Kafka, gives rise to a second "text," which raises the question of the nature of these texts' "working." Both texts return to a self raked by the tension between its poverty and its excess—a self that then gives voice to its suffering by raising the question of the excess which comes to disrupt and to heighten it, a self that situates the excess by asking the question of the suffering "in whose midst" this excess originates.

Kafka provides a nice metaphor to describe this state of affairs in his description of a "real" book: "It must be the axe for the frozen sea in us."[18] One could consider the act of writing (which determines the act of reading) as the stroke of an axe which aims to be decisively liberating and would cut the knot of personality. This view is consistent with Barthes'. But an axe is a blade with two faces that do not fuse. The cutting edge is not a line of one dimension but the infinitesimal difference between two margins. Where it strikes, when it strikes deeply enough, it leaves the impression of two faces. One face of the wedge inscribes the suffering in which the author, says Barthes, could lose himself. But the other, oblique to the oblique space of the first, is the margin of an exorbitant force querying its own nature. Those two inscriptions are separated by the space where they cannot meet—by the *man* who is its author.

Elsewhere Kafka also describes the work of art: "Our art is a way of being dazzled by truth; the light on the flinching grimacing face is true, and nothing else."[19] This imagery of being struck and flinching may do for the first, Barthes' oblique, with its imagery of the flight of identity, the hand that is borne along, and the pure graphemic grimace or trope. But the second oblique, in the fable of the axe, evokes a precisely opposite imagery—of the amazing stroke of the merciful strength of the surplus, and of striking, not flinching back, to advance upon this strength to raise the daring question, What kind of strength is it?

We have, now, a certain perspective on the act of writing in Kafka: it always generates a second, an excessive text oblique to the first. This second text refers back to the negativity (suffering) which precedes the act of writing. With this picture we may be able to advance a little into another question, one which may seem at first, in its pedantic simplicity, remote from the issue at hand and even trivial, but which I do not think is trivial. This is the question of flaws in Kafka's narrative perspective. The problem is one of the kinds and meaning of the "breaks" we find there.

Anthony Wilden, the American interpreter of Lacan, devotes a section of his commentary to the subject of shifters. Shifters include all those elements of a linguistic code—e.g., adverbs of time and place, like "here," "now," and certain tense-indicators of verbs—which do not have general or stable referents and so refer necessarily to the context of the message and hence, finally, to the sender. Words functioning as shifters also include personal pronouns, like Barthes' word "I." This is the "I" which, in Barthes' case, is "nothing more for the scriptor than the instance writing 'I,' " but which for Kafka is that suffering man who feels a surplus of strength.

In raising the question of shifters, Wilden aims to analyze literary narration, unlike Barthes in "The Death of the Author," who in a certain sense means to "neutralize" it. Wilden holds to the notion of a narrative voice within the fiction which, he suggests, has the status of a shifter. The reader is then required to locate "the speaking subject in any one of the various voices of a . . . literary text at any particular moment."[20] Who then is speaking? Is it "the author, the author's second self, the narrator, the questioner, the respondent, the omniscient or the restricted consciousness, the 'I,' the hero"?[21] Barthes stressed that all writing is itself this special voice, consisting of several indiscernible voices; Wilden stresses that they might be distinguished.

Who then speaks in Kafka—especially when we perceive breaks in Kafka's narrative perspective?

In the 30s and 40s the narrative dimension of the Kafkan message was ignored, eclipsed by more striking aspects: the torments of bureaucracy, the bloodthirstiness of family, the neurasthenia of the outcast self—in a word, Kafka's Expressionism. His readers were mainly interested in this confirmation of experience termed existential and even religious but basically political. It is likely, however, that the category of political alienation is not wide enough, being based on a privation of need and not of passion, to encompass Kafka's range and complexity.[22] A good deal of that range is inconspicuous at first; it is only implicated in the easily unnoticed narrative situation. In the beginning the narrative mode did not seem problematical.

It was assumed of Kafka's novels (and typically of the stories written between 1912 and 1914) that, by virtue of the third-person hero and the preterite tense, the subject matter was being narrated from an objective, authoritative standpoint. The text could be read as embodying the intention of the author whose privileged representative was the narrator, however inconspicuous. Consciousness in the novel (all perceiving and valuing) was then divided essentially between the narrator and the hero: the hero provided a deluded but cautionary example; the narrator was clear-sighted, holding up the character's blindness to our judgment.

Beißner's important work in 1952 developed the opposite notion of "singular perspective" (*Einsinnigkeit*).[23] Now, it appeared that the perspective of many of Kafka's works never exceeded that of the hero, was only as knowing and as ignorant as the hero, anchored in his place and time. As a result it became impossible to divide consciousness in the work between higher and lower, deluded and clear. Consciousness was uniform and rather opaque, attuned by the mood of his heroes— worried, captious, and evasive. Their consciousness tended to be repetitive and circular, their projects forever only duplicating obsessive ideas. This impression of truth evaded was one which it was impossible to dispell by an appeal to the narrator, there allegedly being none. Such an argument responds to, indeed itself produces, the critical reception of one aspect of Kafka's writing. In Walter Sokel's formulation, "Kafka's novels and late tales are parabolic formulations of existential questions," yet Kafka refuses to "go beyond the formulation of questions. Kafka's parables show that nothing can be shown. They convey . . . fragmentariness, indeterminacy, and ambiguity as last (not ultimate) meanings to be obtained."[24]

Beißner's narratological account of this situation entails what is nowadays called the undecidability of the work. From inside a figural consciousness that grasps the world immediately, not critically—for which the world is sheer evidence, givenness, just being-there—it is impossible to undertake a critique either of this consciousness or of the world. The reader can reject either one or both, but his judgment is then founded on feelings and beliefs which are not to be found in the novels.

Beißner's discovery helps to account for the narrative mood of neutrality, of hiddenness, in Kafka; but it is not a view of things which can now be stringently maintained. A number of close readers have charted moments in Kafka's fiction which break the perspective of unity and indeed even of "congruence," Martin Walser's revisionary term for Beißner's Einsinnigkeit.[25] Breaks exist between the planes of consciousness of narrator and figure, even in stories without evident authorial intrusion. Here, for example, is one such instance from The Metamorphosis. Gregor is described as struggling to turn the key of the lock in his room with his jaws, "in der Vorstellung, daß . . . ." ("under the impression [i.e., under the mere impression] that . . . [the family] were all following his efforts with suspense").[26] A state of affairs has already been conceived of as "merely an impression." But if the perspective of the story is indeed that of immediacy, the fiction that of naïveté, it is not possible to evaluate a state of affairs in advance of its happening. The consciousness of error can come only in retrospect. Einsinnigkeit requires simultaneity: a perception may not be criticized as inadequate to a state of affairs before that state of affairs has been presented. There are many other such moments of transgression in Kafka's works; the planes of perception and of reflective interpretation momentarily intersect.

In order to treat the passage from The Metamorphosis described above as a break in perspective, one must, of course, construe the word Vorstellung as "mere idea," as delusion. If it is not so construed and is held to the neutral "idea," then there is no break. Here, then, also from The Metamorphosis, is an entirely unequivocal example. At the outset of the third section, we learn that Gregor's mother, upon pointing to Gregor's room, would say, " 'Close that door, Grete'; and when Gregor was back in darkness, . . . the women [in the other room] mingled their tears or stared dry-eyed at the table."[27] Can Gregor have reported these sad facts from behind the closed door? The opening sentence of The Trial offers a more significant example of authorial prejudgment: "Someone must have slandered Joseph K., because without his having done anything wrong, one morning he was arrested." This sentence is, rhetorically speaking, an enthymeme—an abridged syllogism—but one in which the conclusion precedes the omitted major premise, the normal sequence of the syllogism being, if someone is arrested, then someone must have accused him. The story's mythos properly begins with K.'s arrest. The narrator provides a petitio principii by assuming that there must be a primary cause: accusal. Yet in the enthymeme which opens the novel, this assumption precedes, textually although not logically, the performance on which it depends, that is, K.'s arrest. "In this way the text can cry 'Accused!' before the arrest, much in the manner of the White Queen, who screamed before she was struck."[28] For this reason we are not surprised, as we should be, when, in chapter 3, during Joseph K.'s collision with the law student, K. is referred to as "the accused."

Joseph K.'s arrest has been prefigured as the outcome of an accusation. And yet in conversation with the inspector in the first chapter, he is told that the court—or the inspector, at any rate—has no knowledge of his having been accused. The narrator supplies the idea of accusation before he supplies the fact of arrest.

This is a break in perspective. The gist of congruent narration is that no event be presented as already interpreted or presented as if for the second time in the perspective of someone who already has an idea about it. At the outset of *The Trial* we are given an idea about Joseph K.'s arrest before he has been arrested.[29]

There has been, then, a growing number of discussions of Kafka's narrative technique which take into account the kinds and purposes of breaks in perspective. Hartmut Binder, Peter Beicken, Ingeborg Henel, Walter Sokel and most recently Roy Pascal, among others, have been especially informative.[30] None of these studies, however, supplies a systematic organization of the kinds and consequences.

A preliminary classification, I think, would have to begin along these lines. As to *kinds*, at the level of the signifier, the following kinds of words or word-shifts tend to indicate breaks.

1. *Verbs*: (a) verbs belonging to the register of self-reflexive consciousness, like "knowing," especially, "not knowing," "not realizing," and verbs that suggest mere "seeming."

(b) tense shifts. Dorrit Cohn has analyzed at length the remarkable shifts of tense in "A Country Doctor" from past to present to past and again to present—the last shift lending the abandoned wandering of the narrating figure a sort of ghostly immortality.[31]

(c) the pluperfect (except in quoted inner or outer speech).

(d) verbs used to report, as opposed to stage, a scene; reporting can be grasped as an increase in the ratio of narrated time (*erzählte Zeit*) (time covered) to time of narration (*Erzählzeit*) (the time it takes to tell).

2. *Adverbs*: the notable absence of adverbial shifters designating immediate time and place or the substitution, for such shifters, of adverbs stipulating "objective" time spans and localizable places. This is generally true of all Kafka's stories and novels narrated in monopolized perspective. The hero's consciousness tends to be fixed on the objects of its concern "here" and "now." It should be especially true of *The Metamorphosis*. Yet at the beginning of the third section, for example, we read that Gregor had suffered from a serious wound "for over a month."[32]

Can temporal indications having this much objectivity actually be produced, especially toward the close, by a consciousness congruent with
Gregor's, which has lost all track of time?

3. *Personal pronouns*: shifts in personal pronouns are infre-
quent in the published work. The most dramatic example of such a shift
is Kafka's decisive replacement of the first-person protagonist with a third-
person protagonist—"K." for "I"—in *The Castle* on page 43 of the manuscript. He subsequently crossed out all earlier references to an "I."[33] In
The Metamorphosis "Mother" and "Father" become "Mr. and Mrs. Samsa"
or "the Samsas" (*das Ehepaar Samsa*) after Gregor's death.

This latter shift ("break") turns into a shift of significance
produced by the interpretive intrusion of the narrator. This shift in tonality
from "Mother" and "Father" to "Mr. and Mrs. Samsa" is justified by the
work's continuing after the death of the hitherto central intelligence
(Gregor). This sort of break also occurs in the final sentence of *The Judgment*. We have already indicated other breaks in *The Metamorphosis* caused
by reported perceptions of things outside the ken of the protagonist. Such
"things" have a greater or lesser semantic value.

As to *consequences* of breaks in perspective, Ingeborg Henel,
for example, concentrates on striking patterns of contradiction in the re-
sponses and assertions of the hero. These point to a narrator not congruent with the hero and also to a represented world which the character takes to be real but which the reader is meant to decompose into
projections of the hero's "guilty lies."[34]

In general, however, writers on the subject of breaks have
tended to trivialize them. Yet these breaks do and should take us to an
advanced stage of bemusing complexity in our understanding of Kafka's
narrative. The existence of such breaks appears to precipitate within the
text the traces of a superior narrator, inspiring belief in the existence of
an author at once outside and inside the text—Kafka's authorized representative, a logician of the logic of the breaks, holding out to us the
promise of intended meaning. Can it be that when we have once charted
the pattern of his intrusions, the old expectation of the omniscient narrator will after all be fulfilled, requiring of us only that to hear him we
exercise more than usual subtlety?

In fact this is what has often been done, not always with a
surpassing subtlety, let it be quickly noted. If there has arisen a standard reading of, say, *The Trial* and *The Castle*, that reading is squarely
founded on narrative signals which evade the rule of congruence. The
standard reading of *The Trial* confirms the verdict against Joseph K., justifying his execution on the grounds of his unsavory character both before and during his trial. The more important assumption is of his guilty

life before the trial, so that ambiguous behavior during the trial is counted against him. Here a rule of consistency is put into effect before the (bizarre) idea about consistency which the novel produces has been properly considered—the idea, namely, that time is only serial repetition.

Yet it is not out of nowhere that the guilty mood of Joseph K.'s life before his trial arises. We noted the device by which his accusal is conjured before he has been arrested. There are, moreover, a number of straightforward propositions in the first chapter which prefigure his destruction. Kafka writes that "K. had always been inclined to take everything as lightly as possible, to believe in the worst only when the worst happened, to take no precautions for the future, even when everything was threatening."[35] "A few lines further on," notes Keith Leopold, "there is the interpolated statement: 'not as if it had ever been a habit of his to learn from experience.' " "These," continues Leopold, "are the only authorial statements about K.'s character in the whole novel," and, he adds, "Kafka must have been fully aware that these statements stand out because of their authorial character, and yet he did not alter or delete them. They are unique in the novel and consequently cannot be ignored by anyone concerned with the interpretation of Der Prozeβ." Leopold also adduces other breaks in perspective shaping our judgment of K.'s behavior during the trial. But his conclusions seem too hesitant. These breaks do not have to be considered as often or merely "accidental," yet Leopold suggests this possibility when he writes, "One cannot discount the possibility that some [i.e., *only* some] . . . were made deliberately."[36]

A number of writers—Walter Sokel, Dorrit Cohn, Winfried Kudszus, and Richard Sheppard—have shown that a whole texture of intrusions in The Castle invites the conclusion that K. is an aggressive schemer.[37] The narrator of this novel, in Kudszus' phrase, is indeed often *distanziert*, i.e., not congruent with the figural perspective. And so, Kudszus asks us no longer to regard "congruence as purely and simply" the characteristic of Kafka's narration but to acknowledge the presence of a narrator. "To be sure," he continues, "from time to time the case is not one of narrative distance with a meaningful function"; but he concludes—I think, misleadingly—"and is to this extent an oversight of the author."[38] It is misleading to talk of the absence or refusal of overt meaning as a necessarily meaningless oversight. Kudszus' position finally resembles the hesitant position of Leopold which it meant to criticize.

The trouble for the critic who would like to read all of Kafka's breaks strongly is that, however closely examined, they do not fall into a satisfying or indeed intelligible pattern. And given the fact that the novels are unfinished, it is hard to see how they ever can and how deliberately intended breaks could ever finally be distinguished from mistakes. But the problem is not only an empirical one; it is compounded by the complexities of reading. How can we be sure that we have a true break in perspective? It does not always upset our reading. Breaks in perspective may be surprising, but not all breaks are surprising to the same degree. They can alienate us from the hero or involve us more deeply in his fate. They can turn upside down the reading which our inexpungible tendency to interpret has been persistently elaborating, or they can seem to confirm it. Not even "meaningless" breaks will seem equally random or arbitrary: as readers we have a vested interest in diminishing their strangeness.

Randomness as such can be recuperated. Breaks in perspective "without meaningful function" can be read as redoubling and strengthening themes and actions. Consider the vermin Gregor Samsa— Gregor's nonreferential segmented body is constituted by divisible narrative segments. His exoskeleton is articulated in passage after passage. He is a sort of mythic figure of (narrated) narration, of sequential unfolding without real reference. But this narrative sequence is pierced by seemingly random breaks, arbitrarily violated by authorial intrusions.

At the same time, however, throughout the story, on the plane of theme and action, Gregor's body is also arbitrarily punctuated.[39] It is no sooner achieved than it is perforated at random and destroyed. But that, we might conclude, is just as it should be: the formal factor of breakage in narrative perspective is reflected in the thematic of wounding and forgetfulness throughout this story and indeed throughout all of Kafka. Or again the break in narrative perspective following Gregor's death can be "explained." The "flattening" of the narrative perspective and the falseness and banality of the tone of the ending prove that "with the disappearance of Gregor the story has lost its center of orientation."[40]

Other moments of disruption can be recovered as depending on the inevitable exigencies of narrative. Even intrusions without apparent thematic significance suggest the hand of an author guiding the work to an at least formal conclusion. There are limits, however, to this recovery of meaning. Disruptions sometimes remain just that: they seem arbitrary violations of congruence. Now the question must arise of whether even *these* disruptions are deliberately included by Kafka *even as arbitrary breaks of perspective.* The concept of a deliberate and yet arbitrary narrative act may seem strange, even irresponsible. Yet the concept is literally employed by Kafka in a letter to Felice Bauer in which he recalls a "spot on the Graben [in Prague] where because of uneasiness, desire and helplessness, I arbitrarily but deliberately tumbled more than once from the sidewalk into the street" ("*jene Stelle auf dem Graben, wo ich ohne Grund aber absichtlich aus Unruhe, Verlangen und Hilflosigkeit vom Trottoir mehrmals in die Fahrbahn stolperte*").[41] Certainly, it would be presumptuous to declare which of the apparently arbitrary breaks in Kafka's fiction were intended to be arbitrary and which not. This class of disruptions points to an ultimate undecidability. The question is this: Supposing we have resolved the undecidability of a local disruption by concluding that is without meaningful function, hence, arbitrary, can we say that Kafka has intended the break to be arbitrary? Is the fiction controlled or not by an author who decides to suspend congruence at random?

If this undecidability is permanent, we are (so far) forced to the hypothesis that in at least one sector, Kafka's works are not the uniform product of a controlling intention or subjectivity but the disrupted outcome of an impersonal linguistic principle of irony (pure Barthes!). Kafka's fiction emerges as an irony that is not just a controlled trope, for its meaning at the point of disruption is neither recoverable, nor stable, nor finite. At this point we can say no more than that the text "knows" that the author does not know whether these disruptions are intended. We glimpse here, however unsettling the idea, the appropriation of the author Kafka in an impersonal linguistic exchange.

Is this where we must stop? This is the same point to which Barthes took us earlier when he wrote that "writing is that neutral, composite, oblique space where our subject slips away, the negative where all identity is lost."[42] This is precisely the point of decision, where genuine interpretation, however forbidding, has to take place. How adequate is Barthes' essay to the question of breaks in perspective?

The kind of break we are focusing on appears to be insignificant, and therefore critics have called it an unwitting, an unintentional, mistake. Our task is to propose an account of such breaks faithful to Kafka's understanding of the act of writing. The task is imposed by the desideratum that there be a discipline of literary criticism. We cannot too readily call the texts (or parts of the texts) we study oversights or, what is the same thing, unwitting, randomly distributed breaks, while at the same time calling our enterprise a discipline.

With this crux in mind, we shall be well-served by Kafka's full account of the act of writing. The triadic model of sufferer/scription/surplus keeps intact the life of the author—as opposed to Barthes' account, which abolishes the author. If we hold with Barthes' perspective, then what seems meaningless at the level of the "scription" is finally meaningless. A break is—just a bad break.

Kudszus actually operated within Barthes' perspective when

he wrote of many of Kafka's breaks that, because they are without "meaningful function" within the fictive action, they can have been committed only through an oversight. Here Kudszus places value entirely inside the text, keeping the outside void: Kafka's breaks are finally meaningless.

Within Kafka's triadic view, however, a break meaningless at the level of the scription may be purposeful for the subject who suffers and who rings changes from his strength. It is the essentially combative relation of these various intentions composing the text, their unresolved and mutually suspicious character, that provides the frame. The act of writing, for Kafka, takes place with a certain negativity vis-à-vis the sufferer and the surplus subject, the questioner. For writing has no curative effect on the suffering. It reproduces suffering as the poverty of objectification, and its changes yield no answer to the question that arises at their source: What is the nature of this surplus of strength? In this perspective, the so-called scription is inadequate, untrue, a mere construction. Hence it is right that this false construction should be done violence to, that is to say, randomly perforated and broken, its falsity avenged.

The world is acquainted with Kafka's horror of constructions—indeed of all forms of apparent mastery and control.[43] By chiastic logic he usurps the conventional valorization of control at the expense of random activity, as in the aphorism: "Self-control is something for which I do not strive. Self-control means wanting to be effective at some random point in the infinite radiations of my spiritual existence. But if I do have to draw such circles round myself, then it will be better for me to do it passively."[44] The aesthetic parallel to self-control would be the masterful novelistic device of narratorial cunning—Einsinnigkeit.[45] But Kafka deliberately breaks the perfection of this technique, quite as if to rebel against what Nietzsche calls "modern art as an art of tyrannizing.—A coarse and strongly defined logic of delineation . . . the formula tyrannizes."[46] The rule of Kafka's art cannot be adequately expressed in the perfection of a technique, any more than can "the inner rule [or commandment] (das innere Gebot), which is not communicable because it is not graspable and for the same reason . . . strives to be communicated."[47] The outcome must be a communicative structure internally divided, yet not according to some recoverable antithetical scheme: Kafka's repugnance for constructions is rivaled only by his repugnance for antithesis.[48] The truth of the fictive structure, indeed like "the truth of longing, is not so much its truth, rather it is an expression of the lie of everything else."[49]

Imagining Kafka writing, we should see him remote from his

empirical self-consciousness and thematic preoccupation, in a sharply defined metaphysical attitude toward the act of writing, accepting, within the production of demons and forms, as in Nietzsche's astronomy, the disruption of "chance, the uncaused event, the scattering of errors."[50]

In this perspective Kafka's relation to the act of writing is divided between the will to organization and the will to disruption. He is committed to his "strength," and he is committed to the consciousness of precisely what is "diabolical" in this strength and specious in its product.

And who, if this writing is indeed false (or not quite false, but not true either), would be more bent on keeping the construction intact and hence more guilty of complacency than that constructed consciousness—the disembodied, hidden, uncaring narrator, the congruent narrator, the figure of *Einsinnigkeit*? His solidarity with the perspectival hero was only a ruse. The narrator has to be brought in from behind the scenes, and once in play within the fiction, even as a disembodied mind, he is as much subject to inauthenticity and blindness as any character. At such moments the naive, unconscious, but errant hero possesses an ironical superiority over the narrator. His blundering self-love is really no falser than the diabolical aestheticism of the self-effacing narrator. Like the loopholes in bureaucratic procedures which, as Adorno writes, are the institutional equivalent of mercy, random breaks in narrative consistency grant the hero a sort of merciful liberation from the schematism of "character," from the privations of an irremediably personal perspective.

The source of Kafka's text is suffering, suffering that finds its fullest expression in a text to which it could also do violence. This violence sets in motion an interminable hermeneutic endeavor. The reader's effort too should not be to escape suffering: this sometimes pained and sometimes exhilarated effort to interpret extends and enlarges the author's surplus of strength. The life of the author—the tension between his suffering and his excessive interpretation of it—survives, for the reader, on the margin of his breaks. It survives especially in breaks that seem most arbitrary.[51]

To attribute to Kafka an aesthetic of deliberate arbitrariness is not only to stress his radical solitude: it is also to point out his place in, and dialectical distinction from, a tradition of the new. In Monroe Beardsley's view, "One striking . . . feature of the revolution in the arts that has occurred over the past half-century or so is the increasing use of chance, or accident, in the creation of art. . . . If there is . . . an intimate connection between randomness and disorder, we may say that never has the revolt against order been carried further than it has in recent years."[52] Beardsley paraphrases Karlheinz Stockhausen's aesthetic as one of "discovering ways of preventing deliberate intention from playing too large a role in the composition. . . . John Cage praises indeterminancy, which he defines as 'identifying with no matter what eventuality.' "[53] This attitude of identifying with what originates in the act of writing even or especially in spite of a local intention suggests— *mutatis mutandis*—Kafka's aesthetic of suffering.

The aleatory moment, however, is only one moment in Kafka's aesthetic. It marks an artistic world distinctive for the abundance of its structured signs, its "whole orchestration of changes." Kafka's randomness is obliquely expressive of a rigorous poetic intention. What Adorno said of parataxis in Hölderlin could be said of chance language in Kafka: "The language sanctioned by the sacrifice of the subjective intention is not, as it were, simply outside the subject. By cutting through its threads to the subject, language speaks for the subject which for its part can no longer speak."[54]

In Beardsley's view, the contemporary critique of subjectivity considers "chance art . . . as an appropriate response to the chaos of modern life on the part of an artist who values his integrity."[55] For Kafka of course chance is not the servant of a putative commandment that art respond to "the chaos of modern life"; chance serves to express the suffering of a particular consciousness intending to speak the truth of modern life. A modern art including Kafka's might be seen as dwelling amid the ruins of a romantic aesthetic according to which the artist expresses, by free composition, in a form transparent to its theme, the plenitude of a subjectivity. The birth of modern art is thus a straitened birth, the birth of pain as the constitutive feature of man. Adorno writes, "Music, shrunk to the moment, is true as the eruption (*Ausschlag*) of negative experience. It is concerned with real pain, the pain of the real (*sie gilt dem realen Leiden*). . . . What radical music knows is the untransfigured suffering of man."[56]

These topics—art, chance, and suffering—bridge Kafka's world to the moral universe of *Doctor Faustus*, which is no surprise since Mann copies Adorno. In writing of Heine's "wound," Adorno speaks to the predicament of Adrian Leverkühn at the same time that he speaks even more cogently to the predicament of Kafka: "If every expression is the trace of suffering, he was able to transform his own insufficiency, the speechlessness of his speech, into the expression of the break" (Ist aller Ausdruck die Spur von Leiden, so hat er es vermocht, das eigene Ungenügen, die Sprachlosigkeit seiner Sprache, umzuschaffen zum Ausdruck des Bruchs).[57]

To interpret, however, random breaks in Kafka's perspective as an expression of his suffering may indeed be the subterfuge of interpretation, "which abhors the random." [58] It makes us Zeitblom to Kafka's Leverkühn, when the truth may be that Kafka's breaks run "against interpretation." But the thrust counter to interpretation is one which interpretation cannot fail to identify and recover to its purpose, since this thrust belongs, in Kafka's view, ineluctably to interpretation. It is K. who thinks, apropos of the question of the precise value of the texts which the messenger Barnabas delivers, "Chance determines where one stops reflecting, and so even our judgment on them is a matter of chance." [59] To entertain this view and yet to persist in interpreting is a mercy—the merciful effect of the "surplus of strength" of men and women who read.

CHAPTER SIX

Freud as Literature?

The thought of wanting to help
me is a sickness and must be
put to bed to get well.[1]

—Kafka

You have to dive down, as it were,
and sink more rapidly than that
which sinks in advance of you.[2]

—Kafka

Doch konnten wir nicht
hinüberdunkeln zu dir:
es herrschte
Lichtzwang.[3]

—Celan

In the fall of 1977 a convulsive series of events shocked
Germany: the industrialist leader Hanns-Martin Schleyer
was abducted by "terrorists" and was afterward found
dead, bundled in the trunk of an automobile "parked outside a dilapi-
dated tenement in Mulhouse in the French border region of Alsace."[4]
Shortly before his death, other terrorists hijacked a Lufthansa jet, which
they meant to ransom for the freeing of terrorists imprisoned in the
maximum-security prison of Stammheim near Stuttgart. When, a few days
later, the jet was recaptured by German commandos in Somalia, the imprisoned terrorists Baader, Raspe, and Ensslin reportedly committed suicide. All this terror, so concentrated, struck France as a lightning flash
which, for one moment, illuminated the real Germany as a formless mass,

blighted and blasted, a desert, marsh, or lunar landscape—sinister, shadowed, yet lurking too. For the French it was not possible, it seemed, to see anything in Germany except as what the flash of light, the flash of truth, lit up. Germany was darkness, nonbeing—thus unlike the light— but like the light too as light visibly subdued. If the lightning flash was terrible, *terrorist*, so too (wrote Jean Genet) was the real Germany terrible, terribly *violent*. The light flashed and also illuminated the hidden, blind, repressed violence of German nonbeing—German "not becoming," "not wanting." These phrases are Nietzsche's, and with others like them they were much in use.[5]

This was the view from west of the Rhine. But Germany saw too in the French account the familiar French travesty of clarity—what Nietzsche once called the French art of "making thin, simplifying, logicizing" (WP, p. 438). German writers reacted, saying that all the darkness, repression, and indefinite nonbeing that France had seen *in* the German object had been only the effect of the French repression *of* Germany. France had been chiefly bent on denying the interest for France of the German case. Yet the bombs that had gone off had been European explosions, not illuminations of Germany. What they should properly have produced in anyone with eyes to see and senses to feel was not insight but anxiety—terror of violence and of darkness stirring, but of a darkness everywhere, an anxiety for the fate of the whole decent world. French thought had pretended to be not "of" German, of European anxiety, in the genitive sense but in the detached, dissevering ablative—meaning thereby to detach itself from its own anxiety. But by virtue of the circular structure of anxiety, whereby the repression of anxiety (ablative) is itself the effect of the repression of anxiety (genitive), French thought had been, finally, only the effect of French anxiety. An old story: Thought as part of the holding action of repression, revealing nothing of its object and everything of its source, so that what the German reader finally concluded was only a variant of the ready complaint that "the preferred form of French self-criticism is attacking Germany."

According to this German reading, the French had constructed a sign for German terrorism, S/s. For "S," the signifier, read, "the flare-up, the apparent illumination, terroristic clarity and the clarity of terrorism." For "s," the signified, read "the daily landscape of German violence practiced through its repression, of violence that returns to blind itself, of effaced blindness masquerading as order"—the whole of the signified rooted in the Germans' repression of their guilt for the violence of the war. The bar of S/s meanwhile designated, for the French, the trope of litotes: terror is not negated violence, i.e., is the truth of unrepressed violence, whereas the bar designated for Germany (according to the French reading) only a benighted metaphor, of terror as cognate with the violent aggression of a few anarchic individuals.

The Germans did not fail to take their turn at reading the *whole* of the French reading as the new signifier "S'." The French had asserted a litotes whose clever, aggressive, negating style was in reality only the metonymy of French hostility toward Germany. That the French imagined an obscure German repression of German violence was nothing more than an expression of surplus hostility accompanying France's incomplete repression of the German object.[6]

A third reading, neither French nor German, would perceive the abuse (catachresis) in this argument by litotes, the rhetorical figure which asserts sameness through doubled difference or negation. The French action of distinguishing the German crisis as a litotes is the displacement of yet a third trope: France's *identity* with Germany. The displacement aims to dislodge French consciousness of this identity. For France to perceive this sameness would be to recognize the shame of its own repressed daily violence.[7]

Thus French rhetoric designates its own crisis; as often is the case, Germany is involved. What divides these countries, the Rhine, is in times of crisis a mirror with two faces. If from the French side the Germans are *outre-rhin* and thus effectively beyond the pale or *limes*, the French for the Germans are *jenseits des* R(*h*)*ein-en*: unclean. This is one way of avoiding paranoia.[8]

But the effort to shun at all costs the horror of similitude, one's gaze fixed immovably on the "perceived" difference of the other, can mean and meant in the French case self-evasion. The French reader of Baader/Schleyer fully effaced the term of the self and was less a reader than a voyeur. The Germans said that the one genuine access to the German object which the French had gained by the crisis was the annexation to their language of a new signifier: *schadenfreude*. Which brings me by indirections to my subject.

How I understand the French reading of Freud (1856–1939), hence Freud as a literary text, might now be fairly obvious. The parallel between the French reading of Baader/Schleyer and the French reading of Freud is there for the asking. What the French have discovered in the light of their own reading of Freud is Freud's repression of (the discovery of) repression.[9] Suppose we turn French Freud around as the object of an imaginable Freudian analysis. The outcome is the specular doubling of all such closed systems. The new criticism appears violent and aggressive and invites the charge that it is terroristic.[10] Its discovery (of Freud's repression) is not made in the light of truth; it is a glimpse obtained through violent swerving. What the French have uncovered is not

Freud's aversion to repression but their having averted themselves from the *determinist* Freud.

The French mood, the "soldierly" one, of accepting, even welcoming, the small death of self-expropriation in a structure of impersonal exchange, finally embraces Freud the old determinist so as to read the determinist out of him in the name of his more real undecidability. In the margin of undecidability, there is still the small mercy of "negative liberty."[11] It never was really to be supposed that the French were contemplating self-immolation, for their glorification of Freud is too bizarre. The French display of interpretive energy looks like a snook cocked at the father in the guise of model obedience to the father—at Freud the old arbiter.

What, if anything, is truthful in these French and German readings? It would be impossible from *within* such a text, produced by specular relations, to decide this question. Every thesis having the form of litotes, in the sense of deconstruction, "derepression," asserts that some other term ostensibly simple and positive is actually the negation, the exclusion or denial, of what within that very term is contradictory. Every such litotic thesis can be immediately disqualified, however. From another perspective the litotes—the logical figure of deconstruction—is only the catachresis of a virtual identity, namely, the disfigured expression of a will to power bent on masking its own contradiction. In such a system of texts, as in a dream, the principle of *non*contradiction operates, vertiginously. Where from the start no term in a system is self-identical, where none is "demystified from the start" in the sense of assuring the *play* and not the chaotic proliferation of difference between other terms,[12] where all *seeming* identity to self is based only on denial of the actual convergence of, first, what is other with, second, what is always and originally other in the self-same; then questions and answers cannot be distinguished, each being only the "effect" of the other, arrested in a moment of oscillation. Elements of such a pseudostructure do not have enough stability to allow for the stipulation of distinctions or even of "nodal points," let alone of hierarchies; and "leaping from node to node," which Jeffrey Mehlman offers as Leiris' desirable wisdom, is an invitation to vertigo.[13]

Nothing, then, in the pseudostructure of the readings which Freud has generated is properly literary. Freud can be given the stability of a literary text as an organization of ironical practice only by acts of exegetical terrorism. These acts are invited perhaps by the heroic aura of Freud's enterprise but are otherwise sheerly reckless in an order where "mental events are determined, . . . [where] there is nothing arbitrary about them."[14]

The French proposition that the Freudian text repressed its discovery of repression contradicts a "literary" reading of the text, because as a blind text arising from repression, it produces only a repressive discourse. Unlike a literary text, it cannot disabuse the interlocutor by being ahead of him in its understanding; instead it annihilates him every step of the way, declaring each of his questions to be already determined as the effect of repression.[15]

The strong interpretive strategy must aim to organize the current and countercurrent of these effects. If the reversibility of valence attaching to each moment of a specular rhetoric suggests the instability of a dream, then the reading must be waked from its nightmare, cured of its vertigo. Yet "the thought of wanting to help," as Kafka's Hunter Gracchus says, "is a sickness and must be put to bed to get well."[16]

There is no account given in Freud for the therapeutic wonder that pronouncing the name of the determination could break its iron law. It is as if, for Freud, the law of determination produced an endlessly tautological sentence in which the captured subject kept reappearing as the predicate symptom, but the *name* of the determination could then begin another sentence, produce a liberating anacoluthon and a new text in turn.[17] As if too the language with which a nightmare were deciphered, a language inconsistent with the text of the nightmare, could, on being inserted within that first, silent text, awaken the dreamer into a different dream. But if this account is right, and if the therapeutic word is construed on the model of a deciphering (interpreting) phrase, the question arises as how this phrase could be accommodated within the scene of the primary text, which has no place for it, which cannot accept it without being blasted apart, ceasing to contain the captured subject, text, and dream. There could be only languages in parallel, and freedom would indeed be only a leap.

There is moreover a theory of waking and curing already implied in the model of political terror which denies to psychoanalytic discourse any such healing or arresting effect. Reading Baader/Schleyer the French considered the illumination they provided as the bracing lucidity which could wake the Germans from their sleep of reason, cure them of their national melancholy.

By what means does the silent interlocutor (the analyst) produce in the patient the deviant sentence that frees him from the repetition of his suffering, wakes him from the tautology that he lives as helplessly as the dreamer his dream? Where does the French reader find his lights to cure Freud of his tautology, his repression of repression? With what speculum?

Until the text of Freud supplies the instrument with which

the deconstructor can deconstruct Freud without in turn being annihilated by it, there can be no good claim that in Freud we have a literary text. Freud's vertiginous instability is not harmless for the interpreter-subject, who must realize that the ensuing dissolution of the subject is one in which he collaborates only because he does not *live* it.[18] He cannot live this dissolution and also maintain that it is his light in which Freud can be deciphered, let alone be cured of his repression.

Lacan's rereading of Freud—under the banner of a return to Freud—is in fact a turn to, and within, a French intellectual tradition, one characterized by Nietzsche as the "voluptas psychologica," artistic passion, and a flair for mediation (BW, pp. 383ff.) To this one could add the recent acquisition assuring French superiority: intellectual terrorism. It is in the light produced by a self-conscious production of the French spirit, the commentator's own, that Freud is to be deciphered, and indeed cured of his repression (of repression). This cure takes place through the clarity of a psychoanalytical reading. But one worries with Nietzsche:

> How can man know himself? It is . . . a tormenting, a dangerous enterprise to dig at oneself . . . and descend by force on the first route into the shaft of one's being. How easily a man damages himself this way. So |fatally| that no physician can heal him.[19]

Consider, however, the opening of Lacan's "Function of Language in Psychoanalysis," whose confident lucidity—perhaps an intended irony—means to produce a healing. Addressing Freud's "Promethean discovery" (of repression), Lacan writes: "Such awe seizes man when he unveils the lineaments of his power that he turns away from it in the very action employed to lay its features bare."[20]

The word "awe" above conceals more than it reveals. This is the language of "negative pleasure," of the Kantian sublime, but it exalts too high the modality of intimidated blindness, smooths over what Thomas Weiskel called "the logic of terror."[21] The image of the Promethean act of a man laying bare the lineaments of his power is in principle troubled. A Promethean act reveals art and design, illuminates with fire; a human act thus emulating Prometheus' could indeed inspire awe. But it is also an act of defiance and impiety, entailing horrible tortures; the mind that turns away from this implication is not sublime but defensive.[22] "Too concerned with guarding the flame," declares Stuart Schneiderman, and "refusing to repeat the act of theft that acquired fire in the first place, |analysts| let the fire go out |and| . . . turn theory into dogma."[23] Lacan's account represses this implication of defensiveness, but it, rather than the language of sublimity, proves more faithful to the history of the dynamic of repression in Freud. For one can trace in Freud's work the only hesitant process by which the term repression (Verdrän-gung) achieves any sort of meaning independent of that of defense (Ab-wehr).[24]

Thus the picture which reveals Freud's repression of repression itself masks repression as defense. We are still inside the specular circle, where the point is not to stay inside it but to get out of it in the right way. We need a text which operates within the text of recent French criticism and in Freud as the repressed third term. Lacan's image suggests that this text may be Kafka, whom both Freud and the French rewriting of the human sciences in the last twenty years have left strikingly hors compte.[25]

What is the empirical case? Freud nowhere explicitly alludes to Kafka, although it is certain that he knew him, as a visit to his library on the Berggasse confirms. Freud would have been aware of Kafka also, because he read Stekel (who gets mixed reviews in the Interpretation of Dreams),[26] and Stekel devoted a couple of paragraphs in his Pathological Disturbances of the Instinctual and Affective Life of 1917 to The Metamorphosis, diagnosing it as a zooanthropic fantasy (wrong) of transformation into a louse (wrong) and hence as denoting the self-aimed sadistic component of unhappy homosexuality (probably wrong). Kafka wrote to Felix Weltsch on September 22, 1917, asking to read Stekel's comments. If these lines ever did come into his hands, he cannot have been very much instructed.

A more perceptive reader, Hellmuth Kaiser, published in Imago in 1931 an essay on Kafka's "phantasy of punishment" in which the metamorphosis, and in particular the "forcible impregnation" of Gregor's back by two small hard apples fired by his father, represents not the sadistic but the masochistic component: Gregor nearly dies of mingled pleasure and pain at the coitus per anum. The official position of the Freudian school on Kafka was to hammer "given existing pieces" into the machine.

What does it mean for the status of Freud as a literary text that Freud sanctioned so vacuous a reading of the very writer through whom he might have read, in an inspired way, the therapeutist in himself?[27] The image of Freud's fundamentalist corrector Lacan—of man turning in awe from his own Promethean fire—leads one to Kafka for further correction.

Kafka records in his Diaries a moment like that which Lacan describes. Lacan writes of dazzlement at the "unveiling" of man's work of knowledge. For Kafka: "Our art is a way of being dazzled by truth; the light on the flinching grimacing face is true, and nothing else."[28] The light for Kafka is inhuman; the genius provides a maximum of surface, he is the twisted foil for the light. Art includes the moment of being struck, of being wounded, of shrinking back, of being unequal: the wound, a moment between hesitation and flight, generates the productive disparity of the text.

The instant of the copresence of man and illumination in Kafka is negative. The dynamic of occlusion is more humbling than countertransference, as if in the fullest sense of the word an obscure mechanism had to compensate for the presence of a more than ordinary measure of illumination by producing a more than ordinary measure of opacity and disturbance in response to it. From out of the gates of the Law there streams an inextinguishable radiance, but of those who huddle near the light, the doorkeeper has turned his back to it, and the suppliant bribes him with words and implores the fleas on the doorkeeper's fur collar to help him. It is not awe that keeps him from advancing toward the Law. On the bed of the Castle functionary Bürgel, who is on the verge of revealing to the land surveyor K. how one might "enter" the Castle, K. grows drowsy, inattentive, falls asleep. In the early diary entry—" 'You,' I said"—the experience by the bachelor of his "depth" (Grund) forces him to freeze in forgetfulness of the moment.[29]

Kafka's text can be analyzed as a series of cognates of such moments of inequality and disparity *without ethical content*, suggesting that the moment is not one that can in principle ever be cleared-up, made right, enlightened, or controlled.

We have two accounts, then, of the dynamic of repression: on the one hand, that of the French and Freud, that moves between dazzled "awe" and prudent self-defense, both in principle intelligible, auspicious, and contributing to a cure; on the other, an implacable aversion and wounding, incorrigible except for the minimal hope that by a process which Kafka called *Tat-Beobachtung*—"the action of observation," the observation of the trauma of repression—there might be "a leap out of Murderer's Row."[30]

But the leap shown in the "Hunter Gracchus" is only the drifting of a lucid ruin. The wandering Hunter, who cannot die and who suffers from his solitude, says, "I do not shout to summon help, even though at moments—when I lose control over myself . . . —I think seriously of it. But to drive out such thoughts I need only look round me and verify where I am, and—I can safely assert—have been for hundreds of years."[31] What he describes at first is a derepression of desire (the loss of control) and next, a moment of observation, the effect of which is actually to strengthen the original repression. His glance discovers no new object of liberated desire; instead it wounds desire by driving out, as futile, thoughts of freedom. The Hunter continues: "I am here, more than that I do not know, further than that I cannot go." The moment of observation is thus a moment held together by style, and the experience is without practical salvational import: "My ship has no rudder, and it is driven by the wind that blows in the undermost regions of death."

Other features of Kafka's work suggest a model of a literary text with which the text of French Freud can be contrasted. Here are some salient features of the model.

Kafka is supposed to have said, "The dream reveals the reality, which conception lags behind. That is the horror of life—the terror of art." [32] The sentence distinguishes the terror of art from the banal violence (horror) which the French reading of Baader/Schleyer attached to the psychopathology of everyday German life, a psychopathology of everyday repressiveness to which even Freud's discovery succumbed. It is with the values of art that that reading contrived to invest kidnapping and explosives—qualities of fierce, dialectical brilliance which the French reading of Freud displays. But art is a different combustion of the dream.

Art pursues the dream but is not the dream; yet the dream reveals the reality of something terrible distorted by horror, blanketed by ordinary neurosis. [33] Art is the narration of the dream; all of its life is in principle the dream. But as there is no representation in Kafka of a dream that isn't also waking, there is no single action that is dream*like* in his work. Everything, Adorno noted, unlike dream and its prelogical logic is excluded, including "real" dreams themselves. [34]

The difference, now, between the text of the dream in Kafka and the text of the dream in Freud is that Kafka's dream excludes all commentary and deciphering; "the scriptures are unalterable and the comments often enough merely express the commentators' despair." [35] Kafka's script instead calls attention to the act by which it is narrated. There is consciousness *of* dream narration. Kafka develops a fictional language which excludes decipherment even by allusion to the properties of the narrator or to an identification of the dream as dream. There is only the world of the horrible dream distanced in a narrative perspective remarkable for the reticence of its effects. Kafka's superiority is evident in the narrow sector of his work which reveals *that the dream is being narrated*. The fictive consciousness positions itself in the gap between a representation of the content of the dream and a decipherment of the dream: only "the limited circle is pure." [36] What is narrated is accessible in only one way—through the perspective of the narration; its mode of being is a being-towards-narration, which includes its own reflection, flame in a mirror.

Kafka appears to know two things with great clarity: First, the revelation of truth and the swerve from truth is not an affair of intersubjectivity, of "dialogue"; truth is self-authentication, "a great fire . . . in which [everything] perishes and rises up again,"[37] but the swerve is everywhere—"the horror." Second, the condition of registering this truth is writing fiction; this means inscribing within the dream-text, by means of random breaks, the awareness that this text of fire and "flinching" is being narrated.[38]

The repeated point of narrative departure, just outside the dream, does not compose another language except as it communicates the consciousness of a distance. This constructed consciousness is the third term missing from the specular reading of Freud. It is the condition of existence outside the intersubjective relation, a margin which is without life and yet is not painless. "Art for the artist," said Kafka—on Janouch's authority—"is only suffering through which he releases himself for further suffering."[39]

Kafka's last word on the question of cure is, as it ought to be, fictive. "A Country Doctor," which critics have read as an explicit rejection of psychoanalysis, is a literary text par excellence, constituted by two principles: first, consciousness of the narration of fiction (the difference inside narration, the narration of a difference); second, the refusal of a theory of cure—i.e., of intersubjective truth—which would imply the elimination of the constitutive difference of fiction. If we substitute in the formula "Art, for the artist, is only suffering through which he releases himself for further suffering" the words "curing" for "art" and "doctor" for "artist," we could enter the story.

The story thematizes the doctor who cannot cure both his patient and himself. The patient is a wounded boy, "quite blinded by the life within his wound." Kafka, hostile to all forms of superiority, immediately robs the doctor (-narrator) of his vantage point and puts him to bed with the boy, who whispers shrewdly, "Why, you were only blown in here, you didn't come on your own feet. Instead of helping me, you're cramping me on my deathbed. What I'd like best is to scratch your eyes out [your voyeuristic eyes]. . . . 'Right,' I said, 'it is a shame. And yet I am a doctor [a narrator]. What am I to do? Believe me, it is not too easy for me either.'"

Here is the form of the cure, or as much of a cure as we're shown. To the patient who reveals "A fine wound is all I brought into the world, that was my sole endowment," the doctor replies: "My young friend, your mistake is: you have not a wide enough view. . . . Your wound is not so bad. Done in a tight corner with two strokes of the ax. Many a one proffers his side and can hardly hear the ax in the forest, far less that it is coming nearer to him."

The "cure" of the wound, such as it is, is the *knowledge* of its privilege. "It is enough," wrote Kafka in his *Diaries* "that the arrows fit exactly in the wounds that they have made."[40] The sufferer's privilege is that his wound, properly part of a universe of wounding, has been revealed with eminent clarity.

The patient seems pacified, but a striking change missing from the Muir translation occurs at the level of the signifier. The narration suffers a perturbation and passes abruptly into the past tense, then back into the present tense, a present of eternal wounding: the doctor cannot leave the scene of the wounding/cure.

> Slowly, like old men, we crawl through the snowy wastes. . . . Never shall I reach home at this rate; my flourishing practice is done for. Naked, exposed to the frost of this most unhappy of ages . . . , old man that I am, I wander astray. . . . Betrayed! Betrayed! A false alarm (*Fehlläuten*) on the night bell once answered—it cannot be made good, not ever.

Essential Kafka. Essential literature?

The doctor has a truthful consciousness of his failure. This consciousness is enabled for Kafka by the fact that he figures at once as the central perspective, the "perspectival hero," of one of his fictions and as the narrator congruent with his narration. A crucial difference is in play in a narrator who addresses in the first person no other person at all, a margin which assures a disparity of the self to itself and hence the permanence of its "wound." Nowhere does the doctor register the belief that his narrative is a response to the fantasized interlocution operated by the silent image of an auditor.

The fact that he does not cure the other or himself is not of course a *result* of his failure to address another. Only as a speaker whose language is for himself can his assertions be taken seriously: they speak of the impossibility of cure except at the cost of a wound; curing wounds the curer.[41]

Behind this speaker are distinctively Kafkan acts of narrative transgression—arbitrary and inconspicuous. There is yet another consciousness in play, a distance, which to maintain is still not a matter of producing such an effect as cure. Cure, because it implies a crossing over, is avenged by the wound assailing the healer. Both cognitive and therapeutic features of the model are joined in the notion that the cost of noting the wound is being wounded; the condition of understanding suffering is unrelieved suffering. The doctor who cannot close a wound thematizes the scriptor who cannot close the distance to his narration, cannot be allowed to forget that he narrates narrating and that his life is the narrating of a dream.

Supposing Kafka were right: what is the affliction which French Freud has suffered in the course of its confident treatment of Freud?

None—if Lacan's phrase can stand for the rest: The French

stance, whether toward Baader/Schleyer or Freud, is one of being un-
harmed by the cure, secure in "freeplay." Not "man" but French Freud
has protected itself by flinching in awe of the power of its insight. The
turning away, for being sublime, recovers from pain, escapes final
wounding, whereas Kafka—uncertain that there is knowledge—knows that
if there were, it could be had only at the cost of unspeakable suffering.
Genuine thought inflicts the suffering in its object upon the thinker. But,
wrote Kafka, "I have not experienced the eternal hell of the real writer."[42]

Here we would have to study the phantom text in Kafka—
Hölderlin—and proceed to the link, in "When on a Holiday" ("Wie wenn
am Feiertage"), between the terms "self-inflicted wound" (selbstgeschla-
gene Wunde) and the struggle, die Leiden des Stärkeren [mitzuleiden]—this
highest cognitive effort "of suffering the sorrows of the god." For "nothing . . . is more painful than unriddling suffering" (Und nichts ist schmerz-
licher . . . Denn Leiden zu enträtseln).[43]

Postscript

What is distinctively literary about literature? It foregrounds
the act of narration (disrupts it or allows its conventions to occur "naturally," is never naive with respect to it). It makes sharp the noncoincidence between what is being said, and—with a change of a single letter—that (something) is being said.[44]

Freud has been taken as being literary precisely because he
seems to assert the omnipresence of a rhetorical or narrative factor in
psychic life. His awareness of the rhetorical character of psychic manifestations—of behavior, dreams, neurotic symptoms—is seen as paral-
leling the consciousness which writers have and inscribe in their fiction.

But is this understanding properly literary? Freud has discovered the narrated dimension but not narration, not the "that-it-is-being-
said" of what is being said. He is like the first Malte Laurids Brigge, of
Rilke's novel, who says of a jewel case: "I opened it up: it was empty. I
can say this after so long a time. But then, when I had opened it, I saw
only what this emptiness consisted of."[45] Not to distinguish narration
from the narrated is finally to deprive the narrated of its specificity; for
narrating touches differently the points de capiton which "pin or unpin the
signifier onto the signified."[46] It is not enough to declare that object
relations are like the figures in a text. With what consciousness, across
what distance, are they constituted there?

The analyst figure is a Gradiva-like text awakens the patient from his sleep of reason but enters his dream at one special place—a point where the manifest content of the dream and the reality of the awakener coincide. The text is all on the side of the analyst's reality, and here where "narration" is thinnest, least in play, here the membrane around the dreamer can be punctured. In awakening the dreamer, the analyst annihilates dreamer and dream, as if they were uniformly constituted. This fictional psychoanalysis does not specify the "that-it-is-being-dreamt" of the dream content—just as it elides the "that-it-is-being-narrated" of the awakener's reality into which the patient's reality flows. The story does not specify the dream equivalent of narration, of the conscious rhetorical factor in fiction.

Freud is inspired in grasping dream, memory, all transcripts of interiority as not unlike fiction—provoking in turn that reading of his work (by a species of mimicry), by which he is read as the undecidable transcript of a dream not unlike fiction and thus as having the character of literature. But he has only to be faced with an actual fictional text in order to want to insert it into the reality of biological, instinctual life, of genetic and reactive schemes. Freud is "pre-*littéraire*," but "pre-" should not denote nearness to instincts that could be reckoned an origin.

His plainness in aesthetic matters is still preferable to a certain French reading of Freud shaped by Lacan's early reaccentuating of the psychoanalytic interview, in which the patient, as he produces a text before the silent analyst, is viewed as a double agent, offering in between imposing absences of questions not himself but the lineaments of his image of that silence (a silence, true, growing ever noisier as Lacan's ellipses are being filled in). It is then only a short step to read Freud as if he too were addressing ourselves, the reader, in order to disarm us, to bribe us with the profit of a *philosophy of reading*. Kafka offers a different account: "Do you call that conversation if the other is silent and, to keep up the appearance of a conversation, you try to substitute for him, and so imitate him, and so parody him, and so parody yourself?"[47]

Shoshana Felman attributes to literature the power to cure psychoanalysis of its delusions of authority despite its captivation by the master-slave dialectic. Its speculum is "irony," a term which in Felman's discussion has very much the force of my term "consciousness of narration," the effect of the random breaks which bring the self-absorbed narrator into court. Felman explains how

> one crucial feature which is constitutive of literature . . . is essentially lacking in psychoanalytical theory, and indeed in theory as such: irony. Since irony precisely consists in dragging authority as such into a scene which it cannot master, of which it is *not aware* and which, for that very

reason, is the scene of its own self-destruction, literature, by virtue of its ironic force, fundamentally deconstructs the fantasy of authority in the same way, and for the same reasons, that psychoanalysis deconstructs the authority of the fantasy—its claim . . . to power as the sole window through which we behold and perceive reality. . . . Psychoanalysis tells us that the fantasy is a fiction, and that consciousness is itself, in a sense, a fantasy-effect. In the same way, literature tells us that authority is a *language effect*, the product or the creation of its own *rhetorical* power: that authority is the *power of fiction*.[48]

This discussion stresses the power of literary irony to achieve results: such power, like psychoanalysis for Lacan, should indeed strike us with awe. But what is left out of this account is the vulnerability of literary irony to destruction at the hands of its own authority, namely, its irony. Kafka perceives that the cost of exercising a power to cure is being wounded by that power. And indeed the point of Kafka's narrational irony is not that it leaves behind such positive results as that "literature tells us that authority is a *language effect*": what literature "tells" when all the deaths have been counted is that its frame displays the perfect emptiness of consciousness, "the impersonality of consciousness, . . . its utter lack of quality or individuating attributes, its 'nature' as a . . . point without substance or consistency," to which one would have to add the variable factor of its intensity.[49]

Here it is interesting to evoke Kafka's distinction with respect to the effects of his fiction: "I can still have passing satisfaction from works like A *Country Doctor*, provided I can still write such things at all. . . . But happiness only if I can raise the world into the pure, the true, and the immutable."[50] What does this mean, "the pure, the true, the immutable"? An Objective Idealist reference does not seem appropriate. Especially toward the end of his life Kafka conceived of such absolutes in terms of quantity and formality, in the spirit of Nietzsche's apothegm: "from a *quale* grows the desire for an increase in quantum" (WP, p. 304). Kafka wrote, for example, of an autobiographical persona:

He does not live for the sake of his personal life; he does not think for the sake of his personal thoughts. It seems to him that he lives and thinks under the compulsion of a family, which, it is true, is itself superabundant in life and thought, but for which he constitutes, in obedience to some law unknown to him, a formal necessity.[51]

The compulsion might be understood as the factor of consciousness, of proportionality pure and simple, capable of a heightening but not of qualification. This law functions for Kafka as an arbiter allowing him, perhaps, to perceive that "the disproportion in the world is mercifully quantitative."[52]

To an extraordinary degree Kafka identifies his self with the impersonal factor of consciousness; he wants the self to come to light as its light. The self is a surplus with respect to its perceptions, a distance whose strict analogy is the gap between the author and the dream narrated in his text. This factor is clearest in the Kafkan instance of the empty narrator, the narrator of *The Castle*, for example, who is detached from his participation in his narrative only for it to be revealed that "he" knows nothing more than the perspectival hero. His superiority is a matter of difference without quality. One narrative perspective glassily envelops another.

The empty narrator, produced by a break in perspective, reflects the author, whose very being is an affair of the consciousness of narrating, of a superiority impossible to fill in with a value. The sole superiority of consciousness is in perceiving itself as empty. What distinction therefore remains to "the pure, the true, the immutable" beyond the perception of the nullity of cure? Like innocent fire, consciousness can grow to any intensity of light, becoming purer, the great fire in which "everything, . . . the strangest fancies . . . perish and rise up again."[53] This is the surplus of narrative strength at which Kafka anxiously marvels, "a merciful surplus . . . at a moment when suffering has raked me to the bottom of my being and plainly exhausted all my strength. But then what kind of surplus is it?"[54] What dreams arise around this intensity of consciousness? That Kafka cannot answer this question should not suggest that Freud has had the last word.[55]

CHAPTER SEVEN

Heidegger's *Being and Time*: Implications for Poetics

Das Gefühl durchdringt die Poesie,
daß sie die authentische Interpretation
des Lebens selber zu geben habe.[1]
—Dilthey

Poetry is suffused with the feeling
that it has to provide the authentic
interpretation of Life itself.

Poetry is suffused with feeling in
order that it have the task of providing the authentic interpretation
of Life itself.

The work of Martin Heidegger (1889–1976) provokes the question of its fundamental division. Without the illusory rich tensions of lived experience, which organize Mann's work as a "universe," and without the suffering which randomly fragments Kafka's art, Heidegger's work suddenly appears to undergo a "turning" ("Kehre").[2] The moment of turning comes to light shortly after the publication in 1927 of *Being and Time* (*Sein und Zeit*). It occurs without the intrusions of personality, the traces of spiritual ordeal, or the turbulence of crisis.

What is this turning? It appears to have two different senses. On the one hand, it is an "event" in the history of Being, as a consequence of which "Being appears primordially in the light of concealing

withdrawal."[3] On the other, it is a turning within Heidegger's philosophical enterprise. It marks his full response to the turning in the previous
sense—a response which begets "[an]other [mode of] thinking that
abandons subjectivity.[4] In this mode of thinking "every kind of anthropology and all subjectivity of man as subject is . . . left behind."[5] The
movement of this thought, other with respect to the self, is visible in
the 1929 book *What Is Metaphysics?* (*Was ist Metaphysik?*), although it is
plainest in the shorter works which follow. According to Heidegger, "On
the Essence of Truth" ("Vom Wesen der Wahrheit"), 1930, provides "a
certain insight into the thinking of the turning."[6] There thought turns
"from the oblivion of Being, into the truth of Being,"[7] *as* "the simultaneity of disclosure and concealment."[8]

However the turning is described, however fully acknowledged (and indeed Heidegger's language appears to register obstacles
to expression whenever he addresses this event), it undoubtedly has had
an effect. It marks a change of emphasis in Heidegger's conception of
the task of philosophy as "the overcoming of metaphysics" and the kind
of language suited to its ends. Philosophy, for the later Heidegger, is
concerned with raising the question of Being from the standpoint of Being,
of "entreating its unbroken essence . . . into its own truth."[9] *Being and
Time* also raises the question of Being, but takes its point of departure
from the entity that asks this question—the unique, culpable, doomed
human being which Heidegger calls existence or Being-there (*Dasein*).
Hence *Being and Time*, the fruition of the work of the early Heidegger, is
a preparatory analysis of Being, a phenomenology of the questioning
existent. In this phenomenology the category of temporality, of human
time (*Zeitlichkeit*), is central; it does not anticipate the history or temporality (*Temporalität*) of Being.

At the same time the turning should not imply a "change in
standpoint" from *Being and Time*.[10] Heidegger prefers to nuance the change
as follows: "In [the turning] the thinking that was sought, first arrives at
the location of that dimension out of which *Being and Time* is experienced, that is to say, experienced from the fundamental experience of
the oblivion of Being."[11] The oblivion of Being, on the other hand, can
be "located" only with respect to the antithetical experience: the experience of Being (if even in its hiddenness). This experience inspires the
turning.

The later turning is thus a turning to a pure thinking-of-Being,
to a rigorous repetition of the single question of the meaning of Being,
and to a faithful description of what this question brings to light. Both
these "moves" are accomplished in a language of simplicity that intends to displace the language of technical rationality blocking access

to Being. This new language means to arouse a sense of original wonder. The simplicity and intensity of the late Heidegger's language suggests poetry; indeed he calls it "poetic thinking."[12]

The impression that Heidegger's later works aim for the values of poetry is strengthened by the claims he makes on behalf of poetry—particularly poems of Hölderlin, Trakl, and Rilke. These poets were
driven by the very question governing genuine thought: the meaning of
Being. Indeed in the poetry of Hölderlin, Heidegger seems to claim that
Being itself is present, for Hölderlin "speaks the sacred."[13]

The turning in Heidegger's own work, which is different from
his thematizing a turning in the "history of Being," has no objective existence except as a conceptual tool. It can neither be assuredly affirmed
nor denied that Heidegger's thought after 1930 is more adequate to Being
in its hiddenness. If the turning is taken as a sort of caesura, one can
profile differences between the early Heidegger and the late Heidegger.
If evidence for the turning is slighted, then instructive continuities emerge.
How much evidence of continuity is required to gainsay the proleptic
supposition of a turning? How much difference?

Certainly few readers of *Being and Time* would be inclined to
find much poetry in that work, given the systematic character of its production of categories and the overt explicitness of its narrative—questioning, answering, promising a repetition of the answer in yet different
categories. Its language strives to explain, not provoke, ambiguity. For
example, it distinguishes sharply between the concepts of fear and anxiety, which Freud, for one, leaves undecided. It analyzes the structures
of Dasein's phenomenal being; it does not aim to reproduce them in
the immediacy of their being experienced. *Being and Time* uses the German language very strangely at times; it makes central such coinages as
"ownmost" (*eigenst*) and "authenticity" (*Eigentlichkeit*), but its neologisms
are not yet aimed at liberating the experience of thought sedimented in
certain unwonted German words, let alone at "liberating the signifier"
(Barthes). These neologisms belong to a system of analytic categories.
It is true, given the disappearance today of a firmly intuited concept of
poetry, that sharp readers will find in passages of *Being and Time* a typically "poetic" subversion of whole meaning by a free play of ironies. In
section 31, for example, Heidegger abruptly distinguishes between "genuine" (*echt*) and "not genuine" (*unecht*) authenticity! (BT, p. 186).[14] But
this way of approaching *Being and Time* requires a strenuous effort of
reading against the grain.

In exactly this matter, however, of Heidegger's contribution
to poetry and poetics, the question of the turning as a change of tack in
Heidegger's work takes on considerable importance. The evident re-

moteness of the discursive and systematic style of *Being and Time* from the more nearly poetic, incantatory movement of the later works has led almost all those who read *Being and Time* from the later perspective to discount the contribution that work could make to poetic theory. It tends to be assumed instead (as, for example, by a commentator as astute as Hans Gadamer) that Heidegger first addresses poetry in a focused way only after the turning, in *The Origin of the Work of Art* (*Der Ursprung des Kunstwerkes*), 1935, and the *Explications of Hölderlin's Poetry* (*Erläuterungen zu Hölderlins Dichtung*), following 1936.[15] While it is true that *Being and Time* is by no means preoccupied with poetry, it nonetheless contains a theory of poetry. Moreover, it is a valuable theory, differently accented and altogether more realizable than the allusive account in the later work of the origin of poetry from the "foursome" of the gods, the mortals, the heavens, and the earth, with the goal of "eventuating" Being.

The provocative feature of the reception of *Being and Time* is this: Whereas almost no critic has identified its poetics, a good many axioms of recent literary study can be strictly derived from Heidegger's account. The sense, for example, that in poetry, meaning is explicitly figurative, and as such is at once present and elusive, and that poetic language, therefore, is the medium of illumination and diffraction can be founded on Heidegger's description of human existence as "in the truth and in untruth equiprimordially" (BT, p. 272). This admixing of authentic disclosure and retold "scribbling" (*Geschreibe*) (BT, p. 212)—namely, "the 'actual' that is left over, the world-historical that has been, the leavings, and the information about them that is . . . at hand" (BT, p. 443)—has an exact counterpart in literature. It is in the way that literature at once communicates and scatters meaning along the textual genealogical lines of the rhetorical figures it selects. Nor can the fragility of poetic disclosure be stabilized by an existential addition of successive "experiences" of it. The very medium of this integration, namely, history, does not itself have the stability of successiveness (BT, p. 474). Instead it operates a continual effect of alienation and dispersal—of "falling." Poetry, it is said, is that practice of language most aware *of* language—most aware of language as rhetoric and hence as a double agency facilitating and obstructing disclosure.[16] In this, poetry exemplifies the constitutive ambivalence of the movement by which, for Heidegger, truth is disclosed and closed off.

The ontical facts of the case do in fact point to a stubborn penetration of *Being and Time* into the modern poetic consciousness. The effect of *Being and Time* upon poetics during the fifty years of its history has a history of its own.[17] This has come about despite the fact that the work contains few explicit references to literature. For this reason too the idea of drawing implications for poetics from *Being and Time* has met a good deal of intelligent resistance. Beda Allemann, for example, speaks of an "essential absence of connection between *Being and Time* and the phenomenon of literature as such (and not merely as pre-ontological evidence)." But he goes on to concede that "nothing stands in the way of interpreting the results of the existential analytic for the sake of a theory of literature" (HH, pp. 88–89). Continental and, increasingly of late, American criticism bears him out. To judge from the richness and coherence of much poetic thought based on the book, one is no longer inclined to speak of an "essential" absence of connection between *Being and Time* and literature.

In the work of Johannes Pfeiffer, Emil Staiger, Max Bense, Maurice Blanchot, Paul de Man, and Jacques Derrida, to name a few, *Being and Time* has shaped theoretical and practical poetics in decisive ways, and it has done so despite a fundamental and entirely appropriate objection. This objection is based not on the inexplicitness of Heidegger's poetics in *Being and Time* but on the ontological bearing of that enterprise. The book is not just a phenomenology of human existence. It defines the structures which constitute human existence—the "existentials"—as part of an analysis of the understanding of Being which informs the question of Being. The existentials are not meant to organize our experience of some particular phenomenon or to serve as the leading ideas of an ontic discipline, such as the study of literature.

But this argument, while it rightly invokes caution, is not finally strong enough to debar literary speculation based on *Being and Time*. Taken strictly, it amounts to the assertion that ontological discourse and ontic discourse—ontic implying referential discourse—are informed by strictly separate intents. But this assertion is not right. When Heidegger writes, for example, "The history of the signification of the ontical concept cᶜ ⎍are' permits us to see . . . basic structures of Dasein" (BT, p. 243). he describes a relation not of polarity but of hermeneutic circularity. The ontological perspective emerges in and through the ontic conception. The presence of a number of such moments of reciprocal disclosure between the ontological phenomenon and the ontical concept is not accidental. It is based on the fact that "the roots of the existential analytic, on its part, are ultimately . . . *ontical*" (BT, p. 34). "The task of an existential analytic of Dasein has been delineated in advance, as regards both its possibility and its necessity, in Dasein's ontical constitution" (BT, p. 33). This is not to question, even within this circular relation, the priority of the ontological project. The existential analytic in *Being and Time* produces a region of clarity in which literary language could become transparent to its possibilities of ontological disclosure. But such an analysis would also bring to light legitimate ontical features of literature. Indeed, as we shall see, Heidegger designs his analysis this way.

He suggests early an important place for literature within the existential analytic. The "deposition" he selects from "the history of the signification of the ontical concept of 'care' " is a literary text, a fable by the Latin writer Hyginus. In this document, Heidegger asserts, his interpretation of human existence as care has been "sketched out beforehand in elemental ways" (BT, p. 242). True, what is decisive about this document is its character as a self-interpretation of Dasein and not as a literary text. But its literary character is not therefore incidental. Allemann writes, "In *Being and Time* there is not the slightest indication that literature would be particularly conducive to such self-interpretation. Rather, in its bearing on the interpretation of Dasein, literature is grouped together with philosophical psychology, anthropology, ethics, 'political science,' biography and the writing of history" (HH, p. 88). This argument is not convincing. Heidegger justifies his choice of the Hyginus fable as follows: "A deposition which comes from [Dasein's] history and goes back to it, and which, moreover, is *prior* to any scientific knowledge, will have especial weight, even though its importance is never purely ontological" (BT, pp. 241–242). A deposition prior to scientific knowledge could not have come out of the canonical texts of just any of the disciplines named above (although history or biography, it is true, could still qualify). Moreover, Heidegger's note describing how he came to discover the Hyginus fable takes pains to mention that "the fable of *Cura* . . . was taken over from Herder by Goethe and worked up for the second part of his *Faust*" (BT, p. 492). He is undoubtedly conjuring with the authority of Goethe's insight into the literary value of the work as a warrant for its "pre-ontological" importance.[18]

There is, however, an important statement in *Being and Time* which argues further and more decisively for the privilege of "poetic discourse." "In 'poetical' discourse," writes Heidegger, "the communication of the existential possibilities of one's state-of-mind can become an aim in itself, and this amounts to a disclosing of existence" (BT, p. 205). Allemann alludes to this sentence but glosses it with the intent of diminishing its force:[19] "If within the existential analytic, literature does nonetheless acquire a certain importance as the self-expression of Dasein, it should be further noted that Heidegger's concept of existence itself does not possess characteristics derived, say, from the psychology of the artist as the 'creative' human being, as is the case with central concepts (*Life, évolution créatrice*) is the thought of Dilthey and Bergson" (HH, p. 88). This of course is a true criticism, but it is not a devastating one. Heidegger attributes to mood a power to disclose the totality of

Dasein's being-in-the-world—a power more fundamental and also more widely distributed than the large emotions attributed by Dilthey to the artistic personality. Heidegger perceives with considerable originality that the poetic character of language could be its ability to realize the possibilities of disclosure belonging to moods.

Heidegger's insistence on the special privilege of mood runs through a number of works following *Being and Time* (for example, *What is Metaphysics?* and *The Origin of the Work of Art*). The persistence of this theme tends now to speak against the idea of a radical turning in the works after 1930. One example of this repetition may stand for many. In *The Origin of the Work of Art*, Heidegger says, "Perhaps, however, what we call feeling or mood . . . is more reasonable—that is, more intelligently perceptive—because more open to Being than all that reason which, having meanwhile become *ratio*, was misinterpreted as being rational."[20] The importance of this valorization of "feeling or mood" throughout Heidegger's writing should not be discounted because it may now strike us as banal, dated, or even potentially sinister. Certainly it was "in the air" before Heidegger even began thinking of *Being and Time*. In an anonymously published essay, for example, called "The Spiritual Dimension, Modernism, and Metaphysics" ("Das Geistliche, Modernismus und Metaphysik"), 1912, Robert Musil spoke on behalf of "that type of reason which . . . would forget about generating wholly verified truths (*Erkenntnisse*)— . . . but which would strive to find and systematize the truths lending bold new directions to feeling, even if they themselves remain mere plausibilities, hence a Reason for which thought would exist only in order to furnish intellectual scaffolding for as yet uncertain ways of being human."[21] Here, as in Heidegger, "thought" too, together with feeling, is put on the side opposite to "scientific" reason. (Heidegger notes in *Holzwege*: "Thinking begins only after we have experienced that reason is . . . the most stiff-necked adversary of thinking."[22]) Heidegger then, more successfully, I think, than any German thinker belonging to the tradition of "the philosophy of Life" (*Lebensphilosophie*), argues consistently for the dignity of the disclosive power of moods, their power as thought. This valorization of mood is central to *Being and Time*: "In 'poetical discourse' the communication of the existential possibilities of one's state of mind [mood] can become an aim in itself, and this amounts to a disclosing of existence." We shall be exploring the connection of poetry and mood as a vital moment within an epoch of German poetics. Allemann's comment makes a sharp distinction: the locus of the concept is not the psychology of the artist; but this should not diminish the force of Heidegger's statement. The poetics of the philosophy of life, for Dilthey and the George circle, calls for the heightened experience and expressiveness of genius. It could not inspire, except through calculated polemical negation, Heidegger's decision to orient the existential analytic toward *everyday* Dasein at a level where moods disclose existence as a burden and not as a festival.

Heidegger's description of the goal of poetic discourse is everywhere consistent with the existential analytic and has implications extending throughout the entire root system of *Being and Time*. Hence I do not find illuminating Allemann's conclusion that "state-of-mind and understanding as constitutive modes of Da-sein's being are . . . indifferent with respect to the phenomenon of artistic existence" (HH, p. 88). Heidegger says something different in attributing to poetry the possibility of truth precisely by its power of communicating the existential possibilities of states-of-mind through "intonation, modulation, the tempo of talk, 'the way of speaking'" (BT, p. 205).[23] "Way of speaking" means of course rhetoric. In thus founding truth (existential possibilities) on a discourse of moods, Heidegger joins a tradition subverting the western philosophy of language which normally founds meaning on, and subordinates rhetoric to, grammar and logic.[24] "The phenomenon of artistic existence" arises as the concern for making moods transparent to their source, wresting from them their fallen character of revealing only by way of "an evasive turning-away" from existence (BT, p. 175).

Furthermore, "'Understanding' means *to be projecting towards a potentiality-for-being for the sake of which any Dasein exists*." "The most primordial . . . disclosedness, [however,] in which Dasein, as a potentiality-for-Being, can be, is the *truth of existence*," and this "truth of Dasein which is most primordial . . . is resoluteness" (BT, pp. 385, 264, 343). Hence "the phenomenon of artistic existence," aiming at the disclosure of existential resoluteness, pursues the highest fate of understanding.

This highest fate is at once the fate of that "essential attribute of Dasein" we have been pursuing throughout all these chapters—the self (BT, p. 365). In its orientation, artistic existence conveys an understanding of selfhood at an intensifying level of generality, namely, as the "resoluteness [which] constitutes the *loyalty* of existence to its own Self" (BT, pp. 365, 443). Thus "artistic existence" can anticipate, in an exemplary way, "the coming-towards-itself . . . of resoluteness [, which] is at the same time a coming-back to one's ownmost Self" (BT, p. 388). State-of-mind, understanding, and the phenomenon of artistic existence are therefore not "indifferently" related; for artistic existence shapes mood and understanding to Dasein's intent to make a resolute return to the Self.

Allemann's final objection to this view is that an "existentialistic poetics (*Literaturwissenschaft*) basing itself on Heidegger is possible only on the strength of the anthropological misunderstanding" (HH, p. 89). But in light of the central role of the "basic state of mind" of anxiety in *Being and Time*, this objection is not telling either. In attending to literature as a disclosure by mood of existential possibilities, both Heidegger and the literary theorist proceed in basic accord with the project of *Being and Time*. Heidegger motivates his study of anxiety in the existential analytic by the same consideration. "Like any ontological interpretation whatsoever, this analytic can only, so to speak, 'listen in' to some previously disclosed entity as regards its Being. And it will attach itself to Dasein's distinctive and most far-reaching possibilities of disclosure in order to get information about this entity from these" (BT, p. 179). These far-reaching possibilities of disclosure are precisely those developed by the "distinctive" mood of anxiety. "In anxiety there lies the possibility of a disclosure which is quite distinctive; for anxiety individualizes. This individualization brings Dasein back from its falling, and makes manifest to it that authenticity and inauthenticity are possibilities of its Being" (BT, p. 235). The motive which prompts Heidegger to "listen in" to the mood of anxiety applies equally to the literary theorist. "Because of what [and the way in which] it discloses, [a state of mind or mood] is at the same time methodologically significant in principle for the existential analytic" (BT, p. 179). We remember that poetic discourse is defined by its intent to communicate "the existential possibilities of one's state of mind." Literature is par excellence the place and the mode in which the possibilities of moods are revealed. By "listening in" to the thematic disclosures and the mode of revealing accomplished by mood in literature, we will get information about this entity—literature—and the entity toward which it is turned—the Self.

When Heidegger's valorization of poetic discourse is taken as a center, poetics and ontology participate in *Being and Time* in a circle of reciprocal disclosure. The relation between particulars and generals in this text is then formally comparable with the relation of empirical aesthetics and critical thought in Kant's *Critique of Judgment*. Here too "the poetic art" (but also formal gardens and pure arabesques) are held in the play of reciprocal illumination with "something . . . connected with the ground of freedom." [25]

Heidegger's assertion linking poetry, mood, and truth is therefore important in various ways. It is in itself a fruitful beginning for a poetics. Next it focuses an entire system of assertions in *Being and Time* bearing on literary language. This system helps define an earlier Romantic tradition of poetic thought. Finally, when the implications of the system are spelled out, they articulate a stage in Heidegger's poetics which differs importantly from the poetics of subsequent texts. Therefore, to propose that in *Being and Time* "poetry as poetry is not yet in any way expressly thematized" or that "the first evidence of the contribution of what is specifically poetic to the self-interpretation of thought . . . is *The Origin of the Work of Art*" is to overstate matters polemically.[26] This approach diminishes the contribution to poetics of the fruitful complex of mood, temporality, and interpretation on behalf of the problematical effort of Heidegger's later essays to surpass phenomenological and philologically based literary study. Heidegger's later poetics are then attached to the unrepeatable enterprise of "poetic thinking," and literary study is left to court exhaustion through the technologies of linguistics, sociology, and deconstruction.

The key term in Heidegger's account of poetic discourse is "state-of-mind" or "disposition" (*Befindlichkeit*), which he also refers to by its ontic counterpart, mood (*Stimmung*). The term "mood" acquires its main force from its place within the ordonnance of *Being and Time*. But the fact that it figures here in the context of a poetics invokes a diachronic line of force, the "pathetic" tradition in aesthetics.[27]

Western aesthetics may be seen as the history of a single dichotomy modulated in innumerable ways: on the one hand, "an aesthetics of measure and symmetry, *consonantia* and *proportio*, the *unum-multum*, the aesthetics of knowledge, the play of the faculties, totality, form"; on the other, "emotions of pity and fear and their catharsis, enthusiasm, the sublime . . . empathy, expressiveness." Heidegger's *Being and Time* belongs to this second sequence, recognizable as the tradition which, from Greek times, has stressed the feeling dimension of literature. Whatever else may originate or define it, literary communication is, in one of its moments, essentially feeling. The position of the term of feeling varies, but recurs. Plato, in *Ion*, stresses the manic state-of-mind of the poet. Aristotle stresses the feeling object imitated by the tragic poet, "incidents embodying pity and fear," as well as the feelings aroused and purged in the spectator.[28] Kant defines the state of mind arising from the perception of form as a *Gefühl*, a sentiment. For Kant the poem is essentially form, but the analogy of aesthetic form is a feeling of the harmonious interplay of imagination and understanding resistant to final cognition.

If, in poetics, feeling is admitted, it is, however, at once modified; even for Dilthey, in his more radical style, it is "metamorphosed."[29] The tradition distinguishes between actual feelings and the feelings constituting art, which are fictive and whose motive is not personally interesting. Flaubert has Emma Bovary espouse this very distinction: "She knew now how small the passions were that art magnified. So, striving for detachment, Emma resolved to see in this reproduction of her sorrows a mere formal fiction for the entertainment of the eye."[30]

The poetics of feeling stresses the power of literature to reveal, by means of signs having the power to constitute feelings, something different from lived experience. Volkelt speaks of the literary work as *gefühlsanalog*, as analogous to feeling, but ideal, as other than feeling.[31] Literature generates the distinction between the fictive and the lived at the level of feeling; this can be seen in Aristotle. The purgation of tragedy is linked to the fact that what it communicates are not so much feelings (which have an historical existence) as the *possibility* of feelings; on the basis of this difference Aristotle grounds the superiority of poetry to history.

The distinction between feeling as sensation-bound and feeling as disclosure is most clearly accomplished in Kant. Kant describes the aesthetic sentiment as a general structure capable of making a far-reaching discovery. The aesthetic sentiment reveals the attunement (*Einstimmung*) of the cognitive energies enabling all particular cognitions and "finds a reference in itself" to a "ground of unity."[32] Biemel has noted the importance of this point. "Kant," he writes, "allows to feeling, to mood, a revelatory function of judgment which was usually granted only to logical cognition. Kant has demonstrated in the *Critique of Judgment* how feeling is no 'second-rate,' incidental, merely emotional faculty, but how, on the contrary, it mediates for us an experience which has a claim on general validity. He implicitly lends to feeling a 'veritative' significance which had not found its authentic justification until our time with Heidegger and Scheler."[33] Missing from this account is the appropriate stress on the verbal form of Kant's discovery: Kant gives aesthetic feeling, in its formality and transparency, the decisive name *Stimmung* ("mood" and also "attunement").

The elaboration in Kant's third critique of the dimension of mood in art is an exceedingly important yet scarcely assimilated achievement of his aesthetics. Kant identifies the essential character of mood as nonpurposive feeling, as the felt absence of a real-intentional character. Mood is self-reflexive feeling, feeling attuned to the feeling mode.

Spitzer gave the subtitle *Prolegomena to an Interpretation of the Word "Stimmung"* to his monumental *Classical and Christian Ideas of World Harmony*. His essay breaks off just short of Kant. The history of mood in the modern period remains to be written. Rousseau would figure in it decisively, not least as the author of the *Confessions* who conceives his project as a history of moods. "What I write is less the history of these events in themselves as that of my mood (*l'état de mon âme*) in proportion to their occurrence."[34] Such a project requires the invention of "a new language," especially since the moods of his story are original.[35] Yet they are original not because they are particular and personal, but because they are shown as possessing a native thrust toward generality. Rousseau means to communicate the general disclosure in his moods, like, for example, the horror of all injustice in his initial experience of being mistreated. "This feeling [toward violence and injustice] was only a personal one in its origins, but it has since assumed such a consistency and has become so divorced from personal interests that my blood boils at the sight or the tale of any injustice, whoever may be the sufferer and wherever it may have taken place, in just the same way as if I were myself its victim."[36] Rousseau will guarantee the general orientation of his sentiments by "doubly portraying [his] mood."[37] That is, he will include in his portrait of the initial mood the ideal dimension of the mood of writing. This mood allows him to discover in the initial sentiment of injustice a "consistency" or truth which could be established only as a consequence of the act of writing. Rousseau's concern for the ideal or general character of moods also shapes the *Fifth Promenade*. Kant may well have registered this, and the celebrated "sentiment de l'existence" may have guided his phenomenal description of the mood of aesthetic judgment.

The centrality of the term "mood" (*Stimmung* and its cognates *Gefühl, Gemütszustand, sentiment, état d'âme*) in the imaginative work of Rousseau and the systematic work of Kant adumbrates the importance of mood in the poetry and criticism of Romantic writers. The twenty-second letter of Schiller's *Aesthetic Education* connects artistic form with the "aesthetic mood" (*die ästhetische Stimmung des Gemüts*), "which contains the whole of humanity." For Hölderlin, for whom feeling constitutes "the best sobriety and reflection of the poet," "the inner ideal life can be grasped in various moods."[38] These moods then function as the principles of poetic diction, as "tonalities." Wordsworth's "mood of composition" transforms emotions recollected in tranquility into the fictive emotions of his art. The theory of the last two writers helps define the great common themes of their work as mood, temporality, and poetic language, and the form of their work (in Staiger's sense) as a certain "form of temporality."[39] Their poetry exists as the movement through which lived moods are sublated into the moodful language of fictions.

The *history* of mood in the nineteenth century foreshadows the implicit inner connections in *Being and Time* between the terms "mood," "historicity," and "interpretation." A formulation from Lukács' *Theory of the Novel*, describing the alienated situation from which the hero of the novel arises, suggests the necessity of these connections: "The nature of moods . . . presupposes the impossibility of an achieved and meaningful substance, the impossibility that the constitutive subject could find an appropriate constitutive object."[40] The impossibility of the coincidence of the subject with another being, evident in the fragility and strangeness of its moods, establishes the historicity of the subject. For, finally, it is this "necessity of passing through time which prevents the spirit from being master of itself and of its content, of coinciding with itself in the absolute plenitude of a systematic and transparent possession of reality."[41] The common property of post-Kantian philosophical anthropologies in Germany is the revelation through mood of human historicity and hence the necessarily interpretive relation of the self to its content, its "text." More particularly, when the source of literary language is grasped as mood, as the fundamental yet unstable reflex of the temporal self, the historical character of literary *interpretation* becomes explicit. "[Literary] understanding can be called complete only when it becomes aware of its own temporal predicament and realizes that the horizon within which the totalization can take place is time itself. The act of understanding is a temporal act that has its own history."[42] This situation helps originate the rich speculative tradition of nineteenth-century interpretation theory.

Kierkegaard, Dilthey, and Nietzsche are the chief figures of this tradition and Heidegger's immediate precursors. In each, a reflection on the category of mood profiles and organizes a poetics and hermeneutics. In Kierkegaard moods are tones or voices making up the "lyric dialectic" and exacting strenuous interpretations and choices. Dilthey's poetics, especially in *The Poetic Imagination* (*Die Einbildungskraft des Dichters*), profiles mood as the agent of the passage of lived experience (*Erlebnis*) to its historical expression (*Ausdruck*) and its reconstitution through interpretation. This term heightens Dilthey's consciousness of the historicity of textual interpretation but also suggests to him the way in which meaning might be communicated across historical differences. Nietzsche meanwhile represents in the figure of mood that thinking which is not self-reflection but activity and play. The link between a mood-centered aesthetics and Nietzsche's panhermeneutical metaphysics is richly put in an aphorism from *The Dawn* (*Morgenröte*): "Can it be . . . that all our so-called consciousness is a more or less fantastic commentary on an unknown, perhaps unknowable, but *felt* text?"[43] (italics mine).

Between the conceptions of mood in these writers there are vital differences. Yet the term survives in modern European poetics in its crucial difference from that of sensation-bound feeling. Throughout the entire tradition, but clearest in Heidegger, mood stands for a disclosive power whose reach cognitive understanding cannot attain. The affirmation of the centrality of mood is at the same time guarded by a live reluctance to surrender truth to the "squint-eyed gaze" of irrationalism (BT, p. 175). Perhaps something of the optimism engendered by the new discovery attunes the mood which Kant makes exemplary for his demonstration. The aesthetic mood has the tonality of sociability, play, and delight, whereas for Heidegger the exemplary mood is anxiety (BT, p. 204).[44]

What force, then, does Heidegger's connecting poetic discourse with mood exert on the system of *Being and Time*? This demonstration is in principle as long as *Being and Time* itself, for the scope of the terms "discourse," "communication," "existential," "possibility," "disclosure," and, finally, "state of mind" encompasses the entire existential analytic. What follows is a brief account of features of Heidegger's description of these various terms which strike me as particularly interesting or as hitherto unnoted or unstressed.

1. *Discourse* differs from written or spoken language. Along with mood and understanding it constitutes a primordial disposition of being prior to language. Heidegger terms discourse "the articulation of intelligibility"; it accomplishes "the 'significant' articulation of the intelligibility of Being-in-the-world. . . . Vocal utterance, however, is not essential for discourse" (BT, pp. 204, 316). "At this stage of Heidegger's thought," writes Biemel, "*logos* [i.e., discourse], in contradistinction to the usual meaning of the word, is the constitutive moment, and language is the way in which *logos* gets expressed. Language is that through which the *logos* makes itself mundane; through language it becomes an element of the world and can be treated like other things found in the world."[45]

The force of this point is the level at which Heidegger situates the poetic. It is therefore a fundamental orientation toward moods as toward intelligible existence as a whole. It is also the verbal expression of meanings, but "in the factical linguistic form of any definite case of [such] discourse" not every constitutive element of the poetic may appear (BT, p. 206). To this extent literary language could not be grasped as an ensemble of word-things present-at-hand—the canon—nor as a tool functional within a context of "equipment"—the institution. Literature is not an objective fact nor a social function. It would have to be understood principally in terms of an intention aiming at conformity with a goal of which it falls short. As Jan Aler observes, "As soon as understanding manifests itself as a phonetic expression of significations—as an expression in words—one can observe that the project appears [in *Being and Time*] in its being thrown."[46] In the way the poetic disclosure is expressed, there is already a certain opaque understanding deposited in it. "Dasein is constantly delivered over to this interpretedness, which controls and distributes the possibilities of average understanding and of the state-of-mind belonging to it" (BT, p. 211).

The originality of literary language, together with its ineluctable captivation by the world, inspires de Man's view of literature in *Blindness and Insight*.

> With respect to its own specificity (that is, as an existing entity susceptible to historical description), literature exists at the same time in the modes of error and truth; it both betrays and obeys its own mode of being. . . . If literature rested at ease within its own self-definition, it could be studied according to methods that are scientific rather than historical. We are obliged to confine ourselves to history when this is no longer the case, when the entity steadily puts its own ontological status into question.[47]

An entity that seeks to disclose being as the "worldly expression" of significance courts "the desire to break out of literature toward the reality of the moment";[48] whether as a movement of appropriation or of denial of the moment, it is prey, therefore, to the destiny of manipulation, of dissimulation, of idle talk.

Heidegger's poetics shares with certain types of Czech and French structuralism the perception that the true subject of poetics is not poems but "poeticity." But for Heidegger the "poeticity" of literary language consists not in a calculable property but in an intention—one, moreover, which it is possible to describe more richly than in the customary way as self-reflexive and self-distancing in its relation of signifier and signified. The character of poetic language arises from its aim of articulating states-of-mind, that is, moods, with a view toward their fullest possible disclosure; what they disclose are existential possibilities, that is, existence.

The force of Heidegger's situating the poetic at the level of *logos* and not of language might be illustrated in another way. From a variety of critical standpoints, language is nowadays described as literary to the extent that it reveals its character as figurative speech. But following Heidegger the essence of figurative language cannot be located in definite types of verbal entities having the character of objects present-at-hand—say, in metaphorical or metonymic figures. Figurativeness arises from a primordial intention which language can mediate but not realize. The source of poetic figuration is the openness of moods to primary existential possibility, to authentically finite, temporal existence. As language, however, poetry is insistently problematic. "Is [language] a kind of equipment ready-to-hand within the world, or has it Dasein's kind of Being, or is it neither of these?" (BT, p. 209). The possibility that language has Dasein's kind of being is by no means auspicious. It implies that language aiming to communicate the existential possibilities of moods will, like Dasein, find itself "equiprimordially in untruth," in error.

> It is not an accident that the earliest systematic Interpretation of affects that has come down to us is not treated in the framework of 'psychology.' Aristotle investigates the *páthe* (affects) in the second book of his Rhetoric. Contrary to the traditional orientation, according to which rhetoric is conceived as the kind of thing we 'learn in school,' this work of Aristotle must be taken as the first systematic hermeneutic of the everydayness of Being with one another. Publicness, as the kind of Being which belongs to the "they," not only has in general its own way of having a mood, but needs moods and 'makes' them for itself. It is into such a mood and out of such a mood that the orator speaks. He must understand the possibilities of moods in order to rouse them and guide them aright. (BT, p. 178)

Of our quarrels with others we make rhetoric. Poetic discourse runs the danger of manipulating the inauthentic possibilities of moods and as poetic *language* has always already submitted to some extent to this danger. Poetic language is to the same extent rhetoric—but a rhetoric that functions as a *figure* for the intention toward authenticity.

2. Heidegger speaks of poetic discourse as a type of *communication*. This point should not be passed over. It follows a full account of the meaning of communication apropos of assertion and interpretation, and the theme of communication is again picked up in Heidegger's discussion of discourse and language. Here Heidegger writes:

> The phenomenon of *communication* must be understood in a sense which is ontologically broad. 'Communication' in which one makes assertions—giving information, for instance—is a special case of that communication which is grasped in principle existentially. In this more general kind of communication, the Articulation of Being with one another understandingly is constituted. Through it a co-state-of-mind [*Mitbefindlichkeit*] gets 'shared,' and so does the understanding of Being-with. Communication is never anything like a conveying of experiences, such as opinions or wishes, from the interior of one subject into the interior of another. Dasein-with is already essentially manifest in a co-state of mind and a co-understanding. In discourse Being-with becomes 'explicitly' *shared*; that is to say, it *is* already, but it is unshared as something that has not been taken hold of and appropriated. (BT, p. 205)

Poetic discourse is, for Heidegger, the privileged vehicle of a certain kind of communication which shares explicitly the existential possibilities of moods. It is discourse informed by a communicative intent.

In this perspective no act of writing could be described as having put aside the communicative function. The point is Nietzschean. "The ultimate result [of the development of this function] is an excess of this strength and art of communication—as it were a capacity that has gradually been accumulated and now waits for an heir who might squander it. (Those who are called artists are those heirs; so are orators, preachers, writers)" (GS, p. 298). The Dionysian type is marked by "the ease of metamorphosis. . . . It is impossible for him to overlook any sign of an affect . . . , just as he commands the art of communication in the highest degree" (PN, pp. 519–520). This "squandering" of the communicative power to signify affects exceeds need and has an impersonal character. As Fritz Kaufmann writes,

> Contact with the artist himself is not that of personal association but of trans-personal participation in his work. Of course this participation is mediated by communication. But not so that the artist himself communicates his mood to us, manifests himself personally as the vehicle of the mood and the communication . . . ; the mood communicates itself to us from the work, in the way in which it precipitates in this work, as an independent crystallization.[49]

The ineluctability of the communicative intent is maintained even in recent types of critical theory working with the sociological and everyday linguistic analogues to literature and as such most foreign to Heidegger's ontology. To insist on the communicative character of literary discourse is therefore by no means to make the polemically anti-existentialist gesture which many suppose it to be. The notion links Heidegger's program with Habermas' and Watzlawick's and can be paraphrased thus: "The one true *impossibility* of human communicative behavior [is] that *it is impossible not to communicate.*"[50] This point would make unpromising a description of modernism of the Flaubertian strain as "the attempt to escape from the circuit of communication, to make the text a written object and not the physical manifestation of a communicative act."[51] Such an approach itself borrows the formalist tendency to interpret the *lógos* "in a way which is ontologically inadequate, [wherein] the *lógos* gets experienced as something present-at-hand and interpreted as such, while at the same time the entities which it points out have the meaning of presence-of-hand" (BT, p. 203). Culler questions the axiom of the coherence of the literary work in related terms: "The notion that

works of art must be unified and that the task of criticism is to dem-
onstrate this unity derives, at least in part, from the communicative model
and the metaphysics of presence on which it rests."⁵² After *Being and
Time*, of course, this makes for strange reading. The experience of "abysmal" thought, to which "the metaphysics of presence" alludes by contrast, is Heidegger's experience before Derrida's. Not every communicative model rests on a metaphysics of presence.

     Being and Time forges a link between a "communicative model"
and a theory of historicity. As Aler observes: "In linguistic art the sensitive . . . explanation of our Being-in-the-world takes place in such a
way that it also speaks to others. If this had not been touched on in
principle, it would then have been impossible in *Being and Time* to develop the phenomenon of being united by a common fate within the
framework of man's historicity."⁵³

            A poem is a weightless web of
            words which by their ordonnance,
            their sound and their content,
            in fusing the memory of some-
            thing visible and the memory of
            something audible with the element
            of movement, evokes a precisely
            circumscribed, dreamily distinct,
            fleeting state of the soul which
            we call mood.⁵⁴

         3. *Mood*. If a text were only a self-deconstructing motion, a
play of ineffable differences, a representation of nothingness, it could
not weigh heavily enough upon the reader to produce a mood. "What is
told is always the telling"—but what is told is "telling" only as the told
constitutes a world whose construction engages us.⁵⁵ The mood of the
text is precisely the mood of its world—the effect of the text's finitude
on the given reader. Before there is the world of *Combray* or of *The Castle*,
however, there has to be the worldhood of these worlds, there has to be
the communicative situation. The situation arises as a double moment
of world-constitution and unsettlement: the fictional world conveyed must
be unfamiliar, and it must be conveyable. Mood is this burdensome rapport.

     Heidegger's analysis of communication "in a sense which is
ontologically broad" is vital to a discussion of poetic discourse. Poetic
discourse turns on an act of communication, and this act is essentially

the sharing of a mood. To say of a certain kind of discourse that in it "the communication of the existential possibilities of one's state-of-mind can become an aim in itself" is not on the face of it to specify "poetic discourse," since such communication would apparently describe this very section 40 of *Being and Time*, where Heidegger explains the existential possibilities of the basic state-of-mind of anxiety. This explanation, however, is made in the mode of assertion. And it is "assertion" which Heidegger, in the passage above, specifically designates "a special case" of communication and again as "not the primary 'locus' of truth" (BT, p. 269). "Indeed *from the ontological point of view* we must as a general principle leave the primary discovery of the world to 'bare mood' " (BT, p. 177). The distinctiveness and primordiality of poetic discourse are based on the fact that its truth is the truth of moods as it can be communicated *by a mood*.

To the extent that a poem is poetic it thus communicates a mood transparent to its own possibilities. These possibilities vary of course with the mood communicated. But at the basis of each such structure of possibilities is what Heidegger terms "thrownness" (*Geworfenheit*). Literature reveals through moods the dimensions of thrownness. The French translations *déjection* (Wahl) and *déréliction* (de Waehlens) convey something of its negative tonality. As "thrown," Dasein finds itself open to itself and its world but having to endure itself and its world as a burden. Both this openness and this oppression stem from the fact that Dasein does not know its origin or its goal: it is open only to the existence that it has to be in being already "there." When Dasein finds itself thrown, it finds itself moreover "in a way of finding which arises not so much from a direct seeking as rather from a fleeing" (BT, p. 174). In its states-of-mind Dasein turns uneasily away from the fact of existence, its "that it is."

In a valuable paper entitled "Befindlichkeit and Truth" Lawrence Hinman marks out a zone for poetic disclosure.[56] Hinman registers ambiguities in Heidegger's discussion of moods in *Being and Time*. Heidegger's account of anxiety turns on the distinction between anxiety and fear: "Fear," writes Heidegger, "is anxiety, fallen into the 'world,' inauthentic, and, as such, hidden from itself" (BT, p. 234). Like all moods, then, with one exception, fear discloses being-in-the-world as a whole primarily in the manner of an evasive turning away. Anxiety is the exception, for "that in the face of which one has anxiety is Being-in-the world as such." Anxiety "brings Dasein face to face with its *Being-free for* the authenticity of its Being" (BT, p. 232). Fear, then—and indeed any mood other than anxiety—would be inhibited in its disclosure, first, by the manner of the disclosure, for it discloses only as an evasive turning away, and, second, in the content of the disclosure: it is essentially oriented toward things in the world.

Hinman, notices, however, an important ambivalence. Heidegger also writes: "Fear discloses Dasein predominantly in a privative way. . . . Whether privatively or positively, fearing about something, as being afraid in the face of something, always discloses equiprimordially entities within-the-world and Being-in" (BT, p. 181). Hinman concludes therefore, "that there may be instances in which fearing discloses in a non-privative manner, i.e., in which we turn towards rather than away from that which is disclosed."[57] This opens up the possibility of the authentic disclosure of other ontic moods. The zone in which this disclosure could be accomplished is poetry, the poetic discourse which aims to communicate, other than by an evasive turning away, the "positive" existential possibilities of all moods.

Poetic discourse thus brings Dasein face to face with things in the world together with the fact of its contingency, its "thralldom" to existence, brings it back from the "tranquillized supposition that it possesses everything, or that everything is within its reach" (BT, p. 223). It arrests the turbulence with which Dasein falls away from its own destination—its finitude, "the fact 'that it is, and that it has to be . . . the entity which it is' " (BT, p. 321). As finite, Dasein is fundamentally thrown toward its death; it therefore knows the possibility of authentic existence. This possibility is the central disclosure of mood transparent to itself. Toward it is oriented the force of the poetic disclosure of the other "essential characteristics of states-of-mind." "*Mood has already disclosed, in every case, Being-in-the-world as a whole, and makes it possible first of all to direct oneself toward something; . . . [further it] implies a disclosive submission to the world, out of which we can encounter something that matters to us*" (BT, pp. 176–77). Together, these revelations constitute a virtual origin for Dasein, from which it could redirect itself toward something or let something matter to it authentically.

The point becomes strong, I think, if one grasps the literary work as a world. In an exemplary way, the human beings in it are delivered over to that world and none other. The interpreter of the work who shares the existence of its "characters" has the essential experience of what it is to be enthralled by a world. "In the works of Shakespeare and Goethe," as Schopenhauer wrote, "each character, as he acts and speaks, is in the right, even if it is the devil himself! Because each character is so objectively understood that we are drawn into his orbit and compelled to see things as he does. For he is created, just as the works of nature are, from an inner principle, by the power of which his speech and action appear as completely natural, indeed inevitable" (cited in BU, p. 200). At the same time, however, that the interpreter is enthralled, he maintains an interpretive distance from his experience. This distance permits him to grasp the fact of his thralldom to his *own* world and at the same time to reorient himself toward it.

Literature thus becomes the vehicle, for Heidegger, of a possible authenticity. This claim has often been mentioned, especially by those readers of *Being and Time* who from the very start were most interested in finding a connection between it and literature. As a rule, however, no attempt has been made to find in *Being and Time* the justification for the view that literature profiles with any particular clarity or inspires with any particular urgency the existential possibility of authenticity. But this argument is present in various forms.

Poetic discourse seeks to share that articulation of moods which would amount to a disclosure of existence. It thus aims at Dasein's most *authentic* disclosedness, for "the most primordial and indeed most authentic disclosedness in which Dasein . . . can be, is the truth of existence" (BT, p. 264). This truth is Dasein's "resoluteness," its will to return to its own Self. The idea is confirmed by Heidegger's discussion of the discourse which takes a different aim—which issues into assertion and whose truth is *derivative* from existential-hermeneutical disclosure. One way of distinguishing between these two kinds of discourse is by distinguishing the moods that accompany them; linked to different modes of understanding, these practices are differently attuned. Poetic discourse elicits moods of various kinds, including the mood of anxiety. "Apophantical" discourse, issuing into the language of assertions, knows only the mood of theory—the tranquility of just tarrying alongside the world.[58] But this mood is marked by its goal of being without moods. It would be proof against the disclosure which moods could accomplish, including the "quite distinctive" disclosure of anxiety, "that authenticity and inauthenticity are possibilities of Dasein's Being" (BT, p. 235).

In an important way, then, Heidegger's analysis of anxiety merely makes explicit the disclosure he first attributes to poetic discourse. Earlier, we noted the formal analogy that *Being and Time* "listens in" to the possibilities of such distinctive entities as moods. This is the traditional project of poet and hearer. But the affinity is more revealing at the substantive level: Heidegger's analysis of the basic mood of anxiety provides him with "the phenomenal basis for explicitly grasping Dasein's primordial totality of Being" (BT, p. 227). This, however, is exactly the function he earlier assigned to the phenomenon of poetic language. The poetic articulation of moods with communicative intent discloses existence. To prove this affinity, finally, it is not necessary to find that poetic understanding is anxiously attuned. For "along with the sober anxiety," Heidegger declares, "which brings us face to face with our in-dividualized potentiality-for-Being, there goes an unshakable joy in this possibility" (BT, p. 358). This joy could be the essence of poetry and the highest fate of the self.

On Rhetoric, Its Treachery, Confession, and the Desire for Wholeness

> In an autobiography one cannot
> avoid writing "often" where truth
> would require that "once" be written.
> —Kafka

In the late 1940s, I sat in a subway car on my way to Columbia, traveling from the Hamilton Park station in Brooklyn to my destination at Morningside Heights. I had taken from my brother's bookcase a water-stained pamphlet by Max Weber called *The Profession of Science* and Evelyn Waugh's *Brideshead Revisited*; and as I read, and was hurtled along, I imagined with increasing excitement and accuracy that I was myself a student at the Universities of Heidelberg and Cambridge; it seemed that the train I was on was essentially the train that would carry me along to these places in Europe.

Now, long afterward, as I reflect on the years which I did indeed spend at Heidelberg and at Cambridge, I realize that in those years I was never further from my proper destination. It was on the subway train that morning, traveling to Columbia, that I was most myself.

Here, surely, is an autobiographical fragment. Consider these features of its rhetoric: The text identifies a protagonist—the naive self, the pilgrim that travels on subways; it also identifies a narrator—the reflective self that remembers and realizes its old errors. The signs indicating these selves are congruent; both are marked "I." Both signs apparently refer, moreover, to adjacent orders that are themselves congruent. The first self moves in a familiar world in which there figure compatibly subways, books, and persons using them. The self of the narrator, who remembers and realizes, is congruent with the order of the author—*myself*—who by most surface features can have figured then and figures now in that same world of books and subways, and for whom such acts too of remembering and relating are possible.

The bond at the center, of congruent signs of persons having empirical reference—this bond sustained by acts of memory and acts of writing which hearken to memory, all fused into a single identity—invites you to enter a pact and assume autobiographical expectations.

This way you will understand the fragment—Wait!—as *autobiography*? Consider: In the late 1940s I was about fourteen; I have never taken a train from the Hamilton Park station, which in fact does not exist; my brother had no bookcase in the room we shared; *Brideshead Revisited* is not about Cambridge; regrettably, I have never studied either at Heidelberg or at Cambridge. If you entered into an autobiographical pact, you may now feel deceived and that I've broken the pact.

What exactly has happened? Must the pact be dissolved? Consider the text in light of the information I've given: Is it basically deceitful? Has the experience it evokes been destroyed by fabrication, by the illegitimate assumption of autobiographical features? Suppose I mean to construct and preserve such an experience of self-discovery: would it be better to do away with the indicators of autobiography?

No. This point emerges by elimination. For example, I could try to communicate this new, fuller account of what is at work in my text by disrupting the congruence of the two first persons, by rewriting the opening so: "We were in class at Columbia (in the late 1940s) when the teaching assistant came in, followed by the new boy, about fourteen, holding at his knees a hat—one of those headgears of composite order, in which we can find traces of a Cambridge scarf and the peaked shakos worn in dueling fraternities at German universities." I have changed the naive first person to a third person and now have the novelistic situation of the opening of *Madame Bovary*. But this new text is not actually more faithful than the old to the implied meaning, because I do not mean to eliminate from the experience the continuity between the two persons—pilgrim and narrator. Their mutual dependency—their involvement and the lack of any certain priority between them—should remain.

Nor is there any improvement of accuracy, either, in rewriting my fragment so as to dramatize the nonreferential character of the naive self, the fourteen-year old, thus: "Late in the 1940s I sat strapped inside my Spitfire, on my way to Columbia, flying north from the Hamilton Park station." I then have another novelistic situation, something like another Flaubert novel, *The Memoirs of a Madman*, or a paradoxical, deliberately disruptive kind of autobiography, the calculated inverse of the genre in which what would be essential to remember would be only delirium. But this again is not my intent, which is to present "an acquist of true experience" won from a struggle with the world.

What I most nearly have after revealing that I am different from both protagonist and narrator is the situation, say, of Dostoevsky's *Notes from Underground*, where a footnote produces this difference; thus, writes Dostoevsky, "The author of the Notes and the Notes themselves are of course imaginary." Now we have the type of the retrospective *Ich-Roman*, the novel of the retrospective self: a fictive chronicle of memory. But I am not ready to accept in my text so radical a separation of my person from my imagination.

This exercise shows how forms of fiction can be generated from a systematic disruption of autobiographical features. To destroy the congruence of the naive and narrating selves is to produce the novel of interpersonal relations, narrated from a third vantage point; to suspend the referentiality of the naive self is to produce a hallucinatory *journal intime*; to destroy the congruence of the narrating self and author is to produce the fictive autobiography. It's the last transformation that seems most appropriate when I admit that as an autobiographer, I have not been telling the truth.

But neither have I been lying. While it is true that I could not travel to Columbia in the forties, I could and did so in the fifties, from the *Fort* Hamilton *Parkway* subway station. I did ultimately get to read Max Weber and Evelyn Waugh (although at different institutions). I did imagine studying in Europe, and indeed did study there; if I was not a student at Heidelberg and at Cambridge, I've met—with wonderment— some who were; but in their company I have sometimes felt remote, and then felt the absence of my native subway as a place for recovering strength.

Essentially the autobiography is mine; it consists of memories which are mine and other meanings which are not memories only in a trivial way: they are not essentially unlike memories. I have sought to make memory function as a source, however intermittently; I have also written words that do not designate memories, and instead designate fictions or figures, but I mean them to be plausible as my experience.

This last distinction is the one which Rousseau makes in the preface to *La Nouvelle Héloïse*, the drafts of his *Confessions*, and the *Fourth*

Promenade—the distinction between the lie and the fiction. Fictions may be innocent "figurative" language (in which certain states of mind, like love, must express themselves). The lie, on the other hand, includes the consciousness of asserting for profit something to have been the case which memory rejects. Here then is my subject: What happens to the autobiographical pact when autobiography, essentially answerable to memory, veers toward fiction?

The text I began with doesn't serve me anymore, but fails, I hope, in an illustrative way. It raised the question of whether the presence of fiction negates the autobiographical pact, but it did not succeed in raising the question with the right urgency. That is because my stake was too much an entirely cognitive one. I meant to define and have you acknowledge a truth—the superiority of imagination to fulfillment; but whether this cognitive agreement was obtained by an autobiography more or less fictive is not finally crucial. Max Frisch argues that such a thing as experience can come into existence only on the basis of invented fictions. Nevertheless I did insist on keeping the autobiographical status of my text. I wanted the form because I also wanted in my text the reciprocal involvement of two selves, the uncertain priority of one over the other. I wanted its insight to come from empirical experience, and I wanted my person and my imagination to cohere. All these factors point to an intent different from cognitive agreement: the intent, by confessing error, to prove intactness and obtain justification.

The stakes are raised when a text—unlike mine—is powerfully informed by a confessional intent. Such a text carries the illocutionary force of a demand for exculpation. Here it is essential that the persons of the text refer to a personal and historical order surpassing that of "the sole materiality of language, the opaqueness of the text" (the phrase is Eugene Vance's), and it is essential that the narrator not obviously lie. For what is at stake is the justification of the self (despite its shortcomings and errors) by a demonstration of its value in its wholeness, intactness, and integrity. The reader is needed to consent to the success with which a troubled identity is secured.

It is no accident that modern autobiography begins with Rousseau's *Confessions*. This work claims to be guided by memory. But it undertakes, if paradoxically, to depict past *states-of-mind* or *moods*, one vital register of which is moods of self-loss. The shortcoming of these moods—their sad, negative, nostalgic quality—is emphasized by Rousseau's poetics of confession. To define the proper subject of autobiography as the history of one's moods is to be condemned to a disconcerting self-doubling. Rousseau notes: "In surrendering myself at once to the memory of the impression received and my present mood, I shall doubly portray my state of mind." For the mind like Rousseau's which prides itself on "having thought more and better than the kings" and will claim virtue for feats of intellectual force, it must be excruciating to perceive, at the close, how disorderly and lost, how unfaithful to the promise of his past, has been his construction of it. This is the meaning of his appeal at the close that the reader help him find the lost thread of his life.

But the *Confessions* performs amazing feats along the way. Consider Rousseau's problem: How can a confession function as the depiction of moods which cannot be literally represented and whose authenticity is therefore in question? What pact with the reader can be formed on the basis of representations that cannot answer to memory and as such must be mainly lies and/or fictions? Rousseau denies that he has lied (his biographers accuse him not so much of lies as of excuses). He concedes that his depictions of moods are, logically speaking, fictions. As E. T. A. Hoffmann wrote upon rereading the *Confessions* for the thirtieth time, "My head spins too when it becomes a question of grasping feelings in words." Yet the promise of the work to exhibit an authentic self depends on the truth of the feelings represented, hence on the good faith of a narrator who does not himself manipulate or design his subject. If there is design, it must lie in details which act prefiguratively, yet in a spontaneous way; the work must seem to justify a self spontaneously.

Rousseau cannot solve the problem in the manner of Augustine. Augustine confesses a self by enacting the process of exculpation; the moment of conversion is a moment of longing appeal answered by the respondent, the "You" of the text, God. The authority of the conversion, which assures—indeed, is—justification rests with the character of this conversion as a repetition of exemplary conversions in the past. The call to Augustine to take and read Scripture seems to sound spontaneously, but the swiftness with which Augustine responds is the measure of his preparation. Augustine's readiness to comply has its counterpart in the patterning of events (by the narrator) leading up to this moment. These events are stories of conversions: of Victorinus, the powerful Roman orator and scholar who was not ashamed to publish his conversion; of Saint Antony, the Egyptian monk who applied to himself words overheard as the Gospel was being read and was immediately converted; of Ponticianus, whose friends, happening on a life of Antony, all at once resolved to imitate him. And the book which Augustine takes up contains Paul's Epistles. Only then "was [it] as though the light of confidence flooded into my heart and all the darkness of doubt was dispelled."

Augustine makes contact with the experience of the exemplary convert Paul by reading him with the readiness prepared in him by tales of intervenient conversions. He inscribes himself into this series; his experience is authorized by a lineage of conversions—texts of conversions—returning to Scripture. Augustine's human time, a time of error, distraction, and vacillation, is flooded with the sacramental time of typological relations.

Rousseau, however, is cut off from this tradition. Augustine writes, "I should be null and void and could not exist at all if you my God were not in me." Rousseau might be said to have written. "I should be null and void if you my self (*mon vrai Moi*) were not in me." Augustine's warrant for intactness after a life of dispersion is a conversion founded on authenticated conversions; his text echoes older examples. How shall Rousseau, in describing moments of self-recovery, transparency, and coherence, found these sentiments against the charge that his narrator has invented, imagined, designed them so? Rousseau has only himself as an example; he must prove his conversion by founding an account of it, an exemplary experience of selfhood, on an earlier such experience, and by imputing to the first mood—as we shall see—a spontaneously prophetic and prefigurative character.

Rousseau describes an idyll. He has been staying with Madame de Warens; on a holiday he walks outside the city at Annecy, "my heart full of her image and of the ardent desire to spend all my days with her." He knows, however, that for the present this is impossible. Church bells sound; he hears birdsong; the beauty of the day, the loveliness of the scene, the scattered country houses in which he imagines them living together—"all this struck me with an impression so vivid, tender, sad and touching that I saw myself, as if in ecstasy, transported into this happy state, in which my heart possessing all the happiness which could delight it, without even dreaming of the voluptuousness of the senses, enjoyed it with an inexpressible sense of ravishment. I do not remember every being hurtled into the future with so much force and illusion as I was then. If ever the dream of waking man had the air of a prophetic vision, it was assuredly that one." The force and vividness of Rousseau's dream prefigure its future accomplishment.

Rousseau's crucial experience occurs seven years later, on the occasion of another walk, this time *with* Madame de Warens. Once again, it is a holiday: "Everything seemed to conspire in the happiness of the day. It had rained shortly before: no dust; and brooks (*ruisseaux*) flowing freely. The air was pure, the horizon without clouds: serenity ruled in the heavens as in our hearts." They wander freely, botanizing, talking of themselves and of their fate. "Suddenly," writes Rousseau, "an idea which struck me distracted me from the flowers . . . . The mood, the *situation d'âme* in which I found myself, everything we did and said that day, all the objects that had struck me, recalled that sort of dream which wholly awake I had at Annecy seven years before and of which I've given an account in its proper place." Transported, he cries: "Thanks to you, my happiness is at its peak, may it nevermore decline, may it last as long as I savor it! it will not end but with me myself."

His happiness is at a peak; it consists in the fulfillment of a prophecy and has an intensely intellectual character. The prophecy is fulfilled by an idea; the idea is that of a repetition of an experience in the past, but that experience was itself one of imaginative revery. The self is constituted whole by the spectacular coherence of its intellectual power—which prophesies the future as an event of perfect *déjà vu*, with the curious feature that what was seen earlier and recovered was seen in a trance.

At a certain pitch of enactment of intellectual force, the cognitive intent of self-recognition serves the confessional purpose of procuring the subject's integrity. Rousseau converts to selfhood on the basis of the exemplary visionary power of his own prophesying. To alter one word in Pascal's celebrated definition, prophecy for Rousseau is "parler de *Soi* par un sentiment immédiat." A self capable of grasping its own moods as prefiguring their future accomplishment, so that at the heart of the experience of each sentiment is its own thrust into the future—such a self is proof against the narrator who would falsify its design: it is self-designing. The narrator of Rousseau's confessions presents the naive self as forever its own designer, its own prefigurer, its own narrator. The intactness of Rousseau as author, narrator, and naive self is proved.

Supposing that I am reading Rousseau correctly, then the issue of whether his autobiography is essentially cognitive or confessional in intent, and of how these intents are related, and of what is therefore required of the reader, is of no small importance. But since autobiographies will not always declare their intent so plainly, the question of the function of formal features of their rhetoric arises. To what extent are certain forms bound to certain functions? Writers on autobiography, like the late Elizabeth Bruss in *Autobiographical Acts*, are so much aware of the extreme irregularity of the formal features of the genre that they have insisted on an absolute disjunction between form and function. They argue that autobiography, no matter what its form, can function in all the ways that autobiography functions. I don't think this is the case. What I've called the rhetorical features of the mode—stressing always the congruence and referentiality of the protagonist and narrator—strike me as essential indicators and executors of the confessional function. They sustain the effort, since Rousseau, of justifying painful memories by the demonstration of intactness for the sake of exculpation by another. (This other may be the author as subsequent reader.) There is something only loosely called autobiographical writing which might dwindle almost to nothing the confessional intent; such writing would not display the indicators which unvaryingly reveal the intent to unify; the self of experience and thought. If Gertrude Stein calls her autobiography the *Autobiography of Alice* B. *Toklas* or *Everybody's Autobiography*, she is engaged in loosely autobiographical writing; but she is not writing within the strict structure, and hence she does not maximize this possibility of proving intactness of self. The play with one's personae suggests not turpitude of course but simply the fact that the question of justification has already been resolved in one way or another. Either the self has been empirically justified, or else it cannot be.

The decision to disrupt the features of autobiography and in this way to generate characteristic kinds of fiction in each instance redefines the cognitive interest and nuances the cognitive charm of the work, but it cannot serve a confessional intent. The demonstration of the ability to write works of fiction, delirium, or irony says nothing about the virtue, wholeness, or intactness of the self at the order of experience. It points sooner to the claim that "fiction . . . figures . . . as constituting—rather than constituted by—the self" (Jeffrey Mehlman writing on Leiris), an argument that may be extended very likely in the direction of contemporary autobiographical writing, in which the features of referentiality and congruence are systematically disrupted and in which justification is presupposed or simply postponed. Barthes writing on Barthes cites Poe who wrote, "Truth lies in consistency" and adds, "Therefore he who cannot endure consistency cuts himself off from an *ethic* of truth." Especially in autobiographical form, consistency is the mark of ethical concern; the suspension of the form means the deliberate election of an order of fiction or figure—the dizzying freedom of life lived metaphorically, *im Gleichnis*, as conveyed, say, by Thomas Mann's fictive autobiography, *The Adventures of Felix Krull.*

Another way of stating the necessary connection between autobiography, its standard form, and its confessional intent is to recall its sworn dependency on memory. But if, since Freud at least, memory is not a source but a screen, that constellation of terms cannot hold.

Some people might be self-satisfied, some satisfied to be selfless; some find the term "self" excruciating; some, vacuous. On the basis of a thus already interpreted self, anyone can do autobiographical writing, but none can avail himself of standard autobiographical form. In such writers the confessional intent is defunct.

At many points in his *Diaries* Kafka expresses the wish to write an autobiography. He does not do it. He declares that he has no real self and that whatever of his self exists has been alienated through a kind of second death—the act of writing fiction. He claims he does not have real feelings.

Side by side with the expression of his desire to write an autobiography, we find in the early pages of the *Diaries* an imaginary conversation between an I and You which names a primordial disaster: one experiences the basis of one's existence quite as one suddenly notes an abscess on one's body. "[And] if hitherto," Kafka continues, "we were directed with our whole being to the work of our hands, to the things seen by our eyes and the things heard by our ears, to the steps of our feet, we suddenly turn around like a weather cock in the mountains into an element wholly opposed (*ins Entgegengesetzte*)." The turn is the turn to fictions, completed in Kafka at the cost of his bodily life.

Of course Kafka did write a sort of autobiography at an altogether different *niveau*, the "Letter to My Father." But he was to describe his enterprise to Milena as full of "lawyer's tricks." The work pretends to seek exculpation and half does so, in literally addressing the exculpator himself, his father; the intactness which the work demonstrates, though, is curious, feigned, almost conceited. Kafka explicitly portrays himself, more thoroughly than could his father, his adversary, as the wretched product of his father's design: he demonstrates to the world his intactness in being able to imagine his own vileness better than anyone else, and in this way he would sink faster than his persecutor.

This scheme obtains a final twist in the fictive autobiographies of Jerzy Kosinski. Here too a hero—masquerading as a spastic deafmute or as equally woebegone forms of the being which a hostile world has imposed on him—exults at having duped his adversary into supposing that his wretchedness was entirely the doing of that adversary, rather than in part a product of his own feigning. These sinister games are by a final irony not so much free alternatives to life haunted by confession, so much as its sadomasochistic residue. Kosinski's demonstrations of freedom take place in scenes of urban violence: but with this conjuration of Brooklyn, my beginning, and this abjuration of "Brooklyn"—my ending—I close this confession.

Prospect

Such was my reward for
my reading and this dec-
laration.
                                    —Rousseau

"So this whole procession of gallery figures marched to a point is only a moment in an autobiography—the purging of 'Brooklyn'?"

"It is, for the self that rejects the distinction between 'a personal self and a transcendental type of self' and thinks, 'To narrate the modern self is also to narrate myself: in noting this history, I note myself. And if this history is to be autobiography, then it must be ruled by the strict autobiographical intent, the confessional; that form would have to survive the long adventure. I confess that I mean my "German fate" to make me whole.' "

"And so you are made whole, driving out Brooklyn for a German fate?"

"No, I have disowned this speaker."

"You speak then as a 'transcendental self'?"

"A historical self. My German fate is parting from me."

"But confessing this, now you are made whole."

"Flawed by what I must still disown—my German fate."

"I see, there is no end to your confession."

"It has another ending."

Now come into the chapterhouse of history.

Notes

Preface

1. Friedrich Hölderlin, *Sämtliche Werke* (Stuttgart: Kohlhammer, 1961), 4:150.

2. In exploring the various types of self involved in literature, Paul de Man distinguished "the self that judges, the self that reads, the self that writes, and the self that reads itself." Certainly the unity of such a consciousness cannot be taken for granted; "the question of finding the common level on which all these selves meet and thus of establishing [their] unity" is a crucial problem. *Blindness and Insight: Essays in the Rhetoric of Contemporary Criticism*, 2d ed., rev. (Minneapolis: University of Minnesota Press, 1983), p. 39. The writers I study share the desideratum of surviving as such a unity.

3. For Dilthey the work of the poet is always "the faithful expression (*Ausdruck*) of a subjectivity." *Gesammelte Schriften*, 5:320. (This work appears in 18 vols. from 1914–1977. Vols. 1–13, Leipzig: Teubner; Göttingen: Vandenhoeck and Ruprecht. Vols. 14–18, Göttingen: Vandenhoeck and Ruprecht.) Freud holds the poetic intention to be an unconscious wish that seeks and finds "substitutive gratification." The conscious subject of the poet is to some extent excluded from this process because the conscious subject and the unconscious mind are not "co-extensive." But Freud's practice as an interpreter of art invariably follows the postulate of mental continuity, and he bases his interpretation of Michelangelo's Moses—as the "trace [of] the passage of a violent gust of passion left by it on the ensuing calm"—on "what the artist . . . intended either consciously or unconsciously." *On Creativity and the Unconscious: Papers on the Psychology of Art, Literature, Love, Religion*, Benjamin Nelson, ed. (New York: Harper and Row, 1958), pp. 8, 40–41.

4. "An incoherent assumption," wrote Kafka, "is thrust like a board between the actual feeling and the metaphor of the description." *The Diaries of Franz Kafka, 1910–1913*, Joseph Kresh, tr. and Max Brod, ed. (New York: Schocken Books, 1948), p. 200. Yet Kafka was also able to write exultantly of the "coherence" with which his story "The Judgment" had been composed, through "a complete opening out of the body and the soul." *Ibid.*, p. 276. Nietzsche also warned against the "confusion through psychological *contiguity*, . . . a confusion to which an artist himself is only too prone: as if he himself were what he is able to represent, conceive, and express. The fact is that *if* he were it, he would not represent, conceive, and express it. . . . Whoever is completely and wholly an artist is to all eternity separated from the 'real,' the actual." But the unsettling hyperbole of Nietzsche's

critique betrays a mainly polemical intent. He writes of separation in order to condemn Richard Wagner as the artist who could not endure it. "One can understand how [the artist] may sometimes weary to the point of desperation of the eternal 'unreality' and falsity of his innermost existence—and that he may well attempt what is most forbidden him, to lay hold of actuality, for once actually to *be*" (BW, p. 537). In the case of Wagner it is precisely the phenomenon of decadence which establishes the continuity of the artist, his style, and his epoch. And Nietzsche also asserted other continuities as moments of great strength, as "inspirations," in which "one no longer has any notion of what is an image or a metaphor: everything offers itself as the nearest, most obvious, simplest expression" (BW, p. 756–757).

Still the drastic moment of "eternal separation" which Nietzsche introduced between the artist and his work is not to be found in Dilthey, Freud, and early Heidegger.

5. Jacques Derrida, "Differance," in *Speech and Phenomena*, David Allison, tr. (Evanston, Ill.: Northwestern University Press, 1973), p. 152.

6. Jean-Marie Benoist, *The Structural Revolution* (London. Weidenfeld and Nicolson, 1978), pp. 215–216.

7. *Briefe von 1929–1951*, Robert Pick, ed. (Zurich: Rhein, 1957), p. 322. Discussed in Theodore Ziolkowski, *Dimensions of the Modern Novel* (Princeton: Princeton University Press, 1969), p. 141.

Introduction

1. Paul de Man, *Blindness and Insight: Essays in the Rhetoric of Contemporary Criticism*, 2d ed., rev. (Minneapolis: University of Minnesota Press, 1983), p. 9. De Man's phrase, written in 1967, is aimed only at structuralism.

2. *Ibid.*, p. 11.

3. Marcel Mauss, "A Category of the Human Mind: The Notion of Person, the Notion of 'Self,'" in *Sociology and Psychology: Essays by Marcel Mauss*, Ben Brewster, tr. (London: Routledge and Kegan Paul, 1979), p. 90.

4. Emile Benveniste, "Subjectivity in Language," *Problems in General Linguistics* (Miami: University of Miami Press, 1970), pp. 224 ff.

5. Roland Barthes, *Barthes on Barthes*, Richard Howard, tr. (New York: Hill and Wang, 1977), pp. 173–174.

6. Michel Foucault, "Afterword (1983)," in Hubert L. Dreyfus and Paul Rabinow, *Michel Foucault: Beyond Structuralism and Hermeneutics* (Chicago: University of Chicago Press, 1983), p. 252.

7. Jacques Lacan, "Agency of the Letter in the Unconscious," in *Écrits: A Selection*, Alan Sheridan, tr. and ed. (New York: Norton, 1977), pp. 173–174.

8. Jean-Marie Benoist, *The Structuralist Revolution* (London: Weidenfeld and Nicolson, 1978), p. 184. Cf. Anthony Wilden's confident statement that "Lacan's work has surely resulted in the final demise of the *cogito* that Husserl, Merleau-Ponty, and Sartre once struggled with." *The Language of the Self* (Baltimore: Johns Hopkins University Press, 1968), p. 310.

9. Fredric Jameson, *The Political Unconscious: Narrative as a Socially Symbolic Act* (Ithaca: Cornell University Press, 1981), p. 153.

10. Fredric Jameson, "Discussion," in Tak-Wai Wong and M. A. Abbas, eds., *Rewriting Literary History*, pp. 229–230 (Hong Kong: Hong Kong University Press, 1984).

11. Barthes, *Barthes on Barthes*, p. 168.

12. Cf. Martin Jay, who, for instance, writes, "In the name of an impersonal play of intertextuality rather than intersubjectivity, the [recent post-structuralists] have

systematically deconstructed *all* received notions of the subject" (italics mine). "Should Intellectual History Take a Linguistic Turn? Reflections on the Habermas-Gadamer Debate," in Dominick LaCapra and Steven L. Kaplan, eds., *Modern European Intellectual History: Reappraisals and New Perspectives*, p. 89 (Ithaca: Cornell University Press, 1982).

13. Jonathan Culler, *Structuralist Poetics, Structuralism, Linguistics and the Study of Literature* (Ithaca: Cornell University Press, 1975), p. 30.

14. Roland Barthes, *Image, Music, Text* (New York: Hill and Wang, 1977), p. 146.

15. Jonathan Culler, *On Deconstruction: Theory and Criticism After Structuralism* (Ithaca: Cornell University Press, 1982), p. 33.

16. *Thus Spoke Zarathustra*, in PN, p. 147.

17. The work of the late Foucault on the history of the technical practices constituting a self is an eminent contribution to this discussion, as is the work of British cultural materialists like Rosalind Coward and John Ellis, writing on the formation of the subject. The subject is to be grasped as "in process, . . . crossed by the contradictory processes of society. . . . The relation between the subject and meaning in the sign is a stage . . . . continually crossed, destroyed and reformulated." Rosalind Coward and John Ellis, *Language and Materialism: Developments in Semiology and the Theory of the Subject* (Boston: Routledge and Kegan Paul, 1977), pp. 150–152. Kaja Silverman's *Subject of Semiotics* also elaborates "Freudian and Lacanian models of subjectivity, emphasizing the semiotic dimensions of each," and noting "the irreducible distance which separates being from signification" (New York: Oxford University Press, 1983), p. 82. The concern of these writers with the continual destruction and irreducible distance of the self suggests that their enterprises bear a chiefly terminological resemblance to my own. I am opposed to their apodictic and premature rejection of reflection on moments of self-constitution in which self and language are joined—points which situate, in my view, the intentionality of the conscious subject. Nietzsche identifies such moments as "inspirations," when things offer themselves as metaphors (BW, p. 756). A disabusing critic might reply, "Such a claim is false, the claimer is deluded, the subject and his language were never one," to which the claimer responds, "The criticism is false, you do not know of what I speak." The critic: "Only because what you say is unreasonable." The claimer: "To you—but you and I are different, and the difference between us is precisely my claim."

18. Roland Barthes, "L'Effet de réel," *Communications* (1968), no. 11, p. 87. Translated by Fredric Jameson, in *The Political Unconscious*, p. 233.

19. Wylie Sypher, *Loss of the Self in Modern Literature and Art* (New York: Random House, 1962), pp. 148–149.

20. Freud, "Analysis Terminable and Interminable," in *Collected Papers* (London: Hogarth Press, 1950), 5:343.

21. S. T. Coleridge, "Opus Magnum," 3:49, cited in Elinor S. Shaffer, "Iago's Malignity Motivated: Coleridge's Unpublished 'Opus Magnum,' " *Shakespeare Quarterly* (Summer 1968), 19:197.

22. Georg Lukács, *Über die Besonderheit als Kategorie der Ästhetik* (Neuwied and Berlin: Luchterhand, 1967), p. 367. The self is the dialectically opposed "double" of the work of art.

23. This engaging idea was suggested by Fredric Jameson at a conference on "Rewriting Literary History" held at Hong Kong University, December 1982. A mordant example: visitors to Prague wandering down Paris Avenue in search of the apartment building where Kafka, after looking out at the Moldau River and contemplating suicide, composed "The Judgment" in one wild night, will find in its place the poured concrete café of the Hotel Intercontinental.

24. Mauss, *Sociology and Psychology*, pp. 90, 88, 87.

25. Hermann Cohen, *Kants Begründung der Ästhetik* (Berlin: F. Dümmler, 1889), p. 219

26. BT, p. 318.

27. Norman O. Brown, *Life Against Death* (New York: Vintage, 1959), p. 8.

28. See G.W.F. Hegel, *The Phenomenology of Mind*, 2d ed., J. B. Baillie, tr. (London and New York: Macmillan, 1931), p. 144.

29. Friedrich Nietzsche, "Schopenhauer als Erzieher," *Werke in Drei Bänden*, Karl Schlechta, ed. (Munich: Carl Hanser Verlag, 1954), 1:289. For a discussion, see J. M. Kamerbeek, "Dilthey Versus Nietzsche," *Studia Philosophica, Jahrbuch der Schweizerischen Philosophischen Gesellschaft* (1950), 10:56.

30. Jacques Derrida, "Living on Border Lines," in Geoffrey Hartman, ed. *Deconstruction and Criticism*, p. 84 (New York: Seabury Press, 1979).

31. Edward Said, *Beginnings: Intention and Method* (New York: Basic Books, 1975), p. 293.

32. *Beyond Good and Evil*, in BW, p. 418.

33. For an excellent discussion of this Althusserian concept, see Jameson, *The Political Unconscious*, p. 24 ff.

34. E.g., Anthony Wilden's statement, "Montaigne's subjective 'ideology of the self' is in conflict with the actual phenomenology of the self represented in the *Essays*." *System and Structure* (London: Tavistock, 1972), p. 90.

35. Roland Barthes, *S/Z*, Richard Miller, tr. (New York: Hill and Wang, 1974), p. 10.

36. Paul de Man, "Genesis and Genealogy," in *Allegories of Reading* (New Haven: Yale University Press, 1979), p. 80.

37. GS, p. 168. These lines and those which follow will be understood to have a target, but it is not Foucault, who states plainly enough in *Madness and Civilization* that "madness is the absolute break with the work of art; . . . where there is a work of art there is no madness." And yet Foucault also writes of Hölderlin, Nietzsche, and Van Gogh that their "madness is contemporary with the work of art, since it inaugurates the time of its truth. The moment when, together, the work of art and madness are born and fulfilled is the beginning of the time when the world finds itself arraigned by that work of art and responsible before it for what it is" (New York: Vintage, 1973), pp. 287–289. Perhaps these lines could be misunderstood, but still it is not Foucault whom I am thinking of but the weak messianism of American deconstructionism, to which one could add the carnivalesque lunacy of Lacan's texts and public appearances and the comminations of "schizoanalysis," which

> must devote itself with all its strength to the necessary destructions. Destroying beliefs and representations. And when engaged in this task no activity will be too malevolent . . . . [It will] undo all the reterritorializations that transform madness into mental illness. . . . Here madness would no longer exist as madness . . . because it would receive the support of all the other flows, including science and art.

Gilles Deleuze and Felix Guattari, *Anti-Oedipus: Capitalism and Schizophrenia*, Robert Hurley, Mark Seem, and Helen R. Lane, trs. (Minneapolis: University of Minnesota Press, 1983), pp. 314, 321.

38. Lionel Trilling, *The Opposing Self* (New York: Viking, 1955).

39. *Ibid.*, p. ix.

40. *Ibid.*, p. xi.

41. BU, pp. 27–28.

42. Heinrich Mann, *Ein Zeitalter wird besichtigt* (Stockholm: Neuer, 1946), p. 231.

Cited in T. J. Reed, *Thomas Mann: The Uses of Tradition* (Oxford: Oxford University Press, 1974), p. 1.

43. The quotation is from L, p. 97.

44. Friedrich von Schiller, *The Robbers*, F. J. Lamport, tr. (Harmondsworth, Middlesex: Penguin, 1979), pp. 131, 33.

45. Karl Philipp Moritz, *Anton Reiser* (Munich: Wilhelm Goldmann Verlag, 1961), p. 197.

46. Hermann Hesse, *Steppenwolf*, Basil Creighton, tr., rev. by Joseph Mileck and Horst Frenz (New York: Holt, Rinehart and Winston, 1963), pp. 10–11.

47. Franz Kafka, *The Diaries of Franz Kafka*, 1914–1923, Max Brod, ed., and Martin Greenberg, tr. (New York: Schocken, 1949), p. 77.

48. Erich Heller, *The Disinherited Mind* (Harmondsworth, Middlesex: Penguin, 1961); *The Artist's Journey Into the Interior* (London: Secker and Warburg, 1965).

49. Heller, *The Disinherited Mind*, p. x.

50. Heller, *The Artist's Journey*, p. 113.

51. Leo Spitzer, "Milieu and Ambiance," in *Essays in Historical Semantics* (New York: S. F. Vanni, 1947), p. 244.

52. Immanuel Kant, *Sämmtliche Werke*, Karl Rosenkranz and Friedrich Wilhelm Schubert, eds. (Leipzig: Voss, 1842), 11:240.

53. *Ibid.*

54. Jean-Jacques Rousseau, *Oeuvres complètes*, Bibliothèque de la Pléiade (Paris: Gallimard, 1959), 1:1153–1154.

1. Hölderlin and the Question of the Self

1. The first quote is by Georges Poulet, in *Les Métamorphoses du cercle* (Paris: Plon, 1961), p. 136; the second, by Peter Szondi, in *Satz und Gegensatz* (Frankfurt: Insel, 1964), pp. 9–10. Throughout this chapter, I give the term "Romanticism" the wide governance it has for many comparatists: the period ranging from French *pré-romantisme* (the generation of the 1750s) to German *Romantik* (up until the 1830s, the end of the Idealist classical-romantic period).

2. Karl R. Mandelkow, "Vorwort," in *Europäische Romantik I, Neues Handbuch der Literaturwissenschaft* (Wiesbaden: Akademische Verlagsgesellschaft Athenaion, 1982), 14:ix.

3. Paul de Man, "The Sublimation of the Self," in *Blindness and Insight: Essays in the Rhetoric of Contemporary Criticism*, 2d ed., rev. (Minneapolis: University of Minnesota Press, 1983), especially pp. 49–50.

4. Paul de Man, "Wordsworth and Hölderlin," in *The Rhetoric of Romanticism* (New York: Columbia University Press, 1984), p. 50. My own chapter relies explicitly in several places on Paul de Man's writings on Hölderlin. I single out certain texts as more nearly correct in their tendency than others. But such distinctions are also made for narrative and polemical reasons and should not obscure the general responsiveness of this entire chapter to de Man's readings. Indeed the recent publication of *The Rhetoric of Romanticism* makes possible the claim for a concealed unity in de Man's thinking on Romanticism, although he himself disavows any such "secret principle of summation" (p. viii).

5. Paul de Man, "Introduction," *Studies in Romanticism*, (1979), 18:498.

6. David Simpson, *Irony and Authority in Romantic Poetry* (Totowa, N.J.: Rowan and Littlefield, 1979), p. 97.

7. The view received a powerful and sustained impetus from René Girard's analysis of "the Romantic lie" in *Deceit, Desire and the Novel: Self and Other in Literary Structure* (Baltimore: Johns Hopkins University Press, 1965), a translation of *Mensonge romantique et verité romanesque* (Paris: Grasset, 1961).

8. *Materialien zu Hegels Phänomenologie des Geistes*, Hans Fulda, ed. (Frankfurt: Suhrkamp, 1973), pp. 256–257. Hegel frequently quotes from Goethe's poetry. In the *Philosophy of Right*, for example (vol. 7, *Werke in zwanzig Bänden* [Frankfurt: Suhrkamp, 1970], p. 65), he alludes to Goethe's sonnet "Natur und Kunst": "Whoever wants [to accomplish] something great must be able to limit himself." The relevant lines of Goethe are "He who wills great things must pull himself together; / Only in limitation is mastery shown" (*Wer Großes will, mu sich zusammenraffen; / In der Beschränkung zeigt sich erst der Meister*). Again, in the first volume of the *Encyclopedia*, (8:236), Hegel refers to "Natur und Kunst." But here Hegel himself writes poetry against the "sentimental" ethics of Kant: "The laurels of mere willing are dry leaves which have never greened." One should recall too the presence of *Faust* in the composition of the *Phenomenology*, an influence much discussed by Lukács, Ernst Bloch, Walter Kaufmann, Rüdiger Bubner, and others. (I am indebted to a conversation with Mark Roche for this point.)

9. Wilhelm Dilthey, *Gesammelte Schriften*, 5:13. This work appears in 18 vols. from 1914–1977. Vols. 1–13, Leipzig: B. B. Teubner; Göttingen: Vandenhoeck and Ruprecht. Vols. 14–18, Göttingen: Vandenhoeck and Ruprecht.

10. Cited in Cassirer, *The Philosophy of the Enlightenment* (Boston: Beacon Press, 1964), p. 278. The entire passage in Cassirer reads, "Windelband said of Kant's *Critique of Judgment* that it constructs, as it were, *a priori* the concept of Goethe's poetry, and that what the latter presents as achievement and act is founded and demanded in the former by the pure necessity of philosophical thought."

11. Gerhard Kurz, *Mittelbarkeit und Vereinigung: Zum Verhältnis von Poesie, Reflexion and Revolution bei Hölderlin* (Stuttgart: Metzler, 1975), p. 1.

12. De Man's readings of Rousseau in *Allegories of Reading* (New Haven: Yale University Press, 1979) aim to overcome the separation introduced by Rousseau's commentators between those texts allegedly inspired by intellectual analysis and those inspired by sentiment. See, for example, Chapter 10, "Allegory of Reading (*Profession de foi*)," p. 223.

13. Cf. those authors cited on p. 201 of this book as having contributed to the discussion of Heidegger and poetic theory.

14. Cf. Heidegger's *Erläuterungen zu Hölderlins Dichtung* (Frankfurt: V. Klostermann, 1951).

15. In "Genesis and Genealogy (Nietzsche)," in *Allegories of Reading*, de Man attacks the "genetic pattern" according to which Romanticism has been read. Under the head of such a pattern come at least two models of Romantic historiography. The first and less adequate is "a non-dialectical notion of a subject-object dichotomy, revealing a more or less deliberate avoidance of the moment of negation that coincides, for Hegel, with the emergence of the true Subject" (p. 80). Such a moment in Hegel as the following is presumably meant: "Thinking is, indeed, essentially the negation of that which is *immediately* before us." This sort of nondialectical system ends up with "an altogether un-Hegelian concept of the subject as an irrational unmediated experience of particular selfhood (or loss of selfhood)" (p. 80).

On the other hand, even "a dialectical conception of time and history [in the manner of Hegel] can very well be genetic" (p. 80). But it may be precisely the Romantic poets who came closest to undermining the authority of any sort of genetic pattern (p. 82). If it can be shown, as de Man claims to show apropos of Nietzsche, that "genetic models are only one instance of rhetorical mystification among others," then even such values as "the pan-tragic consciousness of the self . . . are made to appear hollow when they are exposed to the clarity of a new ironic light" (p. 102). The weak options for an understanding of a Romantic self-consciousness are therefore the self as, first, the irrational particularity of immediate experience and, second, a negative illusory subject engendered by participation in a speciously genetic teleological process. Is there then no way out of this double bind, no mediation possible between "irrational immediacy" and the "negative subject"?

16. I am thinking of the nearly simultaneous publication in 1966 and 1967 of two works by Derrida. The first to appear was the study of Rousseau's "Essay on the Origin of Language" in *Of Grammatology*, Gayatri Chakravorti Spivak, tr. (Baltimore: Johns Hopkins University Press, 1976). The second was Derrida's essay on Freud, "Freud and the Scene of Writing," in *Writing and Difference*, Alan Bass, tr. (Chicago: University of Chicago Press, 1978), pp. 196–231. In the latter, Derrida writes, "The 'subject' of writing does not exist if we mean by that some sovereign solitude of the author" (p. 226). See, further, Andrzej Warminski's essay on Hölderlin, " 'Patmos': The Sense of Interpretation," in *Modern Language Notes* (April 1976), 91(3):478–500.

17. See further, Derrida: "The interval that constitues in the present [the trace of what is not present] must also, and by the same token, divide the present in itself, thus dividing, along with the present, everything that can be conceived on its basis, that is, every being—in particular, for our metaphysical language, the substance or subject." *Speech and Phenomena*, David Allison, tr. (Evanston, Ill.: Northwestern University Press, 1973), p. 143.

18. De Man, *Allegories of Reading*, p. 299.

19. Cf. Jean Laplanche, in *Hölderlin et la question du père* (Paris: Presses Universitaires de France, 1961): "How describe as other than *narcissistic* this situation in which the subject defines itself uniquely by its dual relation with the Other, where it posits itself as a subject in a specular relation, being itself the other of this Other?" (p. 55). The mirror phase is discussed on p. 43 ff. of this book. Laplanche does not stop here in his constitution of Hölderlin's subjectivity. He reads this narcissism as an early and deficient condition that opens him to schizophrenia. But other critics—e.g., René Girard in *Deceit, Desire and the Novel*—are less generous toward Romantic narcissism. For them the Romantic subject does stop here. "Stendhal too finds in the Romantic *vaniteux* not the generous impulse of a being truly prepared to give itself but rather the tormented recourse of vanity at bay, the centrifugal movement of an ego powerless to desire by itself" (p. 15). An interpretation of the Hegelian dialectic as motivated by resentment is put forward by Gilles Deleuze in his *Nietzsche and Philosophy*, Hugh Tomlinson, tr. (New York: Columbia University Press, 1983). Finally there is this deconstruction of the Romantic metaphysics of antithesis by Glenn Most:

> A concept is valorized as original (primary, natural, metaphysically founded) and another defined as derivative from it (secondary, artificial, merely seeming). What matters then is not so much the one side of the antithesis or the other, but rather antithesis itself as a strategy of self-legitimation. In order to constitute itself through a sort of transcendental litotes, Romanticism first constructs an alternative, then thematizes its [mere] constructedness: this way it justifies the rejection of that alternative and the privileging of the first, defined solely by the fact that it is absolutely non-constructed. Hence the alternative which is acknowledged as the more valuable always lacks the conceptual clarity which characterizes the other, precisely to its disadvantage.

"Des verschieden Gesinnten Sinnesverbindung: zur poetischen Einheit der Alten," in K. Gloy and E. Rudolph, eds., *Einheit als Grundproblem der Philosophie* (Darmstadt: Wissenschaftliche Buchgesellschaft), scheduled to appear in 1985. What this ingenious argument leaves out, however, even as a surmise, is Heidegger's insistence that "to significations words accrue: word-Things do not get supplied with significations" (BT, p. 204). When the Romantic calls a concept originally given, he takes responsibility for its meaning. The deconstruction cannot undo the responsibility entailed by the claimed givenness of a term, both for the Romantic as well as for the writer whose deconstruction takes this term as its prime target. The primary term comes forward for both authors—for the author who believes it and the ironist who dissembles it—with a meaning precisely its own, and not some other. The deconstruction, supposing it to be on good terms with its own principle, can proceed only by addressing something else that has mattered, and what matters enormously is the exact name of the first concept, whether "organism," "self," or something else, for this term decides what term can be derived from it. Hölderlin, for example, unlike Coleridge and Goethe, does not designate "organic" as a first term; it figures for him as the second term, derived from "aorgic," and means "organized" and "artful." Furthermore, the term "self" for him is neither first nor second to its putative alternative, the term of time, but is itself a form of temporality. None of these distinctions can be absorbed under the head of "transcendental litotes."

20. I owe this formulation to Jeffrey Mehlman's *Structural Study of Autobiography* (Ithaca: Cornell University Press, 1976).

21. William Michel, *Hölderlins Abendländische Wendung* (Jena: Eugen Diedrichs, 1923), pp. 8–9.

22. Hölderlin, *Sämtliche Werke* (Stuttgart: Kohlhammer, 1961), 4:216–17.

23. *Ibid.*, 4:235.

24. Summarizing the account given by Beck and Bertaux of Hölderlin's shift of interest from Kant to Fichte, Laplanche writes: "The Kantian categorical imperative gives way to the side of moral feeling, of belief in a law that is less universal than personal, which requires the individual to unfold, to develop, his possibilities, his *forces*, rather than burdening him with the task of making his actions conform to a universally valid maxim." In *Hölderlin et la question du père*, p. 39.

The requirement that Hölderlin endure as a *particular* being persists. In a late letter to von Seckendorf (March 12, 1804), for example, Hölderlin rejects a certain Romanticism of the picturesque. Jochen Schmidt glosses the letter: "The earth has primacy, because Hölderlin's care is for self-assertion, for the preservation of the individual life. And hence the assertion of the concluding strophe of the ode "Ganymede," acutely bent on individuality and particularity: 'And everything blossoms in its own fashion.'" See *Hölderlins Später Widerruf* (Tübingen: Niemeyer, 1978), p. 181.

25. Hölderlin, letter to Bohlendorff, December 4, 1801. *Sämtliche Werke*, 6:426.

26. *Ibid.*, 4:255–256.

27. Cf. H. G. Gadamer's discussion of *Bildung* in *Wahrheit und Methode*, 2d ed. (Tübingen: Mohr, 1960), pp. 7–16.

28. Mehlman, *Structural Study*, p. 67.

29. De Man, *The Rhetoric of Romanticism*, p. 56 (translation modified).

30. De Man, "The Rhetoric of Temporality," in *Interpretation, Theory, and Practice*, Charles Singleton, ed. (Baltimore: Johns Hopkins University Press, 1969), p. 190.

31. *Sämtliche Werke*, 3:212.

32. *Ibid.*, p. 216.

33. Frances Ferguson, in a review article, *Georgia Review* (1977), 31(2):516.

34. Centuries along in the sustained Hölderlinean and Romantic meditation on an "enlightened" reason that would disabuse the self of everything, E. M. Cioran writes: "How match ourselves against ghosts? This is what appearances become when, disabused, we can no longer promote them to the rank of essences. Knowledge . . . produces between them and ourselves a hiatus which is not, unfortunately, a conflict: if it were, all

would be well; no, this hiatus is the suppression of all conflicts, it is the deadly abolition of the tragic." *The Fall Into Time* (Chicago: Quadrangle Books, 1970), p. 155.

35. "A passage written at the end of 1793." Cited in Laplanche, *Hölderlin et la question du père*, p. 32.

36. *Sämtliche Werke*, 6:347–348.

37. *Reflexion, Sämtliche Werke*, 4:234–235. Hölderlin concludes this aphorism by noting an obstacle in the way of truth's successful placement of error within its "system." This obstacle is the special condition which the thinker must achieve, namely, "schneller Begriff" ("quickness of comprehension"), requiring a "durch und durch organisiertes Gefühl" (a "thoroughly developed sensibility"). Indeed, if Hölderlin's thought is dialectical, it is also vertiginously quick; terms cross over with unnerving rapidity. And yet where Hölderlin registers a difficulty in the way of truth, the modern critic sees an impossibility. This substitution impoverishes a prevailing Romantic sensibility that continues to desire a plenitude verging on the unexperienceable, while suffering the consciousness of its impossibility. In a word, the newer criticism demystifies or otherwise etiolates Romantic sublimity.

38. De Man, *Allegories of Reading*, p. 296.

39. A similar version of the critique of the separate integrity of act and interpretation reads: "Non-verbal acts, if such a thing were to be conceivable, are of no concern to [Nietzsche], since no act can ever be separated from the attempt at understanding, from the interpretation, that necessarily accompanies and falsifies it." De Man, *Allegories of Reading*, ch. 6, "Rhetoric of Persuasion (Nietzsche)."

40. *Sämtliche Werke*, 4:150.

41. Michel Foucault, *The Order of Things* (New York: Pantheon, 1970), p. 334. A good deal of recent Hegel criticism rejects a vision of Hegel's *Subjekt* as "bringing its circle to completion." Instead it stresses a pattern of persistent revelation and concealment as the figure of Hegel's thought.

42. "In Hegel the dialectic frequently finishes in an absolute impasse for the individual. If the dialectic picks up again, it is in a 'new figure' in whom the predecessor was only a moment. In Hölderlin the necessity of again taking up the movement toward a synthesis is inherent in the individual; it is as an individual that he is fascinated by the Hen Kai Pan" (Laplanche, *Hölderlin*, p.117).

43. *Sämtliche Werke*, 5:220.

44. Edward Said, *Beginnings: Intention and Method* (New York: Basic Books, 1975), p. 312. Said is here referring to Foucault's argument in "La Pensée du dehors," *Critique* (1966), 22(229):525–527.

45. Cited without source in Michael Ryan, *Marxism and Deconstruction* (Baltimore: Johns Hopkins University Press, 1982), p. vii.

46. Maurice Blanchot, "La Folie par excellence," *Critique* (1951) 7(45):99–118. and "La Parole 'sacrée' de Hölderlin," in *La Part de feu* (Paris: Gallimard, 1949), pp. 118–136.

47. Goethe, letter to Herder (Wetzlar, July 1772). Discussed in G. Lukács, *Essays on Thomas Mann*, Stanley Mitchell, tr. (London: Merlin, 1964), p. 52.

48. Mehlman, *Structural Study*, p. 167.

49. *Sämtliche Werke*, 3:210.

50. Peter Szondi's reading of "When on a Holiday" ("Wie wenn am Feiertage"), which sees Hölderlin's urge to exalt his impoverished self as the obstacle to hymnic poetry, identifies, at its weak side, this important impulse. "Der andere Pfeil," *Hölderlin-Studien* (Frankfurt: Insel, 1967).

51. The extremes of Hölderlinian selfhood can be seen to reflect two notions of selfhood prevalent in Germany at the time of Goethe: Fichtean autonomy and the Spinozistic sublation of individuality. But only with Hölderlin do the modes become existentially problematic. For Goethe "the affirmation of self" (Verselbstigung, as in "Wandrers Sturmlied" and "Prometheus") and "unselfing" (Entselbstigung, as in "Mahomets Gesang" and "Ganymed") are legitimate as long as they are recognized as inevitable modifications of one another. Each is valid when seen as a moment in the context of its necessary reversal. For Hölderlin both the Fichtean and Spinozistic modes lose all legitimacy, be it individually or together, and he is left fighting for another term. (I owe this point to a discussion with Mark Roche.)

52. In Hamlin's lecture at a special session on Hölderlin at the conference of the Modern Language Association in Chicago, 1977.

53. Stuart Schneiderman, Jacques Lacan: The Death of an Intellectual Hero (Cambridge: Harvard University Press, 1983), pp. 6–7.

54. Sämtliche Werke, 4:243.

55. Wolfgang Binder, "Hölderlins Dichtung im Zeitalter des Idealismus," Hölderlin Jahrbuch, (1965–66), 14:57–72.

56. Ibid., pp. 66, 68, 69.

57. In Goethe's Wahlverwandtschaften, for example, renunciation is distinguished from servitude; Ottilie's personal renunciation of a limit-joy produces a liberation from servitude: "Ottilie was delivered (entbunden) from her early sense of confinement, her servitude. . . . Through her division she felt herself freed, also, of the burden of that mishap (Mißgeschick). She no longer required any force over herself; she had forgiven herself . . . only under the condition of complete renunciation."

58. Vincent Descombes, L'Inconscient malgré lui (Paris: Éditions de Minuit, 1977), pp. 98–99.

59. De Man, "The Literary Self as Origin: The Work of Georges Poulet," in Blindness, p. 100.

60. Foucault, The Order of Things, p. 330.

61. Sämtliche Werke, 3:169.

62. Michel Foucault, in Language, Counter-Memory, Practice, D. F. Bouchard, ed. and tr. (Ithaca: Cornell University Press, 1977), p. 138.

63. Michel Foucault, L'Ordre du discours (Paris: Gallimard, 1971), pp. 60–61. Cited in Language, Counter-Memory, Practice, p. 130.

64. Said, Beginnings, p. 157.

65. See Roman Jakobson for an illuminating distinction between Hölderlin's "dialogical" and "monological" language. Under the burden of his illness Hölderlin could produce only a deficient dialogical language, that is, in dialogical situations an opaque language testifying to the loss of a self capable of interpersonal exchange. Hölderlin did, however, possess until the very last year of his life (it is believed) the "monological" language he required to produce poems on demand. In Roman Jakobson and Grete Lübbe-Grothues, "The Language of Schizophrenia: Hölderlin's Speech and Poetry," Poetics Today (1980), 2(1a):137–144.

66. Sämtliche Werke, 6:93.

67. "In lieblicher Bläue," a text of dubious authenticity, Ibid., 2:372. Heidegger makes this sentence the object of a commentary in "Hölderlin und das Wesen der Dichtung," in Erläuterungen, pp. 42–48.

68. Sämtliche Werke, 6:289.

69. Jonathan Culler, The Pursuit of Signs: Semiotics, Literature, Deconstruction (Ithaca: Cornell University Press, 1981), p. 38.

70. Thomas Weiskel, *The Romantic Sublime: Studies in the Structure and Psychology of Transcendence* (Baltimore: Johns Hopkins University Press, 1976), pp. 55–56.

71. Lacan writing on the Schreber case in *La Psychanalyse* (1958), 4:44–45. Cited in Laplanche, *Hölderlin*, p. 46.

72. While noting the particularly compelling possibility of such a link, Foucault, for example, finds it simpler at first to identify degraded formulations of the question. "This approach, pursued to the very heart of madness, is based on the assumption that the meaning of a work, its themes and specific domain, can be traced to a series of events whose details are known to us. The question posed by this nonconceptual eclecticism, as it derives from "clinical" psychology, is whether a chain of significations can be formed to link, without discontinuity or rupture, an individual life to a life's work, events to words, and the mute forms of madness to the most essential aspects of a poem. This possibility . . . must be reformulated." *Language, Counter-Memory, Practice*, p. 71.

73. Jacques Derrida, "La Parole soufflée," *Writing and Difference*, pp. 169–174. Michel Foucault, "The Father's 'No,' " in *Language, Counter-Memory, Practice*.

74. The tone of all these writers in their response to their sources is exceedingly considerate. The distance between Paris and Tübingen is plain in the absence from their work of the virulence of the German contest for Hölderlin. In Germany until recently each new professor of German literature, it seemed, had to pass through the harsh academic rite of presenting a new image of Hölderlin while shattering the images of others. Obviously the agitation that accompanied these discussions came from the fact that Hölderlin had been politicized. Each new reading brought about willy-nilly a repoliticization of him (and of the speaker), even though the speaker chose the political stance of a manifest, scrupulous avoidance of political categories. That the preparation of the new "Red Star" (*Roter Stern*) edition of Hölderlin has been accompanied by radical political polemic is inevitable, perhaps—indeed called for—in light of the long-standing conservative political tradition of Hölderlin studies in Germany. On the other hand, this polarized climate is not always the one in which the most original theorizing is accomplished. French writers have enjoyed the advantage of coming to Hölderlin with chiefly theoretical axes to grind. It is also a fresher wind that blows through discussions of Hölderlin's madness outside Germany. Anyone going through German interpretations of Hölderlin's madness— many of them written in wartime and celebrating as a national epiphany the *dementia praecox catatonica* of "le pauvre Hoelterling"—is bound to be put off this subject as tainted.

Recent French writers have an advantage too in not being excessively familiar with, and hence daunted by, Hölderlin scholarship in German (which tends to be overly technical and high-flown) and for not alleging, either, a more confident understanding of Freud than they are entitled to. (Freud's indignation at the way he was misread in France was nothing compared with the anger he felt at the way he was misread in Germany.)

75. Jacques Lacan, "The Freudian Unconscious and Ours," in *The Four Fundamental Concepts of Psychoanalysis*, Alan Sheridan, tr. (New York: Norton, 1978), p. 20.

76. "In language there are only differences. . . . A difference generally implies positive terms between which the difference is set up; but in language there are only differences *without positive terms*. . . . In language . . . whatever distinguishes one sign from the others constitutes it. *Language is a form and not a substance*." Ferdinand de Saussure, *Course in General Linguistics*, Wade Baskin, tr. (New York: Philosophical Library, 1959), pp. 120–122.

77. Roland Barthes, *The Pleasure of the Text*, Richard Miller, tr. (New York: Hill and Wang, 1975), p. 58.

78. This paragraph is indebted to Jeffrey Mehlman's preface to *French Freud: Structural Studies in Psychoanalysis*, a special edition of *Yale French Studies* (1972), no. 48.

79. Jacques Lacan, "The Function of Language in Psychoanalysis," Anthony

Wilden, tr., in Anthony Wilden, *The Language of the Self* (Baltimore: Johns Hopkins University Press, 1968), p. 21.

80. *Sämtliche Werke*, 3:176–177.

81. Jacques Lacan, "Propos sur la causalité psychique," *Écrits* (Paris: Seuil, 1966), p. 185. Cf. "Stade du miroir," in *Vocabulaire de la psychanalyse* by Jean Laplanche and J.-B. Pontalis (Paris: Presses Universitaires de France), p 452, and Wilden, *The Language of the Self*, pp. 159–177.

82. Lacan, *La Psychanalyse* (1958) 4:44–45; Laplanche, *Hölderlin*, p. 43 ff.

83. Jacques Lacan, "The Function of Language in Psychoanalysis," in Wilden, *The Language of the Self*, p. 41.

84. Laplanche, *Hölderlin*, p. 44.

85. Goethe's *Wilhelm Meister*, the paradigmatic *Bildungsroman*, dramatizes, in the single narrative of a successful *Bildung*, Wilhelm's working through of the paternal signifier, whereby he asserts in the social order his own paternal function. His accession to paternity is shown through incidents ranging from the appearance of a stranger to play the ghost in Wilhelm's *Hamlet*, who counsels Wilhelm to flee the trammels of his earliest associations; to the crucial dream which he soon after has, in which he gladly allows himself to be prevented by the woman who shall become his wife from coming to the aid of his father and his old lover Mariane; to the unexpected "return" to him of the joy of Felix, his illegitimate son, and his acquiring, like Saul, a kingdom richer than his father's patrimony.

86. Laplanche, *Hölderlin*, p. 46.

87. *The Function of Language in Psychoanalysis*," pp. 42–43.

88. *The Four Fundamental Concepts of Psychoanalysis* (New York: Norton, 1978), p. 83.

89. "Jacques Lacan, "Introduction au commentaire de Jean Hyppolite sur la *Verneinung*," *La Psychanalyse* (1956) 1:20. Cited in Wilden, *The Language of the Self*, p. 142.

90. Laplanche, *Hölderlin*, p. 133.

91. Jean Beaufret, "Hölderlin et la question du père," *Les Temps modernes*, (July–December 1962), 194:152–153. This, according to Renate Böschenstein, is too much said; for her "the position of Hölderlin's father-term must be sought *between* 'absence' and the 'fault' *(faille)* |left by| an absence" (my italics). See her "Hölderlin und die Suche nach dem Vater," *Hölderlin-Jahrbuch* (1978–79), 21:346.

92. Foucault, "The Father's 'No,' " in *Language, Counter-Memory, Practice*, p. 77.

93. Derrida, *Of Grammatology*, pp. 68–69.

94. Such categories belong more nearly to the folklore of demonism, to judge from Goethe's definition of the "daemonic" as something which manifested itself only in contradictions and therefore could not be grasped in a concept let alone a word. Richard Rorty disagrees. "Derrida tells us," he writes, "over and over, that *différance* is 'neither a word nor a concept.' This is, however, not true. . . . Any word that has a use automatically signifies a concept." In "Deconstruction and Circumvention," *Critical Inquiry* (September 1984), 11(1):18.

95. Derrida, *Writing and Difference*, p. 170.

96. J.-M. Benoist declares, "Hölderlin's name marks . . . a structuralism which recognizes the activity of lack, of a . . . negativity at the very heart of the function of the symbolic, as the driving force of his trajectory." *The Structural Revolution* (London: Wiedenfeld and Nicolson, 1978), p. 226. But pace Benoist this negativity is anything but "nonmediatizable," and Hölderlin survives, not as a name, but as one who names, and who intends to repair and supplement this lack: "If I have once arrived at that point of . . . seeing, in things that are lacking, less the indefinite pain that they often cause me, than just their peculiar, momentary, particular lack . . . , then my spirit will become calmer and

my activity will make a steadier progress. For when we experience an inadequacy, a lack, only infinitely, then we are naturally inclined, too, to want to repair this lack infinitely, too, and then our strength often exhausts itself . . . in an indefinite, fruitless struggle, because it does not know definitely where the lack is, and how precisely to repair and supplement this lack" (Hölderlin, *Sämtliche Werke*, 6:326).

97. Blanchot, "La Folie par excellence," p. 110.

98. *Ibid.*, p. 111.

99. *Ibid.*, pp. 112–116.

100. Blanchot, *L'Espace littéraire* (Paris: Gallimard, 1955), p. 50.

2. Dilthey's Poetics of Force

1. *Briefwechsel zwischen Wilhelm Dilthey und dem Grafen Paul Yorck von Wartenburg, 1877–1897*, S. von der Schulenberg, ed. (Halle: Niemeyer, 1923), p. 193, cited in BT, p. 451.

2. Roland Barthes, *A Lover's Discourse*, Richard Howard, tr. (New York: Hill and Wang, 1978), p. 133.

3. Rousseau, *Rousseau, Juge de Jean-Jacques*, *Oeuvres complètes*, Bibliothèque de la Pléiade (Paris: Gallimard, 1959), 1:667.

4. "It was the first major study of Hölderlin by a recognized scholar standing outside the coterie of Hölderlin devotees and researchers, and it placed Hölderlin in the mainstream of German intellectual history, linking him with acknowledged masters of the literary tradition." Geoffrey Waite in *Nietzsche/Hölderlin: A Critical Reconstruction* (Berlin: Walter de Gruyter), publication expected in 1985. In *Lived Experience and Poetry* Dilthey typically observes, "In all his poetic work Hölderlin sought to express the character of life itself as it emerged from his experiences [*Erlebnisse*]. . . . Given the kind of being Hölderlin was, the inner history of the hero [Hyperion] had to become the midpoint of the novel." When Hölderlin wrote, the prevailing literary enterprise consisted of "poetic discoveries in the world of the individual and his cultivation of his self [*Selbstbildung*]." *Das Erlebnis und die Dichtung*, 6th ed. (Berlin: Teubner, 1919), pp. 222, 234, 240.

5. *Gesammelte Schriften*, 5:320. (This work appears in 18 volumes from 1914 to 1977. Volumes 1–13, Leipzig: Teubner; Gottingen: Vandenhoeck und Ruprecht. Volumes 14–18, Gottingen: Vandenhoeck und Ruprecht.)

6. This position was advanced with unacceptable bluntness and vehemence by Georg Lukács in *Die Zerstörung der Vernunft: Der Weg des Irrationalismus von Schelling zu Hitler*, *Gesamtausgabe*, vol. 9 (Neuwied: Luchterhand Verlag, 1962). For Lukács Dilthey is the founder of the philosophy of life regnant during the period of German imperialism—an irrationalism propagated by a captive intelligentsia serving the interests of the imperialistic bourgeoisie. Hans-Joachim Lieber asserted this position more tactfully in two important articles: "Geschichte und Gesellschaft im Denken Diltheys," *Kölner Zeitschrift für Soziologie und Sozialpsychologie* (1965) 17:703–742 and "Die deutsche Lebensphilosophie und ihre Folgen," *Universitätstage 1966, Nationalsozialismus und die deutsche Universität* (Berlin: Walter de Gruyter, 1966), pp. 92–108. Lieber's charge that Dilthey's "irrationalism" played into the hands of the Nazis was countered very cogently by Frithjof Rodi in "Die Lebensphilosophie und die Folgen: Zu zwei Aufsätzen von H.-J. Lieber," *Zeitschrift für philosophische Forschung* (1967), 21:600–612.

7. Josef Derbolav discusses Dilthey's subordination of practical energies that aim at real social transformation to theoretical contemplativeness in "Dilthey und das Problem der Geschichtlichkeit," in *Rationalität, Phänomenalität, Individualität. Festgabe, für Hermann und Marie Glockner* (Bonn: Bouvier, 1966), pp. 189–239.

8. Bernd Peschken has described Dilthey's political consciousness as vacuous and conciliatory in *Versuch einer germanistischen Ideologiekritik* (Stuttgart: J. B. Metzlersche Ver-

lagsbuchhandlung, 1972). Christofer Zöckler's study, *Dilthey und die Hermeneutik: Diltheys Begründung der Hermeneutik und die Geschichte ihrer Rezeption* (Stuttgart: J. B. Metzlersche Verlagsbuchhandlung, 1975), speaks with finer nuances on behalf of Dilthey's "oppositionalist" spirit in politics. Zöckler's admirable study marshals a rich range of historical and biographical materials in an effort to define Dilthey's political understanding, but he suspends this venture for the period after 1871, the period that is of course of greatest interest to students of Dilthey's poetics.

My own sense of Dilthey's *Poetic Imagination* has been confirmed by Zöckler's work, which furnishes corroborative evidence for my thesis of the political implications of Dilthey's *Poetics*. On the other hand, I find unintelligible Zöckler's explicit paraphrase of his own argument: "It is the thesis of this study that in this tradition [of Dilthey-Gadamer-Habermas] no positive impulses for literary theory are possible" (p. 9). It simply does not follow from his work—and this I mean to make clear in my own, by reproducing some of his scholarship for the very purpose of focusing Dilthey's study of *The Poetic Imagination*.

9. This work is found on pp. 103–241 of vol. 6 of the *Gesammelte Schriften*, subtitled *Die geistige Welt: Einleitung in die Philosophie des Lebens, Zweite Hälfte: Abhandlungen zur Poetik, Ethik und Pädagogik*. Georg Misch, ed., 2d ed. (Göttingen: Vandenhoeck and Ruprecht, 1957). First published in 1924. References within parentheses are to volumes and pages of the *Gesammelte Schriften*.

For a short bibliography of the secondary literature, see note 19 below.

10. Hans-Georg Gadamer, *Wahrheit und Methode*, 2d ed. (Tübingen: J. C. B. Mohr, 1965), p. 5.

11. In Richard Rorty's recent view, "The notion of knowledge as the assemblage of accurate representations is optional . . . . It may be replaced by a pragmatist conception of knowledge which eliminates the Greek contrast between contemplation and action, between representing the world and coping with it." In *Philosophy and the Mirror of Nature* (Princeton: Princeton University Press, 1979), p. 11. Dilthey's description of knowledge—certainly at least artistic knowledge—is here and elsewhere informed by a pragmatist conception.

12. In light of this passage Edward Said would be required to nuance considerably the following statement in *Beginnings: Intention and Method*: "What puts Vico and Nietzsche to one side of this attitude [that a 'text as an obstruction can be circumvented or dissolved'] is that for them a text is *fundamentally* a fact of power and displacement . . . . [In Dilthey's work, however,] the text presents itself to the historical consciousness as an aspect of 'mental life,' and as such the text's form is a fact of *distribution* in that life, not of threatening obstruction." The text may indeed not be for Dilthey a "threatening obstruction," and of course a "distribution" is what it *is* precisely, but not of (merely) mental life—rather of "strength and force" precipitating "actions." (New York: Basic Books, 1975), p. 205.

13. Zöckler, *Dilthey und die Hermeneutik*, p. 5. The passages from Dilthey cited from vol. 12 and from vol. 1 in the paragraph following are also mentioned by Zöckler on pp. 4–5.

14. Dilthey mitigates the violence of this "rupture." He suggests a continuity of self and life; in self-reflection life comes knowingly to itself. Hence what the great poet experiences ("a kind of splitting of self [*Spaltung des Selbst*] [or] transformation into another person") serves finally to produce forms which objectively represent the spirit of a historical age (6:166, 231).

15. The difference between Nietzsche and Dilthey is never plainer than at this juncture. Nietzsche's fundamental act of defiance of his age takes the form of his defiance

of the legitimacy of *Bildung*. In *Beyond Good and Evil*, published a year before *The Poetic Imagination*, Nietzsche writes:

> And what else is the aim of education and "culture" today? In our very popularity-minded—that is, plebeian—age, "education" and "culture" *have* to be essentially the art of deceiving—about one's origins, the inherited plebs in one's body and soul. An educator who today preached truthfulness above all and constantly challenged his students, "be true! be natural! do not pretend!'"—even such a virtuous and guileless ass would learn after a while to reach for that *furca* of Horace to *naturam expellere*: with what success? "*Plebs usque recurret.*" (BW, p. 404)

16. See the account of Dilthey's intellectual development in J. Kammerbeek, "Dilthey Versus Nietzsche," Studia Philosophica, *Jahrbuch der Schweizerischen Philosophischen Gesellschaft* (1950), 10:52–84.

17. Michel Foucault, cited in *Language, Counter-Memory, Practice*, D. F. Bouchard, ed. (Ithaca: Cornell University Press, 1977), p. 5.

18. Norman Holland, "Transactive Criticism: Re-creation Through Identity," *Criticism* (1976), 18:336.

19. Rudolf Makkreel, *Dilthey: Philosopher of the Human Studies* (Princeton: Princeton University Press, 1975), p. 66. Makkreel's study contains an extensive discussion of *The Poetic Imagination* but gives no account of the political and historical consciousness elaborated in this work. This dimension of Dilthey's thought is consistently absent from other works discussing *The Poetic Imagination*, as, e.g., René Wellek's "Wilhelm Dilthey's Poetics and Literary Theory," *Wächter und Hüter, Festschrift für Hermann J. Weigand* (New Haven: Yale University Press, 1957), pp. 121–32; and Michael Heinen's *Konstitution der Ästhetik in Wilhelm Diltheys Philosophie* (Bonn: Bouvier Verlag Herbert Grundmann, 1974). Kurt Müller-Vollmer, in *Towards a Phenomenological Theory of Literature: A Study of Wilhelm Dilthey's Poetik* (The Hague: Mouton, 1963), mentions a "historical consciousness" in Dilthey's poetics but never his concrete sense of political and institutional forces. Frithjof Rodi's lucid work, *Morphologie und Hermeneutik. Zur Methode von Diltheys Asthetik* (Stuttgart: W. Kohlhammer Verlag, 1969), briefly discusses writers who have reflected on the political character and effect of Dilthey's work, like Lukács and Lieber (see note 6 above). Rodi's own approach, however, eschews all attention to Dilthey's political awareness and effect.

20. On the word "text," cf. Gadamer, *Wahrheit und Methode*, pp. 227ff., especially p. 227: "Dilthey . . . considered his task as that of providing the *Geisteswissenschaften* an epistemological justification by conceiving of the historical world as a text to be deciphered."

21. Peter Hünermann, *Der Durchbruch geschichtlichen Denkens im 19. Jahrhundert* (Freiburg: Herder, 1967), p. 151.

22. Paul de Man, *Allegories of Reading* (New Haven: Yale University Press, 1979), p. 256.

23. Gadamer, *Wahrheit und Methode*, p. 58. My discussion of the history of the word *Erlebnis* is indebted to Gadamer's study of this concept on p. 56ff.

24. *Ibid.*, pp. 59, 57.

25. *Ibid.*, p. 59.

26. Frithjof Rodi, "Grundzüge der Poetik Wilhelm Diltheys," in H. Koopman and J. A. Schmoll-Eisenwerth, eds., *Beiträge zur Theorie der Künste im 19. Jahrhundert*, pp. 79–80 (Frankfurt: V. Klostermann, 1971).

27. *Ibid.*, p. 82.

28. Richard Palmer, *Hermeneutics: Interpretation Theory in Schleiermacher, Dilthey, Heidegger, and Gadamer* (Evanston: Northwestern University Press, 1969), p. 98.

29. Ibid., pp. 100–101.

30. Ibid., p. 102.

31. Ibid., p. 101.

32. Fredric Jameson, "Introduction" to his translation of Dilthey's "The Rise of Hermeneutics," New Literary History (1972), 3:230.

33. Ibid., pp. 231–232.

34. "The kind of Being which Dasein has, as potentiality-for-Being, lies existentially in understanding." BT, p. 183.

35. Victor Lange, in his "Introduction" to New Perspectives in German Literary Criticism, R. E. Amacher and V. Lange, eds. (Princeton: Princeton University Press, 1979), describes as follows the Dilthey-Heidegger nexus:

> From Dilthey, Heidegger derived the conviction that the historical concretizations of life require an understanding from within the phenomena rather than a mere causal explanation, a comprehension of the manner in which 'life' has constituted itself in history. The theory of hermeneutics . . . provided methodological access to this 'understanding from within' by recognizing the historical context of the individual creative act that mirrors the supra-personal presence of life. Heidegger rejects the subjectivist implications of Dilthey's 'Erlebnis'-complex and, in Sein und Zeit, gives to the hermeneutical principle and practice a radical efficacy: it is the fundamental procedure by which man comprehends and articulates his existence. In this sense, Sein und Zeit has been called a hermeneutical phenomenology. (pp. 17–18)

It is hard to say this any better. Yet it appears that for Professor Lange "the subjectivist implications of Dilthey's 'Erlebnis'-complex" are Dilthey's own. For, he continues, " 'Understanding' [for Heidegger] is no longer, as it was for Dilthey, merely a manner of investigation but a constituent element of being-in-the-world. . . . Understanding . . . is not a subjective confrontation of an object, but the way of being of man himself" (p. 18). Here I part company with my eminent colleague. Dilthey believed, in the passage I have earlier stressed, that the object of the Geisteswissenschaften is precisely "not the phenomenon as it is given to the sense, is no mere reflection in consciousness of something real but is itself immediate inner reality and thus indeed, as a context or coherent structure, is experienced from within" (5:317–318).

At the same time it would be quite misleading to attach Dilthey to Heidegger in the period after Being and Time. Indeed the entire antianthropological thrust of Heidegger's later aesthetic and ontology can be identified as an anti-Diltheyan trope. Consider especially Heidegger's critique of the category of Erlebnis in The Origin of the Work of Art (Der Ursprung des Kunstwerkes): "The manner in which man experiences art is supposed to reveal its nature. Experience is the standard source, not only of artistic enjoyment but similarly of artistic creation. Everything is experience. But perhaps experience is the element in which art dies" (Stuttgart: Reclam, 1960), p. 91; first delivered as a lecture in 1936.

And yet the cogency of Diltheyan categories renews itself in cyclical fashion. In 1975 the avant-garde theoretician Hans Jauss wrote: "One of my interests [in aesthetic theory] is to develop categories which no longer refer to what is generally called the history of aesthetic ideas. These categories are not aesthetic ideas, nor literary history in the manner of Lanson. What I seek is a middle category, aesthetic experience" ("Interview," Diacritics [Spring 1975], 5(1):53). Jauss' procedure responds to the Marxist insistence that in questions of aesthetic reception "the relation between art and public is in no way a simple cause-effect relation" (Norbert Krenzlin, Das Werk, "rein für sich": Zur Geschichte des Verhältnisses von Phänomenologie, Ästhetik und Literaturwissenschaft [Berlin: Akademie-Verlag, 1979], p. 71). In Lange's words, concerning "literature in our time, ... neither its subjective nor its objective character is self-evident but demands of its readers a sharp awareness of its modality" (New Perspectives, p. 3). This being the case we can expect approximations of this "modality" to return again and again to Dilthey's arsenal of mediating concepts.

36. Manfred Naumann, "Die Realisierung der Werke durch das 'tätige' Subjekt," in Gesellschaft, Literatur, Lesen, Manfred Naumann, ed. (Berlin-Weimar: Aufbau, 1973), p. 87.

37. BW, p. 122.

38. Cited in Patrick Carnegy, Faust as Musician (New York: New Directions, 1973), p. 36.

39. Compare, on the other hand, Nietzsche's final contribution to Ecce Homo in 1889: "In relation to everything that passes for noblesse today I have a sovereign feeling of distinction; I would not permit the young German Emperor the honor of being my coachman." Cited in Walter Kaufmann, Nietzsche: Philosopher, Psychoanalyst, Antichrist (Princeton: Princeton University Press, 1974), p. 451.

40. Makkreel, Dilthey, p. 81. Dilthey does make statements—in the Introduction to the Historical Sciences, for example, in vol. 1, p. 158—which diminish the institutional character of the arts. On the other hand, he speaks of the process by which a style comes to dominate as a "question of force" (Machtfrage) pure and simple (6:274): the process by which artistic domination arises is the same as in other institutional struggles.

41. Peter Brooks, "Fictions of the Wolfman: Freud and Narrative Understanding," Diacritics (1979), 9:80.

42. One effect of the new poetics on philological practice would be to detach philology from any temptation to found itself on linguistics. It would place philology instead squarely on the basis of an "historical psychology." Dilthey studied linguistics. Müller-Vollmer notes Dilthey's close relation with Lazarus and Steinthal: Dilthey was "involved in [their] venture of founding a journal for social psychology and comparative linguistics, the well-known Zeitschrift für Völkerpsychologie und Sprachwissenschaft" and contributed a number of articles to it" (Towards a Phenomenological Theory, p. 90). If philology in mid-nineteenth-century Germany can be fairly described as inspired by the methodology and specific findings of linguistics, then Dilthey's enterprise is a reassertion of the priority of nonspeculative, nonexperimental poetics over philology and of the necessity of resituating philology. The crucial difference between poetics and linguistics-based philology is based on the fact that "the productive powers which form language are . . . the same as those which can by and large be grasped in the life of the mind: their relation to the speech process (Sprachvorgang), however, is not in any way experienced but is instead arrived at by deduction. On this is founded the relation of the method of linguistics to natural scientific method" ([italics mine] 6:125).

43. See Deric Regin, Freedom and Dignity: The Historical and Philosophical Thought of Schiller (The Hague: Martinus Nijhoff, 1965), p. 28; and also Paul de Man, Blindness and Insight: Essays in the Rhetoric of Contemporary Criticism, 2d ed., rev. (Minneapolis: University of Minnesota Press, 1983): "We can speak of crisis when a 'separation' takes place, by self-reflection, between what, in literature, is in conformity with the original intent and what has irrevocably fallen away from this source" (p. 8).

44. Cf. Zöckler, Dilthey und die Hermeneutik. Dilthey grasped, from 1852 on, that "great men, 'geniuses'—who not only cultivate their inner life but also put this culture into practice—can be produced only by a nation which experiences no obstacle to the unfolding of its power. The universality of Shakespeare and Calderon was made possible only by the 'great fullness of national power' of their nations" (6:235). The inner quote is from Dilthey's 1867 inaugural lecture at Basel, "The Literary and Philosophical Movement in Germany, 1770–1800" (5:14).

45. Peschken, *Versuch*, pp. 11–49; Zöckler, *Dilthey und die Hermeneutik*, pp. 229–236.

46. Peschken, *Versuch*, p. 134.

47. Golo Mann, *The History of Germany Since 1789* (Harmondsworth, Middlesex: Penguin, 1974), p. 297ff, a translation by Marian Jackson of *Deutsche Geschichte des 19. und 20. Jahrhunderts* (Frankfurt: Büchergilde Gutenberg, 1958).

48. "Bismarck, 'sovereign man of action' (7:142), offered Dilthey the hope of lending the German *Weltanschauung*—that Objective Idealism 'intimated' by Goethe—an entirely new validity on the basis of a 'fullness of national force' (5:14)." Zöckler, *Dilthey und die Hermeneutik*, p. 235.

49. Dilthey wrote to Treitschke, in reaction to his militarist-nationalist position: "It does not seem historic to me to declare in every instance those interested in gathering together all forces in the unified purpose of national defense, to be patriots, wise men of vision, having genuine political sense." *Der junge Dilthey: Ein Lebensbild in Briefen und Tagebüchern, 1852–1870*, Clara Misch-Dilthey, ed., 2d ed. (Göttingen: Vandenhoeck und Ruprecht, 1960), p. 290. And further: "The proposition is false that the defense system, as the expression of self-preservation, has the right, until it has reached its saturation point, to injure every other system of culture" (p. 291). Both passages are cited in Zöckler, *Dilthey und die Hermeneutik*, pp. 256–257.

50. Gadamer, *Wahrheit und Methode*, p. 5.

51. Zöckler, *Dilthey und die Hermeneutik*, p. 260.

52. *Ibid.*, p. 223.

53. *Der junge Dilthey*, p. 5.

54. René Girard, *Deceit, Desire, and the Novel: Self and Other in Literary Structure* (Baltimore: Johns Hopkins University Press, 1965).

55. *Ibid.*, p. 294ff.

56. De Man, *Blindness and Insight*, p. 18. Girard's work is presumably targeted again when, in *Allegories of Reading*, de Man writes: "A reversed image of the same model [of a genetically structured, organically determined view of literary history] sees Romanticism as a moment of extreme delusion from which the nineteenth century slowly recovers until it can free itself in the assertion of a new modernity" (p. 81).

57. De Man, "The Rhetoric of Temporality," in *Interpretation, Theory, and Practice*, Charles Singleton, ed., especially pp. 175–185.

58. De Man, *Blindness and Insight*, pp. 22–23. This notion of organic unity proves seductive, tough, and long-lasting, especially when it is found in close connection with an idealization of organic nature. Cf. "I believe that every great creator follows in the course of his life a curve similar to that which Paul Claudel described to me when I asked him why his early dramatic works had appeared under the title of *The Tree*. He pointed out to me the resemblance of the inner ferment and the intense, powerful and irresistible thrust of a personality which asserts itself, to the way in which a tree first attains its full stature, possessed of all its sap and of the whole superstructure of its branches stretching in all directions, crowned with rich foliage, in its fullness and strength. Later comes the *fruit*: the works of the mature man, a regular and perfect crop that follows its own inevitable course." Darius Milhaud in *Poetics of Music* by Igor Stravinsky (London: Oxford University Press, 1947), pp. x–xi.

59. Hölderlin, *Sämtliche Werke*, 3:12.

60. This is an implication flowing out of many of de Man's texts, as, for example, *Blindness and Insight*, p. ix, and "The Rhetoric of Temporality," p. 188.

61. Zöckler, *Dilthey und die Hermeneutik*, p. 232; *Der junge Dilthey*, p. 93.

62. For example, the "point of impression" (*Eindruckspunkt*): "Where life is, there

functions and parts are held together by means of that on which, in its energy and feeling, precisely this particular existence is centered" (6:283).

63. Cf. Wolfgang Heise, *Aufbruch in die Illusion. Zur Kritik der bürgerlichen Philosophie in Deutschland* (Berlin: Akademie Verlag, 1964), p. 371.

64. Gadamer, *Wahrheit und Methode*, p. 211.

65. Jürgen Habermas, *Erkenntnis und Interesse* (Frankfurt: Suhrkamp, 1968), translated as *Knowledge and Human Interests* by Jeremy J. Schapiro (Boston Press, 1971).

66. Makkreel, *Dilthey*, p. 17.

67. This passage comes from a letter written by Dilthey to Count Yorck in July 1886. *Briefwechsel*, p. 58. It is cited in Müller-Vollmer, *Towards a Phenomenological Theory*, p. 136.

68. Golo Mann, *History of Germany*, p. 251.

69. See Zöckler, *Dilthey und die Hermeneutik*, p. 228.

70. "The analysis today of human existence fills all of us with the feeling of fragility, of the might of the dark drive, of suffering from obscurities (*Dunkelheiten*) and illusions, the finitude in everything that is life, even where the loftiest forms of communal life arise from that life" (7:150). "And is there not connected with everything brutal, dreadful, destructive contained in the will to power . . . the consciousness of community, of belonging, the joyous participation in the power of the political whole, experiences which belong to the highest human values?" (7:170). Cited in Zöckler, *Dilthey und die Hermeneutik*, p. 71. Dilthey's stress on the dreadful side of life prompts Gadamer to define Dilthey's intellectual-historical project as the effort, through knowledge, to gain "protection and security, despite the unfathomableness of life" (*Wahrheit und Methode*, p. 226).

71. Cited in Golo Mann, *History of Germany*, p. 209. The sense of crisis among intellectuals of the 1870s and 1880s was due in part to the exacerbation of the chronic feeling of an absence of origins in the German nation-state. What acts or tradition before Bismarck could be pointed to as genuine precursors of the Empire?

72. An effort that, as Zöckler notes, "occurred in connection with [Dilthey's] development of a homogeneous historical-political theory, in which all divergent moments are grasped in their relation to the process of origination and the law of motion of the nation organized by the state, and in this manner are centered" (*Dilthey und die Hermeneutik*, pp. 239–40).

73. Cited in Habermas, *Erkenntnis und Interesse*, p. 192.

74. In fact Dilthey may have had a more vulgar impulse in mind. Recalling the many unreliable reports during the years 1889–1900 concerning Nietzsche's mental illness, Ludwig Doerges wrote: "The motive cannot have been lofty. Should we still hesitate today to call it curiosity [*Neugier*]? Nietzsche often referred all-too-familiar verbal constructions to their real meaning. It was indeed "*Neugier*" as "*Neu-gier*" [a "craving for novelty"] that filled and fulfilled an age bursting with detective flair. We experienced so much novelty that a craving arose for more and still more." In "Kleine Nietzsche-Erinnerungen," *Deutsche Allgemeine Zeitung* (Berlin), October 13, 1934; cited in *Begegnungen mit Nietzsche*, Sander L. Gilman, ed. (Bonn: Bouvier, 1981), p. 656.

75. This point about science in Dilthey has to be further nuanced; science is valorized as the discipline of social thought. Dilthey sees the period following the French Revolution as marked by the increased "importance of the social sciences vis-à-vis the natural sciences" (1:4). Hence Dilthey's systematic "repudiation of the positivistic orientation toward the epistemological model of the natural sciences [read, Comte]." In Lieber, "Geschichte und Gesellschaft," p. 706.

76. René Wellek notes critically Dilthey's normative aesthetics of equilibrium. "Every work of art which seeks to evoke permanent satisfaction must conclude with a situation of equilibrium or with a pleasurable state, in any case with a reconciling final state,

even if this state is only in an idea which lifts us above life" (6:162–63). Cited in "Wilhelm Dilthey's Poetics," p. 122. This would be, for Peschken, the aesthetic reflex of a worldview courting conciliation everywhere, including—lamentably, for Peschken—the political order.

77. Life is the source of art only because life is so egregiously absent from German social life. As what is *unknown*, it can figure precisely as what Barbara Johnson has called the unseen motivating force behind the very deployment of meaning. In *Erlebnis und Dichtung* Dilthey praises Hölderlin's purity and prophetic lucidity as representing his extreme resistance to German social life.

78. Golo Mann, *History of Germany*, p. 387.
79. Heinen, *Konstitution der Ästhetik*, p. 10.
80. Lieber, "Geschichte und Gesellschaft," p. 726.
81. *Briefwechsel Dilthey/Yorck*, p. 183, cited in Rodi, "Lebensphilosophie," p. 608.
82. Golo Mann, *History of Germany*, p. 387.
83. Gadamer, *Wahrheit und Methode*, p. 221.
84. "Entretien avec Günter Grass," *Le Monde*, October 7, 1977, p. 24.

3. Self and Subject in Nietzsche During the Axial Period

1. The "axial period" of 1882–88 is a phrase not often encountered in essays on Nietzsche; I mean by it what is usually meant by "the mature period." The period 1883–87 is a familiar cut because these are the years of the publication of *Thus Spoke Zarathustra* (in PN) and its "commentaries": *Beyond Good and Evil* (1886) and *The Genealogy of Morals* (1887) (both in BW). *Beyond Good and Evil* "says the same things as my *Zarathustra*," wrote Nietzsche to Overbeck, "but differently, very differently" (BW, p. 182). And the *Genealogy* is also offered as a "supplement" and "clarification" of *Beyond Good and Evil* (BW, p. 439). Moreover, the entire third section of the *Genealogy* is devoted, according to Nietzsche, to an exemplary exegesis of a single aphorism from *Zarathustra* (BW, p. 459).

The period 1883–88 is also a familiar cut since it is from the notebooks of these years that the notes making up *The Will to Power* are taken. This period also includes the powerful work "The Case of Wagner," published in 1888. I begin the axial period with 1882, however, so as to take in the whole of *The Gay Science* (first published in 1882, but supplemented by a "Fifth Book" in 1887), which contains a number of aphorisms crucial for my discussion.

2. BW, p. 314.
3. Numbers refer to volume and pages of *Friedrich Nietzsche: Werke in Drei Bänden*, Karl Schlechta, ed. (Munich: Carl Hanser Verlag, 1954–56).

A plain translation of this poem reads: "Now, contorted between two nothingnesses, a question mark, a weary riddle, a riddle for birds of prey: they will 'solve' ['dissolve'] you all right, they are already hungry for your 'solution,' they are already flapping around you, their riddle, around you, hanged man! . . . O Zarathustra . . . *self-knower!* . . . *hangman of your self!* . . ." "Between Birds of Prey," from the *Dithyrambs of Dionysus*, composed before the end of 1888, first published in 1891.

4. Harold Bloom, *Poetry and Repression* (New Haven: Yale University Press, 1976), pp. 135–136. Bloom's response to the Continental attack on the self is mediated by Paul de Man's work on Nietzsche in *Allegories of Reading* (New Haven: Yale University Press, 1979). The notion that Nietzsche's alleged critique of the self occurs on "language-centered grounds" follows de Man's concern "to center a consideration of Nietzsche's relationship to literature on his theory of language" (p. 103). This leads de Man to view Nietzsche as asserting "that the idea of the human subject as a privileged viewpoint is a mere metaphor" (p. 111). Unfortunately this discussion in de Man is vitiated by his failure to distin-

guish between Nietzsche's terms "subject" and "self." Bloom's discussion inherits this fault.

5. All these passages which speak of the self as invented, posited, as un-self-stable—as imaginary, a fiction, a projection, a supplement—are taken from book 3, section 3, of *The Will to Power*, headed "Belief in the 'Ego': The Subject." I take them from this source rather than from the individual published works in which they are elaborated because of the overwhelming impression made by so concentrated a strain of writing against the self in a demystifying way. Walter Kaufmann comments about this third section of *The Will to Power* that "some of the epistemological reflections . . . [have] no close parallel in the works Nietzsche finished" (WP, p. xiv). But what is in fact remarkable (and cautionary) about this subsection on the subject is that *each* of these aphorisms can in fact be traced to more fully elaborated and nuanced versions in the published work. As a result this attack on belief in the subject is nowhere else encountered in so pure a state and will always be found modified by various types of argument on behalf of the self. The reader who relies on *The Will to Power* for Nietzsche's last testament and takes from it a position of radical epistemological nihilism will miss the intricacy of his published statement.

6. The "self . . . is your body" (PN, p. 146). "[Zarathustra's] word pronounced *selfishness* blessed, the wholesome, healthy selfishness that wells from a powerful soul— . . . to which belongs the high body . . . —the supple, persuasive body, the dancer whose parable and epitome is the self-enjoying soul" (PN, p. 302). Further: "It is not at all necessary to get rid of 'the soul' . . . and thus to renounce one of the most ancient and venerable hypotheses—. . . . But the way is open for new versions and refinements of the soul-hypothesis" (BW, p. 210).

7. Other attributes of the ego: It is a "fable, a fiction, a play on words" (PN, p. 495). Its individuality is merely exemplary; it instantiates what is general, indeed, *common* to the species (GS, p. 299). As a subject of "egoism," it is "interesting" and dangerous—but this is also how Nietzsche construes the "self."

The self has few attributes. "Individual psychological observations," writes Ludwig Giesz, "never really treat the self, which precisely is not general. The presupposition of science is that assertions of a categorical kind can be made [only] about an 'exemplary' individual." *Nietzsche: Existenzialismus und Wille zur Macht* (Stuttgart: Deutsche Verlangsanstalt, 1950), p. 45. As that which cannot be known, the self can be described as "there," a "granitic fate" (BW, p. 352), profoundly present and hidden, never lost and therefore never having to be sought (BW, p. 418). Or else it can be represented as insistently problematic, an eternal question. In both cases adequate immediate self-knowledge is impossible (BW, p. 415). The self can be represented, however, by certain more or less inspired metaphors, as we shall see.

8. GS, pp. 297–300. In its main thrust, however, this passage derogates "the thinking that rises to *consciousness*" as "the most superficial and worst part" of all thinking (BW, p. 299). Consciousness is chiefly "superfluous" except for the purpose of communication; as a result it must adopt the "herd perspective" and debase the "incomparably personal, unique, and infinitely individual" character of our actions. (Cf. Kafka: "One cannot express that which one is, since that is precisely what one is; one can only communicate that which is not, i.e., the lie.") "Whatever becomes conscious," continues Nietzsche, "*becomes* by the same token shallow, thin, relatively stupid, general, sign, a herd signal; all becoming conscious involves a great and thorough corruption, falsification, reduction to superficialities, and generalization" (p. 300). This charge applies to *self*-consiousness as well: "The human being inventing signs is at the same time the human being who becomes ever more keenly conscious of himself. It was only as a social animal that man acquired self-consciousness" (p. 299). At the same time this process resembles (or at least precipitates) that famous process of "internalization" (*Verinnerlichung*) which, on the ac-

count given in *The Genealogy of Morals* (BW, pp. 520–521), contributes to more depth, hope, and interest in man than it does to his enfeeblement. Both texts were published of course in the same year—1887.

9. In consecutive episodes of *Thus Spoke Zarathustra*—"On Human Prudence" and "The Stillest Hour"—the vain man sighs, from a sense of modesty, "What am I?" and Zarathustra, perceiving his own smallness next to the superman, says "Who am I? I await the worthier one" (PN, pp. 255, 258). Clearly the choice of pronoun here makes a difference. In the first case it expresses an absolute abjectness of being; the "vain man" feels himself (though unawares) inferior to *anyone* who will praise him. In the second passage the redoubtable Zarathustra speaks as an ego ("A new pride my ego taught me" |PN, p. 144|) and as a self ("Instruments and toys are sense and spirit: behind them still lies the self" |PN, p. 146|), but this identity is only something wanting to perish for a stronger being. The distinction here may not be precisely the one Nietzsche is pointing to in speaking of the "questioner" underlying the will to truth. But these passages support the view that Nietzsche's rhetorical distinction between who and what is significant.

10. BW, p. 199. Nietzsche's mythology of temptresses has its important distinctions in value: the Sphinx is not a Circe. To say the Sphinx is a Circe is to adopt the makeshift consolations of the "skeptic"—"a delicate creature," the product of "nervous exhaustion and sickliness." The skeptic cannot hear "Yes!" He will not "straighten what is crooked," he counsels waiting; "the uncertain has its charms, too," he says; "the sphinx, too, is a Circe; Circe, too, was a philosopher" (BW, pp. 319–320). The encounter of Oedipus and the Sphinx, which is a metaphor of the encounter of the self and the question of its being, is in deadly earnest and in need of solution.

11. In MH, pp. 45–50. Heidegger had read Nietzsche by the time he wrote *Being and Time* in the mid-1920s; his work mentions Nietzsche in connection with notions of Being-toward-death, conscience, and the "use and abuse" of "historiology."

12. The next aphorism (BW, p. 452) speaks literally of "a *fundamental will* of knowledge."

13. MH, p. 48.

14. Martin Heidegger, *Sein und Zeit*, 10th ed. (Tübingen: Max Niemeyer Verlag, 1963), p. 7.

15. The self *wants* itself as a question. In *Zarathustra* (part 2: "On Immaculate Perception") Nietzsche writes, beautifully, "Wo ist Schönheit? Wo ich mit allem Willen *wollen muß*; wo ich lieben und untergehn will, daß ein Bild nicht nur Bild bleibe" (2:379) ("Where is beauty? Where I *must will* with all my will; where I want to love and perish so that an image may not remain a mere image" |PN, p. 235|).

Heidegger reads differently that being which is asked about in the question constituting Dasein. What is asked about is Being, and by this Being a mode of human being is "essentially determined." This is the strong form of the claim; in this section of *Being and Time*, however, it is soon afterward neutralized and almost dissolved. Here is the less strong form: "|'In the question of the meaning of Being'| . . . there is . . . a notable 'relatedness backward or forward' of what is asked about (Being) to asking as a mode of being of a being" (MH, p. 49). The more nearly neutral form reads: "This only means that the being that has the character of Dasein has a relation to the question of Being itself, perhaps even a distinctive one. But have we not thereby demonstrated that a particular being has a priority with respect to Being and that the exemplary being that is to function as what is primarily *interrogated* is pregiven?" (MH, p. 49). Finally the claim is dissolved: "In what we have discussed up to now neither has the priority of Dasein been demonstrated nor has anything been decided about its possible or even necessary function as the primary being to be interrogated" (MH, pp. 49–50). Then the claim is reasserted in a typically Heideggerian manner—at once unassailable, if one is persuaded by the authority of its rhetoric, and vacuous, if one is not. Heidegger writes, "But indeed something like a priority of Dasein has announced itself" (MH, p. 50).

The trouble here is that the basic task at hand is to clarify the meaning of Being as it comes to light in being announced as the object of an insistent question. Such a discussion itself has to be preceded by a clarification of the kind of visibility and evidence which belongs to something thus *announced*. Heidegger begs the question.

16. See previous note.

17. In *The Gay Science* Nietzsche also identifies an unconscious reason, viz., "The development of language and the development of consciousness (*not* of reason but merely of the way reason enters consciousness) go hand in hand" (p. 299).

18. The being of the self, in the moment of its pluralization, is invariably represented by Nietzsche in the images of "society." And, moreover, in such varied and specifically imagined ways as to make Freud's social model of superego/ego seem thin and underrealized. The soul, for example, in *Beyond Good and Evil* is hypothesized as a "social structure of the drives and affects" (BW, p. 210). See *in. al.* the aphorism from *The Will to Power* headed "The Body as a Political Structure" (WP, p. 348).

19. I discount compound words with the prefix "self" (*Selbst*), which have variable value. Thus Nietzsche will discredit a certain kind of introspection which he calls "Selbst-Erkenntnis" (self-knowledge) (BW, p. 414); (see p. 106 of this book) but value that "Selbst-Bekenntnis" (personal confession) which is "what every great philosophy so far has been . . . [:] a kind of involuntary and unconscious memoir" (BW, p. 203).

20. This privilege of the self that is decisively nominal but otherwise obscure gives such confident distinctions as the following their unwitting irony: "In Nietzsche the ego—sometimes called a grammatical fiction, sometimes called a mask—has lost its self-identity." Alphonso Lingis, "The Will to Power," in *The New Nietzsche*, David B. Allison, ed. (New York: Delta, 1977), p. 40.

21. "For one may doubt . . . whether there are any opposites at all, and secondly whether these popular valuations and opposite values on which the metaphysicians put their seal, are not perhaps merely foreground estimates, only provisional perspectives . . . . *Language*, here as elsewhere, will not get over its awkwardness, and will continue to talk of opposites where there are only degrees and many subtleties of gradation" (BW, pp. 200, 225). Cf. Kafka: "My repugnance for antitheses is certain . . . . They make for thoroughness, fullness, completeness, but only like a figure on the 'wheel of life' [a toy with a revolving wheel]; we have chased our little idea around the circle. They are as undifferentiated as they are different." *The Diaries of Franz Kafka: 1910–1923*, Max Brod, ed. (New York: Schocken Books, 1948), p. 157.

22. As, for example: "It is not too much to say that even a partial *diminution of utility*, an atrophying and degeneration, a loss of meaning and purposiveness—in short, death—is among the conditions of an actual *progressus*, which always appears in the shape of a will and a way to greater power and is always carried through at the expense of numerous smaller powers" (BW, p. 514).

23. "For the interpretation itself is a form of the will to power, exists (but not as a 'being' but as a process, a becoming) as an affect" (WP, p. 302).

24. The question is rhetorical; it "cannot be decided . . . . ; for in the course of this analysis the human intellect cannot avoid seeing itself in its own perspectives, and *only* in these. We cannot look around our own corner" (GS, p. 336).

25. The *mise en abîme* is the endless mirror effect shown, for example, on the

Quaker Oats box of my childhood. The quaker is depicted as holding up a box of oats on which he is depicted holding up a box of oats, etc. Valéry's verbal equivalent is M. Teste's confession, "En voyant me voir. . . ."

26. Laurence Rickels writes in a Peircean vein: "A mirror-image is not a total or iconic image but an indexical image, and thus its relation to its object is based not on identity and simultaneity but on sequential difference and connectedness." From his doctoral dissertation, "The Iconic Imagination," Department of German, Princeton University, 1980.

27. I paraphrase here a phenomenological view of the linguistic sign. See Gerald L. Bruns, *Modern Poetry and the Idea of Language* (New Haven: Yale University Press, 1974), p. 233.

I have floated two theories of the origin of a linguistic event, once a personal speaker has been excluded. One theory calls this origin language itself; this is the structuralist position. In effect it replaces the concept of origin by that of an always present synchronic system. As formulated by Paul Ricoeur: "The system of language has no more subject than it has reference. The system is anonymous. Or rather, it is neither personal nor anonymous, since the question 'Who is speaking?' has no longer a meaning. Nobody speaks; the dictionary is mute. The exclusion of the subject results from the closure of a system of signs, since this closure implies the exclusion of the question, 'Who is speaking?' It is rules of the chess game without the moves, without the players" ("Philosophy of Language and Phenomenology," an unpublished lecture delivered at the University of Texas at Austin, November 24, 1968, p. 8). Nietzsche does indeed exclude the question of "Who is speaking?" from the question of the self by mutating it as "What is the self?" This formulation excludes the self as speaking subject. On the other hand, Nietzsche describes the self as "something that *wants* [aims] . . . to *surpass* itself" (WP, p. 270). He therefore lines up with (a version of) another theory of the origin of the linguistic event— the phenomenological.

"What is the sentence for a phenomenological description? First," says Ricoeur, "it is an event. The dictionary is not an event, it is a system. I oppose here event and system" (as indeed does Nietzsche). "A sentence," Ricoeur continues, "is an event because somebody rises up and says something. Something happens, the sentence occurs and disappears. It is historical reality" (p. 10). Moreover it refers to an encompassing reality, to existence as a field of meaning. "In the sentence we experience language not as an object, not as a closed system, but as a mediation, that is to say, that through which we move towards reality, whatever it may be. . . . In the sentence and through the sentence language escapes itself towards what it says. It goes beyond itself and disappears into its intentional referent" (pp. 11–12).

Some of this fits Nietzsche's account of the self, but the *décalage* is instructive. Indeed the self's language transcends itself toward its subject. The subject, however, is not somebody; the way in which it says its question is closer, in the phenomenological account, to the self's primary articulation of the existential field of meaning. The self, indeed, like language in the Husserlian view, "is, in itself, a medium, a mediation, an exchange between the *telos* of logicity [rationality] and the origin in experience" ("Philosophy of Language and Linguistic Analysis," an unpublished lecture delivered at the University of Texas at Austin, November 22, 1968, p. 9). The question of the self articulates the self as an interpreter. Thereafter interpretation involves the self whether it explicitly poses the question of itself. Its being is a question—the transcendental agent of its mutation from a "natural involvement" to a "signifying relation with experience" (p. 13).

28. Giesz, *Nietzsche*, p. xiii. From this perspective, Heidegger himself reads Nietzsche aberrantly; he declares that Nietzsche, who links the self with the will to power,

conceives of the will as "the being of beings." Now in *The Will to Power* and elsewhere Nietzsche gives the will many different names: self-overcomer, creator, commander, even a fiction. But the intelligibility of "the being of beings" is itself only a project of the will to power, indeed a by-product of the fiction of the ego. In a passage which Heidegger is well aware of, but which he slights, Nietzsche writes:

> In its origin language belongs in the age of the most rudimentary form of psychology. We enter a realm of crude fetishism when we summon before consciousness the basic presuppositions of the metaphysics of language, in plain talk, the presuppositions of reason. Everywhere it sees a doer and doing; it believes in will as *the* cause; it believes in the ego, in the ego as being, in the ego as substance, and it projects this faith in the ego-substance upon all things—only thereby does it first *create* the concept of "thing." Everywhere "being" is projected by thought, pushed underneath, as the cause; the concept of being follows, and is a derivative of, the concept of ego. (PN, p. 485)

Heidegger reads this passage as marking Nietzsche's skepticism toward the conventional psychological interpretation of will and hence as requiring that the matter be thought through fundamentally. But Nietzsche's vigilance is somehow not keen enough, according to Heidegger, to protect him against misunderstanding Being as the being of beings. (*Nietzsche*, vol. 1, *The Will to Power as Art*, David Farrell Krell, tr. [New York: Harper and Row, 1979], p. 38.) Yet it is just this error which is sharply identified in the passage. It is remarkable, moreover, that in this passage Nietzsche does not arraign the concept of self. Elsewhere he adds, "We [Germans] hardly believe in the justification of the concept of 'Being' " (GS, p. 306). "Heraclitus will remain eternally right with his assertion that Being is an empty fiction" (PN, p. 481). Further: "To impose upon becoming the character of being—that is the supreme will to power" (BW, p. 330). The word "impose" certainly merits the quotes of pervasive irony.

29. Harold Alderman, *Nietzsche's Gift* (Athens: Ohio University Press, 1977) p. 165.

30. BW, p. 418. This suspension of the explicit question of the self is connected in Nietzsche to the entire complex of ideas that comes under the head of "active forgetfulness"—the condition of action and truth. See especially BW, pp. 493–494, and the early essays "On Truth and Falsity in their Ultramoral Sense," in *The Complete Works of Friedrich Nietzsche*, vol. 2, Oscar Levy, ed. (New York: Macmillan, 1909–1911) (translation is unreliable) and "The Use and Abuse of History," *ibid.*, vol. 5.

31. Again, "One may not ask: 'Who then interprets?' for the interpretation itself is a form of the will to power, exists (but not as a 'being' but as a process, a becoming) as an affect" (WP, p. 302).

32. Nietzsche also asserts the opposite position, but in such a form that I lay my stress where I do. The (opposite) idea is found in *The Will to Power*, viz., "The will to power can manifest itself only against resistances; therefore, it seeks that which resists it" (WP, p. 346). The context of this remark is, however, "the primeval tendency of the protoplasm." The idea reappears in *The Twilight of the Idols*: "How is freedom measured in individuals and peoples? According to the resistance which must be overcome . . . to remain on top" (PN, p. 542). Here again the context disqualifies its general authority. This is the case essentially "five steps from tyranny, close to the threshold of the danger of servitude"— in an extreme situation—and Nietzsche's language is infected by the mood of extremity: "The human being who has *become free*—spits on the contemptible type of well-being dreamed of by shopkeepers, Christians, cows, females, Englishmen, and other democrats" (PN, p. 542). It is wrong to assert, as does Spivak, that the description of the will to power "as a search for what is resistant to itself" is "irreducible." "Translator's Preface," *Of Grammatology*, a translation of *De la Grammatologie* by Jacques Derrida (Baltimore: Johns Hopkins Uni-

versity Press), p. xxvi. Yet this claim passes current as the cardinal axiom in "panironic" readings of Nietzsche. See pp. 115–120 of this book.

33. GS, pp. 244–245. Maire Kurrik makes enlightening distinctions between unconscious negation and the consciousness of negativity in *Literature and Negation* (New York: Columbia University Press, 1979).

34. "For Nietzsche knowledge is a (re)constructed text; the world is the lost original." Bernd Magnus, *Nietzsche's Existential Imperative* (Bloomington: Indiana University Press, 1978), p. 27.

35. *Satzung* (statute, law) and *Setzung* (positing, stake) are central categories in Giesz's discussion of the will to power. Giesz writes of "the structure of the will to power . . . [as] defining at the same time the self-developing Self. This being 'becomes' by producing itself ['We, however, *want to become those we are*—human beings who are new, unique, incomparable, who give themselves laws, who create themselves,' GS, p. 266]. The Self produces itself by relating understandingly to itself (by orienting itself toward something more general). It relates to itself by relating to something else—to contexts of meaning, which it indeed respects as statutes (*Satzungen*) [but] which, however, finally owe their binding character, their 'objectivity,' once again, to the Self which 'created' them" (*Nietzsche*, p. 14). Hence they are only the positings (*Setzungen*) of the Self. The fiction of the stable ego accords with what Nietzsche elsewhere calls "our inevitable need to preserve ourselves[:] to posit a crude world of stability, of 'things,' etc." (WP, p. 380). The ego is that "thing" of the inner life which "still speak[s] most honestly of its being"—the Self (PN, p. 144).

36. Nietzsche's defiance of Goethe should not be represented, of course, as innocent: Nietzsche was well aware of the text of Goethe which he parodies. Speaking against Wagner's assumption in *Parsifal* of the cause of chastity, Nietzsche writes of "all those well-constituted, joyful mortals who are far from regarding their unstable equilibrium between 'animal and angel' as necessarily an argument against existence—the subtlest and brightest among them have even found in it, like Goethe and Hafiz, *one more* stimulus to life" (BW, p. 535). See also BW, p. 300. *The West-Easterly Divan* is inspired by Goethe's reading of the Persian poet Hafiz.

This example nuances Harold Bloom's comment "Nietzsche . . . was the heir of Goethe in his strangely optimistic refusal to regard the poetical past as primarily an obstacle to fresh creation" (*The Anxiety of Influence* [New York: Oxford, 1973] p. 50). Goethe assimilates Hafiz, unafraid. Nietzsche's allusion to Goethe is oddly alienating. It inverts Goethe and suggests that the condition of enduring Goethe is keeping distance. This is not so much acknowledging Goethe's influence as stating that one will go one's own way.

37. Henry David Aiken comments: "In *Zarathustra* . . . the ever-recurrent and combative *ego*, which elsewhere Nietzsche seems to be trying to impose upon the reader, is for once submerged in the creative life, or world, of the work itself. And for this reason, by what is only an apparent paradox, Nietzsche's whole self is able to disport itself more freely . . . [and] more powerfully than in his more explicitly didactic works." "An Introduction to *Zarathustra*," in *Nietzsche: A Collection of Critical Essays*, Robert C. Solomon, ed. (New York: Anchor Books, 1973), p. 116.

38. And would have cost Blake more than a bowel complaint. In the 1814 "Preface" to *The Excursion* Wordsworth quotes lines revealing that to an extravagant degree the subject of his poem is *himself*—"our Minds, . . . the Mind of Man." Upon reading these lines Blake is supposed to have been afflicted by a bowel complaint that nearly killed him. Helen Darbishire, *The Poet Wordsworth* (Oxford: Clarendon, 1958), p. 139.

39. George Santayana, *Egotism in German Philosophy* (New York: Scribner's, 1940), p. 12.

40. In speaking about "the death of the self" in Nietzsche and later too about

what is alleged to be Nietzsche's ubiquitous irony (pp. 115–120 of this book); in speaking about "wild" readers (p. 117 ff.) who have seen in his texts interminable semantic dissonance; in speaking, finally, about the new Nietzsche of poststructuralist French writers, I point to a phenomenon that has moved saliently from the domain of specialist readings into the general (university) discourse about Nietzsche. This view of Nietzsche is now in circulation everywhere, with a force that seems greatly in excess of that exerted by the few essays which have actually advanced this position.

Three essays on Nietzsche in Paul de Man's *Allegories of Reading* (New Haven: Yale University Press, 1979), pp. 79–131, are important. The drift of these essays is suggested by de Man's published comment on the occasion of a Nietzsche symposium in 1974: "Irony . . . puts the notion of the self in question; . . . in Nietzsche we are dealing with a radically ironic rhetorical mode." "Nietzsche and Rhetoric," *Symposium* (1974), 28:45.

De Man's "deconstruction of the subject" in his first essay, on "Genesis and Genealogy" in *The Birth of Tragedy*, proceeds by questioning Nietzsche's presentation of Dionysus as the "father" of all art, of all appearance. The analysis turns on the "voice" which speaks on his behalf, "empowered to decide on matters of truth and falsehood," but with what authority? The claim it advances on behalf of music as the representation of the will is plainly made "in bad faith." Furthermore, the will figures as a subject, a consciousness. How can this subject speak against the category of representative art all the time it is itself a theatrical representation of the will? Finally, the text is discordant on the question of whether Dionysus is true or illusory. Therefore, "the will has been discredited as a self." "The pan-tragic consciousness of the self" is "made to appear hollow when . . . exposed to the clarity of a new ironic light" (p. 102).

De Man's second essay, "Rhetoric of Tropes," means "to put into question the prevalent scheme by which Nietzsche has been read." In this scheme "it seems as if Nietzsche had turned away from the problems of language to questions of the self" (p. 106). In fact, writes de Man, Nietzsche persistently uncovers the "figurality of all language," in which perspective "the idea of individuation, of the human subject as a privileged viewpoint, is a mere metaphor" (p. 111). The subject is then identified with the self.

In the third essay, "Rhetoric of Persuasion," the text which is explored opposes possibility and necessity and "no longer such spatial properties as inside and outside, or categories such as cause and effect, or experiences such a[s] pleasure and pain, all of which figure prominently in the many sections in which consciousness or selfhood are the targets of Nietzsche's critique" (p. 121). This assertion—and much of the argument of the essay on the rhetoric of tropes—is made unintelligible by de Man's equation of subject or consciousness and self.

David Allison's "Introduction" to *The New Nietzsche: Contemporary Styles of Interpretation*, an anthology of recent essays on Nietzsche mainly by French writers, is another text figuring in this discourse (New York: Delta, 1977). In giving an account of Nietzsche's semiotics, Allison writes, typically: "Thus there is nothing [for Nietzsche] beyond language, to guide or subtend linguistic signification from without. Language makes sense because it can draw upon itself" (p. xvi). Here, now, is Nietzsche: "Words are acoustical signs for concepts; concepts, however, are more or less definite image signs for often recurring and associated sensations, for groups of sensations. To understand one another, it is not enough that we use the same words; one also has to use the same words for the same species of inner experiences; in the end one has to have one's experience in common" (BW, p. 406). Language makes sense because it can draw on inner experience.

Allison furthermore sees Nietzsche as deconstructing the "axiomatic system" of "Western thought as such" by exhibiting the *grammatical* necessity producing the terms of thought, viz., "Identity gives rise to the concepts of unity, plurality, specific difference, number, permanence, movement (space and time), subject and substance (self, ego, soul, God, particle)" (p. xxii). In fact Nietzsche maintains a specific difference between "ego" and "self," terming the latter a "plurality with one sense."

Gayatri Spivak's "Translator's Introduction" to her translation of Jacques Derrida's *Of Grammatology* belongs to this wave. Like Allison she also leans heavily on Nietzsche's early essay "On Truth and Falsehood in an Extramoral Sense" (1873) and on Derrida's reading of Nietzsche as one who "contributed a great deal to the liberation of the signifier from its dependance or derivation with respect to the logos, and the related concept of truth or the primary signified" (p. xxi). She writes, "The human being [for Nietzsche] has nothing more to go on than a collection of nerve stimuli" (p. xxii). Yet to substitute the words "collection of nerve stimuli" for the word "experience" in the appropriate passages we have cited would be to distort their sense and resonance. For Spivak Nietzsche's conception of knowledge is of "an unending proliferation of interpretations whose only 'origin' [is] that shudder in the nerve strings" (p. xxiii). (This "shudder" returns to Nietzsche's "nerve-stimulus" in his description of the structural moments of language formation.) Is this true, however, for the being in whom " 'deep down' there is . . . some granite of spiritual *fatum*" (BW, p. 352)? Nietzsche has not interpreted value systems as infinite textuality and does not say that his distinctions between master and slave modes of evaluation are capable of being infinitely reinterpreted or put "under erasure." Spivak writes, "The Nietzschean unconscious is that vast arena of the mind of which the so-called 'subject' knows nothing" (p. xxv). But Nietzsche wrote, "Indeed, the ego and the ego's contradiction and confusion still speak most honestly of its being" (PN, p. 144). Curiously, Spivak appears to want to repair this fault—without too much fanfare, yet with the assertive self-consciousness of a gender claim. She reintroduces the category of the self to account for Nietzsche's (the philosopher's) deliberate reversal of opposed perspectives: "The dissolving of opposites is the philosopher's gesture against that will to power which would mystify her very self" (p. xxviii).

Finally, central to the discourse of the "new" Nietzsche is, of course, Derrida's *Spurs*, for which, in a word, "Nietzsche is a bit lost in the web of the text, like a spider, unequal to what he has produced" (*The New Nietzsche*, p. 186).

41. Ernst Behler, "Nietzsches Auffassung der Ironie," *Nietzsche-Studien* (1975), 4:1–35.

42. This exposure occurs principally in "The Four Great Errors" of *Twilight of the Idols* (PN, pp. 492–501).

43. See p. 113 of this book.

44. "All concepts in which an entire process is semiotically concentrated elude definition" (BW, p. 516).

45. Nietzsche wrote in the early text *Human, All-Too-Human* (*Menschliches Allzumenschliches*), 1878–79: "Immediate self-observation is insufficient by far for self-knowledge: we need history, because the past flows on in a hundred waves in us; indeed we ourselves are no more than what we experience in every moment of this flowing on" (1:823). The notion is developed in *The Gay Science* under the head of "the historical sense" (see p. 118 of this book) and further in *Beyond Good and Evil*. "The past of every form and way of life, of cultures that formerly lay right next to each other or one on top of the other, now flows into us 'modern souls' " (BW, p. 341).

Such passages form the basis of Nietzsche's defense, supposing he needed one, against Dilthey's charge that he lacked a historical sense and maintained that the royal road to human truth was introspection. The charge cannot stand. The debate is interestingly presented in J. Kamerbeek, "Dilthey Versus Nietzsche," *Studia Philosophica, Jahrbuch der Schweizerischen Philosophischen Gesellschaft* (1950), 10:52–84.

46. "And if somebody asked, 'but to a fiction there surely belongs an au-

thor?'—couldn't one answer simply: *why*? Doesn't this 'belongs' perhaps belong to the fiction, too? Is it not permitted to be a bit ironical about the subject no less than the predicate and object?" (BW, p. 237).

47. Jacques Derrida, *Spurs/Éperons*, Barbara Harlow, tr. (Chicago: University of Chicago Press, 1979), p. 81.

48. WP, 337. Or again, " 'The subject' is the fiction that many similar states in us are the effect of one substratum: but it is *we* who first created the 'similarity' of these states" (WP, p. 269; italics mine).

49. Pace Spivak, "Translator's Preface": "The 'subject' is a unified concept and therefore the *result* of 'interpretation' " (p. xxiv; italics mine).

50. *Unschuld des Werdens* II, aphorism 359. Cited in Giesz, *Nietzsche*, p. 6.

51. See note 42, above.

52. Gerald Bruns, *Modern Poetry*, p. 233.

53. There is in every philosophical oeuvre, writes Neal Chandler, "a significant diachrony not identical with the sequential or systematic unfolding of the intentional discourse, but laid down in certain of those disjunctions to which the discourse only *seems* blind. These textual ruptures are not then a product of blindness, but rather of a particular lucidity with which the author forces the discourse—against its own internal logic—to conform to the ambiguities of the ground." In his doctoral dissertation, "Artist-Philosopher, Nietzsche's Poetics of Thought," Department of German, Princeton University, 1977. The discourse—intentional *and* ironical—may still map the ground by means of salient blanks and collisions which criticism identifies.

54. See p. 106 of this book.

55. BW, p. 535; PN, p. 674. Nietzsche's late work *Nietzsche Contra Wagner* is pieced together from passages about Wagner in Nietzsche's earlier works, "perhaps clarified here and there, above all, shortened" ("Preface," PN, p. 662). In the section of *Nietzsche Contra Wagner* entitled "Wagner as an Apostle of Chastity: 3," Nietzsche reprints an earlier aphorism from the *Genealogy of Morals*, 3:3, but omits the sentence I have quoted. Why would Nietzsche not have wanted to reassert in 1888 that the great artist "comes to see himself and his art beneath him?"

56. Giesz, *Nietzsche*, p. 6. As opposed to "the subject" which is "a created entity, a 'thing' like all others, a simplification with the object of defining the force which posits, invents, things" (WP, p. 302).

57. *Selected Short Stories of Franz Kafka*, Willa and Edwin Muir, trs. (New York: Modern Library), pp. 173–174.

58. *Gesammelte Werke*, 3:344. In these early jottings surrounding the composition of *The Birth of Tragedy*, Nietzsche speculates on an "innermost being," a world "core," which is "wholly indecipherable." This is that "power" out of whose "womb a visionary world is generated in the form of the 'will.' " This womb is the "origin of music . . . and lies beyond all individuation." It is, therefore, quite incorrect of Paul de Man, who comments on this text, to assert that once the play of the will has been "shown to be . . . the endless tension of a nonidentity, a pattern of dissonance, . . . [it] contaminates the very source of the will, the will as source" (*Allegories of Reading*, p. 99). It is furthermore untrue that the "unpublished fragments . . . deny this possibility," namely, that "this essence is able to function as origin" (p. 101). The citation from Nietzsche reproduces the very imagery of filiation, indicating the identity of essence and origin.

59. Lewis Thomas, *The Lives of a Cell: Notes of a Biology Watcher* (New York: Bantam Books, 1974), pp. 3, 8, 9, 21, 18. Writing about the self in Nietzsche as related to problems of identity in the biological cell is encouraged by Nietzsche's reflections on the "Biology of the Drive to Knowledge" in *The Will to Power*. See, e.g., WP, p. 272.

60. *The Complete Works*, Oscar Levy, ed., 2:175–176.

61. Reference lost.

62. From Nietzsche's notebooks, cited in Beda Alleman, *Ironie und Dichtung* (Pfullingen: Günther Neske, 1956), p. 105.

63. Cited in De Man, *Allegories of Reading*, p. 94.

64. The point is roughly dramatized by what I hear as the difference between the positions of, say, *Human, All-Too-Human* (their lack of resonance) and those of the works of the axial period. The author of the 1396 aphorisms of *Human, All-Too-Human* is an idea born of Nietzsche's conviction in his solitude that he had better not admit to the solitude of his ego—to his iron restriction to the point of the ego.

65. *The Short Stories of Henry James*, Clifton Fadiman, ed. (New York: Modern Library, 1945), p. 315.

4. Mann as a Reader of Nietzsche

1. "Über die Unverständlichkeit," in *Schriften zur Literatur* (Munich: Deutscher Taschenbuchverlag, 1972), p. 339.

2. L, p. 642.

3. *The Anxiety of Influence: A Theory of Poetry* (New York: Oxford University Press, 1973), p. 50. (Hereafter cited as AI.)

4. BU, p. 84.

5. *Essays of Thomas Mann*, H. T. Lowe-Porter, tr. (New York: Vintage, 1957), p. 322. Cited in AI, p. 54.

6. Cf. Nietzsche, in *Ecce Homo*. "What is necessary does not hurt me; *amor fati* is my inmost nature. But this does not preclude my love of irony, even of world-historical irony" (BW, p. 780).

7. Cf. Heinrich Mann, *Ein Zeitalter wird besichtigt* (Stockholm: Neuer, 1946), p. 231. Cited in T. J. Reed, *Thomas Mann: The Uses of Tradition* (Oxford: Oxford University Press, 1974), p. 1. Cf. further Victor Lange, "Thomas Mann in Exile," in *Thomas Mann: 1875–1955*, Richard Ludwig and Stanley Corngold, eds. (Princeton: Princeton University Library, 1975), p. 40.

8. *Thomas Mann: Briefe 1937–1947*, Erika Mann, ed. (Frankfurt: S. Fischer, 1963), p. 23.

9. "Vorspruch zu einer musikalischen Nietzsche-Feier," in *Reden und Aufsätze*, vol. 2, *Gesammelte Werke*, vol. 10 (Frankfurt: Fisher, 1960), pp. 180–184. (See NM.)

10. "Lebensabriß," in *Reden und Aufsätze*, vol. 3, *Gesammelte Werke* vol. 11, pp. 98–144. (*A Sketch of my Life*, H. T. Lowe-Porter, tr. [New York: Knopf, 1960].)

11. *Thomas Mann's Addresses, 1942–1949* (Washington: Library of Congress, 1963).

12. *Ibid.*, p. 101.

13. A new translation has appeared after the writing of this chapter: *Reflections of a Nonpolitical Man*, Walter D. Morris, tr. (New York: Unger, 1982.)

14. I borrow the rhetoric of this formulation from Jonathan Arac.

15. Dilthey (in *Lived Experience and Poetry*) also thinks of irony as intersubjective polemic. In conjuring Nietzsche's irony, he immediately sees it as the device by which Nietzsche avenged himself against his enemies.

16. Jacques Derrida, "Structure, Sign, and Play in the Discourse of the Human Sciences," in *Writing and Difference*, Alan Bass, tr. (Chicago: University of Chicago Press, 1977), p. 292.

17. *Ibid.*, p. 292.

18. Rousseau, *Les Rêveries du Promeneur Solitaire: Cinquième Promenade*, in *Oeuvres Complètes*, Bibliothèque de la Pléiade (Paris: Gallimard, 1959), 1:1047.

19. Rousseau, *Fragments Autobiographiques: Lettres à Malesherbes*, in *Oeuvres Completès*, 1:1140.

20. Cf. Paul de Man, *The Rhetoric of Romanticism* (New York: Columbia University Press, 1984) p. 21ff.

21. Derrida, "Structure, Sign, and Play," p. 292.

22. If such a humanism is inadequate to the literary-philosophical tradition which Mann tirelessly claims as its source—Goethe, Schopenhauer, and Nietzsche—it will prove especially inadequate to the reality of German life when Life ceases to be the order of a pleasant absence of wit and when the "self-betrayal of spirit on behalf of life" takes the negative turn that Ernst Jünger celebrates: "The best answer to the betrayal of life by Intellect (*Geist*) would be the betrayal of Intellect by Intellect, and one of the great joys of this age is to participate in this work of destruction." (Cited in "Heidegger and Hitler," by Henry Pachter, *Boston University Journal*, 24|3|:52.) Mann's humanism appears in odd distortion in *Doctor Faustus*. There, German life, having ceased to figure as the love object of the bourgeois spirit, is called diabolical *and* equated with German art. There, the only perspective from which Germany can be appreciated is Catholic Latinate late medieval Humanism, and the constitutive irony of Germany, its perpetual self-criticism and self-division, is dismissed as a mad adventure. In this vein Mann would write, in a letter of August 13, 1941: "One would have to drive pretty far upstream along the course of German history before one found no sign of that spirit which today has reached the last degree of baseness and threatens to barbarize and enslave the world. At least as far as the Middle Ages; for Luther . . . already had decidedly Nazistic traits. And what horrors are to be found in Fichte! what menaces in the music, and even more in the writings of Wagner! what a muddle of clarity and obscurity in Schopenhauer and Nietzsche!" (L, p. 370). To be sure, Mann's view in this letter should not be equated with that of Zeitblom, the merely fictional narrator of *Doctor Faustus*. The novel is aware of his stiltedness and partiality, and yet the thrust of their criticism is the same. But now our perspective must return to Mann's less exasperated, ostensibly loving, and "patriotic" stance of 1918.

23. "Nietzsche's Philosophy in the Light of Contemporary Events," *Thomas Mann's Addresses*, p. 103.

24. NM, p. 140. I have modified this translation throughout.

25. Ernst Bertram, *Nietzsche: An Essay in Mythology* (Berlin: G. Bondi, 1918).

26. A *Sketch*, p. 22.

27. The reader may recall, from the discussion of self-development in Hölderlin, the logic of the act of renunciation and the Hesperian turn that brings about an integration of personality. The reappearance of this ethical and aesthetic ideal in Bertram's and Mann's reception of Nietzsche is no accident. Nietzsche was continually read at this time in conjunction with Hölderlin; what was true for Hölderlin became a trope for Nietzsche's commentators.

28. "Nietzsche's Philosophy," p. 76. This essay appeared, in a revised German version, in *Neue Studien* (Stockholm: Fischer, 1948), pp. 103–159.

29. Roland Barthes, S/Z, Richard Miller, tr. (New York: Hill and Wang, 1974), p. 140.

30. Paul de Man, "Nietzsche and Rhetoric," *Symposium* (1974), 28:45.

31. A *Sketch*, p. 22.

32. Hans Egon Holthusen, *Die Welt ohne Transzendenz*, 2d ed. (Hamburg: Verlag Heinrich Ellermann, 1954), p. 60.

33. I copied out this passage in 1974 from a letter by Mann which I can no longer locate. The same idea, however, can be found in a letter to Paul Amann, L, p. 75.

34. Cited in R. A. Nicholls, *Nietzsche in the Early Work of Thomas Mann* (Berkeley: University of California Press, 1955), p. 93.

35. Eugenio Donato, in Richard Macksey and Eugenio Donato, eds., *The Struc-*

turalist Controversy (Baltimore: Johns Hopkins University Press, 1972), p. 96. See pp. 37 and 107 of this book; also compare Spivak, p. xxv.

36. Walter Benjamin, *The Origin of German Tragic Drama*, John Osborne, tr. (London: NLB, 1977), p. 175ff.

37. Derrida, "Structure, Sign, and Play," p. 293.

38. Charles Bernheimer, "Structuralist Plots and Counterplots: A Review of Jeffrey Mehlman's *Structural Study of Autobiography*," *boundary* 2 (1976), 4:979.

39. Certainly the thought that Mann's sense of history might be wanting, a mere construction, was not unknown to him (or to his critics). His decision to write the *Reflections* was preceded and to some extent provoked by critics' negative response to his essay "Frederick and the Grand Coalition," 1915. R. A. Nicholls sums up the situation: "The transition from the moral problem into the political, and the association with the issues of the war, was too facile and too convenient. . . . It may also be that he felt [that] . . . the very artistic control of the material . . . [was] a sign that he was playing with the problem, . . . that in implying parallels with the present crisis he did not appreciate the real earnestness of events. . . . A fearful sense of unreality seemed to overtake him" (*Nietzsche in the Early Work of Thomas Mann*, p. 92).

40. Ernst Jünger, *Rivarol* (Frankfurt: Fischer Bücherei, 1956), p. 88.

5. The Author Survives on the Margin of His Breaks: Kafka's Narrative Perspective

1. *Briefe* (Frankfurt: Fischer; New York: Schocken Books, 1958), p. 384. An especially fine essay by Blanchot, readily available, is "The Diaries: The Exigency of the Work of Art," in Angel Flores and Homer Swander, eds., *Franz Kafka Today*, pp. 195–200 (Madison: University of Wisconsin Press, 1964).

2. *Briefe an Felice*, Erich Heller and Jürgen Born, eds. (Frankfurt: Fischer; New York: Schocken Books, 1967), p. 444.

3. Paul de Man, *Allegories of Reading* (New Haven: Yale University Press, 1979), p. 111.

4. Roland Barthes, "La Mort de l'auteur," *Mantéia* (1968), 12–17. "The Death of the Author," in *Roland Barthes: Image, Music, Text*, Stephen Heath, tr. (New York: Hill and Wang, 1977), pp. 142–148.

5. *Ibid.*, pp. 12, 142. One can choose to see very precisely displayed in this passage the moment of Barthes' "scientific" and universalizing elaboration of Blanchot's metaphysics of artistic impersonality. Cf. p. 51 ff. of this book.

6. *Ibid.*, pp. 15, 145–146.

7. Leslie A. Marchand writes in his "Introduction" to Byron's *Don Juan* (New York: Houghton Mifflin, 1958): "Boisterous effervescence stands side by side with the most serious castigation of war or intolerance, and in the main once one has accepted the genre, though there is little transition, there seems to be no incongruity, for we recognize the voice as we would in a letter or a conversation" (p. xiii).

8. *Ibid.*, pp. 14, 144. This view is also asserted by Gerhard Kurz in *Traum-Schrecken: Kafkas literarische Existenzanalyse* (Stuttgart: Metzler, 1980), viz., "The literary text no longer belongs to the author" (p. 86).

9. *Tagebücher: 1910–1923*, Max Brod, ed. (Frankfurt: Fischer; New York: Schocken Books, 1967), p. 380. I have revised a little Martin Greenberg's translation in *The Diaries of Franz Kafka, 1914–1923* (New York: Schocken Books, 1948), pp. 183–184. In his novel *Hyperion*, Hölderlin's phrase for language itself is "a great surplus" (*ein großer Überfluß*) (3:123). The Kafka passage is suggestively discussed by Maurice Blanchot in "Kafka and Literature," in *The Sirens' Song: Selected Essays by Maurice Blanchot*, Gabriel Josipovici, ed. (Brighton: Harvester, 1982), pp. 36–38.

10. In Dilthey's more radical style, feelings are "metamorphosed" by poetic expression. See *Die Einbildungskraft des Dichters* in *Gesammelte Schriften*, Georg Misch, ed., 2d ed. (Göttingen: Vandenhoeck and Ruprecht, 1924) 6:138. Kafka read Dilthey with keen interest. See his diary entries for January 6, 1914, mentioning *Das Erlebnis und die Dichtung*, and February 11, 1914, mentioning Dilthey's *Goethe* (*Diaries*, 1914–1923, pp. 10 and 18).

11. Anthony Storr, *The Art of Psychotherapy* (London: Secker and Warburg, 1980), cited by Rosemary Dinnage in "Soul-baring Situations," *The Times Literary Supplement* (May 9, 1980), 4024:530.

12. *Dearest Father*, Tania and James Stern, trs. (New York: Schocken Books, 1954), p. 40.

13. Michel Foucault, *The Order of Things: An Archaeology of the Human Sciences* (London: Tavistock, 1974), p. xxiii.

14. Julia Kristeva, "D'une identité l'autre," in *Polylogue* (Paris: Seuil, 1977), p. 149.

15. Kenneth Burke, *Language as Symbolic Action* (Berkeley: University of California Press, 1966), p. 167.

16. *Briefe*, p. 384.

17. Gustav Janouch, *Conversations with Kafka*, Goronwy Rees, tr. (New York: New Directions, 1971), p. 16.

18. *Briefe*, p. 28.

19. *Dearest Father*, p. 41.

20. Anthony Wilden, *The Language of the Self* (Baltimore: Johns Hopkins University Press, 1968), p. 184.

21. *Ibid.*

22. Political acts, as the psychoanalyst Stuart Schneiderman writes, "are one response to the basic structure of human existence, but certainly not the only one that is ethical." *Jacques Lacan: The Death of an Intellectual Hero* (Cambridge: Harvard University Press, 1983), p. 174. The point may be based on the distinction between passion and need—political acts being chiefly responsive to need. De Man offers a related argument about Rousseau, whose preference for "passion over need, as the proper affective metaphor for language," is based on the fact that in need "the referential element is determined" (*Allegories of Reading*, p. 161).

23. Friedrich Beißner, *Der Erzähler Franz Kafka* (Stuttgart: Kohlhammer, 1952) and *Kafka der Dichter* (Stuttgart: Kohlhammer, 1958).

24. Walter Sokel, *The Writer in Extremis: Expressionism in Twentieth-Century Literature* (Stanford: Stanford University Press, 1959), p. 233.

25. Martin Walser, *Beschreibung einer Form* (Munich: Hanser, 1961).

26. *The Metamorphosis by Franz Kafka*, Stanley Corngold, tr. and ed. (New York: Bantam, 1972), p. 14.

27. *Ibid.*, pp. 42–43.

28. Janice Finney, unpublished essay on *The Trial*, Department of German, Princeton University, 1980.

29. Indeed, in his *Diaries*, Kafka himself asserts his belief in Joseph K.'s guilt (T481).

30. Hartmut Binder, *Motiv und Gestaltung bei Franz Kafka* (Bonn: Bouvier, 1966); Peter Beicken, *Perspektive und Sehweise bei Kafka*, unpublished dissertation, Stanford University, 1971; Ingeborg Henel, "Die Deutbarkeit von Kafkas Werken," *Zeitschrift für deutsche Philologie* (1967), 86:250–266; Walter Sokel "Das Verhältnis der Erzählperspektive zu Erzählgeschehen und Sinngehalt in 'Vor dem Gesetz,' 'Schakale und Araber,' und 'Der Prozeß,'" *Zeitschrift für deutsche Philologie* (1967), 86:267–300; Roy Pascal, *Kafka's Narrators: A Study of His Stories and Sketches* (Cambridge: Cambridge University Press, 1982).

31. Dorrit Cohn, "Kafka's Eternal Present: Narrative Tense in 'Ein Landarzt' and Other First-Person Stories," PMLA (1968), 83:144–150.

32. *The Metamorphosis*, p. 40.

33. Dorrit Cohn, "K. Enters the Castle: On the Change of Person in Kafka's Manuscript," *Euphorion* (1968), 62(1):28–45.

34. Henel, "Die Deutbarkeit," p. 257.

35. Keith Leopold, "Breaks in Perspective in Franz Kafka's 'Der Prozeß,'" *German Quarterly* (1963), 36(1):36.

36. *Ibid.*, p. 38.

37. Walter Sokel, *Franz Kafka. Tragik und Ironie. Zur Struktur seiner Kunst* (München/Wien: Albert Langen, Georg Müller, 1964); *Franz Kafka* (New York: Columbia University Press, 1961); Dorrit Cohn, "K. Enters the Castle"; Winfried Kudszus, "Erzählhaltung und Zeitverschiebung in Kafkas 'Prozeß' und 'Schloß,'" *Deutsche Vierteljahrsschrift* (1964), 38:192–207; Richard Sheppard, *On Kafka's Castle* (New York: Barnes and Noble, 1977); "The Trial/The Castle: Towards an Analytical Comparison," in Angel Flores, ed., *The Kafka Debate*, pp. 396–417 (New York: Gordian Press, 1977).

38. Kudszus, "Erzählhaltung," p. 194.

39. When, for example, Gregor, "almost out of his mind . . . lunged forward with all his force, *without caring*, he had picked the wrong direction and slammed himself violently against the lower bedpost, and the searing pain he felt taught him that exactly the lower part of his body was . . . the most sensitive" (*Metamorphosis*, p. 7; italics mine). Again, after seizing the key to his room in his jaws, he "*paid no attention* to the fact that he was undoubtedly hurting himself in some way, for a brown liquid came out of his mouth" (*Metamorphosis*, p. 14; italics mine).

Certainly Gregor's father is something more than an inflictor of random hurts on Gregor's body. It is he who, at the end of part 1, drives Gregor out of the room "as if there were no obstacles," with the result that "one of his flanks was scraped raw . . . |and| one little leg |was| seriously injured in the course of the morning's events" (M, pp. 19–21). On the other hand, "In his father's present state of mind it did not *even remotely occur to him* |Mr. Samsa| to open the other wing of the door in order to give Gregor enough room to pass through" (M, p. 19; italics mine). Mr. Samsa's animosity toward Gregor is certainly somewhat randomly enacted, as witness even his bombardment of Gregor with apples: "He was now pitching one apple after another, for the time being *without taking good aim*" (M, p. 39; italics mine). It is hard to decide whether the apple that finally "literally forced its way into Gregor's back" (M, p. 39) is or is not deliberately aimed.

40. Carsten Schlingmann, "Die Verwandlung—Eine Interpretation." In *Interpretationen zu Franz Kafka: Das Urteil, Die Verwandlung, Ein Landarzt, Kleine Prosastücke* (Munich: Oldenbourg, 1968), p. 89.

41. *Briefe an Felice*, p. 681.

42. Cf. note 5, above.

43. *Diaries, 1910–1913*, p. 318.

44. *Dearest Father*, p. 37.

45. Cf. Maurice Blanchot, who writes: "Patience, accuracy and cool mastery are also faults which, dividing the difficulties and extending them indefinitely, perhaps delay the catastrophe but certainly delay the rescue, constantly transform the infinite into the indefinite, *as it is likewise measure which in the work of art prevents the limitless ever being achieved*" (italics mine). "The Diaries," p. 216.

46. WP, p. 437.

47. *Dearest Father*, p. 92.

48. *Diaries, 1910–1913*, p. 157.

49. *Letters to Milena*, Willy Haas, ed., Tania and James Stern, trs. (New York: Schocken Books, 1953), p. 200.

50. Gottfried Benn, "Nietzsche nach Fünfzig Jahren," in *Gesammelte Werke, Essays, Reden, Vorträge* (Stuttgart: Ernst Klett-Cotta, 1977), 1:490.

51. A critic who prefers to go unnamed questions this appeal to an authorial self produced by and in the breaks of narrative perspective. "Why," he asks, "is this supposed self-production not just a variant of Barthes' 'reality effect' |discussed by Barthes in the essay cited on p. 5 of this book|, which recuperates the meaningless, yet without introducing an authorial self? That is, if we semiotically understand otherwise unmotivated descriptive detail as signs of a 'real world' not artistically dominated, are not narrative breaks of perspective similarly |only| conventional signs of a 'real self' supposedly forcing itself disruptively against fictional form?"

This objection is, I think, answered by an interpretive decision. The semiotic production of "a real self" is not a convention for Kafka, and therefore it should not be one for his reader. From the start I have argued that breaks in perspective, however regarded, are motivated by Kafka's suffering. So whether Kafka's breaks are thought of as a direct expression of his suffering or as a conventional device elected by his suffering, the result is the same: *Kafka survives on the margin of his breaks*.

52. Monroe C. Beardsley, "Order and Disorder in Art," in Paul Kuntz, ed., *The Concept of Order*, p. 193 (Seattle: University of Washington Press, 1968).

53. *Ibid.*, p. 195.

54. Theodor W. Adorno, "Parataxis. Zur späten Lyrik Hölderlins," in Jochen Schmidt, ed., *Über Hölderlin*, p. 367 (Frankfurt: Insel, 1970).

55. Beardsley, "Order and Disorder," p. 196.

56. Theodor W. Adorno, *Philosophie der neuen Musik*, in *Gesammelte Schriften*, (Frankfurt: Suhrkamp, 1975), 12:43, 46–47. Cf. with the figure of an eruption or exanthem (*Ausschlag*) the equally vile figure of disease in these lines from the speech of the "I" in Kafka's *Beschreibung eines Kampfes*, in *Gesammelte Schriften*, vol. 5, Max Brod, ed. (New York, Schocken, 1946). "Now by God I perceive that from the very beginning I suspected the condition you are in. Is not this fever, this seasickness on *terra firma*, a sort of leprosy (*Aussatz*)?" (p. 43). The "I" is a plain persona of the author. He is suffering a crisis of language, cannot be content with the "authentic names of things," and must instead dump onto them random names—dead metaphors.

57. Theodor W. Adorno, "Die Wunde Heine," in *Noten zur Literatur* (Frankfurt: Suhrkamp, 1963), 1:150. I am grateful to Todd Kontje for bringing this passage to my attention.

58. "Now interpretation abhors the random, which is one reason why, in the most modern school of criticism, it has become a dirty word, a word of censure." Frank Kermode, *The Genesis of Secrecy: On the Interpretation of Narrative* (Cambridge: Harvard University Press, 1979), p. 9.

59. Franz Kafka, *The Castle*, Willa and Edwin Muir, trs. (Harmondsworth, Middlesex: Penguin, 1957), p. 216.

6. Freud as Literature?

1. "The Hunter Gracchus," in *Selected Stories of Franz Kafka*, Willa and Edwin Muir, trs. (New York: Modern Library, 1952), p. 187. Translation modified.

2. *The Diaries of Franz Kafka, 1914–1923*, (New York: Schocken Books, 1948), p. 114.

3. "Wir lagen," *Lichtzwang* (Frankfurt: Suhrkamp, 1970), p. 13.

4. *New York Times*, October 20, 1977, p. 1.

5. Although this rhetorical habit was not much commented on. Nietzsche wrote: " 'Being' as universalization of the concept 'life' (breathing), 'having a soul,' 'willing, effecting,' 'becoming'. The antithesis is: 'not to have a soul,' 'not to become,' 'not to will.' Therefore: 'being' is *not* the antithesis of non-being, appearance, nor even of the dead" (WP, p. 312).

6. Each (deluded) reader finds in its image of the other the solidity of the other, with respect to which each asserts its separate identity. But this impression of solidity is won only at the cost of cutting off reflection on the play of difference within the other. The impression of separate identity each has of himself is a litotes, being obtained by denial of the threatening convergence of the other (in his difference) with what is originally other, and hence productive of difference, in himself: "I am *not* divided, i.e., not-unselfsame." The critique of the litotes or denial then takes the form of showing that it is only the blind metaphor of an original *aversion* from self.

7. Consider the unseemly haste with which Croissant, alleged mediator for terrorists, was extradited to Germany.

8. The pseudoexchange I have described (and to which Glucksmann's *Les maîtres penseurs* should be assimilated) belongs to the unwritten history of specular readings of France/Germany, in which two moments are immediately important: (1) Nietzsche's uneasy admiration for French clarity. In 1885, in a preface for the project of *The Will to Power*, Nietzsche describes this work as "a book for *thinking*, nothing else. . . . That it is written in German is untimely, to say the least: I wish I had written it in French so that it might not appear to be a confirmation of the aspirations of the German Reich." A few sentences later, however, he says, "Formerly I wished I had not written my Zarathustra in German." And now? Cited in WP, pp. xxii–xxiii. (2) The mood of conservative Germany during the First World War, which assimilated Nietzsche to an attack on French "enlightenment," French "ideas." Thus Thomas Mann writes in *Reflections of a Nonpolitical Man*, "I well remember the laugh which I had to repress when one day Parisian *literati* whom I sounded out on Nietzsche gave me to understand that *au fond* he had been nothing more than a good reader of the French moralists and aphorists" (BU, p. 82). Mann instead recalls Nietzsche's "depth," his allegiance to Germany as the "recalcitrant" factor in European life.

9. In the *Interpretation of Dreams* Freud himself all but explicitly identifies the process of the repression of repression as the fault of Adler's closed system: His "masculine protest," writes Freud, is nothing else than repression unjustifiably sexualized. I shall not be detailing more than a few moments of this reception, which I imagine is now already understood in its basic directions or can be so understood, thanks mainly to the generous mediation of Jeffrey Mehlman. See his edition of *Yale French Studies* (*French Freud: Structural Studies in Psychoanalysis*) (1972) no. 48, from which the phrase "the repression of the discovery of repression" (p. 7) is taken, and better still his admirable *Structural Study of Autobiography* (Ithaca: Cornell University Press, 1974) and the "Introduction" to his translation of Jean Laplanche's key study, *Life and Death in Psychoanalysis* (Baltimore: Johns Hopkins University Press, 1976).

10. "Deconstruction has been much misrepresented, dismissed as a harmless academic game or denounced as a terrorist weapon." Paul de Man, *Allegories of Reading* (New Haven: Yale University Press, 1979), p. x. But Anthony Wilden, who generally has a fair sense of the intellectual movement in France, describes a "great number" of thinkers associated with or influenced by Lacan as possessing an "intellectual terrorism . . . not unrelated to Lacan's own." *The Language of the Self* (Baltimore: Johns Hopkins University Press, 1968), p. xiv. John Searle notes, "Michel Foucault once characterized Derrida's prose style to me as 'obscurantisme terroriste' " (*New York Review of Books*, October 27, 1983, p. 77). And Richard Howard, the eminent poet and translator of Barthes and others, registers at least

the French rhetorical habit of associating literature and terrorism in his "Note on S/Z": "Only when we know—and it is a knowledge gained by taking pains, by renouncing what Freud calls instinctual gratification—what we are doing when we read, are we free to enjoy what we read. As long as our enjoyment is—or is said to be—instinctive it is not enjoyment, it is terrorism." S/Z (New York: Hill and Wang, 1974), p. i.

11. The cited phrase is Lacan's, in his "Function of Language in Psychoanalysis" (short title), translated by Anthony Wilden, The Language of the Self, pp. 1–87. There the context is madness, and the relevant phrase reads, "In madness, of whatever nature, we must recognize . . . the negative liberty of a Word which has given up trying to make itself understood" (pp. 42–43).

12. Paul de Man, Blindness and Insight (New York: Oxford University Press, 1971), p. 18.

13. Mehlman, A Structural Study of Autobiography, p. 113.

14. Freud, The Interpretation of Dreams, in The Standard Edition of the Complete Psychological Works, James Strachey, ed. (London: Hogarth Press, 1958), 5:514.

15. This is to take seriously the proposition "Freud is (or is not) a literary text," which inside the discourse of French Freud is itself of course entirely vertiginous, since the claim that Freud is or is not a literary text arrives in the rear of the avant-garde polemical statement denying the very distinction between literary and nonliterary texts.

16. Selected Stories, p. 187.

17. Freud provides an analogue to this situation in his account of how the patient undergoes an auspicious and "permanent alteration of his mental economy" through transference. "[Transference] is used to induce the patient to perform a piece of mental work—the overcoming of his transference-resistance. . . . The transference is made conscious to the patient by the analyst, and it is resolved by convincing him that in his transference-attitude he is re-experiencing emotional relations which had their origin in his earliest object-attachments" [Autobiography, James Strachey, tr. (New York: Norton, 1937), p. 85]. If we transform these sentences by metaphorical substitution, we find that the force linking deviant sentences is illocutionary, is rhetorical: The stammering speaker becomes able to thread sentences through his own baby talk when he has once repeated the enabling sentence belonging to another (having been "induced to, convinced").

18. Perhaps the courted dissolution of the subject could be traced to a desire to arrive at a vantage point outside the subject, as the alibi of "objectivity."

19. Cited in J. Kamerbeek, "Dilthey Versus Nietzsche," Studia Philosophica, Jahrbuch der Schweizerischen Philosophischen Gesellschaft (1950), 10:56.

20. "Such awe" translates tel effroi, and indeed the English word mutes more than the French the component of terror in the experience. Lacan, however, approved the translation.

21. Thomas Weiskel, The Romantic Sublime: Studies in the Structure and Psychology of Transcendence (Baltimore: Johns Hopkins University Press, 1976), p. 83ff.

22. Harold Bloom, writing on Derrida's use of hyperbole, sees "the more sublime . . . trope of hyperbole" as indeed having "close relationship to the defense of repression." Map of Misreading (New York: Oxford University Press, 1975), p. 48.

23. Stuart Schneiderman, Jacques Lacan: The Death of an Intellectual Hero (Cambridge: Harvard University Press, 1983), p. 179.

24. Cf. "Refoulement," in Laplanche's and Pontalis' Vocabulaire de la Psychanalyse (Paris: Presses Universitaires de France, 1973), p. 392ff.

25. Some elements in the French case: First, it must have been with some irony or diffidence that Laplanche projected his study of schizophrenia and poetry as Hölderlin (not Kafka) et la question du père. Second, the recalcitrant figure in the deconstructive pro-

gram has been Blanchot who, if he did not explicitly declare the extent of his indebtedness to Kafka, testified to it in writing some of the most accurate pages ever written on him. (Deleuze-Guattari's carefree book on Kafka certainly changes nothing in this reckoning.) Finally, there is but one bare word on Kafka (to my knowledge) in Derrida (*Of Grammatology*, Gayatri C. Spivak, tr. [Baltimore: Johns Hopkins University Press, 1976], p. 272), though Derrida has recently delivered a lecture on Kafka's parable "Before the Law;" and Foucault writes only one bare word in *The Order of Things* (London: Tavistock, 1970), p. 384.

26. *Complete Psychological Works*, 5:350–351.

27. Kafka wrote to Milena, "I consider the therapeutic part of psychoanalysis to be a hopeless error." *Letters to Milena*, Willy Haas, ed., Tania and James Stern, trs. (New York: Schocken Books, 1953), p. 217.

28. *Dearest Father*, Tania and James Stern, trs. (New York: Schocken Books, 1954), p. 41.

29. *Diaries 1910–1913*, p. 26.

30. *Diaries 1914–1923*, p. 212.

31. *Selected Stories*, p. 187.

32. Gustav Janouch, *Conversations with Kafka*, Goronwy Rees, tr. (New York: New Directions, 1971), p. 56.

33. In the relation of dreams to neurosis as explanatory instruments, Freud, in the *Interpretation of Dreams*, privileges neurosis: "Though my own line of approach to the subject of dreams was determined by my previous work on the psychology of the neuroses, I had not intended to make use of the latter as a basis of reference in the present work. Nevertheless I am constantly being driven to do so, instead of proceeding, as I should have wished, in the contrary direction and using dreams as a means of approach to the psychology of the neuroses" (*Complete Psychological Works*, 5:588).

34. Theodor W. Adorno, "Notes on Kafka," in *Prisms*, Samuel and Shierry Weber, trs. (London: Spearman, 1967), p. 250.

35. *The Trial*, Willa and Edwin Muir, trs. (New York: Modern Library, 1956), pp. 272–273.

36. *Diaries, 1910–1913*, p. 300.

37. *Ibid.*, p. 276.

37. Derrida's essay "The Purveyor of Truth," *Yale French Studies* (1975) 52:31–113, which treats Lacan's "Seminar on 'The Purloined Letter' " (in *Yale French Studies* [1971] 48:38–72), also focuses on the deficient treatment in Lacan of the question of narrative. His analysis is linked to a "destruction" of Lacan's familiar absolutization of the intersubjective field, as in Lacan's proposition, "The register of truth . . . is situated strictly speaking at the very foundation of intersubjectivity. It is located there where the subject can grasp nothing but the very subjectivity which constitutes an Other as absolute" (p. 49).

All Kafka's work from 1912 on exists as the project of criticizing, of destroying, this notion. This project originates as the refinement of the narrative form called monopolized perspective (*Einsinnigkeit*), which he scrupulously breaks at points. Derrida writes with great cogency of Lacan's neglect "of the narrator's position, the narrator's involvement in the content of what he seems to be recounting" (p. 100) and of a more "original function" too termed "scription," which guarantees the distinction between "the textual fiction" and narration (p. 52). But how then can Derrida maintain with any force that "the 'form' of the Freudian text . . . belongs no more clearly to the tradition of scientific discourse than to a specific genre of fiction" (p. 38)? The specific genre of the Freudian text does not sufficiently complicate narration so as to bring to light "the invisible but structurally irreducible frame around the narration" that confirms the fiction. Freud does not redouble this frame—as does Kafka, par excellence, on the far edge of the text of the "narrated narrator" oy inscrutable disruptions enacting the distinction between scription and narration. Pace Derrida, the distinction between the scientific text and the literary fiction is "guaranteed . . . from the formal point of view" (p. 50), which discovers the textual staging of a distancing consciousness of narration.

38. *Dearest Father*, p. 41.

39. Janouch, *Conversations*, p. 28.

40. *Diaries 1914–1923*, p. 206.

41. "Why is it meaningless to ask questions? To complain means to put a question and wait for the answer. But the questions that don't answer themselves at the very moment of their asking are never answered. No distance divides the interrogator from the one who answers him" (*Ibid.*, p. 131).

42. *Briefe*, 1902–1924, Max Brod, ed. (Frankfurt: Schocken Books, 1958), p. 98.

43. Hölderlin, *Sämtliche Werke*, 4:21. For Kafka (in the words of Benjamin and Scholem) "the absolute-concrete is of course what is purely and simply the unrealizable." This moment figures as the repetition of a moment of Hölderlin's critique of Fichte: Hölderlin perceives that the requirement of consciousness determines that "the absolute Self shall be (as a self) nothing." *Briefwechsel* 1933–1940, Walter Benjamin and Gershom Scholem (Frankfurt: Suhrkamp, 1980), p. 39; Jean Laplanche, *Hölderlin et la question du père* (Paris: Presses Universitaires de France, 1961), p. 37.

44. I could thus agree with Gadamer that whatever "unity" a literary work possesses—"unity and facility and so, too, its own manner of being true"—is given to it by "an enigmatic form of the nondistinction between what is said and how it is said." "The Eminent Text and Its Truth," in Paul Hernadi, ed., *The Horizon of Literature*, p. 46 (Lincoln: University of Nebraska Press, 1982).

45. *The Notebooks of Malte Laurids Brigge*, M. D. Herter Norton, tr. (New York: Norton, 1964), p. 198.

46. Lacan, cited in Wilden, *The Language of the Self*, p. 273.

47. *Diaries, 1914–1923*, p. 228.

48. Shoshana Felman, "Introduction," *Yale French Studies* (1977), 55/56:8.

49. Fredric Jameson, "Imaginary and Symbolic in Lacan," *Ibid.*, p. 343.

50. *Diaries, 1914–23*, p. 187.

51. *The Great Wall of China*, Willa and Edwin Muir, trs. (New York: Schocken Books, 1970), p. 269.

52. *Dearest Father*, p. 38.

53. *Diaries, 1910–1913*, p. 276.

54. *Diaries, 1914–23*, p. 184.

55. The previous chapter showed Kafka deliberately consenting to a moment of chance in writing; this chapter identifies his truth as pure consciousness without individuation. Both attitudes are meant to characterize his poetic personality, and yet where in any of this is Kafka's self? What in such writing can be recovered as Kafka's subjectivity? The answer is that the poetic display of pure consciousness and Kafka's accession to chance both have in common their affirmation of indifference to the practical concerns of an aimed empirical consciousness. Kafka's self is defined not by particular interests but by its narrating attentiveness to the products of a dream play. The self is precisely its lucid tolerance of whatever arises in the place where control, for the sake of mastery and reward, has been relinquished.

7. Heidegger's Being and Time: Implications for Poetics

1. Dilthey, *Gesammelte Schriften*, Georg Misch, ed. (Göttingen: Vandenhoeck and Ruprecht, 1923), 5:37.

2. *Kehre*, normally "turning," need not mean a radical turnabout. Elisabeth Förster-Nietzsche, for example, describes a *Kehre* as a "popular expression for a bend in the road (*Wendung des Weges*)." *Begegnungen mit Nietzsche*, Sander Gilman, ed. (Bonn: Bouvier, 1981), p. 158.

3. "On the Essence of Truth," in MH, p. 140.

4. "Letter on Humanism," in MH, p. 207.

5. "On the Essence of Truth," in MH, p. 141.

6. *Ibid.*, p. 208.

7. *Die Technik und die Kehre* (Pfullingen: Neske, 1962), p. 42.

8. MH, p. 137.

9. MH, p. 138.

10. Heidegger, "Preface," in William J. Richardson, S. J., *Heidegger: Through Phenomenology to Thought* (The Hague: Nijhoff, 1963), p. xvi.

11. "Letter on Humanism," MH, p. 208.

12. On the subject of "poetic thinking," see the excellent book by David Halliburton, *Poetic Thinking: An Approach to Heidegger* (Chicago: University of Chicago Press, 1981).

13. *Erläuterungen zu Hölderlins Dichtung*, 4th ed. (Frankfurt: Klostermann, 1971), p. 77.

14. "Authentic understanding, no less than that which is inauthentic, *can* be either genuine or not genuine" (BT, p. 186).

15. "Zur Einführung," in Heidegger, *Der Ursprung des Kunstwerkes* (Stuttgart: Reclam, 1960), p. 107.

16. Cf. Paul de Man, *Blindness and Insight: Essays in the Rhetoric of Contemporary Criticism*, 2d ed., rev. (Minneapolis: University of Minnesota Press, 1983),

17. Cf. Halliburton, *Poetic Thinking*, p. viii. A book that singlemindedly suggests a revision of the foundations of *Literaturwissenschaft* on the basis of Heidegger's reflections on temporality is Beda Allemann, *Hölderlin und Heidegger*, 2d ed. (Zurich: Atlantis, 1956), pp. 88–89. Hereafter cited in text as HH.

18. Cf. Jan Aler, "Heidegger's Conception of Language in *Being and Time*," in Joseph J. Kockelmans, ed., *On Heidegger and Language*, p. 44 (Evanston, Ill.: Northwestern University Press, 1972).

19. In his "Beitrag zu Forschungsproblemen: Hölderlin, Heidegger und die Literaturwissenschaft," Hans Joachim Schrimpf also asserts an essential absence of connection between *Being and Time* and poetics but altogether omits mentioning this sentence. *Euphorion*, (1957), 51/3:313ff.

20. MH, p. 155.

21. Cited in *Robert Musil: Ethik und Ästhetik*, Marie-Luise Roth, ed. (Munich: Paul List, 1972), p. 363.

22. *Holzwege*, 6th ed. (Frankfurt: Vittorio Klostermann, 1980), p. 263. This is the concluding sentence of Heidegger's critique of Nietzsche. See Walter Kaufmann's discussion of this sentence in *Nietzsche*, 4th ed. (Princeton: Princeton University Press, 1974), pp. 230–231.

23. Pure Nietzsche. In *Beyond Good and Evil* Nietzsche writes, "What is most difficult to render from one language into another is the *tempo* of its style." He goes on to celebrate French and Italian over German as languages capable of a "bold and merry *tempo*," of *presto*, of *allegrissimo* (BW, p. 230ff).

24. Cf. Newton Garver's informative preface to *Speech and Phenomena* by Jacques Derrida, David B. Allison, tr. (Evanston, Ill.: Northwestern University Press, 1973), pp. xi–xiii.

25. Kant, *The Critique of Judgement*, James Creed Meredith, tr. (Oxford: Clarendon, 1952), p. 224.

26. Schrimpf, *Beitrag*, p. 313.

27. Guido Morpurgo-Tagliabue, *L'Esthétique contemporaraine* (Milan: Marzorati, 1960), p. 597.

28. Aristotle, *Poetics*, Loeb Classical Library (Cambridge: Harvard University Press, 1953), p. 51.

29. Dilthey, *Gesammelte Schriften*, 5:138.

30. Gustave Flaubert, *Madame Bovary*, edited with a substantially new translation by Paul de Man (New York: Norton, 1965), p. 163.

31. Cited in Pfeiffer, *Das lyrische Gedicht als ästhetisches Gebilde* (Halle: Niemeyer, 1931), p. 68.

32. Kant, *The Critique of Judgement*, pp. 224, 14.

33. Walter Biemel, *Die Bedeutung von Kants Begründung der Asthetik für die Philosophie der Kunst* (Köln: Kölner Universitäts-Verlag, 1959), p. 145.

34. Rousseau, *Oeuvres complètes*, Bibliothèque de la Pléiade (Paris: Gallimard, 1959), 1:1150.

35. *Ibid.*, p. 1153.

36. *The Confessions of Jean-Jacques Rousseau*, J. M. Cohen, tr. (Harmondsworth, Middlesex: Penguin, 1953), p. 30.

37. Rousseau, *Oeuvres complètes*, p. 1154.

38. Hölderlin, *Sämtliche Werke* (Stuttgart: Kohlhammer, 1958), 4:243, 257.

39. Emil Staiger, *Die Zeit als Einbildungskraft des Dichters* (Zurich: Max Niehans, 1939), pp. 66–70 and "Schluß."

40. Georg Lukács, *Die Theorie des Romans* (Neuwied: Luchterhand Verlag, 1965), p. 63.

41. Jacques Havet, *Kant et le problème du temps* (Paris: Gallimard, 1953), p. 10.

42. Paul de Man, *Blindness and Insight*, p. 32.

43. Nietzsche, *Morgenröte*, in *Werke in Drei Bänden*, Karl Schlechta, ed. (Munich: Carl Hanser Verlag, 1954), 1:1095.

44. Though perhaps Heidegger here merely inherits a tendency that began with what Nietzsche calls "the decline of cheerfulness around 1770" (WP, p. 56). Kant would then be writing in a mood from memory.

45. Walter Biemel, "Poetry and Language in Heidegger," in Joseph J. Kockelmans, ed., *On Heidegger and Language*, pp. 70–71 (Evanston, Ill.: Northwestern University Press, 1972).

46. Aler, "Heideggers Conception," p. 50.

47. De Man, *Blindness and Insight*, p. 164.

48. *Ibid.*, p. 162.

49. Fritz Kaufman, "Die Bedeutung der künstlerischen Stimmung," in *Jahrbuch für Philosophie und phänomenologische Forschung*, Ergänzungsband (1929), p. 214.

50. Cited in Dieter Krusche, *Kafka und Kafka-Deutung* (Munich: Fink, 1974), p. 156.

51. Jonathan Culler, *Flaubert: The Uses of Uncertainty* (Ithaca: Cornell University Press, 1974), p. 15.

52. *Ibid.*, p. 17.

53. Aler, "Heidegger's Conception," p. 62.

54. Hofmannsthal, "Poesie und Leben" in *Prosa*, (Frankfurt: Fischer, 1950), 1:263.

55. Richard Howard, "A Note on S/Z" (New York: Hill and Wang, 1974), p. xi.

56. Unpublished paper by Professor Lawrence Hinman, Department of Philosophy, University of California at San Diego.

57. Hinman further concludes that there are shortcomings in Heidegger's account of "the truth value of the emotions." Heidegger, he says, loses sight of the possibility of both authentic moods directed toward objects and inauthentic moods directed toward being in the world as such. The expectation that Heidegger should produce such an account comes partly from tensions within *Being and Time* and partly from Hinman's desire that Heidegger provide there an adequate theory of the emotions. The major thrust of *Being and Time* does indeed oppose, however, the notion of "authentic ontic moods directed toward entities within the world." They would in any case be "ungenuine" (BT, p. 186).

58. Cf. Barthes, "Kafka's Answer," in *Critical Essays*, Richard Howard, tr. (Evanston, Ill.: Northwestern University Press, 1972), p. 137. "Any lapse . . . would substitute assertive language for the essentially interrogative function of literature."

Index

The Fate of the Self

German Writers and French Theory

STANLEY CORNGOLD

Recent literary theory has profoundly altered the way in which German writers are read. *The Fate of the Self* examines the poetic self of German intellectual tradition in the light of the main emphases of this new criticism. The focus is on seven major writers: Hölderlin, Dilthey, Nietzsche, Mann, Kafka, Freud, and Heidegger. Their work, Corngold suggests, does not support the theoretical desire to discredit the self as an origin of meaning and value. In all of these writers, the fate of the self resists reduction or abolition in literature.

Hölderlin, for example, wrote that the poetic self must "disown" itself in order to exist. French and American criticism today often dwells on this moment of negativity, rift, and rupture. But Hölderlin also wrote, unless we can "carry over our own spirit and our own experience into a foreign analogous material, nothing at all can be understood or given life." Corngold argues that this claim is typical of the writers studied here.

His book offers a wide range of interpretations on behalf of the self. In a series of rich and intricate analyses, Corngold opposes the work of major writers to tendentious critical readings of them, reconstructing the allegedly fragmented and dispersed poetic self from subtle effects of meaning and style. To read German writers in a perspective opened up by the new French criticism, but explicitly critical of it, is thus the aim of this study. *The Fate of the Self* passionately contests the prejudice against subjectivity in literature, and seeks to discover fresh grounds for affirming what Nietzsche called the "creative self." Engaging, as it does, a topic at the core of current issues in psychoanalysis and the theory